EVALUATION

SEVENTH EDITION

To the memory of Daniel Patrick Moynihan—
intellectual, scholar, policymaker,
and advocate for applied social research

EVALUATION
A Systematic Approach
SEVENTH EDITION

PETER H. ROSSI
University of Massachussets, Amherst

MARK W. LIPSEY
Vanderbilt University, Nashville, TN

HOWARD E. FREEMAN

SAGE Publications
International Educational and Professional Publisher
Thousand Oaks ▪ London ▪ New Delhi

For information:

Sage Publications, Inc.
2455 Teller Road
Thousand Oaks, California 91320
E-mail: order@sagepub.com

Sage Publications Ltd.
6 Bonhill Street
London EC2A 4PU
United Kingdom

Sage Publications India Pvt. Ltd.
B-42, Panchsheel Enclave
Post Box 4109
New Delhi 110 017 India

Printed in the United States of America

Library of Congress Cataloging-in-Publication Data
Rossi, Peter Henry, 1921-
Evaluation : a systematic approach / by Peter H. Rossi, Mark W.
Lipsey, Howard E. Freeman.— 7th ed.
        p. cm.
Includes bibliographical references and index.
ISBN 978-0-7619-0894-4 (cloth)
    1. Evaluation research (Social action programs) I. Lipsey, Mark W.
II. Freeman, Howard E. III. Title.
H62.R666 2004
361.6´1´072—dc222

                                      2003015926

Printed on acid-free paper

            07   08   09   10   9   8   7   6   5

Acquiring Editor:	Lisa Cuevas Shaw
Associate Editor:	Paul Reis
Developmental Editor:	John Bergez
Production Editor:	Claudia A. Hoffman
Copy Editor:	Kate Peterson
Typesetter:	C&M Digitals (P) Ltd.
Indexer:	Molly Hall
Cover Designer:	Michelle Lee Kenny

Contents

PREFACE

This seventh edition contains some new material and extensive revisions of topics that appeared in previous editions. The amendments include an extended treatment of outcome measurement and monitoring, a better exposition of impact assessment designs, a fuller treatment of some key statistical issues in evaluation research, and a more detailed description of meta-analysis. We believe that these changes bring the volume more completely in line with the current leading edge of the field.

However, the central theme of providing an introduction to the field of program evaluation has not been changed. We cover the full range of evaluation research activities used in appraising the design, implementation, effectiveness, and efficiency of social programs. Throughout the many revisions of this book, we retain the ambition to communicate the technical knowledge and collective experiences of practicing evaluators to those who might consider evaluation as a calling and to those who need to know what evaluation is all about. Our intended readers are students, practitioners, sponsors of social programs, social commentators, and anyone concerned with how to measure the successes and failures of attempts to improve social conditions.

We believe that reading this book will provide enough knowledge to understand and assess evaluations. However, it is not intended to be a cookbook of procedures for conducting evaluations, although we identify sources in which such procedures are described in detail, including references to advanced literature for the adventurous. Ultimately, nothing teaches how to do evaluations as well as direct experience in designing and running actual evaluations. We urge all those considering entering the field of evaluation research to seek hands-on experience.

In the 1970s when the first edition of this book was published, evaluation was not yet fully established as a way of assessing social programs. It is quite different now. In the 21st century, evaluation research has become solidly incorporated into the routine activities of all levels of government throughout the world, into the operations of nongovernmental organizations, and into the public discussions of social issues. Hardly a week goes by when the media do not report the results of some evaluation. We believe that evaluation research makes an important contribution to the formation and improvement of social policies. Being an evaluator can be an exciting professional role providing opportunities to participate in the advancement of social well-being along with the exercise of technical and interpersonal skills.

We dedicate this edition to the memory of Daniel Patrick Moynihan, who died recently. Over the last half century, Pat Moynihan held an astonishing array of key positions in academia (Harvard), in federal agencies (Assistant Secretary of Labor in the Kennedy and Johnson administrations), as White House staff adviser on urban issues in the Nixon administration, and two terms as a senator representing New York. He published several influential books on social policy and decision making in the federal government. His presence in the Senate measurably raised the intellectual level of Senate deliberations on social policy. In all the positions he held, the improvement of social policy was his central concern. In addition, he was a firm and eloquent advocate of social research and of evaluation research in particular. (For an example of his advocacy, see Exhibit 1-A in Chapter 1.) Pat Moynihan played a critical role in building and supporting federal evaluation activities as well as advancing the social well-being of our society.

—P.H.R. and M.W.L.

An Overview of Program Evaluation

Chapter Outline

What Is Program Evaluation?

A Brief History of Evaluation
Evaluation Research as a Social Science Activity
The Boom Period in Evaluation Research
Social Policy and Public Administration Movements
     Development of Policy and Public Administration Specialists
The Evaluation Enterprise From the Great Society to the Present Day

The Defining Characteristics of Program Evaluation
Application of Social Research Methods
The Effectiveness of Social Programs
Adapting Evaluation to the Political and Organizational Context
Informing Social Action to Improve Social Conditions

Evaluation Research in Practice
Evaluation and the Volatility of Social Programs
Scientific Versus Pragmatic Evaluation Postures
Diversity in Evaluation Outlooks and Approaches

Who Can Do Evaluations?

In its broadest meaning, to evaluate means to ascertain the worth of or to fix a value on some object. In this book, we use evaluation in a more restricted sense, as program evaluation *or interchangeably as* evaluation research, *defined as a social science activity directed at collecting, analyzing, interpreting, and communicating information about the workings and effectiveness of social programs. Evaluations are conducted for a variety of practical reasons: to aid in decisions concerning whether programs should be continued, improved, expanded, or curtailed; to assess the utility of new programs and initiatives; to increase the effectiveness of program management and administration; and to satisfy the accountability requirements of program sponsors. Evaluations also may contribute to substantive and methodological social science knowledge.*

Understanding evaluation as currently practiced requires some appreciation of its history, its distinguishing concepts and purposes, and the inherent tensions and challenges that shape its practice. Program evaluation represents an adaptation of social research methods to the task of studying social interventions so that sound judgments can be drawn about the social problems addressed, and the design, implementation, impact, and efficiency of programs that address those problems. Individual evaluation studies, and the cumulation of knowledge from many such studies, can make vital contributions to informed social actions aimed at improving the human condition.

Since antiquity organized efforts have been undertaken to describe, understand, and ameliorate defects in the human condition. This book is rooted in the tradition of scientific study of social problems—a tradition that has aspired to improve the quality of our physical and social environments and enhance our individual and collective well-being through the systematic creation and application of knowledge. Although the terms *program evaluation* and *evaluation research* are relatively recent inventions, the activities that we will consider under these rubrics are not. They can be traced to the very beginnings of modern science. Three centuries ago, as Cronbach and colleagues (1980) point out, Thomas Hobbes and his contemporaries tried to calculate numerical measures to assess social conditions and identify the causes of mortality, morbidity, and social disorganization.

Even social experiments, the most technically challenging form of contemporary evaluation research, are hardly a recent invention. One of the earliest "social experiments" took place in the 1700s when a British naval captain observed the lack of scurvy among sailors serving on the ships of Mediterranean countries where citrus fruit was part of the rations. Thereupon he made half his crew consume limes while the other half continued with their regular diet. The good captain probably did not know that he was evaluating a demonstration project nor did he likely have an explicit "program theory" (a term we will discuss later), namely, that scurvy is a consequence of a vitamin C deficiency and that limes are rich in vitamin C. Nevertheless, the intervention worked and British seamen eventually were compelled to consume citrus fruit regularly, a practice that gave rise to the still-popular label *limeys*. Incidentally, it took about 50 years before the captain's "social program" was widely adopted. Then, as now, diffusion and acceptance of evaluation findings did not come easily.

What Is Program Evaluation?

At various times, policymakers, funding organizations, planners, program managers, taxpayers, or program clientele need to distinguish worthwhile **social programs**[1] from ineffective ones and launch new programs or revise existing ones so as to achieve certain desirable results. To do so, they must obtain answers to questions such as the following:

- What are the nature and scope of the problem? Where is it located, whom does it affect, how many are affected, and how does the problem affect them?

- What is it about the problem or its effects that justifies new, expanded, or modified social programs?

- What feasible interventions are likely to significantly ameliorate the problem?

- What are the appropriate target populations for intervention?

- Is a particular intervention reaching its target population?

- Is the intervention being implemented well? Are the intended services being provided?

- Is the intervention effective in attaining the desired goals or benefits?

- Is the program cost reasonable in relation to its effectiveness and benefits?

Answers to such questions are necessary for local or specialized programs, such as job training in a small town, a new mathematics curriculum for elementary schools, or the outpatient services of a community mental health clinic, as well as for broad national or state programs in such areas as health care, welfare, and educational reform. Providing those answers is the work of persons in the program evaluation field. Evaluators use social research methods to study, appraise, and help improve social programs, including the soundness of the programs' diagnoses of the social problems they address, the way the programs are conceptualized and implemented, the outcomes they achieve, and their efficiency. (Exhibit 1-A conveys the views of one feisty senator about the need for evaluation evidence on the effectiveness of programs.)

---

1. Terms in boldface are defined in the Key Concepts list at the end of the chapter and in the Glossary.

EXHIBIT 1-A

A Veteran
Policymaker
Wants to See the
Evaluation Results

But all the while we were taking on this large—and, as we can now say, hugely successful—effort [deficit reduction], we were constantly besieged by administration officials wanting us to *add* money for this social program or that social program. . . . *My* favorite in this miscellany was something called "family preservation," yet another categorical aid program (there were a dozen in place already) which amounted to a dollop of social services and a press release for some subcommittee chairman. The program was to cost $930 million over five years, starting at $60 million in fiscal year 1994. For three decades I had been watching families come apart in our society; now I was being told by seemingly everyone on the new team that one more program would do the trick. . . . At the risk of indiscretion, let me include in the record at this point a letter I wrote on July 28, 1993, to Dr. Laura D'Andrea Tyson, then the distinguished chairman of the Council of Economic Advisors, regarding the Family Preservation program:

Dear Dr. Tyson:

You will recall that last Thursday when you so kindly joined us at a meeting of the Democratic Policy Committee you and I discussed the President's family preservation proposal. You indicated how much he supports the measure. I assured you I, too, support it, but went on to ask what evidence was there that it would have any effect. You assured me there were such data. Just for fun, I asked for two citations.

The next day we received a fax from Sharon Glied of your staff with a number of citations and a paper, "Evaluating the Results," that appears to have been written by Frank Farrow of the Center for the Study of Social Policy here in Washington and Harold Richman at the Chapin Hall Center at the University of Chicago. The paper is quite direct: "Solid proof that family preservation services can affect a state's overall placement rates is still lacking."

Just yesterday, the same Chapin Hall Center released an "Evaluation of the Illinois Family First Placement Prevention Program: Final Report." This was a large scale study of the Illinois Family First initiative authorized by the Illinois Family Preservation Act of 1987. It was "designed to test effects of this program on out-of-home placement and other outcomes, such as subsequent child maltreatment." Data on case and service characteristics were provided by Family First caseworkers on approximately 4,500 cases: approximately 1,600 families participated in the randomized experiment. The findings are clear enough.

(Continued)

EXHIBIT 1-A
(Continued)

Overall, the Family First placement prevention program results in a slight increase in placement rates (when data from all experimental sites are combined). This effect disappears once case and site variations are taken into account. In other words, there are either negative effects or no effects.

This is nothing new. Here is Peter Rossi's conclusion in his 1992 paper, "Assessing Family Preservation Programs." Evaluations conducted to date "do not form a sufficient basis upon which to firmly decide whether family preservation programs are either effective or not." May I say to you that there is nothing in the least surprising in either of these findings? From the mid-60s on this has been the repeated, I almost want to say consistent, pattern of evaluation studies. Either few effects or negative effects. Thus the negative income tax experiments of the 1970s appeared to produce an increase in family breakup.

This pattern of "counterintuitive" findings first appeared in the '60s. Greeley and Rossi, some of my work, and Coleman's. To this day I cannot decide whether we are dealing here with an artifact of methodology or a much larger and more intractable fact of social programs. In any event, by 1978 we had Rossi's Iron Law. To wit: "If there is any empirical law that is emerging from the past decade of widespread evaluation activity, it is that the expected value for any measured effect of a social program is zero."

I write you at such length for what I believe to be an important purpose. In the last six months I have been repeatedly impressed by the number of members of the Clinton administration who have assured me with great vigor that something or other is known in an area of social policy which, to the best of my understanding, is not known at all. This seems to me perilous. It is quite possible to live with uncertainty, with the possibility, even the likelihood that one is wrong. But beware of certainty where none exists. Ideological certainty easily degenerates into an insistence upon ignorance.

The great strength of political conservatives at this time (and for a generation) is that they are open to the thought that matters are complex. Liberals got into a reflexive pattern of denying this. I had hoped twelve years in the wilderness might have changed this; it may be it has only reinforced it. If this is so, current revival of liberalism will be brief and inconsequential.

Respectfully,

Senator Daniel Patrick Moynihan

SOURCE: Adapted, with permission, from D. P. Moynihan, *Miles to Go: A Personal History of Social Policy* (Cambridge, MA: Harvard University Press, 1996), pp. 47-49.

Although this text emphasizes the evaluation of social programs, especially human service programs, program evaluation is not restricted to that arena. The broad scope of program evaluation can be seen in the evaluations of the U.S. General Accounting Office (GAO), which have covered the procurement and testing of military hardware, quality control for drinking water, the maintenance of major highways, the use of hormones to stimulate growth in beef cattle, and other organized activities far afield from human services.

Indeed, the techniques described in this text are useful in virtually all spheres of activity in which issues are raised about the effectiveness of organized social action. For example, the mass communication and advertising industries use essentially the same approaches in developing media programs and marketing products. Commercial and industrial corporations evaluate the procedures they use in selecting, training, and promoting employees and organizing their workforces. Political candidates develop their campaigns by evaluating the voter appeal of different strategies. Consumer products are tested for performance, durability, and safety. Administrators in both the public and private sectors often assess the managerial, fiscal, and personnel practices of their organizations. This list of examples could be extended indefinitely.

These various applications of evaluation are distinguished primarily by the nature and goals of the endeavors being evaluated. In this text, we have chosen to emphasize the evaluation of social programs—programs designed to benefit the human condition—rather than efforts that have such purposes as increasing profits or amassing influence and power. This choice stems from a desire to concentrate on a particularly significant and active area of evaluation as well as from a practical need to limit the scope of the book. Note that throughout this book we use the terms *evaluation, program evaluation,* and *evaluation research* interchangeably.

To illustrate the evaluation of social programs more concretely, we offer below examples of social programs that have been evaluated under the sponsorship of local, state, and federal government agencies, international organizations, private foundations and philanthropies, and both nonprofit and for-profit associations and corporations.

- In several major cities in the United States, a large private foundation provided funding to establish community health centers in low-income areas. The centers were intended as an alternative way for residents to obtain ambulatory patient care that they could otherwise obtain only from hospital outpatient clinics and emergency rooms at great public cost. It was further hoped that by improving access to such care, the clinics might increase timely treatment and thus reduce the need for lengthy and expensive hospital care. Evaluation indicated that centers often were cost-effective in comparison to hospital clinics.

■ Advocates of school vouchers initiated a privately funded program in New York City for poor families with children in the first three grades of disadvantaged public schools. Scholarships were offered to eligible families to go toward tuition costs in the private schools of their choice. Some 14,000 scholarship applications were received, and 1,500 successful candidates were chosen by random selection. The evaluation team took advantage of this mode of selection by treating the program as a randomized experiment in order to compare the educational outcomes among those students who received scholarships and moved to private schools with the outcomes among those students not selected to receive scholarships.

■ In recent decades, the federal government has allowed states to modify their welfare programs provided that the changes were evaluated for their effects on clients and costs. Some states instituted strong work and job training requirements, others put time limits on benefits, and a few prohibited increases in benefits for children born while on the welfare rolls. Evaluation research showed that such policies were capable of reducing welfare rolls and increasing employment. Many of the program features studied were incorporated in the federal welfare reforms passed in 1996 (Personal Responsibility and Work Opportunity Reconciliation Act).

■ Fully two-thirds of the world's rural children suffer mild to severe malnutrition, with serious consequences for their health, physical growth, and mental development. A major demonstration of the potential for improving children's health status and mental development by providing dietary supplements was undertaken in Central America. Pregnant women, lactating mothers, and children from birth through age 12 were provided with a daily high-protein, high-calorie food supplement. The evaluation results showed that children benefited by the program exhibited major gains in physical growth and modest increases in cognitive functioning.

■ In an effort to increase worker satisfaction and product quality, a large manufacturing company reorganized its employees into independent work teams. Within the teams, workers assigned tasks, recommended productivity quotas to management, and voted on the distribution of bonuses for productivity and quality improvements. An evaluation of the program revealed that it reduced days absent from the job, turnover rates, and similar measures of employee inefficiency.

These examples illustrate the diversity of social interventions that have been systematically evaluated. However, all of them involve one particular evaluation activity: assessing the outcomes of programs. As we will discuss later, evaluation may also focus on the need for a program, its design, operation and service delivery, or efficiency.

A Brief History of Evaluation

Although its historical roots extend to the 17th century, widespread systematic evaluation research is a relatively modern 20th-century development. The application of social research methods to program evaluation coincides with the growth and refinement of the research methods themselves as well as with ideological, political, and demographic changes.

Evaluation Research as a Social Science Activity

The systematic evaluation of social programs first became commonplace in education and public health. Prior to World War I, for instance, the most significant efforts were directed at assessing literacy and occupational training programs and public health initiatives to reduce mortality and morbidity from infectious diseases. By the 1930s, social scientists were using rigorous research methods to assess social programs in a variety of areas (Freeman, 1977). Lewin's pioneering "action research" studies and Lippitt and White's work on democratic and authoritarian leadership, for example, were widely influential evaluative studies. The famous Western Electric experiments on worker productivity that contributed the term *Hawthorne effect* to the social science lexicon date from this time as well. (See Bernstein and Freeman, 1975, for a more extended discussion and Bulmer, 1982, Cronbach and Associates, 1980, and Madaus and Stufflebeam, 1989, for somewhat different historical perspectives.)

From such beginnings, applied social research grew at an accelerating pace, with a strong boost provided by its contributions during World War II. Stouffer and his associates worked with the U.S. Army to develop procedures for monitoring soldier morale and evaluate personnel policies and propaganda techniques, while the Office of War Information used sample surveys to monitor civilian morale (Stouffer et al., 1949). A host of smaller studies assessed the efficacy of price controls and media campaigns to modify American eating habits. Similar social science efforts were mounted in Britain and elsewhere around the world.

The Boom Period in Evaluation Research

Following World War II, numerous major federal and privately funded programs were launched to provide urban development and housing, technological and cultural education, occupational training, and preventive health activities. It was also during this time that federal agencies and private foundations made major commitments to international programs for family planning, health and nutrition, and rural development. Expenditures were very large and consequently were accompanied by demands for "knowledge of results."

By the end of the 1950s, program evaluation was commonplace. Social scientists engaged in assessments of delinquency prevention programs, psychotherapeutic and psychopharmacological treatments, public housing programs, educational activities, community organization initiatives, and numerous other initiatives. Studies were undertaken not only in the United States, Europe, and other industrialized countries but also in less developed nations. Increasingly, evaluation components were included in programs for family planning in Asia, nutrition and health care in Latin America, and agricultural and community development in Africa (Freeman, Rossi, and Wright, 1980; Levine, Solomon, and Hellstern, 1981). Expanding knowledge of the methods of social research, including sample surveys and advanced statistical procedures, and increased funding and administrative know-how, made possible large-scale, multisite evaluation studies.

During the 1960s, the number of articles and books about evaluation research grew dramatically. Hayes's (1959) monograph on evaluation research in less developed countries, Suchman's (1967) review of evaluation research methods, and Campbell's (1969) call for social experimentation are a few illustrations. In the United States, a key impetus for the spurt of interest in evaluation research was the federal war on poverty, initiated under Lyndon Johnson's presidency. By the late 1960s, evaluation research had become a growth industry.

In the early 1970s, evaluation research emerged as a distinct specialty field in the social sciences. A variety of books appeared, including the first texts (Rossi and Williams, 1972; Weiss, 1972), critiques of the methodological quality of evaluation studies (Bernstein and Freeman, 1975), and discussions of the organizational and structural constraints on evaluation research (Riecken and Boruch, 1974). The first journal in evaluation, *Evaluation Review,* was launched in 1976 by Sage Publications. Other journals followed in rapid succession, and today there are at least a dozen devoted primarily to evaluation. During this period, special sessions on evaluation studies at meetings of academic and practitioner groups became commonplace, and professional associations specifically for evaluation researchers were founded (see Exhibit 1-B for a listing of the major journals and professional organizations). By 1980, Cronbach and his associates were able to state that "evaluation has become the liveliest frontier of American social science" (pp. 12-13).

As evaluation research matured, a qualitative change occurred. In its early years, evaluation was shaped mainly by the interests of social researchers. In later stages, however, the consumers of evaluation research exercised a significant influence on the field. Evaluation is now sustained primarily by funding from policymakers, program planners, and administrators who use the findings and by the interests of the general public and the clients of the programs evaluated. Evaluation results may not make front-page headlines, but they are often matters of intense concern to informed citizens, program sponsors, and decisionmakers, and those whose lives are affected, directly or indirectly, by the programs at issue.

EXHIBIT 1-B
Major Evaluation
Journals and
Professional
Organizations

Journals devoted primarily to program and policy evaluation:
   Evaluation Review: A Journal of Applied Social Research
      (Sage Publications)
   American Journal of Evaluation (JAI Press) (formerly *Evaluation
      Practice*, before 1998)
   New Directions for Evaluation (Jossey-Bass)
   *Evaluation: The International Journal of Theory, Research, and
      Practice* (Sage Publications)
   Evaluation and Program Planning (Pergamon)
   Journal of Policy Analysis and Management (John Wiley)
   Canadian Journal of Program Evaluation (University of
      Calgary Press)
   Evaluation Journal of Australasia (Australasian Evaluation Society)
   Evaluation & the Health Professions (Sage Publications)
   Educational Evaluation and Policy Analysis (American Educational
      Research Association)
   Assessment and Evaluation in Higher Education (Carfax Publishing Ltd.)

Professional organizations for program and policy evaluators:
   American Evaluation Association
      (Web page: http://www.eval.org/)
   Association for Public Policy Analysis and Management
      (Web page:)
   American Educational Research Association (Evaluation Division)
      (Web page: http://aera.net)
   Canadian Evaluation Association (Web page:
      http://www.unites.uqam.ca/ces/ces-sce.html)
   Australasian Evaluation Society
      (Web page: http://www.parklane.com.au/aes/)
   European Evaluation Society
      (Web page: http://www.europeanevaluation.org)
   UK Evaluation Society
      (Web page: http://www.evaluation.org.uk)
   German Evaluation Society
      (Web page: http://www.fal.de/tissen/geproval.htm)
   Italian Evaluation Society
      (Web page: http://www.valutazione.it/)

Incorporation of the consumer perspective into evaluation research has moved the field beyond academic social science. Evaluation has now become a political and managerial activity that makes significant input into the complex mosaic from which emerge policy decisions and resources for starting, enlarging, changing, or sustaining programs to better the human condition. In this regard, evaluation research must be seen as an integral part of the social policy and public administration movements.

Social Policy and Public Administration Movements

Social programs and the associated evaluation activities have emerged from the relatively recent transfer of responsibility for the nation's social and environmental conditions, and the quality of life of its citizens, to government bodies. As Bremner (1956) has described, before World War I, except for war veterans, the provision of human services was seen primarily as the obligation of individuals and voluntary associations. Poor people, physically and mentally disabled persons, and troubled families were the clients of local charities staffed mainly by volunteers drawn from the ranks of the more fortunate. Our image of these volunteers as wealthy matrons toting baskets of food and hand-me-down clothing to give to the poor and unfortunate is only somewhat exaggerated. Along with civic associations, charity hospitals, county and state asylums, locally supported public schools, state normal schools, and sectarian old-age homes, volunteers were the bulwark of our human service "system." Indeed, government—particularly the federal government—was comparatively small before the 1930s. The idea of annual federal expenditures of billions of dollars to provide medical care for the aged and the poor, for instance, would have been mind-boggling for the government official of the 1920s. More dollars for public education currently flow from Washington in a few months than were spent by the federal treasury for that purpose in the entire first decade of the 20th century.

Correspondingly, there was little demand for social and economic information. Even in the late 1930s, federal expenditures for social science research and statistics were only $40-$50 million, as compared to many magnitudes that amount today. Also, before the 1930s key government officials typically were selected without regard to objective competence criteria; indeed, there were few ways of objectively determining competence. The professional civil service was a fraction of the size it is today, most jobs did not require technical know-how, and formal training programs were not widely available.

All this began to change in the 1930s. Human services grew at a rapid pace with the advent of the Great Depression, and so, of course, did government. In part because of the unwieldiness that accompanied this accelerated growth, there was strong pressure to apply the concepts and techniques of so-called scientific management, which were well regarded in industry, to government programs and activities. These ideas first took hold in the Department of Defense and then diffused to other government organizations, including human service agencies. Concepts and procedures for planning, budgeting, quality control, and accountability, as well as later, more sophisticated notions of cost-benefit analysis and system modeling, became the order of the day in the human services area.

Development of Policy and Public Administration Specialists

During this same period, scholars with social science training began to investigate the political, organizational, and administrative decision making that took place in executive departments and other government agencies. In part, their interests were purely academic—they wanted to understand how government worked. However, individuals in leadership positions in government agencies, who were groping for ways to deal with their large staffs and full coffers of funds, recognized a critical need for orderly, explicit ways to handle their policy, administrative, program, and planning responsibilities. They found many of the concepts, techniques, and principles from economics, political science, psychology, and sociology useful. The study of the public sector thus grew into the largely applied research specialty that is now most commonly called "policy science" or "policy analysis."

As government became increasingly complex and technical, its programs could no longer be adequately managed by people hired as intelligent generalists or because of their connections with political patrons, relatives, or friends. Most middle management jobs and many senior executive positions required specific substantive and technical skills, and those who filled them needed either training or extensive experience to do their work competently (see Exhibit 1-C). In response, many graduate schools of management, public health, and social work began programs to train students for government positions and more specialized schools, generally with "public administration" in their titles, were established or expanded.

The importance of evaluation is now widely acknowledged by those in political and administrative roles in government. Many federal agencies have their own evaluation units, as do a large number of their state counterparts. In addition, federal, state, and local agencies regularly contract for program evaluation with university researchers or research firms and consultants. Although evaluation research continues to have an academic side oriented toward training, methodology, theory, and study of the nature and effects of social programs, it is now generally practiced in a context of policy making, program management, or client advocacy. Thus, not only is its history intertwined with the social policy and public administration movements, but its practice typically occurs in the same political and organizational arenas as policy analysis and public administration.

The Evaluation Enterprise From the Great Society to the Present Day

Evaluation activities increased rapidly during the Kennedy and Johnson presidencies of the 1960s, when social programs undertaken under the banners of the War on Poverty and the Great Society provided extensive resources to deal with unemployment, crime, urban deterioration, access to medical care, and mental health treatment

EXHIBIT 1-C
The Rise of
Policy Analysis

The steady growth in the number, variety, complexity, and social importance of policy issues confronting government is making increasing intellectual demands on public officials and their staffs. What should be done about nuclear safety, teenage pregnancies, urban decline, rising hospital costs, unemployment among black youth, violence toward spouses and children, and the disposal of toxic wastes? Many of these subjects were not on the public agenda 20 years ago. They are priority issues now, and new ones of a similar character emerge virtually every year. For most elected and appointed officials and their staffs, such complicated and controversial questions are outside the scope of their judgment and previous experience. Yet the questions cannot be sidestepped; government executives are expected to deal with them responsibly and effectively.

To aid them in thinking about and deciding on such matters, public officials have been depending to an increasing extent on knowledge derived from research, policy analysis, program evaluations, and statistics to inform or buttress their views. More often than in the past, elected and appointed officials in the various branches and levels of government, from federal judges to town selectmen, are citing studies, official data, and expert opinion in at least partial justification for their actions. Their staffs, which have been increasing in size and responsibility in recent decades, include growing numbers of people trained in or familiar with analytic techniques to gather and evaluate information. Increasing amounts of research, analysis, and data gathering are being done.

Because the power to influence policy is widely shared in our system of government, public officials seeking to influence policy—to play the policy game well—must be persuasive. Because of the changing character of policy issues, it is probably harder to be persuasive than it used to be. Seniority, affability, and clever "wheeling and dealing" may be relatively less influential than being generally knowledgeable and tough-minded, having the ability to offer ideas and solutions that can attract a wide following, or having a reputation as a well-informed critic. Increasingly, officials from the president on down lose influence in policy debates when they cannot get their numbers right or when their ideas and arguments are successfully challenged by opposing experts. Indeed, thorough and detailed command of an issue or problem is often mandatory. Legislatures are requiring executives to be experts in the programs and issues under their jurisdiction. Judges are requiring detailed proof that administrative decisions are not arbitrary and capricious. Budget officials demand positive program evaluations. The public demands accountability. Thus the dynamic processes whereby our political system confronts social problems are perceptibly, if not dramatically, raising the standards of substantive and managerial competence in the performance of public responsibilities.

SOURCE: Adapted, with permission, from Laurence E. Lynn, Jr., *Designing Public Policy* (Santa Monica, CA: Scott, Foresman, 1980).

The year 1965 was an important one in the evolution of "policy analysis and evaluation research" as an independent branch of study. Two developments at the federal government level—the War on Poverty-Great Society initiative and the Executive Order establishing the Planning-Programming-Budgeting (PPB) system—were of signal importance in this regard. Both offered standing, legitimacy, and financial support to scholars who would turn their skills and interests toward examining the efficiency with which public measures allocate resources, their impacts on individual behavior, their effectiveness in attaining the objectives for which they were designed, and their effects on the well-being of rich versus poor, minority versus majority, and North versus South.

The War on Poverty-Great Society developments initiated in 1965 represented a set of social interventions on an unprecedented scale. All impacted by them wanted to know if they were working, and who was being affected by them and how. Those with the skills to answer these questions found both financial support and an interested audience for their efforts. And the social science community responded. The same year saw government-wide adoption of the formal evaluation and analysis methods that had earlier been applied in Robert McNamara's Defense Department in the Planning-Programming-Budgeting system. A presidential Executive Order gave employment and financial support to thousands who wished to apply their analytical skills to such efficiency, effectiveness, and equity questions.

SOURCE: Robert H. Haveman, "Policy Analysis and Evaluation Research After Twenty Years," *Policy Studies Journal*, 1987, 16:191-218.

(see Exhibit 1-D). These programs were often hurriedly put into place, and a significant portion were poorly conceived, improperly implemented, or ineffectively administered. Findings of limited effectiveness and poor benefit-to-cost ratios prompted widespread reappraisal of the magnitude of effects that can be expected from social programs.

Partly as a consequence of the apparent ineffectiveness of many initiatives, along with increasing expenditures for social programs in the face of rising fiscal conservatism, the decade of the 1970s was marked by increasing resistance to the expansion of government programs (Freeman and Solomon, 1979). This, in turn, brought about a change in emphasis in the evaluation field. In particular, increased attention was given to assessing the expenditures of social programs in comparison to their benefits and to demonstrating fiscal accountability and effective management. In the process, many fiscal and political conservatives, often skeptical about social science, joined the advocates of social programs in pressing for the information that evaluations provide.

Beginning with the Reagan presidency in the 1980s, and continuing to the present day, domestic federal expenditures were curtailed in an attempt to control inflation and reduce the federal deficit. Many of the largest cutbacks targeted social programs. Many states and cities adopted a similar posture; indeed, some of the local and state reactions to their deteriorating economic situations were particularly severe. These developments were partly a consequence of the distrust, hostility, and political actions of community members dismayed with the painful bite of income and property taxes. As we have indicated, however, they were also influenced by disenchantment with the modest effects and poor implementation of many of the programs most ardently championed by public officials, planners, and politicians in prior decades.

As should be apparent, social programs and, consequently, the evaluation enterprise are powerfully shaped by changing times. Political perspectives during recent decades, not only in the United States but also in a number of Western European countries, have been especially concerned with the balance of benefits and costs for social programs. On the intellectual front, both conservative and liberal critiques of the Great Society programs have had an impact on the evaluation field. Although these criticisms were sometimes based more on ideology than evidence, they also have drawn on evaluation results in condemning social programs. The evaluation field has thus been thrust into the middle of contentious debates about the very concept of social intervention and faced with new challenges to demonstrate that any major program initiative can be effective.

As we move into the 21st century, national policy is dominated by fiscal conservatism, the devolution of responsibility to the states, and continuing skepticism about social programs. These trends have mixed implications for evaluation. On the one hand, revisions and reforms in social programs require evaluation if anything is to be learned about their fiscal and social impacts, and a number of major national evaluations are under way (Rossi, 2001). On the other hand, much of the responsibility for conducting evaluation has devolved to the states along with the programs. Despite a steady increase in the amount and quality of evaluation conducted at state and local levels, many states do not have the capability to undertake rigorous evaluation on a regular basis or the means to develop such capability.

Regardless of political trends, two points seem clear about the current environment for evaluation. First, restraints on resources will continue to require funders to choose the social problem areas on which to concentrate resources and the programs that should be given priority. Second, intensive scrutiny of existing programs will continue because of the pressure to curtail or dismantle those that do not demonstrate that they are effective and efficient. Moreover, both dissatisfaction with existing programs and shifts in political currents will result in new and modified programs that come forward with promises of being more effective and less costly. All these circumstances create an important role for evaluation research.

The Defining Characteristics of Program Evaluation

With the benefit of some historical context, we will now provide a fuller description of the nature of the program evaluation enterprise in contemporary context. We begin, as a proper textbook should, with a definition:

Program evaluation is the use of social research methods to systematically investigate the effectiveness of social intervention programs in ways that are adapted to their political and organizational environments and are designed to inform social action to improve social conditions. By elaborating on the components of this definition, we can highlight the major themes that we believe are integral to the practice of program evaluation.

Application of Social Research Methods

The concept of evaluation entails, on the one hand, a description of the performance of the entity being evaluated and, on the other, some standards or criteria for judging that performance (see Exhibit 1-E). It follows that a central task of the program evaluator is to construct a valid description of program performance in a form that permits incisive comparison with the applicable criteria. Failing to describe program performance with a reasonable degree of validity may distort a program's accomplishments, deny it credit for its successes, or overlook shortcomings for which it should be accountable. Moreover, an acceptable description must be detailed and precise. An unduly vague or equivocal description of program performance may make it impossible to determine with confidence whether the performance actually meets the appropriate standard.

Social research methods and the accompanying standards of methodological quality have been developed and refined over the years explicitly for the purpose of constructing sound factual descriptions of social phenomena. In particular, contemporary social science techniques of systematic observation, measurement, sampling, research design, and data analysis represent rather highly evolved procedures for producing valid, reliable, and precise characterizations of social behavior. Social research methods thus provide an especially appropriate approach to the task of describing program performance in ways that will be as credible and defensible as possible.

Regardless of the type of social intervention under study, therefore, evaluators will typically employ social research procedures for gathering, analyzing, and interpreting evidence about the performance of a program. In any event, commitment to the rules of social research is at the core of the perspective on evaluation presented in this book and is what is meant by the subtitle, *A Systematic Approach.* This is not to say, however, that we believe evaluation studies must follow some particular social research style or combination of styles, whether quantitative or qualitative, experimental or ethnographic, "positivistic" or "naturalistic." Nor does this commitment to the methods of social science mean that we

EXHIBIT 1-E

The Two Arms
of Evaluation

Evaluation is the process of determining the merit, worth, and value of things, and evaluations are the products of that process. . . . Evaluation is not the mere accumulation and summarizing of data that are clearly relevant for decision making, although there are still evaluation theorists who take that to be its definition. . . . In all contexts, gathering and analyzing the data that are needed for decision making—difficult though that often is—comprises only one of the two key components in evaluation; absent the other component, and absent a procedure for combining them, we simply lack anything that qualifies as an evaluation. *Consumer Reports* does not just test products and report the test scores; it (i) *rates or ranks* by (ii) *merit or cost-effectiveness*. To get to that kind of conclusion requires an input of something besides data, in the usual sense of that term. The second element is required to get to conclusions about merit or net benefits, and it consists of evaluative premises or standards. . . . A more straightforward approach is just to say that evaluation has two arms, only one of which is engaged in data-gathering. The other arm collects, clarifies, and verifies relevant values and standards.

SOURCE: Quoted, with permission, from Michael Scriven, *Evaluation Thesaurus*, 4th ed. (Newbury Park, CA: Sage, 1991), pp. 1, 4-5.

think current methods are beyond improvement. Evaluators must often innovate and improvise as they attempt to find ways to gather credible, defensible evidence about social programs. In fact, evaluators have been, and will likely continue to be, especially productive contributors to methodological development in applied social research.

Finally, this view does not imply that methodological quality is necessarily the most important aspect of an evaluation nor that only the highest technical standards, without compromise, are always appropriate for evaluation research. As Carol Weiss (1972) once observed, social programs are inherently inhospitable environments for research purposes. The circumstances surrounding specific programs, and the particular issues the evaluator is called on to address, frequently compel evaluators to compromise and adapt textbook methodological standards. The challenges to the evaluator are to match the research procedures to the evaluation questions and circumstances as well as possible and, whatever procedures are used, to apply them at the highest possible standard feasible to those questions and circumstances.

The Effectiveness of Social Programs

By definition, social programs are activities whose principal reason for existing is to "do good," that is, to ameliorate a social problem or improve social conditions. It follows that it is appropriate for the parties who invest in social programs to hold them accountable for their contribution to the social good. Correspondingly, any evaluation of such programs that is worthy of the name must evaluate—that is, judge—the quality of a program's performance as it relates to some aspect of its effectiveness in producing social benefits. More specifically, the evaluation of a program generally involves assessing one or more of five domains: (1) the need for the program, (2) the program's design, (3) its implementation and service delivery, (4) its impact, or outcomes, and (5) its efficiency. Subsequent chapters will address how evaluators make these assessments.

Adapting Evaluation to the Political and Organizational Context

Program evaluation is not a cut-and-dried activity like putting up a prefabricated house or checking a document with a word processor's spelling program. Rather, evaluators must tailor the initial evaluation plan to the particular program and its circumstances and then typically revise and modify their plan as needed. The specific form and scope of an evaluation depend primarily on its purposes and audience, the nature of the program being evaluated, and, not least, the political and organizational context within which the evaluation is conducted. Here we focus on the last of these factors, the context of the evaluation.

The evaluation plan is generally organized around the questions posed about the program by those who commission the evaluation, called the **evaluation sponsor,** and other pertinent **stakeholders**—individuals, groups, or organizations that have a significant interest in how well a program functions. These questions may be stipulated in very specific, fixed terms that allow little flexibility, as in a detailed contract for evaluation services. More often, however, the evaluator must negotiate with the evaluation sponsors and stakeholders to develop and refine the questions. Although these parties presumably know their own interests and purposes, they will not necessarily formulate their concerns in ways that the evaluator can use to structure an evaluation plan. For instance, the initial questions may be vague, overly general, or phrased in program jargon that must be translated for more general consumption. Occasionally, the evaluation questions put forward are essentially pro forma (e.g., is the program effective?) and have not emerged from careful reflection regarding the relevant issues. In such cases, the evaluator must probe thoroughly to determine what the question means to the evaluation sponsor and program stakeholders and why they are concerned about it.

Equally important are the reasons the questions about the program are being asked, especially the uses that will be made of the answers. An evaluation must provide information that addresses the issues that matter, develop that information in a way that is timely and meaningful for the decisionmakers, and communicate it in a form that is

EXHIBIT 1-F

Where Politics
and Evaluation Meet

Evaluation is a rational enterprise that takes place in a political context. Political considerations intrude in three major ways, and the evaluator who fails to recognize their presence is in for a series of shocks and frustrations:

First, the policies and programs with which evaluation deals are the creatures of political decisions. They were proposed, defined, debated, enacted, and funded through political processes, and in implementation they remain subject to pressures—both supportive and hostile—that arise out of the play of politics.

Second, because evaluation is undertaken in order to feed into decision making, its reports enter the political arena. There, evaluative evidence of program outcomes has to compete for attention with other factors that carry weight in the political process.

Third, and perhaps least recognized, evaluation itself has a political stance. By its very nature, it makes implicit political statements about such issues as the problematic nature of some programs and the unchallenge-ability of others, the legitimacy of program goals and program strategies, the utility of strategies of incremental reform, and even the appropriate role of the social scientist in policy and program formation.

Knowing that political constraints and resistance exist is not a reason for abandoning evaluation research; rather, it is a precondition for usable evaluation research. Only when the evaluator has insight into the interests and motivations of other actors in the system, into the roles that he himself is consciously or inadvertently playing, the obstacles and opportunities that impinge upon the evaluative effort, and the limitations and possibilities for putting the results of evaluation to work—only with sensitivity to the politics of evaluation research—can the evaluator be as creative and strategically useful as he should be.

SOURCE: From Carol H. Weiss, "Where Politics and Evaluation Research Meet," *Evaluation Practice*, 1993, 14(1):94, where the original 1973 version was reprinted as one of the classics in the evaluation field.

usable for their purposes. For example, an evaluation might be designed one way if it is to provide information about the quality of service as feedback to the program director, who will use the results to incrementally improve the program, and quite another way if it is to provide the same kind of information to an external funder, who will use it to decide whether to renew the program's funding. In all cases, however, evaluators must design and conduct evaluations in a way that is sensitive to the political context (see Exhibit 1-F).

These assertions assume that an evaluation would not be undertaken unless there was an audience interested in receiving and, at least potentially, using the findings.

Unfortunately, sponsors sometimes commission evaluations with little intention of using the findings. For example, an evaluation may be conducted because it is mandated by program funders and then used only to demonstrate compliance with that requirement. Responsible evaluators try to avoid being drawn into such situations of "ritualistic" evaluation. An early step in planning an evaluation, therefore, is a thorough inquiry into the motivation of the evaluation sponsors, the intended purposes of the evaluation, and the uses to be made of the findings.

As a practical matter, an evaluation must also be tailored to the organizational makeup of the program. In designing the evaluation, the evaluator must take into account any number of organizational factors, such as the availability of administrative cooperation and support; the ways in which program files and data are kept and access permitted to them; the character of the services provided; and the nature, frequency, duration, and location of the contact between the program and its clients. In addition, once an evaluation is launched, it is common for changes and "in-flight" corrections to be required. Modifications, perhaps even compromises, may be necessary in the types, quantity, or quality of the data collected as a result of unanticipated practical or political obstacles, changes in the operation of the program, or shifts in the interests of the stakeholders.

Informing Social Action to Improve Social Conditions

We have emphasized that the role of evaluation is to provide answers to questions about a program that will be useful and will actually be used. This point is fundamental to evaluation—its purpose is to inform action. An evaluation, therefore, primarily addresses the audience (or, more accurately, audiences) with the potential to make decisions and take action on the basis of the evaluation results. The evaluation findings may assist such persons to make go/no-go decisions about specific program modifications or, perhaps, about initiation or continuation of entire programs. They may bear on political, practical, and resource considerations or make an impression on the views of individuals with influence. They may have direct effects on judgments of a program's value as part of an oversight process that holds the program accountable for results. Or they may have indirect effects in shaping the way program issues are framed and the nature of the debate about them.

Program evaluations may also have social action purposes that are beyond those of the particular programs being evaluated. What is learned from an evaluation of one program, say, a drug use prevention program implemented at a particular high school, also tells us something about the whole category of similar programs, such as weight reduction or antismoking programs. Many of the parties involved with social interventions must make decisions and take action that relates to types of programs rather than individual instances. A congressional committee may deliberate the merits of compensatory education programs, a state correctional department may consider instituting boot camps for juvenile offenders, or a philanthropic foundation may decide to promote and underwrite programs that provide visiting nurses to single mothers. The body of evaluation findings for programs of each of these types is very pertinent to decisions and social actions of similar sorts.

One important form of evaluation research is that which is conducted on demonstration programs, that is, social intervention projects designed and implemented explicitly to test the value of an innovative program concept. In such cases, the findings of the evaluation are significant because of what they reveal about the program concept and are used primarily by those involved in policy making and program development at levels broader than any one program. Another significant evaluation-related activity is the integration of the findings of multiple evaluations of a particular type of program into a synthesis that can inform policy making and program planning.

Evaluation thus informs social action, contributing information for planning and policy purposes, indicating whether certain innovative approaches to community problems are worth pursuing, or demonstrating the utility of some principle of professional practice. Evaluation research may even help shape our general understanding of how to bring about planned social change by testing the effects of certain broad forms of intervention. The common denominator in all evaluation research is that it is intended to be both useful and used, either directly and immediately or as an incremental contribution to a cumulative body of practical knowledge.

Evaluation Research in Practice

We have outlined the general considerations, purposes, and approaches that shape evaluation research and guide its application to any program situation. In practice, applying these concepts involves a balancing act between competing forces. Paramount among these is the inherent conflict between the requirements of systematic inquiry and data collection associated with evaluation research and the organizational imperatives of a social program devoted to delivering services and maintaining essential routine activities. The planning phase of evaluation and, especially, the data collection phase necessarily place unusual and sometimes unwelcome demands on a program's personnel and processes. Data collection, for instance, may require access to files, clients, staff, and facilities that disrupts normal program processes and distracts from or even compromises the service functions that are the program's primary obligation.

Every evaluation plan, therefore, must negotiate a middle way between optimizing the situation for research purposes and minimizing the disruption caused to normal operations. We use the word *negotiate* quite deliberately here, because the best approach is for the evaluator to develop the evaluation plan in consultation with program personnel. If the needs and purposes of the evaluation are spelled out in detail before the research begins, and those personnel who will be affected (not just the administrators) are given an opportunity to react, make input, and otherwise help shape the data collection plan, the result is usually a more workable plan and better cooperation in the face of the inevitable strains the evaluation will place on the program's administrators and staff.

In addition to the conflict between the needs of the evaluation and the functions of the program, there are other inherent tensions in the practice of evaluation that warrant comment. Here we introduce a few of the more notable dilemmas the evaluator must confront: the incompatibility of a fixed evaluation plan with the volatility of social programs; the strain between a press for evaluations to be scientific, on the one hand, and pragmatic, on the other; and the competing approaches to evaluation offered up by a field of great diversity and little consensus.

Evaluation and the Volatility of Social Programs

One of the most challenging aspects of program evaluation is the continually changing decision-making milieu of the social programs that are evaluated. The resources, priorities, and relative influence of the various sponsors and stakeholders of social programs are dynamic and frequently change with shifts in political context and social trends. The 1996 welfare reform legislation, for example, has drastically altered the nature of income support for poor families. A program reconfiguration of this magnitude requires evaluations of family income support programs to be defined differently than in the past, with new outcomes and quite different program components at issue.

The priorities and responsibilities of the organizations implementing a program can also change in significant ways. For example, a school system relieved by the courts from forced school busing may lose interest in its programs to increase white students' acceptance of assignment to predominantly minority schools. Or unanticipated problems with the intervention may require modifying the program and, consequently, the evaluation plan as well. A program to reduce the absence rates of low-income high school students by providing comprehensive medical care might be thwarted if a large proportion of the eligible students refuse the services.

Somewhat ironically, preliminary findings from the evaluation itself may stimulate changes in a program that render the remainder of the evaluation plan obsolete. Consider, for example, a study of the impact of an alcohol treatment program that included six-month and one-year follow-ups of the clients. When the six-month follow-up revealed high rates of alcohol use among the treatment group, the program's staff markedly modified the intervention.

The evaluator must attempt to anticipate such program changes and prepare for them to the extent possible. More important, perhaps, is to match the evaluation to the program circumstances and prospects at the time the evaluation is planned. It would generally make little sense to design a rigorous assessment of the impact of a program that is under consideration for significant revision by relevant decisionmakers. Of equal importance, however, is the flexibility the evaluator brings to the evaluation task. Knowing the dynamic nature of programs, evaluators must be prepared to modify an evaluation if it becomes apparent that the original plan is no longer appropriate to the circumstances. This often involves difficult issues associated with the availability of resources for the evaluation, the time lines for producing results, and the relationships with the program administrators and evaluation sponsors, so it is not to be taken lightly. Social programs are not research laboratories, however, and evaluators must expect to be buffeted about by forces and events outside their control.

The contrast between the image of a research laboratory and the reality of social programs as places to conduct social research leads us directly to another of the inherent tensions in evaluation, that between a scientific and a pragmatic perspective on the process.

Scientific Versus Pragmatic Evaluation Postures

Perhaps the single most influential article in the evaluation field was written by the late Donald Campbell and published in 1969. This article outlined a perspective that Campbell advanced over several decades: Policy and program decisions should emerge from continual social experimentation that tests ways to improve social conditions. Campbell asserted that the technology of social research made it feasible to extend the experimental model to evaluation research to create an "experimenting society." Although he tempered his position in later writing, it is fair to characterize him as fitting evaluation research into the scientific research paradigm (see Exhibit 1-G).

Campbell's position was challenged by Lee Cronbach, another giant in the evaluation field. While acknowledging that scientific investigation and evaluation may use some of the same research procedures, Cronbach (1982) argued that the purpose of evaluation sharply differentiates it from scientific research. In his view, evaluation is more art than science and should be oriented toward meeting the needs of program decisionmakers and stakeholders. Whereas scientific studies strive principally to meet research standards, Cronbach thought evaluations should be dedicated to providing the maximally useful information that the political circumstances, program constraints, and available resources allow (see Exhibit 1-H).

One might be inclined to agree with both these views—that evaluations should meet high standards of scientific research and at the same time be dedicated to serving the information needs of program decisionmakers. The problem is that in practice

EXHIBIT 1-G

Reforms as
Experiments

> The United States and other modern nations should be ready for an experimental approach to social reform, an approach in which we try out new programs designed to cure specific social problems, in which we learn whether or not these programs are effective, and in which we retain, imitate, modify, or discard them on the basis of apparent effectiveness on the multiple imperfect criteria available.

SOURCE: Quoted from Donald Campbell, "Reforms as Experiments," *American Psychologist*, April 1969, 24:409.

EXHIBIT 1-H

Evaluators
as Teachers

> An evaluative study of a social program is justified to the extent that it facilitates the work of the polity. It therefore is to be judged primarily by its contribution to public thinking and to the quality of service provided subsequent to the evaluation. . . . An evaluation pays off to the extent that it offers ideas pertinent to pending actions and people think more clearly as a result. To enlighten, it must do more than amass good data. Timely communications—generally not "final" ones—should distribute information to the persons rightfully concerned, and those hearers should take the information into their thinking. To speak broadly, an evaluation ought *to inform and improve the operations of the social system.*

SOURCE: Quoted from Lee J. Cronbach and Associates, *Toward Reform of Program Evaluation* (San Francisco: Jossey-Bass, 1980), pp. 65-66.

these two goals often are not especially compatible. Conducting social research at a high scientific standard generally requires resources that exceed what is available for evaluation projects. These resources include time, because high-quality research cannot be done quickly, whereas program decisions often have to be made on short notice. They also include the funding needed for the expertise and level of effort required for high-quality scientific research. Moreover, research within the scientific framework may require structuring the inquiry in ways that do not mesh well with the perspectives of those who make decisions about the program. For example, specifying variables so that they are well defined and measurable under scientific standards may appear to trivialize what policymakers see as complex and dynamic facets of the program. Similarly, scientific standards for inferring causality, as when investigating program outcomes (was the program the cause of an observed change?), may require such elaborate experimental controls that what is studied is no longer the program's typical services, but some constrained version of uncertain relevance to the actual program.

Nor can one blithely dismiss scientific concerns in evaluation. Properly understood, the scientific approach is a very considered attempt to produce conclusions that are valid and credible. Even when an evaluation falls short of this ideal—as all do to some extent—science-based findings make an important contribution to a decision-making context that is otherwise rife with self-interested perceptions and assertions, ideological biases, and undocumented claims. But this statement, in turn, assumes that the evaluation conclusions meaningfully address the situation of concern to decisionmakers; if not, they may be praiseworthy for their validity and credibility, but still be irrelevant.

In practice, therefore, the evaluator must struggle to find a workable balance between the emphasis placed on procedures that ensure the validity of the findings and those that make the findings timely, meaningful, and useful to the consumers. Where that balance point should be will depend on the purposes of the evaluation, the nature of the program, and the political or decision-making context. In many cases, evaluations will justifiably be undertaken that are "good enough" for answering relevant policy and program questions even though program conditions or available resources prevent them from being the best possible designs from a scientific standpoint.

A further complication is that it is often unclear who the ultimate users of the evaluation will be and which of the potential users should be given priority in the design. An evaluation generally has various audiences, some with very immediate interests in particular aspects of the program under investigation, some with broader interests in the type of intervention the particular program represents, and others falling somewhere in between. Occasionally, the purposes and priority users of an evaluation are defined so clearly and explicitly in advance that the evaluator has relatively little difficulty in balancing scientific and pragmatic considerations. However, many evaluation situations are not so clear-cut. Evaluation may be routinely required as part of funding or contract arrangements with the presumption that it will be generally informative to a program's managers, the evaluation sponsors, and other interested parties. Or it may evolve from a collaboration between a service agency with a need for information for management purposes and a researcher with broader interests in the type of intervention that a particular program provides. Under such circumstances, the trade-offs between utility for program decisionmakers and scientific rigor are such that it is rarely possible to design an evaluation that serves both interests well.

Some evaluation theorists champion **utilization of evaluation** as the overriding concern and advocate evaluation that is designed around the information needs of specific stakeholding consumers with whom the evaluator collaborates very closely (e.g., Patton, 1997). A contrary view is advanced by the authors of review articles in applied research journals who attempt to synthesize available research on the effectiveness of various interventions. These scholars generally deplore the poor methodological quality of evaluation studies and urge a higher standard. Some commentators want to have it both ways and press the view that evaluations should strive to have utility to program stakeholders and contribute to cumulative knowledge about social intervention (Lipsey, 1997). Our outlook, for the didactic purposes of this book, is that all these options are defensible, but not necessarily equally defensible in any given evaluation situation. This, then, presents yet another issue for which the evaluator must make a judgment call and attempt to tailor the evaluation design to the particular purposes and circumstances.

Diversity in Evaluation Outlooks and Approaches

As the preceding discussion illustrates, the field of evaluation is diverse and contentious. The fundamental differences represented historically by Campbell and Cronbach represent but one instance of this diversity. Evaluation practitioners are drawn from a wide range of academic disciplines and professions with different orientations and methods, and this mix has contributed significantly to the multiplicity of perspectives. Other differences in outlook are related to the motivations of evaluators and the settings in which they work. The solo practitioner who undertakes short-term evaluations on contract with local agencies and the tenured professor with long-term foundation funding will likely have quite divergent views on their evaluation activities.

As the field of evaluation has matured and become institutionalized, interest has developed in explicating the different postures toward evaluation and the methods preferred by leaders in various "camps." There is growing interest in identifying congruent elements among different perspectives to advance what is referred to as "evaluation theory" (Shadish, Cook, and Leviton, 1991). Advocates of the evaluation theory movement envision the development of a theory that will serve as the basis for decision making by evaluators as they proceed with their work (see Exhibit 1-I).

At present, we must acknowledge that evaluation is at least as much art as science, and perhaps should be and always will be. Inevitably, the evaluator's task is to creatively weave together many competing concerns and objectives into a tapestry in which different viewers can find different messages. We recognize, too, the difficulty of teaching an art form, especially via the written word. Teaching evaluation is analogous to training physicians to be diagnosticians. Any intelligent person can be taught to understand the results from laboratory tests, but a doctor becomes an astute diagnostician only through practice, experience, and attention to the idiosyncrasies of each individual case. In this sense, learning from a text can provide only part of the knowledge needed to become a capable evaluator.

Who Can Do Evaluations?

Systematic evaluation is grounded in social science research techniques; hence, most evaluation specialists have had some social research training. Beyond that

EXHIBIT 1-1

The Ideal
Evaluation Theory

The ideal (never achievable) evaluation theory would describe and justify why certain evaluation practices lead to particular kinds of results across situations that evaluators confront. It would (a) clarify the activities, processes, and goals of evaluation; (b) explicate relationships among evaluative activities and the processes and goals they facilitate; and (c) empirically test propositions to identify and address those that conflict with research and other critically appraised knowledge about evaluation.

SOURCE: Quoted from William R. Shadish, Thomas D. Cook, and Laura C. Leviton, *Foundations of Program Evaluation: Theories of Practice* (Newbury Park, CA: Sage, 1991), pp. 30-31.

commonality, evaluators are very diverse in their disciplinary backgrounds and professional training (see Exhibit 1-J). Ideally, every evaluator should be familiar with the full repertoire of social research methods. It is also critical for an evaluator to be knowledgeable about the target problem area the program addresses (e.g., crime, health, drug abuse) and about the findings from evaluations of previous interventions. This is necessary, first, for the evaluator to understand the issues and context with which the program deals and, second, for the evaluator to develop an appropriate evaluation plan that reflects the reality of the program and existing knowledge relevant to such programs.

At the most complex level, evaluation activities can be so technically complicated, sophisticated in conception, costly, and of such long duration that they require the dedicated participation of highly trained specialists at ease with the latest in social science theory, program knowledge, data collection methods, and statistical techniques. Such complex evaluations are usually conducted by specialized evaluation staffs. At the other extreme, there are many evaluation tasks that can be easily carried out by persons of modest expertise and experience.

It is the purpose of this book to provide an introduction to the field for those whose current positions, professional interests, or natural curiosity inspire them to want to learn how evaluations are conducted. Studying this text is, of course, only a start along the path to becoming an expert in evaluation—there is no substitute for experience. We also aim to provide persons responsible for administering and managing human services programs with sufficient understanding of evaluation concepts and methods to be able to judge for themselves what kinds of evaluations are appropriate to their programs and projects and to comprehend the results of those studies. In brief, we have tried to provide a text that is helpful to those who conduct evaluations, those who commission them, those who oversee evaluation staffs, and those who are consumers of evaluation research.

EXHIBIT 1-J
Diversity of the Members of the American Evaluation Association (in percentages)

Major Activity	2003	Organizational Setting	2003	Primary Discipline	1993
Evaluation	39	College or university	36	Education	22
Research	15	Private business	18	Psychology	18
Administration	10	Nonprofit organization	17	Evaluation	14
Teaching	8	Federal government agency	7	Statistical methods	10
Consulting	10	State/local government agency	6	Sociology	6
Student	6	School system	3	Economics and political science	6
Other	4	Other	6	Organizational development	3
Unknown	9	Unknown	8	Other and unknown	21

SOURCE: Data for 2003 based on 3,429 members, as reported by Susan Kistler, AEA (February 19, 2003). Data for 1993 adapted from *Evaluation Practice News* (October 1993); based on 2,045 AEA members as of June 1993.

Summary

■ Program evaluation is the use of social research methods to systematically investigate the effectiveness of social intervention programs. It draws on the techniques and concepts of social science disciplines and is intended to be useful for improving programs and informing social action aimed at ameliorating social problems.

■ Modern evaluation research grew from pioneering efforts in the 1930s and burgeoned in the years after World War II as new methodologies were developed that could be applied to the rapidly growing social program arena. The social policy and public administration movements have contributed to the professionalization of the field and to the sophistication of the consumers of evaluation research.

■ The need for program evaluation is undiminished in the current era and may even be expected to grow. Indeed, contemporary concern over the allocation of scarce resources makes it more essential than ever to evaluate the effectiveness of social interventions.

■ Evaluation requires an accurate description of the program performance or characteristics at issue and assessment of them against relevant standards or criteria.

■ Evaluation typically involves assessment of one or more of five program domains: (1) the need for the program, (2) the design of the program, (3) program implementation and service delivery, (4) program impact or outcomes, and (5) program efficiency. An evaluation must be tailored to the political and organizational context of the program being evaluated.

■ In practice, program evaluation presents many challenges to the evaluator. Program circumstances and activities may change during the course of an evaluation, an appropriate balance must be found between scientific and pragmatic considerations in the evaluation design, and the wide diversity of perspectives and approaches in the evaluation field provide little firm guidance about how best to proceed with an evaluation.

■ Most evaluators are trained either in one of the social sciences or in professional schools that offer applied social research courses. Highly specialized, technical, or complex evaluations may require specialized evaluation staffs. A basic knowledge of the evaluation field, however, is relevant not only to those who will perform evaluations but also to the consumers of evaluation research.

KEY CONCEPTS

Evaluation sponsor

The person, group, or organization that requests or requires the evaluation and provides the resources to conduct it.

Program evaluation

The use of social research methods to systematically investigate the effectiveness of social intervention programs in ways that are adapted to their political and organizational environments and are designed to inform social action in ways that improve social conditions.

Social program; social intervention

An organized, planned, and usually ongoing effort designed to ameliorate a social problem or improve social conditions.

Social research methods

Procedures for studying social behavior devised by social scientists that are based on systematic observation and logical rules for drawing inferences from those observations.

Stakeholders

Individuals, groups, or organizations having a significant interest in how well a program functions, for instance, those with decision-making authority over the program, funders and sponsors, administrators and personnel, and clients or intended beneficiaries.

Utilization of evaluation

The use of the concepts and findings of an evaluation by decisionmakers and other stakeholders whether at the day-to-day management level or at broader funding or policy levels.

2

Tailoring Evaluations

Chapter Outline

What Aspects of the Evaluation Plan Must Be Tailored?
What Features of the Situation Should the Evaluation Plan Take Into Account?
    The Purposes of the Evaluation
        Program Improvement
        Accountability
        Knowledge Generation
        Hidden Agendas
    The Program Structure and Circumstances
        Stage of Program Development
        Administrative and Political Context of the Program
        Conceptual and Organizational Structure of the Program
    The Resources Available for the Evaluation

The Nature of the Evaluator-Stakeholder Relationship
Evaluation Questions and Evaluation Methods
    Needs Assessment
    Assessment of Program Theory
    Assessment of Program Process
    Impact Assessment
    Efficiency Assessment

Every evaluation must be tailored to a specific set of circumstances. The tasks that evaluators undertake depend on the purposes of the evaluation, the conceptual and organizational structure of the program being evaluated, and the resources available. Formulating an evaluation plan requires the evaluator to first explore these aspects of the evaluation situation with the evaluation sponsor and other key stakeholders. Based on this reconnaissance, the evaluator can then develop a plan that identifies the evaluation questions to be answered, the methods for answering them, and the relationships to be developed with the stakeholders during the course of the evaluation.

No hard-and-fast guidelines direct the process of designing an evaluation. Nonetheless, achieving a good fit between the evaluation plan and the program circumstances involves attention to certain critical themes. It is essential that the evaluation plan be responsive to the purposes of the evaluation as understood by the evaluation sponsor and key stakeholders. An evaluation intended to provide feedback to program decisionmakers for improving a program will take a different approach than one intended to help funders determine whether a program should be terminated. In addition, the evaluation plan must reflect an understanding of how the program is designed and organized so that the questions asked and the data collected will be appropriate to the circumstances. Finally, of course, any evaluation will have to be designed within the constraints of available time, personnel, and funding.

Although the particulars are diverse, the situations confronting the evaluator typically present one of a small number of variations. In practice, therefore, tailoring an evaluation is usually a matter of selecting and adapting one or another of a set of familiar evaluation schemes to the circumstances at hand. One set of evaluation schemes centers around the nature of the evaluator-stakeholder relations. Another distinct set of approaches is organized around common combinations of evaluation questions and the usual methods for answering them. This chapter provides an overview of the issues and considerations the evaluator should take into account when tailoring an evaluation plan.

O ne of the most challenging aspects of evaluation is that there is no "one size fits all" approach. Every evaluation situation has a different and sometimes unique profile of characteristics. The evaluation design must, therefore, involve an interplay between the nature of the evaluation situation and the evaluator's repertoire of approaches, techniques, and concepts. A good evaluation design is one that fits the circumstances while yielding credible and useful answers to the questions that motivate it. We begin our discussion of how to accomplish this goal by taking inventory of the aspects of the evaluation plan that need to be tailored to the program and the context of the evaluation.

What Aspects of the Evaluation Plan Must Be Tailored?

Evaluation designs may be quite simple and direct, perhaps addressing only one narrow question such as whether using a computerized instructional program helps a class of third graders read better. Or they may be prodigiously complex, as in a national evaluation of the operations and effects of a diverse set of programs for reducing substance abuse in multiple urban sites. Fundamentally, however, we can view any evaluation as structured around three issues that will be introduced in this chapter and elaborated in the chapters to come:

The questions the evaluation is to answer. A large number of questions might be raised about any social program by interested parties. There may be concerns about such matters as the needs of the **targets** (persons, families, or social groups) to which a program is directed and whether they are being adequately served, the management and operation of the program, whether the program is having the desired impact, and its costs and efficiency. No evaluation can, nor generally should, attempt to address all such concerns. A central feature of an evaluation design, therefore, is specification of its guiding purpose and the corresponding questions on which it will focus.

The methods and procedures the evaluation will use to answer the questions. A critical skill for the evaluator is knowing how to obtain useful, timely, and credible information about the various aspects of program performance. A large repertoire of social research techniques and conceptual tools is available for this task. An evaluation design must identify the methods that will be used to answer each of the questions at issue and organize them into a feasible work plan. Moreover, the methods selected must be practical as well as capable of providing meaningful answers to the questions with the degree of scientific rigor appropriate to the evaluation circumstances.

The nature of the evaluator-stakeholder relationship. One of the most important lessons from the first several decades of experience with systematic evaluation is that there is nothing automatic about the use of evaluation findings by the relevant stakeholders. Part of an evaluation design, therefore, is a plan for working with stakeholders to identify and clarify the issues, conduct the evaluation, and make effective use of the findings. This interaction may be collaborative, with the evaluator serving as a consultant or facilitator to stakeholders who take primary responsibility for planning, conducting, and using the evaluation. Alternatively, the evaluator may have that responsibility but seek essential guidance and information from stakeholders. An evaluation plan should also indicate which audiences are to receive information at what times, the nature and schedule of written reports and oral briefings, and how broadly findings are to be disseminated beyond the evaluation sponsor.

What Features of the Situation Should the Evaluation Plan Take Into Account?

In developing an evaluation plan, the evaluator must be guided by a careful analysis of the context of the evaluation. The most significant features of the situation to consider have to do with (1) the purposes of the evaluation, (2) the program's structure and circumstances, and (3) the resources available for the evaluation.

The Purposes of the Evaluation

Evaluations are initiated for many reasons. They may be intended to help management improve a program; support advocacy by proponents or critics; gain knowledge about the program's effects; provide input to decisions about the program's funding, structure, or administration; or respond to political pressures. One of the first determinations the evaluator must make is just what the purposes of a specific evaluation are. This is not always a simple matter. A statement of the purposes generally accompanies the initial request for an evaluation, but these announced purposes rarely tell the whole story and sometimes are only rhetorical. Furthermore, evaluations may be routinely required in a program situation or sought simply because it is presumed to be a good idea without any distinct articulation of the sponsor's intent (see Exhibit 2-A).

The prospective evaluator must attempt to determine who wants the evaluation, what they want, and why they want it. There is no cut-and-dried method for doing this, but it is usually best to approach this task the way a journalist would dig out a story. The evaluator should examine source documents, interview key informants with different vantage points, and uncover pertinent history and background. Generally, the purposes of the evaluation will relate mainly to program improvement, accountability, or knowledge generation (Chelimsky, 1997), but sometimes quite different motivations are in play.

Program Improvement

An evaluation intended to furnish information for guiding program improvement is called a **formative evaluation** (Scriven, 1991) because its purpose is to help form or shape the program to perform better (see Exhibit 2-B for an example). The audiences for formative evaluations typically are program planners, administrators, oversight boards, or funders with an interest in optimizing the program's effectiveness. The information desired may relate to the need for the program, the program's design, its implementation, its impact, or its efficiency. The evaluator in this situation will

EXHIBIT 2-A

Does Anybody
Want This
Evaluation?

> Our initial meetings with the Bureau of Community Services administrators produced only vague statements about the reasons for the evaluation. They said they wanted some information about the cost-effectiveness of both New Dawn and Pegasus and also how well each program was being implemented. . . . It gradually became clear that the person most interested in the evaluation was an administrator in charge of contracts for the Department of Corrections, but we were unable to obtain specific information concerning where or how the evaluation would be used. We could only discern that an evaluation of state-run facilities had been mandated, but it was not clear by whom.

SOURCE: Quoted from Dennis J. Palumbo and Michael A. Hallett, "Conflict Versus Consensus Models in Policy Evaluation and Implementation," *Evaluation and Program Planning*, 1993, 16(1):11-23.

EXHIBIT 2-B

A Stop-Smoking
Telephone Line
That Nobody Called

> Formative evaluation procedures were used to help design a "stop smoking" hotline for adult smokers in a cancer control project sponsored by a health maintenance organization (HMO). Phone scripts for use by the hotline counselors and other aspects of the planned services were discussed with focus groups of smokers and reviewed in telephone interviews with a representative sample of HMO members who smoked. Feedback from these informants led to refinement of the scripts, hours of operation arranged around the times participants said they were most likely to call, and advertising of the service through newsletters and "quit kits" routinely distributed to all project participants. Despite these efforts, an average of less than three calls per month was made during the 33 months the hotline was in operation. To further assess this disappointing response, comparisons were made with similar services around the country. This revealed that low use rates were typical but the other hotlines served much larger populations and therefore received more calls. The program sponsors concluded that to be successful, the smoker's hotline would have to be offered to a larger population and be intensively publicized

SOURCE: Adapted from Russell E. Glasgow, H. Landow, J. Hollis, S. G. McRae, and P. A. La Chance, "A Stop-Smoking Telephone Help Line That Nobody Called," *American Journal of Public Health*, February 1993, 83(2): 252-253.

usually work closely with program management and other stakeholders in designing, conducting, and reporting the evaluation. Evaluation for program improvement characteristically emphasizes findings that are timely, concrete, and immediately useful.

Correspondingly, the communication between the evaluator and the respective audiences may occur regularly throughout the evaluation and be relatively informal.

Accountability

The investment of social resources such as taxpayer dollars by human service programs is justified by the presumption that the programs will make beneficial contributions to society. Program managers are thus expected to use resources effectively and efficiently and actually produce the intended benefits. An evaluation conducted to determine whether these expectations are met is called a **summative evaluation** (Scriven, 1991) because its purpose is to render a summary judgment on the program's performance (Exhibit 2-C provides an example). The findings of summative evaluations are usually intended for decisionmakers with major roles in program oversight, for example, the funding agency, governing board, legislative committee, political decisionmaker, or upper management. Such evaluations may influence significant decisions about the continuation of the program, allocation of resources, restructuring, or legal action. For this reason, they require information that is sufficiently credible under scientific standards to provide a confident basis for action and to withstand criticism aimed at discrediting the results. The evaluator may be expected to function relatively independently in planning, conducting, and reporting the evaluation, with stakeholders providing input but not participating directly in decision making. In these situations, it may be important to avoid premature or careless conclusions, so communication of the evaluation findings may be relatively formal, rely chiefly on written reports, and occur primarily at the end of the evaluation.

Knowledge Generation

Some evaluations are undertaken to describe the nature and effects of an intervention as a contribution to knowledge. For instance, an academic researcher might initiate an evaluation to test whether a program designed on the basis of theory, say, an innovative science curriculum, is workable and effective (see Exhibit 2-D for an example). Similarly, a government agency or private foundation may mount and evaluate a demonstration program to investigate a new approach to a social problem, which, if successful, could then be implemented more widely. Because evaluations of this sort are intended to make contributions to the social science knowledge base or be a basis for significant program innovation, they are usually conducted using the most rigorous methods feasible. The audience for the findings will include the sponsors of the research as well as a broader audience of interested scholars and policymakers. In these situations, the findings of the evaluation are most likely to be disseminated

EXHIBIT 2-C
U.S. General
Accounting Office
Assesses Early
Effects of the
Mammography
Quality Standards
Act

The Mammography Quality Standards Act of 1992 required the Food and Drug Administration (FDA) to administer a code of standards for mammogram-screening procedures in all the states. When the act was passed, Congress was concerned that access to mammography services might decrease if providers choose to drop them rather than upgrade to comply with the new standards. The U.S. General Accounting Office (GAO) was asked to assess the early effects of implementing the act and report back to Congress. It found that the FDA had taken a gradual approach to implementing the requirements, which had helped to minimize adverse effects on access. The FDA inspectors had not closed many facilities that failed to meet the standards but, instead, had allowed additional time to correct the problems found during inspections. Only a relatively small number of facilities had terminated their mammography services and those were generally small providers located within 25 miles of another certified facility. The GAO concluded that the Mammography Quality Standards Act was having a positive effect on the quality of mammography services, as Congress had intended.

SOURCE: Adapted from U.S. General Accounting Office, *Mammography Services: Initial Impact of New Federal Law Has Been Positive.* Report 10/27/95, GAO/HEHS-96-17 (Washington, DC: General Accounting Office, 1995).

through scholarly journals, research monographs, conference papers, and other professional outlets.

Hidden Agendas

Sometimes the true purpose of the evaluation, at least for those who initiate it, has little to do with actually obtaining information about the program's performance. Program administrators or boards may launch an evaluation because they believe it will be good public relations and might impress funders or political decisionmakers. Occasionally, an evaluation is commissioned to provide a rationale for a decision that has already been made behind the scenes to terminate a program, fire an administrator, and the like. Or the evaluation may be commissioned as a delaying tactic to appease critics and defer difficult decisions.

Virtually all evaluations involve some political maneuvering and public relations, but when these are the principal purposes, the prospective evaluator is presented with a difficult dilemma. The evaluation must either be guided by the political or public relations purposes, which will likely compromise its integrity, or focus on program performance issues that are of no real interest to those commissioning the evaluation and may even be threatening to them. In either case, the evaluator is well advised to try to avoid

EXHIBIT 2-D

Testing an
Innovative
Treatment Concept
for Pathological
Gambling

Pathological gambling is characterized by a loss of control over gambling impulses, lying about the extent of gambling, family and job disruption, stealing money, and chasing losses with additional gambling. Recent increases in the availability of gambling have led to corresponding increases in the prevalence of pathological gambling, but few treatment programs have been developed to help the victims of this disorder. Research on the psychology of gambling has shown that problem gamblers develop an illusion of control and believe they have strategies that will increase their winnings despite the inherent randomness of games of chance. A team of clinical researchers in Canada hypothesized that treatment based on "cognitive correction" of these erroneous beliefs would be an effective therapy. Because excessive gambling leads to financial problems and interpersonal difficulties, they combined their cognitive intervention with problem-solving and social skills training.

To test their concept, the researchers recruited 40 pathological gamblers willing to accept treatment. These were randomly assigned to a treatment or control group and measures of pathological gambling, perception of control, desire to gamble, feelings of self-efficacy, and frequency of gambling were taken before and after treatment. The results showed significant positive changes in the treatment group on all outcome measures with maintenance of the gains at 6- and 12-month follow-up. However, the results may have been compromised by high attrition—8 of the 20 gamblers who began treatment and 3 of the 20 in the control group dropped out, a common occurrence during intervention for addictive problems. Despite this limitation, the researchers concluded that their results were strong enough to demonstrate the effectiveness of their treatment concept.

SOURCE: Adapted from Caroline Sylvain, Robert Ladouceur, and Jean-Marie Boisvert, "Cognitive and Behavioral Treatment of Pathological Gambling: A Controlled Study," *Journal of Consulting and Clinical Psychology*, 1997, 65(5):727-732.

such situations. If a lack of serious intent becomes evident during the initial exploration of the evaluation context, the prospective evaluator may wish to decline to participate. Alternatively, the evaluator might assume a consultant role at that point to help the parties clarify the nature of evaluation and redirect their efforts toward approaches more appropriate to their purposes.

The Program Structure and Circumstances

No two programs are identical in their organizational structure and environmental, social, and political circumstances, even when they appear to provide the "same" service. The particulars of a program's structure and circumstances constitute major features of the evaluation situation to which the evaluation plan must be tailored. Three broad categories of such particulars are especially important to evaluators: the stage of program development, the administrative and political context of the program, and the conceptualization and organizational structure of the program.

Stage of Program Development

The life of a social program can be viewed as a progression in which different questions are at issue at different stages and, correspondingly, different evaluation approaches are needed (see Exhibit 2-E). Assessment of programs in the early stages of planning will be distinctly different from assessment of well-established programs. Similarly, assessment of an established program for which restructuring is contemplated or under way will be different from one for a program that is presumed to be stable in its basic operations and functions.

When new programs are initiated, especially innovative ones, evaluators are often called on to examine the social needs the program addresses, the program's design and objectives, the definition of its target population, the expected outcomes, and the means by which the program intends to attain those outcomes. The evaluator, therefore, may function as a planning consultant before the program is launched or when it is in an early stage of implementation by helping to assess and improve the program design.

Sometimes evaluations of new programs are expected to address questions of impact and efficiency, but the unsettled nature of programs in their beginning years most often makes those issues premature. It can easily take a year or more for a new program to establish facilities, acquire and train staff, make contact with the target population, and develop its services to the desired level. During this period, it may not be realistic to expect much impact on the social conditions that the program is intended to affect. Formative evaluation aimed at clarifying the needs of the target population, improving program operations, and enhancing the quality of service delivery, using approaches such as those discussed later in Chapters 4-6, is more likely to fit these cases.

Although the evaluation of new programs represents an important activity, by far the greater effort goes into assessing established programs, usually in terms of implementation issues. Evaluation of established, stable programs rarely focuses on assessing the underlying conceptualization of the program, that is, the rationale that went into the original design of the program. Stakeholders in well-established social programs are generally very reluctant to alter the programs' traditional forms and approaches unless some crisis compels them to consider fundamental change. So, for example, stakeholders take for granted the value of such well-entrenched programs as Social Security pensions, guidance counselors in schools, vocational programs for disabled persons, parole

EXHIBIT 2-E
Stages of Program Development and Related Evaluation Functions

Stage of Program Development	Question to Be Asked	Evaluation Function
1. Assessment of social problems and needs	To what extent are community needs and standards met?	Needs assessment; problem description
2. Determination of goals	What must be done to meet those needs and standards?	Needs assessment; service needs
3. Design of program alternatives	What services could be used to produce the desired changes?	Assessment of program logic or theory
4. Selection of alternative	Which of the possible program approaches is best?	Feasibility study; formative evaluation
5. Program implementation	How should the program be put into operation?	Implementation assessment
6. Program operation	Is the program operating as planned?	Process evaluation; program monitoring
7. Program outcomes	Is the program having the desired effects?	Outcome evaluation
8. Program efficiency	Are program effects attained at a reasonable cost?	Cost-benefit analysis; cost-effectiveness analysis

SOURCE: Adapted from S. Mark Pancer and Anne Westhues, "A Developmental Stage Approach to Program Planning and Evaluation," *Evaluation Review*, 1989, 13(1):56-77.

supervision for released convicts, and community health education for the prevention of diseases. In addition, long-standing programs that provide services to virtually the entire eligible population can be difficult to evaluate for their impact and efficiency. In such cases, the evaluator has limited ability to compare the outcomes and costs of the program to alternative situations that indicate what things would be like in the absence of the program. Accordingly, the evaluation of universally available programs is often directed toward assessing the extent to which their objectives are explicit and relevant to the interests of program sponsors, staff, and other stakeholders; whether the programs are well implemented and conform to plan; and whether they actually reach all of their target population. For example, the U.S. Department of Agriculture conducts periodic studies of the food stamps program to measure the extent to which eligible households are enrolled and to guide outreach efforts to increase participation (Trippe, 1995).

Sometimes, however, evaluation is sought for established programs because the program status quo has been called into question. This may result from political attack, competition, mounting program costs, changes in the target population, or dissatisfaction with program performance. When that happens, restructuring may be an option and evaluation may be sought to guide that change. Under these circumstances, the evaluation may focus on any aspect of the program—whether it is needed, its conceptualization and design, its operations and implementation, or its impact and efficiency.

The federal food stamps program, for instance, has been a national program for more than three decades. It is intended to increase the quantity and quality of food consumed by providing poor households with food stamps redeemable for approved foods purchased at grocery stores. At one point, the Department of Agriculture contemplated issuing checks instead, thereby eliminating the high costs of printing, distributing, and redeeming the food stamps. To test this concept, it launched four experiments comparing the food consumption in households receiving food stamps with that in households receiving checks for the same dollar amount of benefits (Fraker, Martini, and Ohls, 1995). The results showed that households receiving checks purchased less food than those receiving food stamps. The Department of Agriculture therefore decided to retain food stamps despite their higher processing costs.

Administrative and Political Context of the Program

Except possibly for academic researchers who conduct evaluation studies on their own initiative for the purpose of generating knowledge, evaluators are not free to establish their own definitions of what the program is about, its goals and objectives, and what evaluation questions should be addressed. The evaluator works with the evaluation sponsor, program management, and other stakeholders to develop this essential background. Different perspectives from these various groups are to be expected. In most instances, the evaluator will solicit input from all the major stakeholders and attempt to incorporate their concerns so that the evaluation will be as inclusive and informative as possible.

If significant stakeholders are not in substantial agreement about the mission, goals, or other critical issues for the program, evaluation design becomes very difficult (see Exhibit 2-F). The evaluator can attempt to incorporate the conflicting perspectives into the design, but this may not be easy. The evaluation sponsors may not be willing to embrace the inclusion of issues and perspectives from groups they view as adversaries. Furthermore, these perspectives may be so different that they cannot be readily incorporated into a single evaluation plan with the time and resources available.

Alternatively, the evaluator can plan the evaluation from the perspective of only one of the stakeholders, typically the evaluation sponsor. This, of course, will not be

EXHIBIT 2-F
Stakeholder Conflict
Over Home Arrest
Program

In an evaluation of a home arrest program using electronic monitoring for offenders on parole, the evaluators made the following comments about stakeholder views:

There were numerous conflicting goals that were considered important by different agencies, including lowering costs and prison diversion, control and public safety, intermediate punishment and increased options for corrections, and treatment and rehabilitation. Different stakeholders emphasized different goals. Some legislators stressed reduced costs, others emphasized public safety, and still others were mainly concerned with diverting offenders from prison. Some implementers stressed the need for control and discipline for certain "dysfunctional" individuals, whereas others focused on rehabilitation and helping offenders become reintegrated into society. Thus, there was no common ground for enabling "key policymakers, managers, and staff" to come to an agreement about which goals should have priority or about what might constitute program improvement.

SOURCE: Dennis J. Palumbo and Michael A. Hallett, "Conflict Versus Consensus Models in Policy Evaluation and Implementation," *Evaluation and Program Planning,* 1993, 16(1): 11-23.

greeted with enthusiasm by stakeholders with conflicting perspectives and they will likely oppose the evaluation and criticize the evaluator. The challenge to the evaluator is to be clear and straightforward about the perspective represented in the evaluation and the reasons for it, despite the objections. It is not necessarily inappropriate for an evaluation sponsor to insist that the evaluation emphasize its perspective, nor is it necessarily wrong for an evaluator to conduct an evaluation from that perspective without giving strong representation to conflicting views.

Suppose, for instance, that the funders of a job training program for unemployed persons have concerns about whether the program is mainly taking cases that are easy to work with and, additionally, is providing only vocational counseling services rather than training in marketable job skills. The sponsors may appropriately commission an evaluation to examine these questions. Program managers, in contrast, will likely have a sharply conflicting perspective that justifies their selection of clients, program activities, and management practices. A conscientious evaluator will listen to the managers' perspective and encourage their input so that the evaluation can be as sensitive as possible to their legitimate concerns about what the program is doing and why. But the evaluation design should, nonetheless, be developed primarily from the perspective of the program funders and the issues that concern them. The evaluator's primary obligations are to be forthright about the perspective the evaluation takes, so there is no misunderstanding, and to treat the program personnel fairly and honestly.

Another approach to situations of stakeholder conflict is for the evaluator to design an evaluation that attempts to facilitate better understanding among the conflicting parties about the aspects of the program at issue. This might be done through efforts to clarify the nature of the different concerns, assumptions, and perspectives of the parties. For instance, parents of special education children may believe that their children are stigmatized and discriminated against when mainstreamed in regular classrooms. Teachers may feel equally strongly that this is not true. A careful observational study by an evaluator of the interaction of regular and special education children may reveal that there is a problem, as the parents claim, but that it occurs outside the classroom on the playground and during other informal interactions among the children, thus accounting for the teachers' perspective.

Where stakeholder conflict is deep and hostile, it may be based on such profound differences in political values or ideology that an evaluation, no matter how comprehensive and ecumenical, cannot reconcile them. One school of thought in the evaluation field holds that many program situations are of this sort and that differences in values and ideology are the central matter to which the evaluator must attend. In this view, the social problems that programs address, the programs themselves, and the meaning and importance of those programs are all social constructions that will inevitably differ for different individuals and groups. Thus, rather than focus on program objectives, decisions, outcomes, and the like, evaluators are advised to directly engage the diverse claims, concerns, issues, and values put forth by the various stakeholders.

Guba and Lincoln (1987, 1989, 1994), the leading proponents of this particular construction of evaluation, have argued that the proper role of the evaluator is to encourage interpretive dialogue among the program stakeholders. From this perspective, the primary purpose of an evaluation is to facilitate negotiations among the stakeholders from which a more shared construction of the value and social significance of the program can emerge that still respects the various ideologies and concerns of the different stakeholders.

Finally, evaluators must realize that, despite their best efforts to communicate effectively and develop appropriate, responsive evaluation plans, program stakeholders owe primary allegiance to their own positions and political alignments. This means that sponsors of evaluation and other stakeholders may turn on the evaluator and harshly criticize the evaluation if the results contradict the policies and perspectives they advocate. Thus, even those evaluators who do a superb job of working with stakeholders and incorporating their views and concerns in the evaluation plan should not expect to be acclaimed as heroes by all when the results are in. The multiplicity of stakeholder perspectives makes it likely that no matter how the results come out, someone will be unhappy. It may matter little that everyone agreed in advance on the evaluation questions and the plan for answering them, or that each stakeholder group understood that honest results might not favor its position. Nonetheless, it is highly advisable for the evaluator to give early attention to identifying stakeholders, devising strategies for minimizing discord due to their different perspectives, and conditioning their expectations about the evaluation results.

Conceptual and Organizational Structure of the Program

It is a simple truism that if stakeholders do not have a clear idea about what a program is supposed to be doing, it will be difficult to evaluate how well it is doing it. One factor that shapes the evaluation design, therefore, is the conceptualization of the program, or the **program theory**, that is, its plan of operation, the logic that connects its activities to the intended outcomes, and the rationale for why it does what it does. As we will discuss later in this chapter, this conceptual structure can itself be a focus of evaluation. The more explicit and cogent the program conceptualization, the easier it will be for the evaluator to identify the program functions and effects on which the evaluation should focus. If there is significant uncertainty about whether the program conceptualization is appropriate for the social problem the program addresses, it may make little sense for the evaluation design to focus on how well the conceptualization has been implemented. In such cases, the evaluation may be more usefully devoted to assessing and better developing the program plan. In the planning stages of a new program, an evaluator can often help sharpen and shape the program design to make it both more explicit and more likely to effectively achieve its objectives.

When a program is well established, everyday practice and routine operating procedures tend to dominate, and key stakeholders may find it difficult to articulate the underlying program rationale or agree on any single version of it. For instance, the administrators of a counseling agency under contract to a school district to work with children having academic problems may be quite articulate about their counseling theories, goals for clients, and therapeutic techniques. But they may have difficulty expressing a clear view of how their focus on improving family communication is supposed to translate into better grades. It may then become the task of the evaluator to help program personnel to formulate the implicit but unarticulated rationale for program activities.

At a more concrete level, evaluators also need to take into consideration the organizational structure of the program when planning an evaluation. Such program characteristics as multiple services or multiple target populations, distributed service sites or facilities, or extensive collaboration with other organizational entities have powerful implications for evaluation. In general, organizational structures that are larger, more complex, more decentralized, and more geographically dispersed will present greater practical difficulties than their simpler counterparts. In such cases, a team of evaluators is often needed, with resources and time proportionate to the size and complexity of the program. The challenges of evaluating complex, multisite programs are sufficiently daunting that they are distinct topics of discussion in the evaluation literature (see Exhibit 2-G; Turpin and Sinacore, 1991).

Equally important are the nature and structure of the particular intervention or service the program provides. The easiest interventions to evaluate are those that involve discrete, concrete activities (e.g., serving meals to homeless persons) expected to have relatively immediate and observable effects (the beneficiaries of the program are not hungry). The organizational activities and delivery systems for such interventions are usually straightforward (soup kitchen), the service itself is uncomplicated

EXHIBIT 2-G

Multisite Evaluations in Criminal Justice: Structural Obstacles to Success

Besides the usual methodological considerations involved in conducting credible evaluations, the structural features of criminal justice settings impose social, political, and organizational constraints that make multisite evaluations difficult and risky. To begin, the system is extremely decentralized. Police departments, for example, can operate within the province of municipalities, counties, campuses, public housing, mass transit, and the states. The criminal justice system is also highly fragmented. Cities administer police departments and jails; counties administer sheriffs' and prosecutors' offices, jails, and probation agencies; state governments run the prisons. Agencies are embedded in disparate political settings, each with its own priorities for taxing and spending. In addition, criminal justice agencies foster a subculture of secrecy concerning their work that has serious consequences for evaluators, who are readily seen as "snoops" for management, the courts, or individuals with political agendas. Line staff easily adopt an "us against them" mentality toward outside evaluators. Also, criminal justice agencies generally exist in highly charged political environments. They are the most visible components of local government, as well as the most expensive, and their actions are frequently monitored by the media, who historically have assumed a watchdog or adversarial posture toward the system. Finally, the criminal justice system operates within a context of individual rights–legal constraint in procedural issues, an unwillingness to risk injustice in individual cases, and a stated (though not actually delivered) commitment to providing individualized treatment. This translates, for example, into a general aversion to the concept of random or unbiased assignment, the hallmark of the best designs for yielding interpretable information about program effects.

SOURCE: Adapted from Wesley G. Skogan and Arthur J. Lurigio, *Multisite Evaluations in Criminal Justice Settings: Structural Obstacles to Success,* New Directions for Evaluation, no. 50 (San Francisco: Jossey-Bass, summer 1991), pp. 83-96.

(hand out meals), and the outcomes are direct (people eat). These features greatly simplify the evaluation questions likely to be raised, the data collection required to address them, and the interpretation of the findings.

The most difficult interventions to evaluate are those that are diffuse in nature (e.g., community organizing), extend over long time periods (an elementary school math curriculum), vary widely across applications (psychotherapy), or have expected outcomes that are long term (preschool compensatory education) or indistinct (improved quality of life). For such interventions, many evaluation questions dealing with a program's process and outcome can arise because of the ambiguity of the services and their potential effects. The evaluator may also have difficulty developing measures that capture the critical aspects of the program's implementation and outcomes. Actual data collection, too, may be challenging if it must take place over extended time periods or involve many different variables and observations. All these factors have implications for the evaluation plan and, especially, for the effort and resources required to complete the plan.

The Resources Available for the Evaluation

Conducting a program evaluation requires resources of various kinds. Personnel must be allocated to the evaluation activities and arrangements must be made for materials, equipment, and facilities to support data collection, analysis, and reporting. These resources may be drawn from the existing capabilities of the program or evaluation sponsor, or they may be separately funded. An important aspect of planning an evaluation, therefore, is to break down the tasks and construct timelines for accomplishing them so that a detailed estimate can be made of the personnel, materials, and funds that are needed. The sum total of the resources required must then, of course, fit within what is available or changes in either the plan or the resources must be made. Useful advice on how to go about resource planning, budgeting, and determining timelines can be found in Hedrick, Bickman, and Rog (1992), Card, Greeno, and Peterson (1992), and Fink (1995, chap. 9).

Although available funding is, of course, a critical resource around which the evaluation must be planned, it is important to recognize that it is not the only resource that should concern the evaluator. Specialized expertise is often necessary and must be made available if the evaluation is to be done well and, in a large project, a considerable number of proficient evaluators, data collectors, data managers, analysts, and assistants may be required to do a quality job. Even with generous funding, it will not always be easy to obtain the services of sufficient persons with the requisite expertise. This is why large, complex evaluation projects are often done through contracts with research firms that maintain appropriate personnel on their permanent staffs.

Another critical resource for an evaluation is support from program management, staff, and other closely related stakeholders. For instance, the degree of assistance in data collection that program personnel will provide can have considerable influence on how much an evaluation can accomplish. Barriers to access and lack of cooperation from the program or, worse, active resistance, are very expensive to the evaluation effort. It can take a substantial amount of time and effort to overcome these obstacles sufficiently to complete the evaluation. In the most severe cases, such resistance may compromise the scope or validity of the evaluation or even make it impossible to complete.

It is especially important for the evaluator to have access to program records, documents, and other such internal data sources that identify the number and characteristics of clients served, the type and amount of services they received, and the cost of providing those services. Information that can be confidently obtained from program records need not be sought in a separate, and almost certainly more expensive, data collection administered by the evaluator. However, program records vary in how easy they are to use for the purposes of evaluation. Records kept in writing often require considerable amounts of coding and processing while those kept in machine-readable databases can usually be used with relatively little adaptation. It is often advisable to inspect a sample of actual program records to try out the procedures for accessing and working with them and determine their completeness and quality.

The crucial point is that the evaluator must view cooperation from program personnel, access to program materials, and the nature, quality, and availability of data from program records as resource issues when planning an evaluation. The potential for misunderstanding and resistance can be lowered considerably if the evaluator spells out the resources and support needed for the evaluation in early discussions with the evaluation sponsors and program personnel (Hatry, 1994).

Experienced evaluators also know that one of the most precious resources is time. The time allotted for completion of the evaluation and the flexibility of the deadlines are essential considerations in evaluation planning but are rarely determined by the evaluator's preferences. The scheduling imperatives of the policy process usually control the time allowed for an evaluation because results typically must be available by a given date to play a role in a decision; after that they may be relatively useless. Further complicating the situation is the tendency for evaluation sponsors to underestimate the time needed to complete an evaluation. It is not uncommon for sponsors to request an evaluation that encompasses an imposing range of issues and requires considerable effort and then expect results in a matter of a few months.

The trade-offs here are quite significant. An evaluation can have breadth, depth, and rigor but will require proportionate funding and time. Or it can be cheap and quick but will, of necessity, deal with narrow issues or be relatively superficial (or both). All but the most sophisticated evaluation sponsors usually want evaluations that have breadth, depth, and rigor and that are also cheap and quick. Too often the result is overburdened evaluators working frantically against deadlines with inadequate resources and frustrated evaluation sponsors perturbed about delays in receiving the product they have paid for. An especially direct relationship exists between the time and technical expertise available for the evaluation and the methods and procedures that can be realistically planned. With few exceptions, the higher the scientific standard to be met by the evaluation, the greater the time, expertise, effort, and program cooperation required.

It is generally better for an evaluation to answer a few important questions well than a larger number poorly. The best way for the evaluator to prevent disappointment is to negotiate very explicitly with the evaluation sponsor about the resources to be made available to the evaluation and the trade-offs associated with the inevitable constraints on those resources.

The Nature of the Evaluator-Stakeholder Relationship

Every program is necessarily a social structure in which various individuals and groups engage in the roles and activities that constitute the program: program managers administer, staff provides service, participants receive service, and so forth. In addition, every program is a nexus in a set of political and social relationships among those with an association or interest in the program, such as relevant policymakers, competing programs, and advocacy groups. Early in the planning process, evaluators should give explicit attention to the nature of their relationship with these and other stakeholders who may participate in the evaluation or who have an interest in the evaluation process or results. More specifically, the primary stakeholders the evaluator may need to consider include the following:

- *Policymakers and decisionmakers:* Persons responsible for deciding whether the program is to be started, continued, discontinued, expanded, restructured, or curtailed.

- *Program sponsors:* Organizations that initiate and fund the program. They may also overlap with policymakers and decisionmakers.

- *Evaluation sponsors:* Organizations that initiate and fund the evaluation (sometimes the evaluation sponsors and the program sponsors are the same).

- *Target participants:* Persons, households, or other units that receive the intervention or services being evaluated.

- *Program managers:* Personnel responsible for overseeing and administering the intervention program.

- *Program staff:* Personnel responsible for delivering the program services or in supporting roles.

- *Program competitors:* Organizations or groups that compete with the program for available resources. For instance, an educational program providing alternative schools will attract the attention of the public schools because the new schools are seen as competitors.

- *Contextual stakeholders:* Organizations, groups, and individuals in the immediate environment of a program with interests in what the program is doing or what happens to it (e.g., other agencies or programs, public officials, or citizens' groups in the jurisdiction in which the program operates).

- *Evaluation and research community:* Evaluation professionals who read evaluations and pass judgment on their technical quality and credibility and researchers who work in areas related to a program.

All these groups or only a few may be involved in any given evaluation. But, whatever the assortment of stakeholders, the evaluator must be aware of their concerns and include in the evaluation planning appropriate means for interacting with at least the major stakeholders (Exhibit 2-H provides suggestions about how to do that).

At the top of the list of stakeholders is the evaluation sponsor. The sponsor is the agent who initiates the evaluation, usually provides the funding, and makes the decisions about how and when it will be done and who should do it. Various relationships with the evaluation sponsor are possible and will largely depend on the sponsor's preferences and whatever negotiation takes place with the evaluator. A common situation is one in which the sponsor expects the evaluator to function as an independent professional practitioner who will receive guidance from the sponsor, especially at the beginning, but otherwise take full responsibility for planning, conducting, and reporting the evaluation. For instance, program funders often commission evaluations by publishing a request for proposals (RFP) or applications (RFA) to which evaluators respond with statements of their capability, proposed design, budget, and time line, as requested. The evaluation sponsor then selects an evaluator from among those responding and establishes a contractual arrangement for the agreed-on work.

Other situations call for the evaluator to work more collaboratively with the evaluation sponsor. The sponsor may want to be involved in the planning, implementation, and analysis of results, either to react step by step as the evaluator develops the project or to actually participate with the evaluator in each step. Variations on this form of

EXHIBIT 2-H
Stakeholder
Involvement in
Evaluation:
Suggestions for
Practice

Based on experience working with school district staff, one evaluator offers the following advice for bolstering evaluation use through stakeholder involvement:

- *Identify stakeholders:* At the outset, define the specific stakeholders who will be involved with emphasis on those closest to the program and who hold high stakes in it.

- *Involve stakeholders early:* Engage stakeholders in the evaluation process as soon as they have been identified because many critical decisions that affect the evaluation occur early in the process.

- *Involve stakeholders continuously:* The input of key stakeholders should be part of virtually all phases of the evaluation; if possible, schedule regular group meetings.

- *Involve stakeholders actively:* The essential element of stakeholder involvement is that it be active; stakeholders should be asked to address design issues, help draft survey questions, provide input into the final report, and deliberate about all important aspects of the project.

- *Establish a structure:* Develop and use a conceptual framework based in content familiar to stakeholders that can help keep dialogue focused. This framework should highlight key issues within the local setting as topics for discussion so that stakeholders can share concerns and ideas, identify information needs, and interpret evaluation results.

SOURCE: Adapted from Robert A. Reineke, "Stakeholder Involvement in Evaluation: Suggestions for Practice," *Evaluation Practice,* 1991, 12(1):39-44.

relationship are typical for internal evaluators who are part of the organization whose program is being evaluated. In such cases, the evaluator generally works closely with management in planning and conducting the evaluation, whether management of the evaluation unit, the program being evaluated, someone higher up in the organization, or some combination.

In some instances, the evaluation sponsor will ask that the evaluator work collaboratively but stipulate that the collaboration be with another stakeholder group. For instance, private foundations often want evaluations to be developed in collaboration with the local stakeholders of the programs they fund. An especially interesting variant of this approach is when it is required that the recipients of program services take the primary role in planning, setting priorities, collecting information, and interpreting the results of the evaluation.

The evaluator's relationship to the evaluation sponsor and other stakeholders is so central to the evaluation context and planning process that a special vocabulary has arisen to describe various circumstances. The major recognized forms of evaluator-stakeholder relationships are as follows:

Independent evaluation. In an **independent evaluation**, the evaluator takes the primary responsibility for developing the evaluation plan, conducting the evaluation, and disseminating the results. The evaluator may initiate and direct the evaluation quite autonomously, as when a social scientist undertakes an evaluation for purposes of knowledge generation with research funding that leaves the particulars to the researcher's discretion. More often, the independent evaluator is commissioned by a sponsoring agency that stipulates the purposes and nature of the evaluation but leaves it to the evaluator to do the detailed planning and conduct the evaluation. In such cases, however, the evaluator generally confers with a range of stakeholders to give them some influence in shaping the evaluation.

Participatory or collaborative evaluation. A **participatory or collaborative evaluation** is organized as a team project with the evaluator and representatives of one or more stakeholder groups constituting the team (Greene, 1988; Mark and Shotland, 1985). The participating stakeholders are directly involved in planning, conducting, and analyzing the evaluation in collaboration with the evaluator whose function might range from team leader or consultant to that of a resource person called on only as needed. One particularly well-known form of participatory evaluation is Patton's (1986, 1997) utilization-focused evaluation. Patton's approach emphasizes close collaboration with those who will use the evaluation findings to ensure that the evaluation is responsive to their needs and produces information that they can and will actually use.

Empowerment evaluation. Some evaluators have advanced a view of evaluator-stakeholder relations that emphasizes the initiative, advocacy, and self-determination of the stakeholders (Fetterman, Kaftarian, and Wandersman, 1996). In an **empowerment evaluation**, the evaluator-stakeholder relationship is participatory and collaborative. In addition, however, the evaluator's role includes consultation and facilitation directed toward developing the capabilities of the participating stakeholders to conduct evaluations on their own, to use the results effectively for advocacy and change, and to experience some sense of control over a program that affects their lives. The evaluation process, therefore, is directed not only at producing informative and useful findings but also at enhancing the self-development and political influence of the participants. As these themes imply, empowerment evaluation most appropriately involves those stakeholders who otherwise have little power in the context of the program, usually the program recipients or intended beneficiaries.

A significant contribution of the participatory and empowerment perspectives is to call into question the assumption that an independent evaluation is always appropriate. Participation by the evaluation sponsor or other stakeholder groups may ensure that the evaluation results will more closely address their concerns and be useful to them. Moreover, it can create a sense of ownership in the evaluation that amplifies the significance of its findings and reduces its potential to engender resistance. And, as the empowerment theorists point out, when stakeholder groups with little formal power are able to conduct and use an evaluation, it can alter the balance of power in a program context by enhancing their influence and sense of efficacy. It is thus appropriate for the evaluation sponsors and the evaluator to explicitly consider the way evaluation responsibilities will be assigned and the arrangements for organizing the evaluator-stakeholder collaboration.

Whether the evaluation is planned and conducted by an independent evaluator or a team of stakeholders has a considerable effect on the nature of the decision making, the evaluator's role, and, most likely, the focus and character of the evaluation. The result, nonetheless, should represent an application of established evaluation concepts and methods to the program. We thus distinguish the process of working with stakeholders, whether as an independent evaluator, collaborator, facilitator, or resource person, from the evaluation plan that results from that process. The features of a good plan for the evaluation context and the program at issue should be much the same whatever the process through which the planning and implementation is done. In the remainder of this chapter, therefore, we will discuss general planning issues and, when reference is made to the evaluator's role, assume that can mean either an independent evaluator or a collaborative team.

In addition to the evaluator-stakeholder relationship, the evaluation plan should make some provision for the communication and dissemination of the findings of the evaluation. To be useful, evaluation findings must be communicated to those with interest in the program, especially to those with responsibility for making important decisions. It is difficult to communicate evaluation findings in fine detail and there is often inherent uncertainty about what information will be of most interest to stakeholders. It is usually best, therefore, to discuss this issue with the major stakeholders and develop an organized communication and dissemination plan from the beginning. Useful advice for planning effective communication and dissemination activities is found in Torres, Preskill, and Piontek (1996; also see Exhibit 2-I).

Evaluation Questions and Evaluation Methods

A program evaluation is essentially information gathering and interpretation to answer questions about a program's performance and effectiveness. An important step in

EXHIBIT 2-1
Successful
Communication
With Stakeholders

Torres, Preskill, and Piontek (1996) surveyed and interviewed members of the American Evaluation Association about their experiences communicating with stakeholders and reporting evaluation findings. The respondents identified the following elements of effective communication:

- Ongoing, collaborative communication processes were the most successful. Periodic meetings and informal conversations can be used to maintain close contact throughout the evaluation, and interim memos and draft reports can be used to convey findings as they develop.

- It is important to use varied formats for communication. These might include short reports and summaries, verbal presentations, and opportunities for informal interaction.

- The content of the communication should be tailored to the audience and be easy for them to understand. Communication should use clear language, graphs and charts, and vivid, concrete illustrations. It should present contextual information about the program and the evaluation, cover both positive and negative findings, and be specific about recommendations.

SOURCE: Adapted from Rosalie T. Torres, Hallie S. Preskill, and Mary E. Piontek, *Evaluation Strategies for Communicating and Reporting: Enhancing Learning in Organizations* (Thousand Oaks, CA: Sage, 1996), pp. 4-6.

designing an evaluation, therefore, is determining the questions the evaluation must answer. This is sometimes done in a very perfunctory manner, but we advocate that it be given studious and detailed attention. A carefully developed set of **evaluation questions** gives structure to the evaluation, leads to appropriate and thoughtful planning, and serves as a basis for essential discussions about who is interested in the answers and how they will be used. Indeed, constructing such questions and planning how to answer them is the primary way in which an evaluation is tailored to the unique circumstances associated with each program that comes under scrutiny.

Because the evaluation questions to be addressed are so pivotal to evaluation planning, Chapter 3 is devoted entirely to discussing the form they should take, how they are generated, and how they are winnowed, organized, and integrated to provide the structure for the evaluation design. For present purposes, we will assume that an appropriate set of evaluation questions has been identified and consider some of the broader implications of their character for tailoring and planning the evaluation. In this regard, it is useful to recognize that evaluation questions generally fall into recognizable types according to the program issues they address. Five such types are commonly distinguished:

- *Needs assessment:* Questions about the social conditions a program is intended to ameliorate and the need for the program.

- *Assessment of program theory:* Questions about program conceptualization and design.

- *Assessment of program process (or process evaluation):* Questions about program operations, implementation, and service delivery.

- *Impact assessment (impact evaluation or outcome evaluation):* Questions about program outcomes and impact.

- *Efficiency assessment:* Questions about program cost and cost-effectiveness.

These forms of evaluation are discussed in detail in Chapters 4-11. Here we will only provide some guidance regarding the circumstances for which each is most appropriate.

Needs Assessment

The primary rationale for a social program is to alleviate a social problem. The impetus for a new program to increase literacy, for example, is likely to be recognition that a significant proportion of persons in a given population are deficient in reading skills. Similarly, an ongoing program may be justified by the persistence of a social problem: Driver education in high schools receives public support because of the continuing high rates of automobile accidents among adolescent drivers.

One important form of evaluation, therefore, assesses the nature, magnitude, and distribution of a social problem; the extent to which there is a need for intervention; and the implications of these circumstances for the design of the intervention. These diagnostic activities are referred to as **needs assessment** in the evaluation field but overlap what is called social epidemiology and social indicators research in other fields (McKillip, 1987; Reviere et al., 1996; Soriano, 1995; Witkin and Altschuld, 1995). Needs assessment is often a first step in planning a new program or restructuring an established one to provide information about what services are needed and how they might best be delivered. Needs assessment may also be appropriate to examine whether established programs are responsive to the current needs of the target participants and provide guidance for improvement. Exhibit 2-J provides an example of one of the several approaches that can be taken. Chapter 4 discusses the various aspects of needs assessment in detail.

Assessment of Program Theory

Given a recognized problem and need for intervention, it does not follow that any program, willy-nilly, will be appropriate for the job. The conceptualization and design of

EXHIBIT 2-J
Needs for Help
Among Homeless
Men and Women

A representative sample of 1,260 homeless men and women were interviewed in New York City's municipal shelters for single adults to determine their perception of their needs. The interview covered 20 items, each indicating need for help in a particular area. Most respondents identified multiple needs, averaging 6.3. The need for help in finding a place to live and having a steady income were the most commonly cited needs overall, closely followed by the need for help in finding a job and improving job skills. Compared to women, men more often reported needs for help with drinking problems, drug problems, learning how to handle money, getting veterans benefits, problems with the police, getting along better with other people, and finding a place to live. Women more frequently reported needs for help with health and medical problems and learning self-protection skills. The evaluators pointed out that for programs to be truly responsive to these multiple needs, they must have the capacity to deliver or broker access to a comprehensive range of services.

SOURCE: Adapted by permission from Daniel B. Herman, Elmer L. Struening, and Susan M. Barrow, "Self-Reported Needs for Help Among Homeless Men and Women," *Evaluation and Program Planning*, 1994, 17(3):249-256. Copyright © 1998, John Wiley & Sons, Inc.

the program must reflect valid assumptions about the nature of the problem and represent a feasible approach to resolving it. Put another way, every social program is based on some plan or blueprint that represents the way it is "supposed to work." This plan is rarely written out in complete detail but exists nonetheless as a shared conceptualization among the principal stakeholders. Because this program plan consists essentially of assumptions and expectations about how the program should conduct its business in order to attain its goals, we will refer to it as the program theory. If this theory is faulty, the intervention will fail no matter how elegantly it is conceived or how well it is implemented (Chen, 1990; Weiss, 1972).

An **assessment of program theory** focuses on questions relating to the way the program is conceptualized and designed. This type of assessment involves, first, describing the program theory in explicit and detailed form. Then, various approaches are used to examine how reasonable, feasible, ethical, and otherwise appropriate it is. The sponsors of this form of evaluation are generally funding agencies or other decisionmakers attempting to launch a new program. Exhibit 2-K describes an examination of the conceptual foundation for family preservation programs that indicated that programs based on those notions had little prospect for success. Chapter 5 provides further discussion of program theory and the ways in which it can be evaluated.

EXHIBIT 2-K
A Flaw in the
Design of Family
Preservation
Programs

As part of an evaluability assessment (see Chapter 5), evaluators working under contract to the U.S. Department of Health and Human Services reviewed the design of family preservation programs (FPPs). FPPs are time-limited, intensive home-based services to families in crisis that are intended to prevent the placement of children in foster care. The evaluators held discussions with the staff of federal and national private sector agencies about the definition of FPPs, reviewed available literature, obtained descriptions of state and local programs, and made site visits to four programs. From this information they developed "models" of how the programs were supposed to operate and then obtained the views of policymakers, program managers, and operating-level staff on four key dimensions: (a) program goals, (b) aspects of the child welfare system that affect the programs, (c) the target population, and (d) the characteristics that distinguish FPPs from other home-based services. Based on their own analysis and discussions with an expert advisory committee, the evaluators concluded that, as currently designed, FPPs could not achieve the policymakers' primary goal of preventing placement in foster care. The major flaw found in the program design was the practical difficulty of identifying children at "imminent risk" of placement; this meant that programs could not consistently target families with children truly at risk of placement.

SOURCE: Adapted from Joseph S. Wholey, "Assessing the Feasibility and Likely Usefulness of Evaluation," in *Handbook of Practical Program Evaluation*, eds. J. S. Wholey, H. P. Hatry, and K. E. Newcomer (San Francisco: Jossey-Bass, 1994), pp. 29-31. Wholey's account, in turn, is based on Kaye and Bell (1993).

Assessment of Program Process

Given a plausible theory about how to intervene in an accurately diagnosed social problem, a program must still be implemented well to have a reasonable chance of actually improving the situation. It is not unusual to find that programs are not implemented and executed according to their intended design. A program may be poorly managed, compromised by political interference, or designed in ways that are impossible to carry out. Sometimes appropriate personnel are not available, facilities are inadequate, or program staff lack motivation, expertise, or training. Possibly the intended program participants do not exist in the numbers required, cannot be identified precisely, or are not cooperative.

A basic and widely used form of evaluation, **assessment of program process**, assesses the fidelity and effectiveness of a program's implementation. Such process assessments evaluate the activities and operations of the program and are commonly referred to as **process evaluation** or, when the evaluation is an ongoing function, **program monitoring**. Process evaluation investigates how well the program is operating. It might examine how consistent the services actually delivered are with the goals of the program, whether services are delivered to appropriate recipients, how well service delivery is organized, the effectiveness of program management, the use of program resources, and other such matters (Exhibit 2-L provides an example).

EXHIBIT 2-L

Failure on the Front Lines: Implementing Welfare Reform

> Work Pays is a state-level welfare reform demonstration program in California designed to establish incentives to work and disincentives for staying on the Aid to Families with Dependent Children (AFDC) welfare program. The program administrators recognized that to realize the policymakers' intent, the workers in local welfare offices would have to inform their clients about the new policy and present this information in a positive, individualized way that would reinforce clients' understanding of their obligations and choices about work and welfare. An implementation assessment was therefore conducted in which researchers interviewed welfare workers about the Work Pays program and observed a number of meetings with clients. This information revealed that the type of transaction expected between welfare workers and their clients under the new policy was exceedingly rare. In more than 80% of their interviews with clients, workers did not provide and interpret information about the new policy. Most workers continued their routine patterns of collecting and verifying eligibility information and providing scripted recitations of welfare rules. However, the evaluators also found that the workers had been given only minimal information about the Work Pays program and no additional time or resources for educating their large caseloads about the changes. These findings demonstrated that welfare reform was not fully implemented at the street level in California and revealed some of the reasons why it was not.

SOURCE: Adapted from Marcia K. Meyers, Bonnie Glaser, and Karin MacDonald, "On the Front Lines of Welfare Delivery: Are Workers Implementing Policy Reforms?" *Journal of Policy Analysis and Management,* 1998, 17(1):1-22.

Process evaluation is the most frequent form of program evaluation. It is used both as a freestanding evaluation and in conjunction with impact assessment (discussed below) as part of a more comprehensive evaluation. As a freestanding evaluation, it yields quality assurance information, assessing the extent to which a program is implemented as intended and operating up to the standards established for it. When the program model employed is one of established effectiveness, a demonstration that the program is well implemented can be presumptive evidence that the expected outcomes are produced as well. When the program is new, a process evaluation provides valuable feedback to administrators and other stakeholders about the progress that has been made implementing the program plan. From a management perspective, process evaluation provides the feedback that allows a program to be managed for high performance (Wholey and Hatry, 1992), and the associated data collection and reporting of key indicators may be institutionalized in the form of a management information system (MIS) to provide routine, ongoing performance feedback.

In its other common application, process evaluation is an indispensable adjunct to impact assessment. The information about program outcomes that evaluations of impact provide is incomplete and ambiguous without knowledge of the program activities and services that produced those outcomes. When no impact is found, process evaluation has significant diagnostic value by indicating whether this was because of implementation failure, that is, the intended services were not provided hence the expected benefits could not have occurred, or theory failure, that is, the program was implemented as intended but failed to produce the expected effects. On the other hand, when program effects are found, process evaluation helps confirm that they resulted from program activities, rather than spurious sources, and identify the aspects of service most instrumental to producing the effects. Process evaluation is described in more detail in Chapter 6.

Impact Assessment

An **impact assessment**, sometimes called an impact evaluation or outcome evaluation, gauges the extent to which a program produces the intended improvements in the social conditions it addresses. Impact assessment asks whether the desired outcomes were attained and whether those changes included unintended side effects.

The major difficulty in assessing the impact of a program is that usually the desired outcomes can also be caused by factors unrelated to the program. Accordingly, impact assessment involves producing an estimate of the *net effects* of a program—the changes brought about by the intervention above and beyond those resulting from other processes and events affecting the targeted social conditions. To conduct an impact assessment, the evaluator must thus design a study capable of establishing the status of program recipients on relevant outcome measures and also estimating what their status would be had they *not* received the intervention. Much of the complexity of impact assessment is associated with obtaining a valid estimate of the latter status, known as the *counterfactual* because it describes a condition contrary to what actually happened to program recipients (Exhibit 2-M presents an example of impact evaluation).

Determining when an impact assessment is appropriate and what evaluation design to use present considerable challenges to the evaluator. Evaluation sponsors often believe that they need an impact evaluation and, indeed, it is the only

EXHIBIT 2-M
No Impact
on Garbage

Taiwan is a high-density island country with a garbage problem. Garbage accumulation has increased exponentially in recent years, 26 rivers are polluted by garbage, and the number of landfill sites is increasingly limited. Consequently, in 1993 a garbage reduction demonstration program (GRD) was launched in Nei-fu, a suburb of Taipei, and evaluated for its impact on the amount of waste produced. Garbage is collected daily in Taiwan and the plan of the GRD was to disrupt this routine by suspending Tuesday collections. The theory was that requiring residents to store garbage one day a week in their homes, which are ill equipped for that function, would create sufficient inconvenience and unpleasantness to raise awareness of the garbage problem. As a result, it was expected that residents would make efforts to reduce the volume of garbage they produced. A process evaluation established that the program was implemented as planned.

The impact assessment was conducted by obtaining records of the daily volume of garbage for Nei-fu and the similar, adjacent suburb of Nan-kan for a period beginning four months prior to the program onset and continuing four months after. Analysis showed no reduction in the volume of garbage collected in Nei-fu during the program period relative to the preprogram volume or that in the comparison community. The evidence indicated that residents simply saved their customary volume of Tuesday garbage and disposed of it on Wednesday, with no carryover effects on the volume for the remainder of each week. Interviews with residents revealed that the program theory was wrong—they did not report the inconvenience or unpleasantness expected to be associated with storing garbage in their homes.

SOURCE: Adapted from Huey-Tsyh Chen, Juju C. S. Wang, and Lung-Ho Lin, "Evaluating the Process and Outcome of a Garbage Reduction Program in Taiwan," *Evaluation Review,* 1997, 21(1):27-42.

way to determine if the program is having the intended effects. However, an impact assessment is characteristically very demanding of expertise, time, and resources and is often difficult to set up properly within the constraints of routine program operation. If the need for outcome information is sufficient to justify an impact assessment, there is still a question of whether the program circumstances are suitable for conducting such an evaluation. For instance, it makes little sense to establish the impact of a program that is not well structured or cannot be adequately described. Impact assessment, therefore, is most appropriate for mature, stable programs with a well-defined program model and a clear use for the results that justifies the effort required. Chapters 7-10 discuss impact assessment and the various ways in which it can be designed and conducted.

Efficiency Assessment

Finding that a program has positive effects on the target problem is often insufficient for assessing its social value. Resources for social programs are limited so their accomplishments must also be judged against their costs. Some effective programs may not be attractive because their costs are high relative to their impact in comparison to other program alternatives (Exhibit 2-N presents an example).

Exhibit 2-N

The Cost-Effectiveness of Community Treatment for Persons With Mental Disabilities

If provided with supportive services, persons with mental disabilities can often be maintained in community settings rather than state mental hospitals. But is such community treatment more costly than residential hospital care? A team of researchers in Ohio compared the costs of a community program that provides housing subsidies and case management for state-certified severely mentally disabled clients with the costs of residential patients at the regional psychiatric hospital. Program clients were interviewed monthly for more than two years to determine their consumption of mental health services, medical and dental services, housing services, and other personal consumption. Information on the cost of those services was obtained from the respective service providers and combined with the direct cost of the community program itself. Costs for wards where patients resided 90 or more days were gathered from the Ohio Department of Mental Health budget data and subdivided into categories that corresponded as closely as possible to those tabulated for the community program participants. Mental health care comprised the largest component of service cost for both program and hospital clients. Overall, however, the total cost for all services was estimated at $1,730 per month for the most intensive version of community program services and about $6,250 per month for residential hospital care. Community care, therefore, was much less costly than hospital care, not more costly.

SOURCE: Adapted from George C. Galster, Timothy F. Champney, and Yolonda Williams, "Costs of Caring for Persons With Long-Term Mental Illness in Alternative Residential Settings," *Evaluation and Program Planning*, 1994,17(3):239-348.

An **efficiency assessment** takes account of the relationship between a program's costs and its effectiveness. Efficiency assessments may take the form of a **cost-benefit analysis** or a **cost-effectiveness analysis**. Typical issues include whether a program produces sufficient benefits in relation to its costs and whether other interventions or delivery systems can produce the benefits at a lower cost.

Efficiency assessment can be tricky and arguable because it requires making assumptions about the dollar value of program-related activities and, sometimes, imputing monetary value to a program's benefits. Nevertheless, such estimates are often essential for decisions about the allocation of resources to programs and identification of the program models that produce the strongest results with a given amount of funding.

Like impact assessment, efficiency assessment is most appropriate for mature, stable programs with a well-structured program model. This form of evaluation builds on process and impact assessment. A program must be well implemented and produce the desired outcomes before questions of efficiency become relevant. Given the specialized financial expertise required to conduct efficiency assesments, it is also apparent that it should be undertaken only when there is a clear need and identified user for the information. With the high level of concern about program costs in many contexts, however, this may not be an unusual circumstance. Chapter 11 discusses efficiency assessment methods in more detail.

Summary

■ Every evaluation must be tailored to a specific set of circumstances so that it will be capable of yielding credible and useful answers to the questions at issue while still being sufficiently practical to actually implement within the resources available.

■ Key aspects of the evaluation plan that must be tailored include the questions the evaluation is to answer, the methods and procedures to be used in answering those questions, and the nature of the evaluator-stakeholder relationship.

■ Three principal features of the evaluation context must be taken into account in an evaluation plan: the purpose of the evaluation, the structure and circumstances of the program being evaluated, and the resources available for the evaluation.

■ The overall purpose of the evaluation necessarily shapes its focus, scope, and construction. Evaluation is generally intended to provide feedback to program managers and sponsors, establish accountability to decisionmakers, or contribute to knowledge about social intervention.

■ The evaluation plan must also be responsive to a program's structure and circumstances, including how new or open to change the program is, the degree of consensus or conflict among stakeholders about the nature and mission of the program, the values and concepts inherent in the program rationale, and the way in which the program is organized and administered.

■ The evaluation plan must accommodate the inevitable limitations on the resources available for the evaluation effort. The critical resources include not only funding but also the time allowed for completion of the work, pertinent technical expertise, program and stakeholder cooperation, and access to important records and program material. A balance must be found between what is most desirable from an evaluation standpoint and what is feasible in terms of available resources.

■ An often neglected but critical aspect of an evaluation plan involves spelling out the appropriate relationship between the evaluator and the evaluation sponsor and other major stakeholders. The three major types of evaluator-stakeholder relationships are (1) independent evaluation, in which the evaluator takes primary responsibility for designing and conducting the evaluation; (2) participatory or collaborative evaluation, in which the evaluation is conducted as a team project involving stakeholders; and (3) empowerment evaluation, in which the evaluation is designed to help develop the capabilities of the participating stakeholders in ways that enhance their skills or political influence.

■ The questions an evaluation is designed to address generally fall into recognizable categories. Evaluators have developed relatively distinct conceptual and methodological approaches for these different issues. The main types of concerns addressed by evaluations and the associated methods are (1) the need for services (needs assessment), (2) the conceptualization and design of the program (assessment of program theory), (3) the implementation of a program (assessment of program process, also called process evaluation or program monitoring), (4) the program's outcomes (impact assessment), and (5) the program's efficiency (efficiency assessment). In practice, much of evaluation planning consists of identifying the approach corresponding to the type of questions to be answered, then tailoring the specifics to the program situation.

KEY CONCEPTS

Assessment of program process

An evaluative study that answers questions about program operations, implementation, and service delivery. Also known as a process evaluation or an implementation assessment.

Assessment of program theory

An evaluative study that answers questions about the conceptualization and design of a program.

Cost-benefit analysis

Analytical procedure for determining the economic efficiency of a program, expressed as the relationship between costs and outcomes, usually measured in monetary terms.

Cost-effectiveness analysis

Analytical procedure for determining the efficacy of a program in achieving given intervention outcomes in relation to the program costs.

Efficiency assessment

An evaluative study that answers questions about program costs in comparison to either the monetary value of its benefits or its effectiveness in terms of the changes brought about in the social conditions it addresses.

Empowerment evaluation

A participatory or collaborative evaluation in which the evaluator's role includes consultation and facilitation directed toward the development of the capabilities of the participating stakeholders to conduct evaluation on their own, to use it effectively for advocacy and change, and to have some influence on a program that affects their lives.

Evaluation questions

A set of questions developed by the evaluator, evaluation sponsor, and other stakeholders; the questions define the issues the evaluation will investigate and are stated in terms such that they can be answered using methods available to the evaluator in a way useful to stakeholders.

Formative evaluation

Evaluative activities undertaken to furnish information that will guide program improvement.

Impact assessment

An evaluative study that answers questions about program outcomes and impact on the social conditions it is intended to ameliorate. Also known as an impact evaluation or an outcome evaluation.

Independent evaluation

An evaluation in which the evaluator has the primary responsibility for developing the evaluation plan, conducting the evaluation, and disseminating the results.

Needs assessment

An evaluative study that answers questions about the social conditions a program is intended to address and the need for the program.

Participatory or collaborative evaluation

An evaluation organized as a team project in which the evaluator and representatives of one or more stakeholder groups work collaboratively in developing the evaluation plan, conducting the evaluation, and disseminating and using the results.

Process evaluation

A form of program monitoring designed to determine whether the program is delivered as intended to the target recipients. Also known as implementation assessment.

Program monitoring

The systematic documentation of aspects of program performance that are indicative of whether the program is functioning as intended or according to some appropriate standard. Monitoring generally involves program performance related to program process, program outcomes, or both.

Program theory

The set of assumptions about the manner in which a program relates to the social benefits it is expected to produce and the strategy and tactics the program has adopted to achieve its goals and objectives. Within program theory we can distinguish *impact theory*, relating to the nature of the change in social conditions brought about by program action, and *process theory*, which depicts the program's organizational plan and service utilization plan.

Summative evaluation

Evaluative activities undertaken to render a summary judgment on certain critical aspects of the program's performance, for instance, to determine if specific goals and objectives were met.

Target

The unit (individual, family, community, etc.) to which a program intervention is directed. All such units within the area served by a program comprise its target population.

3

Identifying Issues and Formulating Questions

Chapter Outline

What Makes a Good Evaluation Question?
Dimensions of Program Performance
Evaluation Questions Must Be Reasonable and Appropriate
Evaluation Questions Must Be Answerable
Criteria for Program Performance
Typical Evaluation Questions
The Evaluation Hierarchy

Determining the Specific Questions the Evaluation Should Answer
Representing the Concerns of the Evaluation Sponsor and Major Stakeholders
Obtaining Input From Stakeholders
Topics for Discussion With Stakeholders
Analysis of Program Assumptions and Theory

Collating Evaluation Questions and Setting Priorities

The previous chapter presented an overview of the many considerations that go into tailoring an evaluation. Although all those matters are important to evaluation design, the essence of evaluation is generating credible answers to questions about the performance of a social program. Good evaluation questions must address issues that are meaningful in relation to the nature of the program and also of concern to key stakeholders. They must be answerable with the research techniques available to the evaluator and formulated so that the criteria by which the corresponding program performance will be judged are explicit or can be determined in a straightforward way.

A set of carefully crafted evaluation questions, therefore, is the hub around which evaluation revolves. It follows that a careful, explicit formulation of those questions greatly facilitates the design of the evaluation and the use of its findings. Evaluation questions may take various forms, some of which are more useful and meaningful than others for stakeholders and program decisionmakers. Furthermore, some forms of evaluation questions are more amenable to the evaluator's task of providing credible answers, and some address critical program effectiveness issues more directly than others.

This chapter discusses practical ways in which evaluators can fashion effective evaluation questions. An essential step is identification of the decisionmakers who will use the evaluation results, what information they need, and how they expect to use it. The evaluator's own analysis of the program is also important. One approach that is particularly useful for this purpose is articulation of the program theory, a detailed account of how and why the program is supposed to work. Consideration of program theory focuses attention on critical events and premises that may be appropriate topics of inquiry in the evaluation.

A critical phase in an evaluation is the identification and formulation of the questions the evaluation is to address. One might assume that this step would be very straightforward, indeed, that the questions would be stipulated routinely as part of the process of commissioning the evaluation. As described in Chapter 2, however, it is rare for final, workable evaluation questions to be specified clearly by the evaluation sponsor at the beginning of an evaluation. Nor can the evaluator usually step in and define those questions solely on the basis of his or her professional expertise. That maneuver would increase the risk that the evaluation would not be responsive to stakeholder concerns, would not be useful or used, and would be attacked as irrelevant or inappropriate.

To ensure that the evaluation will focus on the matters of greatest concern to the pertinent decisionmakers and stakeholders, the initial evaluation questions are best formulated through discourse and negotiation with them. Equally important, engaging key stakeholders increases the likelihood that they will understand, appreciate, and make effective use of the findings when they become available.

Although input from stakeholders is critical, the evaluator should not depend solely on their perspective to identify the issues the evaluation will address. Sometimes the evaluation sponsors are very knowledgeable about evaluation and will have formulated a complete and workable set of questions to which the evaluation should attend. More often, however, the evaluation sponsors and program stakeholders are not especially expert at evaluation or, if so, have not done all the groundwork needed to focus the evaluation. This means that the evaluator will rarely be presented at the outset with a finished list of issues the evaluation should address for the results to be useful, interpretable, and complete. Nor will the questions that are put forward generally be formulated in a manner that permits ready translation into research design.

The evaluator, therefore, also has a crucial role in the framing of evaluation questions. The stakeholders will be the experts on the practical and political issues facing the program, but the evaluator should know the most about how to analyze a program and focus an evaluation. The evaluator must be prepared to raise issues that otherwise might be overlooked, identify aspects of the program's operations and outcomes that might warrant inquiry, and work with stakeholders to translate their concerns into questions that evaluation research can actually answer.

It is generally wise for the evaluator to develop a written summary of the specific questions that will guide the evaluation design. This provides a useful reference to consult while designing the evaluation and selecting research procedures. Perhaps more important, the evaluator can discuss this summary statement with the evaluation sponsor and key stakeholders to ensure that it encompasses their concerns. Such a procedure also can safeguard against later misunderstanding of what the evaluation was supposed to accomplish.

The remainder of this chapter examines the two most important topics related to specifying the questions that will guide an evaluation: (1) how to formulate evaluation questions in such a way that they can be addressed using the research procedures available to the evaluator, and (2) how to determine the specific questions on which the evaluation should focus.

What Makes a Good Evaluation Question?

The form that evaluation questions should take is shaped by the functions they must perform. Their principal role is to focus the evaluation on the areas of program performance at issue for key decisionmakers and stakeholders. They should also be able to facilitate the design of a data collection procedure that will provide meaningful information about that area of performance. In particular, a good evaluation question must identify a distinct dimension of relevant program performance and do so in such a way that the quality of the performance can be credibly assessed. Such assessment, in turn, requires an accurate description of the nature of the performance and some standard by which it can be evaluated (see Exhibit 3-A). Each of these aspects of good evaluation questions warrants further discussion.

There are different kinds of inquiry across practice areas, such as that which is found in law, medicine, and science. Common to each kind of inquiry is a general pattern of reasoning or basic logic that guides and informs the practice. . . . Evaluation is one kind of inquiry, and it, too, has a basic logic or general pattern of reasoning [that has been put forth by Michael Scriven]. . . . This general logic of evaluation is as follows:

1. *Establishing criteria of merit.* On what dimensions must the evaluand [thing being evaluated] do well?

2. *Constructing standards.* How well should the evaluand perform?

3. *Measuring performance and comparing with standards.* How well did the evaluand perform?

4. *Synthesizing and integrating data into a judgment of merit or worth.* What is the merit or worth of the evaluand?

. . . To evaluate anything means to assess the merit or worth of something against criteria and standards. The basic logic explicated by Scriven reflects what it means when we use the term to *evaluate*.

SOURCE: Quoted from Deborah M. Fournier, *Establishing Evaluative Conclusions: A Distinction Between General and Working Logic,* New Directions for Evaluation, no. 68 (San Francisco: Jossey-Bass, 1995), p. 16.

Dimensions of Program Performance

Good evaluation questions must first of all be *reasonable and appropriate.* That is, they must identify performance dimensions that are relevant to the expectations stakeholders hold for the program and that represent domains in which the program can realistically hope to have accomplishments. It would hardly be fair or sensible, for instance, to ask if a low-income housing weatherization program reduced the prevalence of drug dealing in a neighborhood. Nor would it generally be useful to ask a question as narrow as whether the program got a bargain in its purchase of file cabinets for its office. Furthermore, evaluation questions must be *answerable;* that is, they must involve performance dimensions that are sufficiently specific, concrete, practical, and measurable that meaningful information can be obtained about their status. An evaluator would have great difficulty determining whether an adult literacy program improved a community's competitiveness in the global economy or whether the counselors in a drug prevention program were sufficiently caring in their relations with clients.

Evaluation Questions Must Be Reasonable and Appropriate

Program advocates often proclaim grandiose goals (e.g., improve the quality of life for children), expect unrealistically large effects, or believe the program to have accomplishments that are clearly beyond its actual capabilities. Good evaluation questions deal with performance dimensions that are appropriate and realistic for the program. This means that the evaluator must often work with relevant stakeholders to scale down and focus the evaluation questions. The manager of a community health program, for instance, might initially ask, "Are our education and outreach services successful in informing the public about the risk of AIDS?" In practice, however, those services may consist of little more than occasional presentations by program staff at civic club meetings and health fairs. With this rather modest level of activity, it may be unrealistic to expect the public at large to receive much AIDS information. If a question about this service is deemed important for the evaluation, a better version might be something such as "Do our education and outreach services raise awareness of AIDS issues among the audiences addressed?" and "Do those audiences represent community leaders who are likely to influence the level of awareness of AIDS issues among other people?"

There are two complementary ways for an evaluator, in collaboration with pertinent stakeholders, to assess how appropriate and realistic a candidate evaluation question is. The first is to examine the question in the context of the actual program activities related to it. In the example above, for instance, the low-key nature of the education and outreach services was clearly not up to the task of "informing the public about the risk of AIDS," and there would be little point in having the evaluation attempt to determine if this was the actual outcome. The evaluator and relevant stakeholders should identify and scrutinize the program components, activities, and personnel assignments that relate to program performance and formulate the evaluation question in a way that is reasonable given those characteristics.

The second way to assess whether candidate evaluation questions are reasonable and appropriate is to analyze them in relationship to the findings reported in applicable social science and social service literature. For instance, the sponsor of an evaluation of a program for juvenile delinquents might initially ask if the program increases the self-esteem of the delinquents, in the belief that inadequate self-esteem is a problem for these juveniles and improvements will lead to better behavior. Examination of the applicable social science research, however, will reveal that juvenile delinquents do not generally have problems with self-esteem and, moreover, that increases in self-esteem are not generally associated with reductions in delinquency. In light of this information, the evaluator and the evaluation sponsor may well agree that the question of the program's impact on self-esteem is not appropriate.

The foundation for formulating appropriate and realistic evaluation questions is detailed and complete program description. Early in the process, the evaluator should become thoroughly acquainted with the program—how it is structured, what activities take place, the roles and tasks of the various personnel, the nature of the participants, and the assumptions inherent in its principal functions. The stakeholder groups with whom the evaluator collaborates (especially program managers and staff) will also have knowledge about the program, of course. Evaluation questions that are inspired by close consideration of actual program activities and assumptions will almost automatically be appropriate and realistic.

Evaluation Questions Must Be Answerable

It is obvious that the evaluation questions around which an evaluation plan is developed should be answerable. Questions that cannot be answered may be intriguing to philosophers but do not serve the needs of evaluators and the decisionmakers who intend to use the evaluation results. What is not so obvious, perhaps, is how easy it is to formulate an unanswerable evaluation question without realizing it. This may occur because the terms used in the question, although seemingly commonsensical, are actually ambiguous or vague when the time comes for a concrete interpretation ("Does this program enhance family values?"). Or sensible-sounding questions may invoke issues for which there are so few observable indicators that little can be learned about them ("Are the case managers sensitive to the social circumstances of their clients?"). Also, some questions lack sufficient indication of the relevant criteria to permit a meaningful answer ("Is this program successful?"). Finally, some questions may be answerable only with more expertise, data, time, or resources than are available to the evaluation ("Do the prenatal services this program provides to high-risk women increase the chances that their children will complete college?").

For an evaluation question to be answerable, it must be possible to identify some evidence or "observables" that can realistically be obtained and that will be credible as the basis for an answer. This generally means developing questions that involve measurable performance dimensions stated in terms that have unambiguous and noncontroversial definitions. In addition, the relevant standards or criteria must be specified with equal clarity. Suppose, for instance, that a proposed evaluation question for a compensatory education program like Head Start is, "Are we reaching the children most in need of this program?" To affirm that this is an answerable question, the evaluator should be able to do the following:

1. Define the group of children at issue (e.g., those in census tract such and such, four or five years old, living in households with annual income under 150% of the federal poverty level).

2. Identify the specific measurable characteristics and cutoff values that represent the greatest need (e.g., annual income below the federal poverty level, single parent in the household with educational attainment of less than high school).

3. Give an example of the evaluation finding that might result (e.g., 60% of the children currently served fall in the high-need category; 75% of the high-need children in the **catchment area**—the geographic area being served by the program—are not enrolled in the program).

4. Stipulate the evaluative criteria (e.g., to be satisfactory, at least 90% of the children in the program should be high need and at least 50% of the high-need children in the catchment area should be in the program).

5. Have the evaluation sponsors and other pertinent stakeholders (who should be involved in the whole process) agree that a finding meeting these criteria would, indeed, answer the question.

If such conditions can be met and, in addition, the resources are available to collect, analyze, and report the applicable data, then the evaluation question can be considered answerable.

Criteria for Program Performance

Beginning a study with a reasonable, answerable question or set of questions, of course, is customary in the social sciences (where the questions often are framed as hypotheses). What distinguishes evaluation questions is that they have to do with performance and are associated, at least implicitly, with some criteria by which that performance can be judged. Identifying the relevant criteria was mentioned above as part of what makes an evaluation question answerable. However, this is such an important and distinctive aspect of evaluation questions that it warrants separate discussion.

When program managers or evaluation sponsors ask such things as "Are we targeting the right client population?" or "Do our services benefit the recipients?" they are not only asking for a description of the program's performance with regard to serving appropriate clients and providing services that yield benefits. They are also asking if that performance is good enough according to some standard or judgment. There is likely little doubt that at least a few of the "right client population" receive services or that some recipients receive some benefit from services. But is it enough? Some criterion level must be set by which the numbers and amounts can be evaluated on those performance dimensions.

One implication of this distinctive feature of evaluation is that good evaluation questions will, when possible, convey the **performance criterion** or standard that is applicable as well as the performance dimension that is at issue. Thus, evaluation questions should be much like this: "Is at least 75% of the program clientele appropriate for services?" (by some explicit definition of appropriate) or "Do the majority of those who receive the employment services get jobs within 30 days of the conclusion of training that they keep at least three months?" In addition, the performance standards represented in these questions should have some defensible, though possibly indirect, relationship to the social needs the program addresses. There must be some reason why attaining that standard is meaningful, and the strongest rationale is that it represents a level of performance sufficient for that program function to contribute effectively to the overall program purpose of improving the target social conditions.

A considerable complication for the evaluator is that the applicable performance criteria may take different forms for various dimensions of program performance (see Exhibit 3-B). Moreover, it is not always possible to establish an explicit, consensual performance standard in advance of collecting data and reporting results. Nonetheless, to the extent that the formulation of the initial evaluation questions includes explicit criteria on which key stakeholders agree, evaluation planning is made easier and the potential for disagreement over the interpretation of the evaluation results is reduced.

We stress that the criterion issue cannot be avoided. An evaluation that only describes program performance, and does not attempt to assess it, is not truly an evaluation (by definition, as indicated in Exhibit 3-A). At most, such an evaluation only pushes the issue of setting criteria and judging performance onto the consumer of the information.

With these considerations in mind, we turn attention to the kinds of performance criteria that are relevant to the formulation of useful evaluation questions. Perhaps the most common criteria are those based on program goals and objectives. In this case, certain desirable accomplishments are identified as the program aims by program officials and sponsors. Often these statements of goals and objectives are not very specific with regard to the nature or level of program performance they represent. (As will be

EXHIBIT 3-B

Many Criteria May Be Relevant to Program Performance

The standards by which program performance may be judged in an evaluation include the following:

- The needs or wants of the target population
- Stated program goals and objectives
- Professional standards
- Customary practice; norms for other programs
- Legal requirements
- Ethical or moral values; social justice, equity
- Past performance; historical data
- Targets set by program managers
- Expert opinion
- Preintervention baseline levels for the target population
- Conditions expected in the absence of the program (counterfactual)
- Cost or relative cost

---

noted later in this chapter, evaluators should distinguish between general program goals and specific, measurable objectives.) One of the goals of a shelter for battered women, for instance, might be to "empower them to take control of their own lives." Although reflecting commendable values, this statement gives no indication of the tangible manifestations of such empowerment or what level of empowerment constitutes attainment of this goal. Considerable discussion with stakeholders may be necessary to translate such statements into mutually acceptable terminology that describes the intended outcomes concretely, identifies the observable indicators of those outcomes, and specifies the level of accomplishment that would be considered a success in accomplishing the stated goal.

Some program objectives, on the other hand, may be very specific. These often come in the form of administrative objectives adopted as targets for routine program functions. The target levels may be set according to past experience, the experience of comparable programs, a judgment of what is reasonable and desirable, or maybe only a "best guess." Examples of administrative objectives may be to complete intake actions for 90% of the referrals within 30 days, to have 75% of the clients complete the full term of service, to have 85% "good" or "outstanding" ratings on a client satisfaction questionnaire, to provide at least three appropriate services to each person under case management, and the like. There is typically a certain amount of arbitrariness in these criterion levels. But, if they are administratively stipulated or can be established through stakeholder consensus, and if they are reasonable, they are quite serviceable in the formulation of evaluation questions and the interpretation of the subsequent findings. However, it is not generally wise for the evaluator to press for specific statements of target performance levels if the program does not have them or cannot readily and confidently develop them. Setting such targets with little justification only creates a situation in which they are arbitrarily revised when the evaluation results are in.

In some instances, there are established professional standards that can be invoked as performance criteria. This is particularly likely in medical and health programs, where practice guidelines and managed care standards have developed that may be relevant for setting desirable performance levels. Much more common, however, is the situation where there are no established criteria or even arbitrary administrative objectives to invoke. A typical situation is one in which the performance dimension is clearly recognized but there is ambiguity about the criteria for good performance on that dimension. For instance, stakeholders may agree that the program should have a low drop-out rate, a high proportion of clients completing service, a high level of client satisfaction, and the like, but only nebulous ideas as to what level constitutes "low" or "high." Sometimes the evaluator can make use of prior experience or find information in the evaluation and program literature that provides a reasonable basis for setting a criterion level. Another approach is to collect judgment ratings from relevant stakeholders to establish the criterion levels or, perhaps, criterion ranges, that can be accepted to distinguish, say, high, medium, and low performance.

Establishing a criterion level can be particularly difficult when the performance dimension in an evaluation question involves outcome or impact issues. Program stakeholders and evaluators alike may have little idea about how much change on a given outcome variable (e.g., a scale of attitude toward drug use) is large and how much is small. By default, these judgments are often made on the basis of statistical criteria; for example, a program is judged to be effective solely because the measured effects are statistically significant. This is a poor practice for reasons that will be more fully examined when impact evaluation is discussed later in this volume. Statistical criteria have no intrinsic relationship to the practical significance of a change on an outcome dimension and can be misleading. A juvenile delinquency program that is found to have the statistically significant effect of lowering delinquency recidivism by 2% may not make a large enough difference to be worthwhile continuing. Thus, as much as possible, the evaluator should use the techniques suggested above to attempt to determine and specify in practical terms what "success" level is appropriate for judging the nature and magnitude of the program's effects.

Typical Evaluation Questions

As is evident from the discussion so far, well-formulated evaluation questions are very concrete and specific to the program at issue and the circumstances of the prospective evaluation. It follows that the variety of questions that might be relevant to some social program or another is enormous. As noted in Chapter 2, however, evaluation questions typically deal with one of five general program issues. Some of the more common questions in each category, stated in summary form, are as follows.

Questions about the need for program services (needs assessment):

- What are the nature and magnitude of the problem to be addressed?

- What are the characteristics of the population in need?

- What are the needs of the population?

- What services are needed?

- How much service is needed, over what time period?

- What service delivery arrangements are needed to provide those services to the population?

Questions about the program's conceptualization or design (assessment of program theory):

- What clientele should be served?

- What services should be provided?

- What are the best delivery systems for the services?

- How can the program identify, recruit, and sustain the intended clientele?

- How should the program be organized?

- What resources are necessary and appropriate for the program?

Questions about program operations and service delivery (assessment of program process):

- Are administrative and service objectives being met?

- Are the intended services being delivered to the intended persons?

- Are there needy but unserved persons the program is not reaching?

- Once in service, do sufficient numbers of clients complete service?

- Are the clients satisfied with the services?

- Are administrative, organizational, and personnel functions handled well?

Questions about program outcomes (impact assessment):

- Are the outcome goals and objectives being achieved?

- Do the services have beneficial effects on the recipients?

- Do the services have adverse side effects on the recipients?

- Are some recipients affected more by the services than others?

- Is the problem or situation the services are intended to address made better?

Questions about program cost and efficiency (efficiency assessment):

- Are resources used efficiently?

- Is the cost reasonable in relation to the magnitude of the benefits?

- Would alternative approaches yield equivalent benefits at less cost?

There is an important relationship among these categories of questions that the evaluator must recognize. Each successive type of question draws much of its meaning from the answers to the questions in the prior set. Questions about a program's conceptualization and design, for instance, depend very much on the nature of the need the program is intended to address. Different needs are best met by different types of programs. If the need a program targets is lack of economic resources, the appropriate program concepts and the evaluation questions that might be asked about them will be different than if the program is intended to reduce drunken driving. Moreover, the most appropriate criteria for judging the program design relate to how well it fits with the need and the circumstances of those in need.

Similarly, a central set of questions about program operations and service delivery has to do with how well the program design is actually implemented in practice. Correspondingly, the principal basis for assessing program operations and service delivery is in terms of fidelity to the intended program design. Key evaluation questions, therefore, relate to whether the program *as intended* has actually been implemented. This means that the criteria for assessing implementation are drawn, at least in part, from assumptions about how the program is intended to function, that is, from its basic conceptualization and design. If we know the basic concept of a program is to feed the homeless through a soup kitchen, we readily recognize a problem with program operations if no food is actually distributed to homeless individuals.

Questions about program outcome, in turn, are meaningful only if the program design is well implemented. Program services that are not actually delivered, or are not the intended services, cannot generally be expected to produce the desired outcomes. Evaluators call it **implementation failure** when the outcomes are poor because the program activities assumed necessary to bring about the desired improvements did not actually occur. It would be an implementation failure if there were no improvements in the nutritional status of the homeless because the soup kitchen was so rarely open that few homeless individuals were actually able to eat there.

A program may be well implemented and yet fail to achieve the desired results because the program concepts embodied in the corresponding services are faulty. When the program conceptualization and design are not capable of generating the desired outcomes no matter how well implemented, evaluators refer to **theory failure.** In the sequence of evaluation questions shown above, therefore, those relating to outcomes are meaningful only when program operations and services are well implemented. Good implementation, in turn, is meaningful only if the program design that identifies the intended operations and services represents an appropriate response to the social problem and needs the program is attempting to alleviate. If the plan for the soup kitchen locates it a great distance from where homeless individuals congregate, it will provide little benefit to them no matter how well it is implemented. In this case, a key aspect of the basic design of the program (location) does not connect well with the needs of the target population.

The last set of evaluation questions in the list above relating to program cost and efficiency also draw much of their significance from the issues that precede them on the list. A program must produce at least minimal outcomes before questions about the cost of attaining those outcomes or more efficient ways of attaining them are interesting. We might, for instance, assess the costs of a soup kitchen for feeding the homeless. However, if there are no benefits because no homeless individuals are actually fed, then there is little to say except that any cost is too much. The lack of positive outcomes, whether resulting from poor implementation or faulty program design, makes the cost issues relatively trivial.

The Evaluation Hierarchy

The relationships among the different types of evaluation questions just described define a hierarchy of evaluation issues that has implications beyond simply organizing categories of questions. As mentioned in the overview of kinds of evaluation studies in Chapter 2, the types of evaluation questions and the methods for answering them are sufficiently distinct that each constitutes a form of evaluation in its own right. These groupings of evaluation questions and methods constitute the building blocks of evaluation research and, individually or in combination, are recognizable in virtually all evaluation studies. As shown in Exhibit 3-C, we can think of these evaluation building blocks in the form of a hierarchy in which each rests on those below it.

EXHIBIT 3-C
The Evaluation Hierarchy

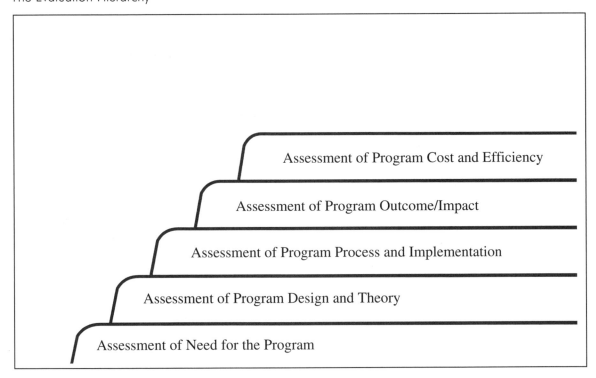

The foundational level of the evaluation hierarchy relates to the need for the program. Assessment of the nature of the social problem and the need for intervention produces the diagnostic information that supports effective program design, that is, a program theory for how to address the social conditions the program is intended to improve. Given a credible program theory, the next level of evaluation is to assess how well it is implemented. This is the task of process or implementation evaluation.

If we know that the social need is properly understood, the program theory for addressing it is reasonable, and the corresponding program activities and services are well implemented, then it may be meaningful to assess program outcomes. Undertaking an impact evaluation to assess outcomes thus necessarily presupposes acceptable results from assessments of the issues below it on the evaluation hierarchy. If assessments have not actually been conducted on the logically prior issues when an impact evaluation is done, its results are interpretable only to the extent that justifiable assumptions can be made about those issues.

At the top of the hierarchy we have assessment of program cost and efficiency. Pursuing questions about these matters is a relatively high-order evaluation task that assumes knowledge about all the supporting issues below it in the hierarchy. This is because answers about cost and efficiency issues are generally interpretable only when there is also information available about the nature of the program outcomes, implementation, theory, and the social problem addressed.

It follows that a major consideration in identifying the evaluation questions to be answered in a program evaluation is what is already known or can be confidently assumed about the program. It would not be sensible for the evaluation to focus on the assessment of outcomes, for instance, if there was uncertainty about how well the program was conceptualized and implemented in relation to the nature of the social conditions it was intended to improve. If there are relevant questions about these more fundamental matters, they must be built into the evaluation plan along with the outcome questions.

When developing the questions around which the plan for an evaluation will revolve, therefore, it is best for the evaluator to start at the bottom of the evaluation hierarchy and consider first what is known and needs to be known about the most fundamental issues. When the assumptions that can be safely made are identified and the questions that must be answered are defined, then it is appropriate to move to the next level of the hierarchy. There the evaluator can determine if the questions at that level will be meaningful in light of what will be available about the more fundamental issues.

By keeping in mind the logical interdependencies between the levels in the evaluation hierarchy and the corresponding evaluation building blocks, the evaluator can focus the evaluation on the questions most appropriate to the program situation. At the same time, many mistakes of premature attention to higher-order evaluation questions can be avoided.

Determining the Specific Questions the Evaluation Should Answer

The families of evaluation questions relating to the need, design, implementation, outcomes, and cost of a program are not mutually exclusive. Questions in more than one category could be relevant to a program for which an evaluation was being planned. To develop an appropriate evaluation plan, the many possible questions that might be asked about the program must be narrowed down to those specific ones that are most relevant to the program's circumstances. (See Exhibit 3-D for an example of specific evaluation questions for an actual program.)

As we emphasized in Chapter 2, the concerns of the evaluation sponsor and other major stakeholders should play a central role in shaping the questions that structure the evaluation plan. In the discussion that follows, therefore, we first examine the matter of obtaining appropriate input from the evaluation sponsor and relevant stakeholders prior to and during the design stage of the evaluation.

However, it is rarely appropriate for the evaluator to rely only on input from the evaluation sponsor and stakeholders to determine the questions on which the evaluation should focus. Because of their close familiarity with the program, stakeholders may overlook critical, but relatively routine, aspects of program performance. Also, the experience and knowledge of the evaluator may yield distinctive insights into program issues and their interrelations that are important for identifying relevant evaluation questions. Generally, therefore, it is desirable for the evaluator to make an independent analysis of the areas of program performance that may be pertinent for investigation. Accordingly, the second topic addressed in the discussion that follows is how the evaluator can analyze a program in a way that will uncover potentially important evaluation questions for consideration in designing the evaluation. The evaluation hierarchy, described above, is one tool that can be used for this purpose. Especially useful is the concept of program theory. By depicting the significant assumptions and expectations on which the program depends for its success, the program theory can highlight critical issues that the evaluation should look into.

Representing the Concerns of the Evaluation Sponsor and Major Stakeholders

In planning and conducting an evaluation, evaluators usually find themselves confronted with multiple stakeholders who hold different and sometimes conflicting views on the program or its evaluation and whose interests will be affected by the outcome (see Exhibit 3-E for an illustration). Recall from Chapter 2 that the stakeholders typically encountered include policymakers and decisionmakers, program and evaluation sponsors, target participants, program managers and staff, program competitors, contextual stakeholders, and the evaluation and research community. At the planning stage, the evaluator usually attempts to identify all the stakeholders with an important point of view on what questions should be addressed in the evaluation, set priorities among those viewpoints, and integrate as many of the relevant concerns as possible into the evaluation plan.

EXHIBIT 3-D

Evaluation Questions for a Neighborhood Afterschool Program

An afterschool program located in an economically depressed area uses the facilities of a local elementary school to provide free afterschool care from 3:30 to 6:00 for the children of the neighborhood. The program's goals are to provide a safe, supervised environment for latchkey children and to enhance their school performance through academic enrichment activities. The following are examples of the questions that an evaluation might be designed to answer for the stakeholders in this program, together with the standards that make the questions answerable:

Is there a need for the program?

Question: How many latchkey children reside within a radius of 1.5 miles of the school? Latchkey children are defined as those of elementary school age who are without adult supervision during some period after school at least once a week during the school year.

Standard: There should be at least 100 such children in the defined neighborhood. The planned enrollment for the program is 60, which should yield enough children in attendance on any given day for efficient staffing, and it is assumed that some eligible children will not enroll for various reasons.

Question: What proportion of the children enrolled in the program are actually latchkey children?

Standard: At least 75% of the enrolled children should meet the definition for latchkey children. This is an administrative target that reflects the program's intent that a large majority of the enrollees be latchkey children while recognizing that other children will be attracted to, and appropriate for, the program even though not meeting that definition.

Is the program well designed?

Question: Are the planned educational activities the best ones for this clientele and the purposes of enhancing their performance in school?

Standard: There should be indications in the educational research literature to show that these activities have the potential to be effective. In addition, experienced teachers for the relevant grade levels should endorse these activities.

Question: Is there a sufficient number of staff positions in the program?

Standard: The staff-student ratio should exceed the state standards for licensed child care facilities.

(Continued)

EXHIBIT 3-D
(Continued)

Is the program implemented effectively?

Question: What is the attendance rate for enrolled children?

Standard: All enrolled children should either be in attendance every afternoon for which they are scheduled or excused with parental permission.

Question: Is the program providing regular support for school homework and related tasks?

Standard: There should be an average of 45 minutes of supervised study time for completion of homework and reading each afternoon, and all the attending children should participate.

Does the program have the intended outcomes?

Question: Is there improvement in the attitudes of the enrolled children toward school?

Standard: At least 80% of the children should show measurable improvement in their attitudes toward school between the beginning and end of the school year. Norms for similar students show that their attitudes tend to get worse each year of elementary school; the program objective is to reverse this trend, even if the improvement is only slight.

Question: Is there an improvement in the academic performance of the enrolled children in their regular school work?

Standard: The average term grades on academic subjects should be at least a half letter grade better than they would have been had the children not participated in the program.

Is the program cost-effective?

Question: What is the cost per child for running this program beyond the fixed expenses associated with the regular operation of the school facility?

Standard: Costs per child should be near or below the average for similar programs run in other school districts in the state.

Question: Would the program be equally effective and less costly if staffed by community volunteers (except the director) rather than paid paraprofessionals?

Standard: The annual cost of a volunteer-based program, including recruiting, training, and supporting the volunteers, would have to be at least 20% less than the cost of the current program with no loss of effectiveness to justify the effort associated with making such a change.

EXHIBIT 3-E

Diverse Stakeholder
Perspectives on an
Evaluation of a
Multiagency Program
for the Homeless

The Joint Program was initiated to improve the accessibility of health and social services for the homeless population of Montreal through coordinated activities involving provincial, regional, and municipal authorities and more than 20 nonprofit and public agencies. The services developed through the program included walk-in and referral services, mobile drop-in centers, an outreach team in a community health center, medical and nursing care in shelters, and case management. To ensure stakeholder participation in the evaluation, an evaluation steering committee was set up with representatives of the different types of agencies involved in the program and which, in turn, coordinated with two other stakeholder committees charged with program responsibilities.

Even though all the stakeholders shared a common cause to which they were firmly committed—the welfare of the homeless—they had quite varied perspectives on the evaluation. Some of these were described by the evaluators as follows:

> The most glaring imbalance was in the various agencies' different organizational cultures, which led them to experience their participation in the evaluation very differently. Some of the service agencies involved in the Joint Program and its evaluation were front-line public organizations that were accustomed to viewing their actions in terms of a mandate with a target clientele. They were familiar with the evaluation process, both as an administrative procedure and a measurement of accountability. Among the nonprofit agencies, however, some relative newcomers who had been innovators in the area of community-based intervention were hoping the evaluation would recognize the strengths of their approach and make useful suggestions for improvement. Other nonprofit groups were offshoots of religious or charitable organizations that had been involved with the homeless for a very long time. For those groups the evaluation (and the logical, planning-based program itself) was a procedure completely outside of anything in their experience. They perceived the evaluators as outsiders meddling in a reality that they had managed to deal with up until now, under very difficult conditions. Their primary concern was the client. More than the public agencies, they probably saw the evaluation as a waste of time, money, and energy. Most of the day centers involved in the program fell into this category. They were the ones who were asked to take part in a process with which they were unfamiliar, alongside their counterparts in the public sector who were much better versed in research procedures. (p. 471)

SOURCE: From Céline Mercier, "Participation in Stakeholder-Based Evaluation: A Case Study," *Evaluation and Program Planning,* 1997, 20(4):467-475.

The starting point, of course, is the evaluation sponsors. Those who have commissioned and funded the evaluation rightfully have priority in defining the issues it should address. Sometimes evaluation sponsors have stipulated the evaluation questions and methods completely and want the evaluator only to manage the practical details. In such circumstances, the evaluator should assess which, if any, stakeholder perspectives are excluded by the sponsor's questions and whether those perspectives are sufficiently distinct and important that omitting them would compromise the evaluation. If so, the evaluator must decide whether to conduct the evaluation under the specified constraints, reporting the limitations and biases along with the results, or attempt to negotiate an arrangement whereby the evaluation is broadened to include additional perspectives.

More often, however, the evaluation sponsors' initial specifications are not so constrained or nonnegotiable that they rule out consideration of the concerns of other stakeholders. In this situation, the evaluator typically makes the best attempt possible within the constraints of the situation to consult fully with all stakeholders, set reasonable priorities, and develop an evaluation plan that will enhance the information available about the respective concerns of all parties.

Given the usual multiplicity of program stakeholders and their perspectives, and despite an evaluator's efforts to be inclusive, there is considerable inherent potential for misunderstandings to develop between the evaluator and one or more of the stakeholders about what issues the evaluation should address. It is especially important, therefore, that there be full and frank communication between the evaluator and the stakeholder groups from the earliest possible point in the planning process. Along with obtaining critical input from the stakeholders about the program and the evaluation, this exchange should emphasize realistic, shared understanding of what the evaluation will and will not do, and why. Most essentially, the evaluator should strive to ensure that the key stakeholders understand, and find acceptable, the nature of the evaluation process, the type of information the evaluation will produce, what it might mean if the results come out one way or another, and what ambiguities or unanswered questions may remain.

Obtaining Input From Stakeholders

The major stakeholders, by definition, have a significant interest in the program and the evaluation. It is thus generally straightforward to identify them and obtain their views about the issues and questions to which the evaluation should attend. The evaluation sponsor, program administrators (who may also be the evaluation sponsor), and intended program beneficiaries are virtually always major stakeholders. Identification of other important stakeholders can usually be accomplished by analyzing the network of relationships surrounding a program. The most revealing relationships involve the flow of money to or from the program, political influence on and by the program, those whose actions affect or are affected by the program, and the set of direct interactions between the program and its various boards, patrons, collaborators, competitors, clients, and the like.

A *snowball* approach may be helpful in identifying the various stakeholder groups and persons involved in relationships with the program. As each such representative is identified and contacted, the evaluator asks for nominations of other persons or groups with a significant interest in the program. Those representatives, in turn, are asked the same question. When this process no longer produces important new nominations, the evaluator can be reasonably assured that all major stakeholders have been identified.

If the evaluation is structured as a collaborative or participatory endeavor with certain stakeholders directly involved in designing and conducting the evaluation (as described in Chapter 2), the participating stakeholders will, of course, have a firsthand role in shaping the evaluation questions. Similarly, an internal evaluator who is part of the organization that administers the program will likely receive forthright counsel from program personnel. Even when such stakeholder involvement is built into the evaluation, however, this arrangement is usually not sufficient to represent the full range of pertinent stakeholder perspectives. There may be important stakeholder groups that are not involved in the participatory structure but have distinct and significant perspectives on the program and the evaluation. Moreover, there may be a range of viewpoints among the members of groups that are represented in the evaluation process so that a broader sampling of opinion is needed than that brought by the designated participant on the evaluation team.

Generally, therefore, formulating responsive evaluation questions requires discussion with members of stakeholder groups who are not directly represented on the evaluation team. Fewer such contacts may be needed by evaluation teams that represent many stakeholders and more by those on which few or no stakeholders are represented. In cases where the evaluation has not initially been organized as a collaborative endeavor with stakeholders, the evaluator may wish to consider configuring such an arrangement to ensure that key stakeholders are engaged and their views fully represented in the design and implementation of the evaluation. Participatory arrangements might be made through stakeholder advisory boards, steering committees, or simply regular consultations between the evaluator and key stakeholder representatives. More information about the procedures and benefits of such approaches can be found in Fetterman, Kaftarian, and Wandersman (1996), Greene (1988), Mark and Shotland (1985), and Patton (1997).

Outside of organized arrangements, evaluators generally obtain stakeholder views about the important evaluation issues through interviews. Because early contacts with stakeholders are primarily for orientation and reconnaissance, interviews at this stage typically are unstructured or, perhaps, semistructured around a small set of themes of interest to the evaluator. Input from individuals representing stakeholder groups might also be obtained through focus groups (Krueger, 1988). Focus groups have the advantages of efficiency in getting information from a number of people and the facilitative effect of group interaction in stimulating ideas and observations. They also may have some disadvantages for this purpose, notably the potential for conflict in politically volatile situations and the lack of confidentiality in group settings. In some cases, stakeholders may speak more frankly about the program and the evaluation in one-on-one conversations with the evaluator.

The evaluator will rarely be able to obtain input from every member of every stakeholder group, nor will that ordinarily be necessary to identify the major issues and questions with which the evaluation should be concerned. A modest number of carefully selected stakeholder informants who are representative of significant groups or distinctly positioned in relation to the program is usually sufficient to identify the principal issues. When the evaluator no longer hears new themes in discussions with diverse stakeholders, the most significant prevailing issues have probably all been discovered.

Topics for Discussion With Stakeholders

The issues identified by the evaluation sponsor when the evaluation is requested usually need further discussion with the sponsor and other stakeholders to clarify what these issues mean to the various parties and what sort of information would usefully bear on them. The topics that should be addressed in these discussions will depend in large part on the particulars of the evaluation situation. Here we will review some of the general topics that are often relevant.

Why is an evaluation needed? It is usually worthwhile for the evaluator to probe the reasons an evaluation is desired. The evaluation may be motivated by an external requirement, in which case it is important to know the nature of that requirement and what use is to be made of the results. The evaluation may be desired by program managers to determine whether the program is effective, to find ways to improve it, or to "prove" its value to potential funders, donors, critics, or the like. Sometimes the evaluation is politically motivated, for example, as a stalling tactic to avoid some unpleasant decision. Whatever the reasons, they provide an important starting point for determining what questions will be most important for the evaluation to answer and for whom.

What are the program goals and objectives? Inevitably, whether a program achieves certain of the goals and objectives ascribed to it will be pivotal questions for the evaluation to answer. The distinction between goals and objectives is critical. A **program goal** relates to the overall mission of the program and typically is stated in broad and rather abstract terms. For example, a program for the homeless may have as its goal "the reduction of homelessness" in its urban catchment area. Although easily understood, such a goal is too vague to determine whether it has been met. Is a "reduction of homelessness" 5%, 10%, or 100%? Does "homelessness" mean only those living on the streets or does it include those in shelters or temporary housing? For evaluation purposes, broad goals must be translated into concrete statements that specify the condition to be dealt with together with one or more measurable criteria of success. Evaluators generally refer to specific statements of measurable attainments as **program objectives**. Related sets of objectives identify the particular accomplishments presumed necessary to attain the program goals. Exhibit 3-F presents helpful suggestions for specifying objectives.

An important task for the evaluator, therefore, is to collaborate with relevant stakeholders to identify the program goals and transform overly broad, ambiguous, or idealized representations of them into clear, explicit, concrete statements of objectives. The more closely the objectives describe situations that can be directly and reliably observed, the more likely it is that a meaningful evaluation will result. Furthermore, it is essential that the evaluator and stakeholders achieve a workable agreement on which program objectives are most central to the evaluation and the criteria to be used in assessing whether those objectives have been met. For instance, if one stated objective of a job training program is to maintain a low drop-out rate, the key stakeholders should agree to its importance before it is accepted as one of the focal issues around which the evaluation will be designed.

If consensus about the important objectives is not attained, one solution is to include all those put forward by the various stakeholders and, perhaps, additional objectives drawn from current viewpoints and theories in the relevant substantive field (Chen, 1990). For example, the sponsors of a job training program may be interested solely in the frequency and duration of postprogram employment. But the evaluator may propose that stability of living arrangements, competence in handling finances, and efforts to obtain additional education be considered as program outcomes because these lifestyle features also may undergo positive change with increased employment and job-related skills.

What are the most important questions for the evaluation to answer? We echo Patton's (1997) view that priority should be given to evaluation questions that will yield information most likely to be used. Evaluation results are rarely intended by evaluators or evaluation sponsors to be "knowledge for knowledge's sake." Rather, they are intended to be useful, and to be used, by those with responsibility for making decisions about the

EXHIBIT 3-F
Specifying
Objectives

Four techniques are particularly helpful for writing useful objectives: (1) using strong verbs, (2) stating only one purpose or aim, (3) specifying a single end-product or result, and (4) specifying the expected time for achievement. (Kirschner Associates, 1975).

A "strong" verb is an action-oriented verb that describes an observable or measurable behavior that will occur. For example, "to increase the use of health education materials" is an action-oriented statement involving behavior which can be observed. In contrast, "to promote greater use of health education materials" is a weaker and less specific statement.

A second suggestion for writing a clear objective is to state only a single aim or purpose. Most programs will have multiple objectives, but within each objective only a single purpose should be delineated. An objective that states two or more purposes or desired outcomes may require different implementation and assessment strategies, making achievement of the objective difficult to determine. For example, the statement "to begin three prenatal classes for pregnant women and provide outreach transportation services to accommodate twenty-five women per class" creates difficulties. This objective contains two aims—to provide prenatal classes and to provide outreach services. If one aim is accomplished but not the other, to what extent has the objective been met?

Specifying a single end-product or result is a third technique contributing to a useful objective. For example, the statement "to begin three prenatal classes for pregnant women by subcontracting with City Memorial Hospital" contains two results, namely, the three classes and the subcontract. It is better to state these objectives separately, particularly since one is a higher-order objective (to begin three prenatal classes) which depends partly on fulfillment of a lower order objective (to establish a subcontract).

A clearly written objective must have both a single aim and a single end-product or result. For example, the statement "to establish communication with the Health Systems Agency" indicates the aim but not the desired end-product or result. What constitutes evidence of communication— telephone calls, meetings, reports? Failure to specify a clear end-product makes it difficult for assessment to take place.

Those involved in writing and evaluating objectives need to keep two questions in mind. First, would anyone reading the objective find the same purpose as the one intended? Second, what visible, measurable, or tangible

(Continued)

EXHIBIT 3-F
(Continued)

results are present as evidence that the objective has been met? Purpose or aim describes what will be done; end-product or result describes evidence that will exist when it has been done. This is assurance that you "know one when you see one."

Finally, it is useful to specify the time of expected achievement of the objective. The statement "to establish a walk-in clinic as soon as possible" is not a useful objective because of the vagueness of "as soon as possible." It is far more useful to specify a target date, or in cases where some uncertainty exists about some specific date, a range of target dates—for example, "sometime between March 1 and March 30."

SOURCE: Adapted, with permission, from Stephen M. Shortell and William C. Richardson, *Health Program Evaluation* (St. Louis, MO: C. V. Mosby, 1978), pp. 26-27.

program, whether at the day-to-day management level or at broader funding or policy levels (see Exhibit 3-G for an evaluation manager's view of this process).

Unfortunately, the experience of evaluators is replete with instances of evaluation findings that were virtually ignored by those to whom they were reported. There are numerous reasons why this may happen, many of which are not within the control of the evaluator. Program circumstances may change between the initiation of the evaluation and its completion in ways that make the evaluation results irrelevant when they are delivered. But lack of utilization may also occur because the evaluation does not actually provide information useful for the decisions that must be made. This can happen rather innocently as well as through ineptness. An evaluation plan may look like it will produce relevant information but, when that information is generated, it is not as useful as the recipients expected. It may also happen that those to whom the evaluation results are directed are not initially clear in their own minds about what information they need for what purposes.

With these considerations in mind, we advocate that in developing evaluation questions evaluators use *backward mapping*. This technique starts with a specification of the desired endpoint then works backward to determine what must be done to get there (Elmore, 1980). Taking this approach, the essential discussion with the evaluation sponsor and other key stakeholders must establish who will use the evaluation results and for what purposes. Note that the question is not who is *interested* in the evaluation findings but who will *use* them. The evaluator wants to understand, in an explicit, detailed fashion, who specifically will use the evaluation and what specifically they will use it for. For instance, the administrator and board of directors

EXHIBIT 3-G

Lessons Learned
About the Utilization
of Evaluation

An evaluation manager for a social services organization summarized his observations about the use of evaluation findings by program decision-makers as follows:

1. The utilization of evaluation or research does not take care of itself. Evaluation reports are inanimate objects, and it takes human interest and personal action to use and implement evaluation findings and recommendations. The implications of evaluation must be transferred from the written page to the agenda of program managers.

2. Utilization of evaluation, through which program lessons are identified, usually demands changed behaviors or policies. This requires the shifting of priorities and the development of new action plans for the operational manager.

3. Utilization of evaluation research involves political activity. It is based on a recognition and focus on who in the organization has what authority to make x, y, or z happen. To change programs or organizations as a result of some evaluation requires support from the highest levels of management.

4. Ongoing systems to engender evaluation use are necessary to legitimate and formalize the organizational learning process. Otherwise, utilization can become a personalized issue and evaluation advocates just another self-serving group vying for power and control.

SOURCE: Quoted from Anthony Dibella, "The Research Manager's Role in Encouraging Evaluation Use," Evaluation Practice, 1990, 11(2):119.

of the program may intend to use the evaluation results to set administrative priorities for the next fiscal year. Or the legislative committee that oversees a program area may desire the evaluation as input to its deliberations about continued funding for the program. Or the program monitors in the government agency that has initiated the program may want to know if it represents a successful model that should be disseminated to other sites.

In each case, the evaluator should work with the respective evaluation users to describe the range of potential decisions or actions that they might consider taking and the form and nature of information that they would find pertinent in their deliberation. To press this exercise to the greatest level of specificity, the evaluator might even generate dummy information of the sort that the evaluation will produce (e.g., "20% of the clients who complete the program relapse within 30 days") and discuss with the prospective users what this would mean to them and how they would use such information.

A careful specification of the intended use of the evaluation results and the nature of the information expected to be useful leads directly to the formulation of questions the evaluation must attempt to answer (e.g., "What proportion of the clients who complete the program relapse during the first month?") and helps to set priorities identifying questions that are most important. At this juncture, consideration must also be given to matters of timing. It may be that some questions must be answered before others can be asked, or users may need answers to some questions before others because of their own timetable for decision making. The important questions can then be organized into related groups, combined and integrated as appropriate, sequenced in appropriate time lines, and worked into final form in consultation with the designated users. With this in hand, developing the evaluation plan is largely a matter of working backward to determine what measures, observations, procedures, and the like must be undertaken to provide answers to the important questions in the form that the users require by the time they are needed.

Analysis of Program Assumptions and Theory

As we remarked at the outset of this discussion, in addition to consulting with stakeholders, the evaluator should normally perform an independent analysis of the program in designing appropriate and relevant evaluation questions. Most evaluation questions are variations on the theme of "Is what's supposed to be happening actually happening?" Familiar examples include "Are the intended target participants being reached?" "Are the services adequately delivered?" and "Are the goals being met?" Consequently, a very useful analysis for purposes of identifying important evaluation questions is to delineate in some detail just what it is that is supposed to be happening. The evaluator can construct a conceptual model of how the program is expected to work and the connections presumed between its various activities and functions and the social benefits it is intended to produce. This representation can then be used to identify those aspects of the program most essential to effective performance. These, in turn, raise evaluation-related questions about whether the key assumptions and expectations are reasonable and appropriate and, if so, whether the program is enacting them in an effective manner.

What we are describing here is an explication of the program theory, the set of assumptions about the relationships between the strategy and tactics the program has adopted and the social benefits it is expected to produce. *Theory* has a rather grandiose sound, and few program directors would claim that they were working from any distinct theory. Among the dictionary definitions of theory, however, we find "a particular conception or view of something to be done or of the method of doing it." It is generally this sense of the word that evaluators mean when they refer to program theory. It might alternatively be called the program conceptualization or, perhaps, the program plan, blueprint, or design.

Evaluators have long recognized the importance of program theory as a basis for formulating and prioritizing evaluation questions, designing evaluation research, and interpreting evaluation findings (Bickman, 1987; Chen and Rossi, 1980; Weiss, 1972; Wholey, 1979). However, it is described and used under various different names, for example, logic model, program model, outcome line, cause map, action theory, and so forth. Moreover, there is no general consensus about how best to depict or represent program theory, and many different versions can be found in the evaluation literature, although all show common elements. Because program theory is itself a potential object for evaluation, we will defer our full discussion of how it can be represented and evaluated to Chapter 5, which is solely devoted to this topic.

What we wish to emphasize here is the utility of program theory as a tool for analyzing a program for the purpose of formulating evaluation questions. One common depiction of program theory, for instance, is in the form of a *logic model*, which lays out the expected sequence of steps going from program services to client outcomes. Exhibit 3-H shows a logic model for a teen mother parenting program. For that program, the service agency and local high school are expected to recruit pregnant teens who will attend parenting classes. Those classes are expected to teach certain topics and the teen mothers, in response, are expected to become more knowledgeable about prenatal nutrition and how to care for their babies. That knowledge, in turn, is expected to lead to appropriate dietary and child care behavior and, ultimately, to healthy babies.

Simply laying out the logic of the program in this form makes it relatively easy to identify questions the evaluation might appropriately address. For example: How many eligible pregnant teens are in the catchment area of the program, and how deficient is their knowledge of nutrition and child care? What proportion actually participates in the program? Do the classes actually cover all the intended topics and is the nature of the instruction suited to the teen audience? What do the teens actually learn from the classes and, more important, what changes do they make in their behavior as a result? And finally, are their babies healthier at 12 months than they would have been without the program experience?

Each of these questions can be refined further into the more specific terms the evaluator needs in order to use them as a basis for evaluation design. The expectations for program performance in each of the corresponding domains can also be further explored to develop more specific criteria for assessing that performance. If the logic model or some other form of theory depiction has been developed in collaboration with key stakeholders and represents a consensus view, the resulting evaluation questions are quite likely to be viewed as relevant and potentially important. What makes this

EXHIBIT 3-H

Logic Model for a Teen Mother Parenting Program

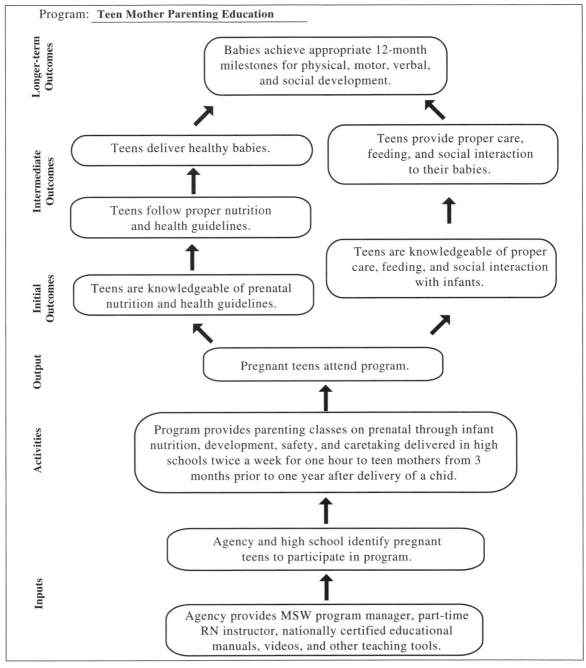

SOURCE: Adapted from United Way of America Task Force on Impact, *Measuring Program Outcomes: A Practical Approach.* Alexandria, VA: Author, 1996, p. 42. Used by permission, United Way of America.

technique especially useful to the evaluator, however, is that it will often bring out significant program issues and questions that would not otherwise have been recognized by either the stakeholders or the evaluator. It has the additional advantage of permitting a systematic review of all aspects of the program to help the evaluator ensure that no critical issues have been overlooked.

Collating Evaluation Questions and Setting Priorities

The evaluator who thoroughly explores stakeholder concerns and conducts an analysis of program issues guided by carefully developed descriptions of program theory will turn up many questions that the evaluation might address. The task at this point becomes one of organizing those questions according to distinct themes and setting priorities among them.

Organization of evaluation questions is generally rather straightforward. Evaluation questions tend to cluster around different program functions (e.g., recruitment, services, outcomes) and, as already discussed, around different evaluation issues (need, design, implementation, impact, efficiency). In addition, evaluation questions tend to show a natural structure in which very specific questions (e.g., "Are elderly homebound persons in the public housing project aware of the program?") are nested under broader questions ("Are we reaching our target population?").

Setting priorities to determine which questions the evaluation should be designed to answer can be much more challenging. Once articulated, most of the questions about the program that arise during the planning process are likely to seem interesting to some stakeholder or another, or to the evaluators themselves. Rarely will resources be available to address them all, however. At this juncture, it is especially important for the evaluator to focus on the main purposes of the evaluation and the expected uses to be made of its findings. There is little point to investing time and effort in developing information that is of little use to any stakeholder.

That said, we must caution against an overly narrow interpretation of what information is useful. Evaluation utilization studies have shown that practical, instrumental use for program decision making is only one of the contributions evaluation information makes (Leviton and Hughes, 1981; Rich, 1977; Weiss, 1988). Equally important in many cases are conceptual and persuasive uses—the contribution of evaluation findings to the way in which a program and the social problems to which it responds are understood and debated. Evaluations often identify issues, frame analysis, and sharpen the focus of discussion in ways that are influential to the decision-making process even when there is no direct connection evident between any evaluation finding and any specific program decision. A fuller discussion of this issue is presented in Chapter 12; our purpose here is only to point out the possibility that some evaluation questions may be important to answer even though no immediate use or user is evident.

With the priority evaluation questions for a program selected, the evaluator is ready to design the substantial part of the evaluation that will be devoted to trying to answer them. Most of the remainder of this book discusses the approaches, methods, and considerations related to that task. The discussion is organized to follow the natural logical progression of evaluation questions we identified earlier in the evaluation hierarchy. It thus addresses, in turn, how to assess the need for a program, the program theory or plan for addressing that need, the implementation of the program plan and the associated program process, the impact or outcome of the program implementation on the social need, and the efficiency with which the program attains its outcomes.

Summary

- A critical phase in evaluation planning is the identification and formulation of the questions the evaluation will address. Those questions focus the evaluation on the areas of program performance most at issue for key stakeholders and guide the design so that it that will provide meaningful information about program performance.

- Good evaluation questions must be reasonable and appropriate, and they must be answerable. That is, they must identify clear, observable dimensions of program performance that are relevant to the program's goals and represent domains in which the program can realistically be expected to have accomplishments.

- What most distinguishes evaluation questions is that they involve performance criteria by which the identified dimensions of program performance can be judged. If the formulation of the evaluation questions can include performance standards on which key stakeholders agree, evaluation planning will be easier and the potential for disagreement over the interpretation of the results will be reduced.

- Evaluation issues can be arranged in a useful hierarchy, with the most fundamental issues at the bottom. Generally, questions at higher levels of the hierarchy presuppose either knowledge or confident assumptions about issues at lower levels.

- To ensure that the matters of greatest significance are covered in the evaluation design, the evaluation questions are best formulated through interaction and negotiation with the evaluation sponsors and other stakeholders representative of significant groups or distinctly positioned in relation to program decision making.

- Although stakeholder input is critical, the evaluator must also be prepared to identify program issues that might warrant inquiry. This requires that the evaluator conduct an independent analysis of the assumptions and expectations on which the program is based.

- One useful way to reveal aspects of program performance that may be important is to make the program theory explicit. Program theory describes the assumptions inherent in a program about the activities it undertakes and how those relate to the social benefits it is expected to produce. Critical analysis of program theory can surface important evaluation questions that might otherwise have been overlooked.

- When these various procedures have generated a full set of candidate evaluation questions, the evaluator must organize them into related clusters and draw on stakeholder input and professional judgment to set priorities among them. With the priority evaluation questions for a program determined, the evaluator is then ready to design the part of the evaluation that will be devoted to answering them.

Key Concepts

Catchment area

The geographic area served by a program.

Implementation failure

The program does not adequately perform the activities specified in the program design that are assumed to be necessary for bringing about the intended social improvements. It includes situations in which no service, not enough service, or the wrong service is delivered, or the service varies excessively across the target population.

Performance criterion

The standard against which a dimension of program performance is compared so that it can be evaluated.

Program goal

A statement, usually general and abstract, of a desired state toward which a program is directed. Compare *program objectives.*

Program objectives

Specific statements detailing the desired accomplishments of a program together with one or more measurable criteria of success.

Theory failure

The program is implemented as planned but its services do not produce the immediate effects on the participants that are expected or the ultimate social benefits that are intended, or both.

4

Assessing the Need for a Program

Chapter Outline

Evaluation questions about the nature of a social problem a program is intended to alleviate are fundamental to the evaluation of that program. The evaluation activities that address these questions are usually called needs assessment. *From a program evaluation perspective, needs assessment is the means by which an evaluator determines whether there is a need for a program and, if so, what program services are most appropriate to that need. Such an assessment is critical to the effective design of new programs. However, it is equally relevant to established programs when it cannot be assumed that the program is needed or that the services it provides are well suited to the nature of the need.*

Needs assessment is fundamental because a program cannot be effective at ameliorating a social problem if there is no problem to begin with or if the program services do not actually relate to the problem. This chapter focuses on the role of evaluators in diagnosing social problems through systematic and reproducible procedures in ways that can be related to the design and evaluation of intervention programs.

A s we stated in Chapter 1, effective programs are instruments for improving social conditions. In evaluating a social program, it is therefore essential to ask whether it addresses a significant social need in a plausible way and does so in a manner that is responsive to the circumstances of those in need.

Answering these questions for a given program first requires a description of the social problem that the program addresses. The evaluator can then ask whether the program theory embodies a valid conceptualization of the problem and an appropriate means of remedying it. If that question is answered in the affirmative, attention can turn to whether the program is actually implemented in line with the program theory and, if so, whether the intended improvements in the social conditions actually result and at what cost. Thus, the logic of program evaluation builds upward from careful description of the social problem the program is expected to ameliorate.

The family of procedures used by evaluators and other social researchers to systematically describe and diagnose social needs is generally referred to as *needs assessment*.

The essential task for the program evaluator as needs assessor is to describe the "problem" that concerns major stakeholders in a manner that is as careful, objective, and meaningful to all groups as possible, and help draw out the implications of that diagnosis for structuring effective intervention. This task involves constructing a precise definition of the problem, assessing its extent, defining and identifying the targets of interventions, and accurately describing the nature of the service needs of that population. This chapter describes these activities in detail.

The Role of Evaluators in Diagnosing Social Conditions and Service Needs

In the grand scheme of things, evaluators' contributions to the identification and alleviation of social problems are modest compared with the weightier actions of political bodies, advocacy groups, investigative reporters, and charismatic public figures. The impetus for attending to social problems most often comes from political and moral leaders and community advocates who have a stake, either personally or professionally, in dealing with a particular condition. Thus, the post–World War II attention to mental illness was heavily influenced by the efforts of a single congressman; federal programs for mental retardation received a major boost during John F. Kennedy's presidency because he had a mentally retarded sister; improved automobile safety can be credited to a considerable degree to Ralph Nader's advocacy; and efforts to control fraud and improprieties in the delivery of health and welfare services have most often come about because of exposés in the mass media and the activities of interest and pressure groups, including the organized efforts of those in need themselves.

Nevertheless, evaluators do contribute significantly to efforts to improve the human and social condition, though not by mobilizing the disaffected, storming the barricades, or shooting from the lip. Rather, they contribute in mundane but essential ways by applying their repertoire of research techniques to systematically describe the nature of social problems, gauge the appropriateness of proposed and established intervention programs, and assess the effectiveness of those programs for improving social conditions.

The importance of the resulting diagnostic information cannot be overstated. Speculation, impressionistic observations, political pressure, and even deliberately biased information may spur policymakers, planners, and funding organizations to initiate action, support ongoing programs, or withdraw support from programs. But if sound judgment is to be reached about such matters, it is essential to have an adequate understanding of the nature and scope of the problem the program is meant to address as well as precise information about the corresponding program targets and the context in which the intervention operates or will operate. Here are a few examples of what can happen when adequate diagnostic procedures are ignored.

The problem of high unemployment rates in inner-city neighborhoods frequently has been defined as reflecting the paucity of employment opportunities in those neighborhoods. Programs have therefore been established that provided substantial incentives to businesses for locating in inner-city neighborhoods. Subsequent experiences often found that most of the workers these businesses hired came from outside the neighborhood that was supposed to be helped.

Planners of many of the urban renewal projects undertaken during the 1960s assumed that persons living in what the planners regarded as dilapidated buildings also viewed their housing as defective and would therefore support the demolition of their homes and accept relocation to replacement housing. In city after city, however, residents of urban renewal areas vigorously opposed these projects.

Media programs designed to encourage people to seek physical examinations to detect early signs of cancer often had the effect of swamping health centers with more clients than they could handle. The media effort stimulated many hypochondriacal persons without cancer symptoms to believe they were experiencing warning signs.

In an effort to improve the clinical identification of AIDS, community physicians were provided with literature about the details of diagnosing the syndrome among high-risk patients using blood tests. Only after the materials had been disseminated was it recognized that few physicians take sex histories as a routine practice. Most physicians were therefore unlikely to know which of their patients were high risk. Consequently, the only way they could make use of their new knowledge was by testing all their patients. The result was an excessive amount of testing, at high cost and some risk to the patients.

A birth control project was expanded to reduce the reportedly high rate of abortion in a large urban center, but the program failed to attract many additional participants. Subsequently, it was found that most of the intended urban clients were already being adequately served and a high proportion practiced contraception. The high abortion rate was caused mainly by young women who came to the city from rural areas to have abortions.

The problem of criminal use of handguns has led to legislation forbidding the sale of such guns to persons convicted of felony offenses. However, most criminals do not purchase their guns from legitimate gun dealers but obtain them through the "black market" or theft.

In all of these examples, a good needs assessment would have prevented programs from implementing inappropriate or unneeded services. In some cases, unnecessary programs were designed because the problem did not exist. In others, the intervention was not effective because the target population did not desire the services provided, was incorrectly identified, or was unlikely or unable to act in the way the program expected.

All social programs rest on a set of assumptions concerning the nature of the problem they address and the characteristics, needs, and responses of the target population they intend to serve. Any evaluation of a plan for a new program, a change in an existing program, or the effectiveness of an ongoing program must necessarily consider those assumptions. Of course, the problem diagnosis and target population description may already be well established, in which case the evaluator can move forward with that as a given. Or the nature of the evaluation task may be stipulated in such a way that the nature of the need for the program is not a matter for independent investigation. Program personnel and sponsors often believe they know the social problems and target population so well that further inquiry is a waste of time. Such situations must be approached cautiously. As the examples above show, it is remarkably easy for a program to be based on faulty assumptions, either through insufficient initial problem diagnosis, changes in the problem or target population since the program was initiated, or selective exposure or stereotypes that lead to distorted views.

In all instances, therefore, the evaluator should scrutinize the assumptions about the target problem and population that shape the nature of a program. Where there is any ambiguity, it may be advisable for the evaluator to work with key stakeholders to formulate those assumptions explicitly. Often it will also be useful for the evaluator to conduct at least some minimal independent investigation of the nature of the program's target problem and population. For new program initiatives, or established programs whose utility has been called into question, it may be essential to conduct a very thorough needs assessment.

It should be noted that needs assessment is not always done with reference to a specific social program or program proposal. The techniques of needs assessment are also used as planning tools and decision aids for policymakers who must prioritize among competing needs and claims. For instance, a regional United Way or a metropolitan city council might commission a needs assessment to help it determine how funds should be allocated across various service areas. Or a state department of mental health might assess community needs for different mental health services to distribute resources optimally among its service units. Thus, needs assessment often includes rankings of needs according to how serious, neglected, or salient they are. Although these broader needs assessments are different in scope and purpose from the assessment of the need for a particular program, the relevant methods are much the same, and such assessments also are generally conducted by evaluation researchers.

Exhibit 4-A provides an overview of the steps in a needs assessment. Note that this exhibit includes steps that stress the involvement of stakeholders in needs assessment, which we have discussed at length elsewhere and need not consider in detail in this chapter. Useful book-length discussion of needs assessment applications and techniques can be found in McKillip (1987), Reviere et al. (1996), Soriano (1995), and Witkin and Altschuld (1995).

Defining the Problem to Be Addressed

Proposals for policy changes, new or modified programs, or evaluation of existing programs typically arise out of some stakeholder dissatisfaction with the effectiveness of existing policies and programs or concern that a new social problem has emerged. Either case means that a social problem has been identified and defined, a matter that

EXHIBIT 4-A
Steps in
Analyzing Need

1. *Identification of users and uses.* The users of the analysis are those who will act on the basis of the results and the audiences who may be affected by it. The involvement of both groups will usually facilitate the analysis and implementation of its recommendations. Knowing the uses of the need assessment helps the researcher focus on the problems and solutions that can be entertained, but also may limit the problems and solutions identified in Step 3, below.

2. *Description of the target population and service environment.* Geographic dispersion, transportation, demographic characteristics (including strengths) of the target population, eligibility restrictions, and service capacity are important. Social indicators are often used to describe the target population either directly or by projection. Resource inventories detailing services available can identify gaps in services and complementary and competing programs. Comparison of those who use services with the target population can reveal unmet needs or barriers to solution implementation.

3. *Need identification.* Here problems of the target population(s) and possible solutions are described. Usually, more than one source of information is used. Identification should include information on expectations for outcomes; on current outcomes; and on the efficacy, feasibility, and utilization of solutions. Social indicators, surveys, community forums, and direct observation are frequently used.

4. *Need assessment.* Once problems and solutions have been identified, this information is integrated to produce recommendations for action. Both quantitative and qualitative integration algorithms can be used. The more explicit and open the process, the greater the likelihood that results will be accepted and implemented.

5. *Communication.* Finally, the results of the need analysis must be communicated to decisionmakers, users, and other relevant audiences. The effort that goes into this communication should equal that given the other steps of the need analysis.

SOURCE: Adapted from Jack McKillip, "Need Analysis: Process and Techniques," in *Handbook of Applied Social Research Methods,* eds. L. Bickman and D. J. Rog (Thousand Oaks, CA: Sage, 1998), pp. 261-284.

is not as straightforward as it may seem. Indeed, the question of what defines a social problem has occupied spiritual leaders, philosophers, and social scientists for centuries. Thorny issues in this domain revolve around deciding what is meant by a need in contrast, say, to a want or desire, and what ideals or expectations should provide the benchmarks for distinguishing a need (cf. McKillip, 1998; Scriven, 1991). For our purposes, the key point is that social problems are not themselves objective phenomena. Rather, they are social constructions involving assertions that certain conditions constitute problems that require public attention and ameliorative programs. In this sense, community members, together with the stakeholders involved in a particular issue, literally create the social reality that constitutes a recognized social problem (Miller and Holstein, 1993; Spector and Kitsuse, 1977).

It is generally agreed, for example, that poverty is a social problem. The observable facts are the statistics on the distribution of income and assets. However, those statistics do not define poverty, they merely permit one to determine how many are poor when a definition is given. Nor do they establish poverty as a social problem; they only characterize a situation that individuals and social agents may view as problematic. Moreover, both the definition of poverty and the goals of programs to improve the lot of the poor can vary over time, between communities, and among stakeholders. Initiatives to reduce poverty, therefore, may range widely—for example, from increasing employment opportunities to simply lowering the expectations of persons with low income.

Defining a social problem and specifying the goals of intervention are thus ultimately political processes that do not follow automatically from the inherent characteristics of the situation. This circumstance is illustrated nicely in an analysis of legislation designed to reduce adolescent pregnancy that was conducted by the U.S. General Accounting Office (GAO, 1986). The GAO found that none of the pending legislative proposals defined the problem as involving the fathers of the children in question; every one addressed adolescent pregnancy as an issue of young mothers. Although this view of adolescent pregnancy may lead to effective programs, it nonetheless clearly represents arguable assumptions about the nature of the problem and how a solution should be approached.

The social definition of a problem is so central to the political response that the preamble to proposed legislation usually shows some effort to specify the conditions for which the proposal is designed as a remedy. For example, two contending legislative proposals may both be addressed to the problem of homelessness, but one may identify the homeless as needy persons who have no kin on whom to be dependent, whereas the other defines homelessness as the lack of access to conventional shelter. The first definition centers attention primarily on the social isolation of potential clients; the second focuses on housing arrangements. The ameliorative actions that are justified in terms of these definitions will likely be different as well. The first definition, for instance, would support programs that attempt to reconcile homeless persons with alienated relatives; the second, subsidized housing programs.

It is usually informative, therefore, for an evaluator to determine what the major political actors think the problem is. The evaluator might, for instance, study the definitions given in policy and program proposals or in enabling legislation. Such information may also be found in legislative proceedings, program documents, newspaper and magazine articles, and other sources in which discussions of the problem or the program appear. Such materials may explicitly describe the nature of the problem and the program's plan of attack, as in funding proposals, or implicitly define the problem through the assumptions that underlie statements about program activities, successes, and plans.

This inquiry will almost certainly turn up information useful for a preliminary description of the social need to which the program is presumably designed to respond. As such, it can guide a more probing needs assessment, both with regard to how the problem is defined and what alternative perspectives might be applicable.

An important role evaluators may play at this stage is to provide policymakers and program managers with a critique of the problem definition inherent in their policies and programs and propose alternative definitions that may be more serviceable. For example, evaluators could point out that a definition of the problem of teenage pregnancies as primarily one of illegitimate births ignores the large number of births that occur to married teenagers and suggest program implications that follow from that definition.

Specifying the Extent of the Problem: When, Where, and How Big?

Having clearly defined the problem a program is to address, evaluators can then assess the extent of the problem. Clearly, the design and funding of a social program should be geared to the size, distribution, and density of the target problem. In assessing, ay, emergency shelters for homeless persons, it makes a very significant difference whether the total homeless population in the community is 350 or 3,500. It also matters whether homelessness is located primarily in family neighborhoods or in rooming house districts and how many of the homeless have mental illness, chronic alcoholism, and physical disabilities.

It is much easier to establish that a problem exists than to develop valid estimates of its density and distribution. Identifying a handful of battered children may be enough to convince a skeptic that child abuse exists. But specifying the size of the problem and where it is located geographically and socially requires detailed knowledge about the population of abused children, the characteristics of the perpetrators, and the distribution of the problem throughout the political jurisdiction in question. For a problem such as child abuse, which is not generally public behavior, this can be difficult. Many social problems are mostly "invisible," so that only imprecise estimates of their rates are possible. In such cases, it is often necessary to use data from several sources and apply different approaches to estimating incidence rates (e.g., Ards, 1989).

It is also important to have at least reasonably representative samples to estimate rates of occurrence. It can be especially misleading to draw estimates from populations, such as those found in service programs, that are at greater risk than the population as a whole. Estimation of the rate of spousal abuse during pregnancy based on reports of residents of battered women's shelters, for instance, results in overestimation of the frequency of occurrence in the general population of pregnant women. An estimate from a more representative sample still indicates that battering of pregnant women is a serious problem, but places the extent of the problem in a realistic perspective (see Exhibit 4-B).

EXHIBIT 4-B

Estimating the Frequency of Domestic Violence Against Pregnant Women

All women are at risk of being battered; however, pregnancy places a woman at increased risk for severe injury and adverse health consequences, both for herself and her unborn infant. Local and exploratory studies have found as many as 40%-60% of battered women to have been abused during pregnancy. Among 542 women in a Dallas shelter, for example, 42% had been battered when pregnant. Most of the women reported that the violence became more acute during the pregnancy and the child's infancy. In another study, interviews of 270 battered women across the United States found that 44% had been abused during pregnancy.

But most reports on battering during pregnancy have come from samples of battered women, usually women in shelters. To establish the prevalence of battering during pregnancy in a representative obstetric population, McFarlane and associates randomly sampled and interviewed 290 healthy pregnant women from public and private clinics in a large metropolitan area with a population exceeding three million. The 290 Black, White, and Latina women ranged in age from 18 to 43 years; most were married, and 80% were at least five months pregnant. Nine questions relating to abuse were asked of the women, for example, whether they were in a relationship with a male partner who had hit, slapped, kicked, or otherwise physically hurt them during the current pregnancy and, if yes, had the abuse increased. Of the 290 women, 8% reported battering during the current pregnancy (one out of every twelve women interviewed). An additional 15% reported battering before the current pregnancy. The frequency of battering did not vary as a function of demographic variables.

SOURCE: Adapted from J. McFarlane, "Battering During Pregnancy: Tip of an Iceberg Revealed," *Women and Health*, 1989, 15(3):69-84.

Using Existing Data Sources to Develop Estimates

For some social issues, existing data sources, such as surveys and censuses, may be of sufficient quality to be used with confidence for assessing certain aspects of a social problem. For example, accurate and trustworthy information can usually be obtained about issues on which information is collected by the Current Population Survey of the U.S. Bureau of the Census or the decennial U.S. Census. The decennial Census volumes contain data on census tracts (small areas containing about 4,000 households) that can be aggregated to get neighborhood and community data. As an illustration, Exhibit 4-C describes the use of vital statistics records and census data to assess the nature and magnitude of the problem of poor birth outcomes in a Florida county. This needs assessment was aimed at estimating child and maternal health needs so that appropriate services could be planned. Even when such direct information about the problem of interest is not available from existing records, indirect estimates may be possible if the empirical relationships between available information and problem indicators are known (e.g., Ciarlo et al., 1992). For example, the proportion of schoolchildren in a given neighborhood who are eligible for free lunches is often used as an indicator of the prevalence of poverty in that neighborhood.

When evaluators use sources whose validity is not as widely recognized as that of the census, they must assess the validity of the data by examining carefully how they were collected. A good rule of thumb is to anticipate that, on any issue, different data sources will provide disparate or even contradictory estimates.

Using Social Indicators to Identify Trends

On some topics, existing data sources provide periodic measures that chart historical trends in the society. For example, the Current Population Survey of the Bureau of the Census collects annual data on the characteristics of the U.S. population using a large household sample. The data include measures of the composition of households, individual and household income, and household members' age, sex, and race. The regular Survey of Income and Program Participation provides data on the extent to which the U.S. population participates in various social programs: unemployment benefits, food stamps, job training programs, and so on.

A regularly occurring measure such as those mentioned above, called a **social indicator**, can provide important information for assessing social problems and needs in several ways. First, when properly analyzed, the data can often be used to estimate the size and distribution of the social problem whose course is being tracked over time. Second, the trends shown can be used to alert decisionmakers to whether certain social conditions are improving, remaining the same, or deteriorating. Finally, the social indicator trends can be used to provide a first, if crude, estimate of the effects of social

EXHIBIT 4-C

Using Vital
Statistics and
Census Data to
Assess Child
and Maternal
Health Needs

The Healthy Start Initiative in Florida, a series of legislative measures intended to improve pregnancy and birth outcomes within the state, provides for the establishment of community-based prenatal and infant health care coalitions composed of representatives of relevant community, government, provider, and consumer groups. Each coalition was required to conduct a needs assessment within its service delivery area and develop a service delivery plan. The needs assessment of the Gadsden Citizens for Healthy Babies, representing a small, rural, mostly African American county in north Florida, used existing data to estimate the magnitude and distribution of child and maternal health problems in the county.

First, pregnancy outcomes and related maternal characteristics within the county were investigated using Florida Vital Statistics data collected annually on births and deaths. In particular, the following indicators were examined:

- *Infant mortality.* The county's rate was far higher than national or state rates.
- *Fetal mortality.* The rate for the county was higher than the state goal, and the rate for African American mothers was higher than for white mothers.
- *Neonatal mortality.* The rates were higher than the state goal for white mothers but below the state goal for African American mothers.
- *Postneonatal mortality.* The rates were below state goals.
- *Low birth weight babies.* There was a higher incidence for adolescents and women over age 35.
- *Very low birth weight births.* The overall rate was twice that for the whole state and exceeded state goals for both African American and white mothers.
- *Adolescent pregnancy.* The proportion of births to teens was over twice the state average; the rate for African American teens was more than twice that for white teens.
- *Age of mother.* The infant mortality and low birth rates were highest among children born to mothers 16-18 years of age.
- *Education of mother.* Mothers with less than a high school education were slightly more likely to have low birth weight newborns but almost eight times more likely to have newborns identified as high risk on infant screening measures.

Based on these findings, three groups were identified with high risk for poor birth outcomes:

- Mothers less than 19 years of age
- Mothers with less than a high school education
- African American mothers

(Continued)

EXHIBIT 4-C
(Continued)

U.S. Census data were then used to identify the number of women of childbearing age in each of these risk categories, the proportions in low-income strata, and their geographic concentrations within the county. This information was used by the coalition to identify the major problem areas in the county, set goals, and plan services.

SOURCE: Adapted from E. Walter Terrie, "Assessing Child and Maternal Health: The First Step in the Design of Community-Based Interventions," in *Needs Assessment: A Creative and Practical Guide for Social Scientists,* eds. R. Reviere, S. Berkowitz, C. C. Carter, and C. G. Ferguson (Washington, DC: Taylor & Francis, 1996), pp. 121-146.

programs that have been in place. For example, the Survey of Income and Program Participation can be used to estimate the coverage of such national programs as food stamps or job training.

Social indicator data are often used to monitor changes in social conditions that may be affected by social programs. Considerable effort has gone into the collection of social indicator data on poor households in an effort to judge whether their circumstances have worsened or improved after the radical reforms in welfare enacted in the Personal Responsibility and Work Opportunity Reconciliation Act of 1996. Repeated special surveys concentrating on the well-being of children are being conducted by the Urban Institute and the Manpower Development Research Corporation. In addition, the Bureau of the Census has extended the Survey of Income and Program Participation to constitute a panel of households repeatedly interviewed before and after the welfare reforms were instituted (Rossi, 2001).

Unfortunately, the social indicators currently available are limited in their coverage of social problems, focusing mainly on issues of poverty and employment, national program participation, and household composition. For many social problems, no social indicators exist. In addition, those that do exist support only analysis of national and regional trends and cannot be broken down to provide useful indicators of trends in states or smaller jurisdictions.

Estimating Problem Parameters Through Social Research

In many instances, no existing data source will provide estimates of the extent and distribution of a problem of interest. For example, there are no ready sources of information about household pesticide misuse that would indicate whether it is a problem, say, in households with children. In other instances, good information about a problem may be available for a national or regional sample that cannot be disaggregated to a relevant local level. The National Survey of Household Drug Use, for instance, uses a nationally representative sample to track the nature and extent of substance abuse. However, the number of respondents from most states is not large enough to provide good state-level estimates of drug abuse, and no valid city-level estimates can be derived at all.

When pertinent data are nonexistent or insufficient, the evaluator must consider collecting new data. There are several ways of making estimates of the extent and distribution of social problems, ranging from expert opinion to a large-scale **sample survey**. Decisions about the kind of research effort to undertake must be based in part on the funds available and how important it is to have precise estimates. If, for legislative or program design purposes, it is critical to know the precise number of malnourished infants in a political jurisdiction, a carefully planned health interview survey may be necessary. In contrast, if the need is simply to determine whether there is any malnutrition among infants, input from knowledgeable informants may be all that is required. This section reviews three types of sources that evaluators can mine for pertinent data.

Agency Records

Information contained in records of organizations that provide services to the population in question can be useful for estimating the extent of a social problem (Hatry, 1994). Some agencies keep excellent records on their clients, although others do not keep records of high quality or do not keep records at all. When an agency's clients include all the persons manifesting the problem in question and records are faithfully kept, the evaluator need not search any further. Unfortunately, these conditions do not occur often. For example, it might be tempting to try to estimate the extent of drug abuse in a certain locality by extrapolating from the records of persons treated in drug abuse clinics. To the extent that the drug-using community is fully covered by existing clinics, such an estimate may be accurate. However, since it is generally doubtful that all drug abusers are in fact served by the clinics, the problem is likely to be much more widespread than such an estimate would indicate. A more accurate estimate might be provided by a sample survey of all the residents in the locality in question. (The different estimates obtained from a served population and a sample survey of the general population were illustrated in the example of battered pregnant women in Exhibit 4-B.)

Surveys and Censuses

When it is necessary to get very accurate information on the extent and distribution of a problem and there are no existing credible data, the evaluator may need to undertake original research using sample surveys or censuses (complete enumerations). Because they come in a variety of sizes and degrees of technical complexity, either of these techniques can involve considerable effort and skill, not to mention a substantial commitment of resources.

To illustrate one extreme, Exhibit 4-D describes a needs assessment survey undertaken to estimate the size and composition of the homeless population of Chicago. The survey covered both persons in emergency shelters and homeless persons who did not use shelters. Surveying the latter involved searching Chicago streets in the middle of the night. The survey was undertaken because the Robert Wood Johnson Foundation and the Pew Memorial Trust were planning a program for increasing the access of homeless persons to medical care. Although there was ample evidence that serious medical conditions existed among the homeless populations in urban centers, no reliable information was available about either the size of the homeless population or the extent of their medical problems. Hence, the foundations funded a research project to collect that information.

Usually, however, needs assessment research is not as elaborate as that described in Exhibit 4-D. In many cases, conventional sample surveys can provide adequate information. If, for example, reliable information is required about the number and distribution of children needing child care so that new facilities can be planned, it will usually be feasible to obtain it from sample surveys conducted on the telephone. Exhibit 4-E describes a telephone survey conducted with more than 1,100 residents of Los Angeles County to ascertain the extent of public knowledge about the effectiveness of AIDS prevention behaviors. For mass media educational programs aimed at increasing awareness of ways to prevent AIDS, a survey such as this identifies both the extent and the nature of the gaps in public knowledge.

Many survey organizations have the capability to plan, carry out, and analyze sample surveys for needs assessment. In addition, it is often possible to add questions to regularly conducted studies in which different organizations buy time, thereby reducing costs. Whatever the approach, it must be recognized that designing and implementing sample surveys can be a complicated endeavor requiring high skill levels. Indeed, for many evaluators, the most sensible approach may be to contract with a reputable survey organization. For further discussion of the various aspects of sample survey methodology, see Fowler (1993) and Henry (1990).

Key Informant Surveys

Perhaps the easiest, though by no means most reliable, approach to estimating the extent of a social problem is to ask **key informants**, persons whose position or experience should provide them with some knowledge of the magnitude and distribution

Exhibit 4-D

Using Sample
Surveys to Study the
Chicago Homeless

Most sample surveys are based on the assumption that all persons can be enumerated and surveyed in their dwellings, an assumption that fails by definition in any study of the homeless. The strategy devised for the Chicago study therefore departed from the traditional survey in that persons were sampled from non-dwelling units and interviews were conducted at times when the separation between the homed and homeless was at a maximum. Two complementary samples were taken: (1) a probability sample of persons spending the night in shelters provided for homeless persons and (2) a complete enumeration of persons encountered between the hours of midnight and 6 a.m. in a thorough search of non-dwelling-unit places in a probability sample of Chicago census blocks. Taken together, the shelter and street surveys constitute an unbiased sample of the homeless of Chicago.

A person was classified as homeless at the time of the survey if that person was a resident of a shelter for homeless persons or was encountered in the block searches and found not to rent, own, or be a member of a household renting or owning a conventional dwelling unit. Conventional dwelling units included apartments, houses, rooms in hotels or other structures, and mobile homes.

In the after-midnight street surveys, teams of interviewers, accompanied by off-duty Chicago policemen, searched all places on each sampled block to which they could obtain access, including all night businesses, alleys, hallways, roofs and basements, abandoned buildings, and parked cars and trucks. All persons encountered in the street searches were awakened if necessary and interviewed to determine whether or not they were homeless. In the shelter samples, all persons spending the night in such places were assumed to be homeless. Once identified, homeless persons were interviewed to obtain data on their employment and residence histories as well as their sociodemographic characteristics. All cooperating respondents were paid $5.00.

SOURCE: Adapted from P. H. Rossi, *Down and Out in America: The Origins of Homelessness* (Chicago: University of Chicago Press, 1989).

of the problem. Key informants can often provide very useful information about the characteristics of a target populations and the nature of service needs. Unfortunately, few are likely to have a vantage point or information sources that permit very good estimation of the actual number of persons affected by a social condition or the demographic and geographic distribution of those persons. Well-placed key informants, for instance, may have experience with the homeless, but it will be difficult

EXHIBIT 4-E

Assessing the Extent
of Knowledge About
AIDS Prevention

To gauge the extent of knowledge about how to avoid HIV infection, a sample of Los Angeles County residents was interviewed on the telephone. The residents were asked to rate the effectiveness of four methods that "some people use to avoid getting AIDS through sexual activity" (see table). Their highest effectiveness rating was for monogamous sex between HIV-negative people, although 12% felt that even in these circumstances there were no assurances of safety. Condom use, despite reported problems with breakage, leakage, and misuse, was rated as very effective by 42% of the respondents and as somewhat effective by another 50%. Respondents were much less certain about the effectiveness of spermicidal agents, regardless of whether they were used in conjunction with an alternative method.

Percentage Distribution of Ratings of the Effectiveness of Different Prevention Methods

Prevention Method	Very Effective	Somewhat Effective	Not at All Effective	Don't Know
Monogamous sex between HIV-negative individuals	73	14	12	1
Using a condom alone	42	50	7	1
Using a diaphragm with spermicide	9	35	50	6
Using spermicide alone	7	32	53	8

SOURCE: Adapted with permission from D. E. Kanouse, S. H. Berry, E. M. Gorman, E. M. Yano, S. Carson, and A. Abrahamse, *AIDS-Related Knowledge, Attitudes, Beliefs, and Behaviors in Los Angeles County* R-4054-LACH (Santa Monica, CA: RAND, 1991).

for them to extrapolate from that experience to an estimate of the size of the total population. Indeed, it has been shown that selected informants' guesses about the numbers of homeless in their localities vary widely and are generally erroneous (see Exhibit 4-F).

On the grounds that key informants' reports of the extent of a problem are better than no information at all, evaluators may wish to use a key informant survey when a better approach is not feasible. Under such circumstances, the survey must be conducted as cautiously as possible. The evaluator should choose persons to be surveyed who have the necessary expertise and ensure that they are questioned in a careful manner (Averch, 1994).

EXHIBIT 4-F

Using Key Informant Estimates of the Homeless Population

To ascertain how close "expert" estimates of the number of homeless persons in downtown Los Angeles came to actual counts of homeless persons "on the streets," in shelters, or in single-room occupancy (SRO) hotels, a team of researchers asked eight service providers in the Skid Row area—shelter operators, social agency officials, and the like—to estimate the total homeless population in that 50-block area. The estimates obtained were as follows:

Provider 1: 6,000 to 10,000
Provider 2: 200,000
Provider 3: 30,000
Provider 4: 10,000
Provider 5: 10,000
Provider 6: 2,000 to 15,000
Provider 7: 8,000 to 10,000
Provider 8: 25,000

Clearly, the estimates were all over the map. Two providers (4 and 5) came fairly close to what the researchers estimated as the most likely number, based on shelter, SRO, and street counts.

SOURCE: Adapted from Hamilton, Rabinowitz, and Alschuler, Inc., *The Changing Face of Misery: Los Angeles' Skid Row Area in Transition—Housing and Social Services Needs of Central City East* (Los Angeles: Community Redevelopment Agency, July 1987).

Forecasting Needs

Both in formulating policies and programs and in evaluating them, it is often necessary to estimate what the magnitude of a social problem is likely to be in the future. A problem that is serious now may become more or less serious in later years, and program planning must attempt to take such trends into account. Yet the forecasting of future trends can be quite risky, especially as the time horizon lengthens.

There are a number of technical and practical difficulties in forecasting that derive in part from the necessary assumption that the future will be related to the present and past. For example, at first blush a projection of the number of persons in a population that will be 18 to 30 years of age a decade from now seems easy to construct from the age structure in current population data. However, had demographers made such forecasts 20 years ago for central Africa, they would have been substantially off the mark because of the unanticipated and tragic impact of the AIDS epidemic among young adults.

Projections with longer time horizons wouldbe even more problematic because they would have to take into account trends in fertility, migration, and mortality.

We are not arguing against the use of forecasts in a needs assessment. Rather, we wish to warn against accepting forecasts uncritically without a thorough examination of how they were produced. For simple extrapolations of existing trends, the assumptions on which a forecast is based may be relatively few and easily ascertained. For sophisticated projections such as those developed from multiple-equation, computer-based models, examining the assumptions may require the skills of an advanced programmer and an experienced statistician. In any event, evaluators must recognize that all but the simplest forecasts are technical activities that require specialized knowledge and procedures.

Defining and Identifying the Targets of Interventions

Understanding the nature of a social problem and estimating the size and characteristics of a target population are prerequisite to documenting the need for a program. To be effective, however, a program must not only know what its target population is but also be able to readily direct its services to that population and screen out individuals who are not part of that population. Consequently, delivering service to a target population requires that the definition of the target population permit targets to be distinguished from nontarget units in a relatively unambiguous and efficient manner as part of the program's normal operating procedures.

Specifying a program's target population is complicated by the fact that the definition and corresponding estimates of the size of the population may change over time. During the early 1980s, for instance, the homeless were identified as individuals who lived in streets and alleyways or shacks they constructed for themselves. As advocates of the homeless became increasingly active and programs began to emerge, the definition of the homeless population soon included persons without stable housing who lived for brief periods with relatives, friends, and sometimes strangers. For some stakeholders, the homeless population also encompassed the large number of individuals who lived in single rooms paid for daily or weekly without the protection of leases or other contractual arrangements. These varying definitions result in quite different notions of exactly what population a program for the homeless is intended to serve.

What Is a Target?

The targets of a social program are usually individuals. But they also may be groups (families, work teams, organizations), geographically and politically related areas (such as communities), or physical units (houses, road systems, factories). Whatever the target, it is imperative at the outset of a needs assessment to clearly define the relevant units.

In the case of individuals, targets are usually identified in terms of their social and demographic characteristics or their problems, difficulties, and conditions. Thus, targets of an educational program may be designated as children aged 10 to 14 who are one to three years below their normal grade in school. The targets of a maternal and infant care program may be defined as pregnant women and mothers of infants with annual incomes less than 150% of the poverty line.

When aggregates (groups or organizations) are targets, they are often defined in terms of the characteristics of the individuals that constitute them: their informal and formal collective properties and their shared problems. For example, an organizational-level target for an educational intervention might be elementary schools (kindergarten to eighth grade) with at least 300 pupils in which at least 30% of the pupils qualify for the federal free lunch program.

Direct and Indirect Targets

Targets may also be regarded as direct or indirect, depending on whether services are delivered to them directly by the program or indirectly through activities the program arranges. Most programs specify direct targets, as when medical interventions treat persons with a given affliction. However, in some cases, either for economic or feasibility reasons, programs may be designed to affect a target population by acting on an intermediary population or condition that will, in turn, have an impact on the intended target population. A rural development project, for example, might select influential farmers for intensive training with the intention that they will communicate their new knowledge to other farmers in their vicinity who, thus, are the indirect targets of the program.

Specifying Targets

At first glance, specifying the target population for a program may seem simple. However, although target definitions are easy to write, the results often fall short when the program or the evaluator attempts to use them to identify who is properly included or excluded from program services. There are few social problems that can be easily and convincingly described in terms of simple, unambiguous characteristics of the individuals experiencing the problem.

Take a single illustration: What is a resident with cancer in a given community? The answer depends on the meanings of both "resident" and "cancer." Does "resident" include only permanent residents, or does it also include temporary ones (a decision that would be especially important in a community with a large number of vacationers, such as Orlando, Florida). As for "cancer," are "recovered" cases to be included, and, whether they are in or out, how long without a relapse constitutes recovery? Are cases of cancer to be defined only as diagnosed cases, or do they also include persons whose cancer had not yet been detected? Are all cancers to be included regardless of type or severity? While it should be possible to formulate answers to these and similar questions for a given program, this illustration shows that the evaluator can expect a certain amount of difficulty in determining exactly how a program's target population is defined.

Target Boundaries

Adequate target specification establishes boundaries, that is, rules determining who or what is included and excluded when the specification is applied. One risk in specifying target populations is to make a definition too broad or overinclusive. For example, specifying that a criminal is anyone who has ever violated a law is useless; only saints have not at one time or another violated some law, wittingly or otherwise. This definition of criminal is too inclusive, lumping together in one category trivial and serious offenses and infrequent violators with habitual felons.

Definitions may also prove too restrictive, or underinclusive, sometimes to the point that almost no one falls into the target population. Suppose that the designers of a program to rehabilitate released felons decide to include only those who have never been drug or alcohol abusers. The extent of substance abuse is so great among released prisoners that few would be eligible given this exclusion. In addition, because persons with long arrest and conviction histories are more likely to be substance abusers, this definition eliminates those most in need of rehabilitation as targets of the proposed program.

Useful target definitions must also be feasible to apply. A specification that hinges on a characteristic that is difficult to observe or for which existing records contain no data may be virtually impossible to put into practice. Consider, for example, the difficulty of identifying the targets of a job training program if they are defined as persons who hold favorable attitudes toward accepting job training. Complex definitions requiring detailed information may be similarly difficult to apply. The data required to identify targets defined as "farmer members of producers' cooperatives who have planted barley for at least two seasons and have an adolescent son" would be difficult, if not impossible, to gather.

Varying Perspectives on Target Specification

Another issue in the definition of target populations arises from the differing perspectives of professionals, politicians, and the other stakeholders involved—including, of course, the potential recipients of services. Discrepancies may exist, for instance, between the views of legislators at different levels of government. At the federal level, Congress may plan a program to alleviate the financial burden of natural disasters for a target population viewed as all areas in which 100-year floods may occur. True to their name, however, 100-year floods occur in any one place on average only once in every century. From the local perspective a given flood plain may not be viewed as a part of the target population, especially if it means that the local government must implement expensive flood control measures.

Similarly, differences in perspective can arise between the program sponsors and the intended beneficiaries. The planners of a program to improve the quality of housing available to poor persons may have a conception of housing quality much different from those of the people who live in those dwellings. The program's definition of what constitutes the target population of substandard housing for renewal, therefore, could be much broader than that of the residents of those dwellings who find them adequate.

Although needs assessment cannot establish which perspective on program targets is "correct," it can help eliminate conflicts that might arise from groups talking past each other. This is accomplished by investigating the perspectives of all the significant stakeholders and helping ensure that none is left out of the decision process through which the target population is defined. Information collected about needs from varying perspectives may lead to a reconceptualization of the target population or of the program.

Describing Target Populations

The nature of the target population a program attempts to serve naturally has a considerable influence on the program's approach and the likelihood of success. In this section, we discuss a range of concepts useful to the evaluator for describing target populations in ways that have important implications for program design and implementation.

Risk, Need, and Demand

A public health concept, **population at risk**, is helpful in specifying program targets in projects that are preventive in character. The population at risk consists of those persons or units with a significant probability of having or developing the condition that the program intends to address. Thus, the population at risk in birth control programs is usually defined as women of childbearing age. Similarly, projects designed to mitigate the effects of typhoons and hurricanes may define its targets as those communities located in the typical paths of such storms.

A population at risk can be defined only in probabilistic terms. Women of child-bearing age may be the population at risk in a birth control project, but a given woman may or may not conceive a child within a given period of time. In this instance, specifying the population at risk simply in terms of age results unavoidably in overinclusion. That is, the definition includes many women as targets who may not be in need of family planning efforts because they are not sexually active or are otherwise incapable of getting pregnant.

The targets of programs may also be specified in terms of current need rather than risk. A **population in need** is a group of target units in a specified area that currently manifest the condition of concern to the program. A population in need can be most exactly identified through direct measures of their condition. For instance, there are reliable and valid literacy tests that can be used to specify a target population of functionally illiterate persons. For projects directed at alleviating poverty, the population in need may be defined as families whose annual income, adjusted for family size, is below a certain specified minimum. The fact that individuals are members of a population in need does not mean that they necessarily want the program at issue. Desire for a service and willingness to participate in a program define the extent of the demand for a particular service, a concept that only partially overlaps need. Community leaders and service providers, for instance, may define a need for overnight shelter among homeless persons sleeping on the streets when some significant number of these persons do not want to use such facilities. Thus, the need may not be equivalent to the demand.

Some needs assessments undertaken to estimate the extent of a problem are actually *at-risk assessments* or *demand assessments* according to the definitions just offered. Such assessments may do duty for true needs assessments, either because it is technically infeasible to measure need or because it is impractical for the program to deal only with the population in need. For example, although only sexually active individuals are immediately appropriate for family planning information, the target population for most family planning programs is women assumed to be at risk, generally defined by an age span such as 15 to 50. It would be difficult and intrusive for a program to attempt to identify and designate only those who are sexually active as its target population. Similarly, whereas the in-need group for an evening educational program may be all functionally illiterate adults, only those who are willing or who can be persuaded to participate can be considered the target population (an "at demand" definition). The distinctions between populations at risk, in need, and at demand are therefore important for estimating the scope of a problem, estimating the size of the target population, and designing, implementing, and evaluating the program.

Incidence and Prevalence

A useful distinction for describing the conditions a program aims to improve is the difference between incidence and prevalence. **Incidence** refers to the number of new cases of a particular problem that are identified or arise in a specified area or context during a specified period of time. **Prevalence** refers to the total number of existing cases in that area at a specified time. These concepts come from the field of public health, where they are sharply distinguished. To illustrate, the incidence of influenza during a particular month would be defined as the number of new cases reported during that month. Its prevalence during that month would be the total number of people afflicted, regardless of when they were first stricken. In the health sector, programs generally are interested in incidence when dealing with disorders of short duration, such as upper-respiratory infections and minor accidents. They are more interested in prevalence when dealing with problems that require long-term management and treatment efforts, such as chronic conditions and long-term illnesses.

The concepts of incidence and prevalence also apply to social problems. In studying the impact of crime, for instance, a critical measure is the incidence of victimization—the number of new victims in a given area per interval of time. Similarly, in programs aimed at lowering drunken-driver accidents, the incidence of such accidents may be the best measure of the need for intervention. But for chronic conditions such as low educational attainment, criminality, or poverty, prevalence is generally the appropriate measure. In the case of poverty, for instance, prevalence may be defined as the number of poor individuals or families in a community at a given time, regardless of when they became poor.

For other social problems, both prevalence and incidence may be relevant characteristics of the target population. In dealing with unemployment, for instance, it is important to know its prevalence, the proportion of the population unemployed at a particular time. If the program's concern is with providing short-term financial support for the newly unemployed, however, it is the incidence rate that defines the target population.

Rates

In some circumstances, it is useful to be able to express incidence or prevalence as a **rate** within an area or population. Thus, the number of new crime victims in a community during a given period (incidence) might be described in terms of the rate per 1,000 persons in that community (e.g., 23 new victims per 10,000 residents). Rates are especially handy for comparing problem conditions across areas or groups. For example, in describing crime victims, it is informative to have estimates by sex and age group. Although almost every age group is subject to some kind of crime victimization, young people are much more likely to be the victims of robbery and assault, whereas older persons are more likely to be the victims of burglary and larceny; men are considerably less likely than women to be the victims of sexual abuse, and so on. The ability to identify program targets with different profiles of problems and risks allows a needs assessment to examine the way a program is tailored (or not) to those different groups.

In most cases, it is customary and useful to specify rates by age and sex. In communities with cultural diversity, differences among racial, ethnic, and religious groups may also be important aspects of a program's target population. Other variables that may be relevant for identifying characteristics of the target population include socioeconomic status, geographic location, and residential mobility. (See Exhibit 4-G for an example of crime victimization rates broken down by sex, age, and race.)

Describing the Nature of Service Needs

As described above, a central function of needs assessment is to develop estimates of the extent and distribution of a given problem and the associated target population. However, it is also often important for such research to yield useful descriptive information about the specific character of the need within that population. Often it is not sufficient for a social program to merely deliver some standard services in some standard way presumed to be responsive to a given problem or need. To be effective, a program may need to adapt its services to the local nature of the problem and the distinctive circumstances of the target population. This, in turn, requires information about the way in which the problem is experienced by those in that population, their perceptions and attributions about relevant services and programs, and the barriers and difficulties they encounter in attempting to access services.

A needs assessment might, for instance, probe why the problem exists and what other problems are linked with it. Investigation of low rates of foreign language study by high school students may reveal that many schools do not offer such courses. Thus, part of the problem is that the opportunities to learn foreign languages are insufficient. Similarly, the fact that many primary school children of low socioeconomic backgrounds appear tired and listless in class may be explained with a finding that many regularly do not eat breakfast. Of course, different stakeholders are likely to have different views about the nature and source of the problem so it is important that the full range of perspectives be represented (see Exhibit 4-H for an example of diverse stakeholder perspectives).

Cultural factors or perceptions and attributions that characterize a target population may be especially relevant to the effectiveness of a program's outreach

EXHIBIT 4-G

Rates of Violent Crime Victimization by Sex, Age, and Race

Characteristic of Victim	Victimization per 1,000 Persons Age 12 or Older: 2001				
	All Violent Crimes	Rape; Sexual Assault	Robbery	Aggravated Assault	Simple Assault
Sex					
Male	27.3	0.2	3.8	6.5	16.7
Female	23.0	1.9	1.7	4.2	15.1
Age					
12-15	55.1	1.7	5.2	8.7	39.6
16-19	55.8	3.4	6.4	12.3	33.8
20-24	44.7	2.4	4.2	10.7	27.4
25-34	29.3	1.1	3.6	6.5	18.1
35-49	22.9	1.0	2.1	5.2	14.5
50-64	9.5	0.2	1.2	2.0	6.2
65+	3.2	0.1	1.3	0.4	1.4
Race					
White	24.5	1.0	2.6	5.1	15.7
Black	31.2	1.1	3.6	8.1	18.3
Hispanic	29.5	1.1	5.3	6.6	16.6
Other	18.2	1.6	2.4	2.6	11.6
All persons	25.1	1.1	2.8	5.3	15.9

Data obtained by the National Crime Victimization Survey, conducted by the Bureau of the Census for the Bureau of Justice Statistics. All persons 12 or older (about 80,000) in about 40,000 households are interviewed concerning whether each was a victim of crime over the previous six-month period. The survey constitutes a probability sample of the non-institutionalized U.S. population.

SOURCE: U.S. Department of Justice, Office of Justice Programs, Bureau of Justice Statistics, *Criminal Victimization in the United States, 2001 Statistical Tables* (Washington, DC: U.S. Department of Justice, January 2003). Accessed through www.ojp.doj.gov/bjs.

EXHIBIT 4-H
Stakeholders
Have Different
Perceptions of the
Problems With Local
Health Services

Telephone interviews were conducted in three rural Colorado communities to identify health service problems related to cancer. In each community the study participants included (1) health care providers (physicians, nurses, public health personnel), (2) community influentials (teachers, librarians, directors of community agencies, business leaders), and (3) patients or family members of patients who had a cancer experience. While there was general agreement about problems with availability and access to services, each stakeholder group had somewhat different perceptions of the nature of the problems:

Physicians and health care providers:
  Regional facilities only accept paying patients or close down.
  The remoteness of the community creates a lack of services.
  Physician shortage exists because of low salaries, large workloads, and difficult patients.
  We don't have training or equipment to do high-tech care.

Community influentials:
  People are on waiting lists for services for several months.
  There are not enough professionals or volunteers here.
  There is inadequate provider knowledge about specialized services.

Patients and family members:
  A time or two we have had no doctor here.
  We have a doctor here now but his patients have no money and I hear he's going to leave.
  We need treatment locally.
  I was on a waiting list for three weeks before the mammography van got here.

SOURCE: Adapted from Holly W. Halvorson, Donna K. Pike, Frank M. Reed, Maureen W. McClatchey, and Carol A. Gosselink, "Using Qualitative Methods to Evaluate Health Service Delivery in Three Rural Colorado Communities," *Evaluation & the Health Professions*, 1993, 16(4):434-447.

to members of the target population and the way in which it delivers its service. A thorough needs assessment on poverty in Appalachian mountain communities, for instance, should reflect the sensitivities of the target population about their self-sufficiency and independence. Programs that are construed as charity or that give what are perceived as handouts are likely to be shunned by needy but proud families.

Another important dimension of service needs may involve difficulties some members of the target population have in using services. This may result from transportation problems, limited service hours, lack of child care, or a host of similar obstacles. The difference between a program with an effective service delivery to needy persons and an ineffective one is often chiefly a matter of how much attention is paid to overcoming these barriers. Job training programs that provide child care to the participants, nutrition programs that deliver meals to the homes of elderly persons, and community health clinics that are open during evening hoursall illustrate approaches that have based service delivery on a recognition of the complexity of their clients' needs.

Qualitative Methods for Describing Needs

While much social research is quantitative (involving numerical representation of the objects of interest), qualitative (nonnumerical) research can be especially useful for obtaining detailed, textured knowledge of the specific needs in question. Such research can range from interviews of a few persons or group discussions to elaborate ethnographic (descriptive) research such as that conducted by anthropologists. As an example of the utility of such research, qualitative data on the structure of popular beliefs can contribute substantially to the effective design of educational campaigns. What, for instance, are the trade-offs people believe exist between the pleasures of cigarette smoking and the resulting health risks? A good educational program must be adapted to those perceptions.

Carefully and sensitively conducted qualitative studies are particularly important for uncovering information relevant to how program services are configured. Thus, ethnographic studies of disciplinary problems within high schools will not only indicate how widespread disciplinary problems are but also suggest why some schools have fewer disciplinary problems than others. The findings on how schools differ might have implications for the ways programs are designed. Or consider qualitative research on household energy consumption that reveals that few householders have any information about the energy consumption characteristics of their appliances. Not knowing how they consume energy, these householders cannot very well develop effective strategies for reducing their consumption.

A useful technique for obtaining rich information about a social problem is the **focus group**. Focus groups bring together selected persons for a discussion of a particular topic or theme under the supervision of a facilitator (Dean, 1994; Krueger, 1988). Appropriate participant groups generally include such stakeholders as knowledgeable community leaders, directors of service agencies, line personnel in those agencies who deal firsthand with clients, representatives of advocacy groups, and persons experiencing the social problem or service needs directly. With a careful selection and grouping of individuals, a modest number of focus groups can provide a wealth of descriptive information about the nature and nuances of a social problem and the service needs of those who experience it. (Exhibit 4-I provides a helpful protocol for a needs assessment focus group.) A range of other group techniques for eliciting information for needs assessment can be found in Witkin and Altschuld (1995).

EXHIBIT 4-I

Sample Protocol for a Needs Assessment Focus Group

A focus group protocol is a list of topics that is used to guide discussion in a focus group session. The protocol should (1) cover topics in a logical, developmental order so that they build on one another; (2) raise open-ended issues that are engaging and relevant to the participants and that invite the group to make a collective response; and (3) carve out manageable "chunks" of topics to be examined one at a time in a delimited period. For example, the following protocol is for use in a focus group with low-income women to explore the barriers to receiving family support services:

- Introduction: greetings; explain purpose of the session; fill out name cards; introduce observers, ground rules, and how the focus group works (10 minutes).

- Participant introductions: first names only; where participants live, age of children; which family support services are received and for how long; other services received (10 minutes).

- Introduce idea of barriers to services: ask participants for their views on the most important barriers to receipt of family support services (probe regarding transportation, treatment by agency personnel, regulations, waiting lists); have they discontinued any services or been unable to get ones they want? (30 minutes).

- Probe for reasons behind their choices of most important barriers (20 minutes).

- Ask for ideas on what could be done to overcome barriers: what would make it easier to enter and remain in the service loop? (30 minutes).

- Debrief and wrap up: moderator summary, clarifications, and additional comments or questions (10 minutes).

SOURCE: Adapted from Susan Berkowitz, "Using Qualitative and Mixed-Method Approaches," in *Needs Assessment: A Creative and Practical Guide for Social Scientists,* eds. R. Reviere, S. Berkowitz, C. C. Carter, and C. G. Ferguson (Washington, DC: Taylor & Francis, 1996), pp. 121-146.

Any use of key informants in needs assessment must involve a careful selection of the persons or groups whose perceptions are going to be taken into account. A useful way to identify such informants is the "snowball" approach described in Chapter 3. More formally, in **snowball sampling**, an initial set of appropriate informants is located through some reasonable means and surveyed. The informants are then asked to identify other informants whom they believe are knowledgeable about the matter at issue. These other informants are then contacted and asked, in turn, to identify still others. Because those persons active and involved in any matter of public interest in a community tend to know of each other, snowball sampling works especially well for key informant surveys about social problems. When the process no longer produces relevant new names, it is likely that most of those who would qualify as key informants have been identified.

An especially useful group of informants that should not be overlooked in a needs assessment consists of a program's current clientele or, in the case of a new program, representatives of its potential clientele. This group, of course, is especially knowledgeable about the characteristics of the problem and the associated needs as they are experienced by those whose lives are affected by the problem. Although they are not necessarily in the best position to report on how widespread the problem is, they are the key witnesses with regard to how seriously the problem affects individuals and what dimensions of it are most pressing. Exhibit 4-J illustrates the unique perspective of potential service beneficiaries.

EXHIBIT 4-J

Homeless Men and Women Report Their Needs for Help

As efforts to help the homeless move beyond the provision of temporary shelter, it is important to understand homeless individuals' perspectives on their needs for assistance. Responses from a representative sample of 1,260 homeless men and women interviewed in New York City shelters revealed that they had multiple needs not easily met by a single service. The percentage reporting a need for help on each of 20 items was as follows:

Finding a place to live	87.1
Having a steady income	71.0
Finding a job	63.3
Improving my job skills	57.0
Learning how to get what I have coming from agencies	45.4
Getting on public assistance	42.1
Health and medical problems	41.7
Learning how to manage money	40.2
Getting along with my family	22.8
Getting on SSI/SSD	20.8

(Continued)

EXHIBIT 4-J
(Continued)

Problems with drugs	18.7
Learning to get along better with other people	18.5
Nerves and emotional problems	17.9
Learning how to protect myself	17.6
Learning how to read and fill out forms	17.3
Legal problems	15.0
Drinking problems	13.0
Getting around town	12.4
Getting veteran's benefits	9.6
Problems with the police	5.1

SOURCE: Adapted with permission from Daniel B. Herman, Elmer L. Struening, and Susan M. Barrow, "Self-Reported Needs for Help Among Homeless Men and Women," *Evaluation and Program Planning,* 1994, 17(3):249-256.

Because of the distinctive advantages of qualitative and quantitative approaches, a useful and frequently used strategy is to conduct needs assessment in two stages. The initial, exploratory stage uses qualitative research approaches to obtain rich information on the nature of the problem (e.g., Mitra, 1994). The second stage, estimation, builds on this information to design a more quantitative assessment that provides reliable estimates of the extent and distribution of the problem.

Summary

- Needs assessment attempts to answers questions about the social conditions a program is intended to address and the need for the program, or to determine whether a new program is needed. More generally, it may be used to identify, compare, and prioritize needs within and across program areas.

- Adequate diagnosis of social problems and identification of the target population for interventions are prerequisites to the design and operation of effective programs.

- Social problems are not objective phenomena; rather, they are social constructs. Evaluators can play a useful role in assisting policymakers and program managers to refine the definition of the social problem being addressed by a program.

- To specify the size and distribution of a problem, evaluators may gather and analyze data from existing sources, such as the U.S. Census, or use ongoing social indicators to identify trends. Because the needed information often cannot be obtained from such sources, evaluators frequently conduct their own research on a social problem. Useful approaches include studies of agency records, surveys, censuses, and key informant surveys. Each of these has its uses and limitations; for example, key informant surveys may be relatively easy to conduct but of doubtful reliability; agency records generally represent persons in need of services but may be incomplete; surveys and censuses can provide valid, representative information but can be expensive and technically demanding.

■ Forecasts of future needs are often very relevant to needs assessment but are complex technical activities ordinarily performed by specialists. In using forecasts, evaluators must take care to examine the assumptions on which the forecasts are based.

■ Appropriate definitions and accurate information about the numbers and characteristics of the targets of interventions are crucial throughout the intervention process, from initial planning through all the stages of program implementation. Targets may be individuals, groups, geographic areas, or physical units, and they may be defined as direct or indirect objects of an intervention.

■ Good target specifications establish appropriate boundaries, so that an intervention correctly addresses the target population and is feasible to apply. In defining targets, care must be taken to allow for the varying perspectives of different stakeholders. Useful concepts in target definition include population at risk, population in need, population at demand, incidence and prevalence, and rates.

■ For purposes of program planning or evaluation, it is important to have detailed information about the local nature of a social problem and the distinctive circumstances of those in need of program services. Such information is usually best obtained through qualitative methods such as ethnographic studies or focus groups with selected representatives of various stakeholders and observers.

KEY CONCEPTS

Focus group

A small panel of persons selected for their knowledge or perspective on a topic of interest that is convened to discuss the topic with the assistance of a facilitator. The discussion is used to identify important themes or to construct descriptive summaries of views and experiences on the focal topic.

Incidence

The number of new cases of a particular problem or condition that arise in a specified area during a specified period of time. Compare *prevalence*.

Key informants

Persons whose personal or professional position gives them a knowledgeable perspective on the nature and scope of a social problem or a target population and whose views are obtained during a needs assessment.

Population at risk

The individuals or units in a specified area with characteristics indicating that they have a significant probability of having or developing a particular condition.

Population in need

The individuals or units in a specified area that currently manifest a particular problematic condition.

Prevalence

The total number of existing cases with a particular condition in a specified area at a specified time. Compare *incidence*.

Rate

The occurrence or existence of a particular condition expressed as a proportion of units in the relevant population (e.g., deaths per 1,000 adults).

Sample survey

A survey administered to a sample of units in the population. The results are extrapolated to the entire population of interest by statistical projections.

Snowball sampling

A nonprobability sampling method in which each person interviewed is asked to suggest additional knowledgeable people for interviewing. The process continues until no new names are suggested.

Social indicator

Periodic measurements designed to track the course of a social condition over time.

5

Expressing and Assessing Program Theory

Chapter Outline

In Chapter 3, we advocated that evaluators analyze a program's theory as an aid in identifying potentially important evaluation questions. In this chapter, we return to the topic of program theory, not as a framework for identifying evaluation questions, but as a constituent part of the program that is being evaluated.

The social problems that programs address are often so complex and difficult that bringing about even small improvements may pose formidable challenges. A program's theory is the conception of what must be done to bring about the intended social benefits. As such, it is the foundation on which every program rests.

A program's theory can be a good one, in which case it represents the "know-how" necessary for the program to attain the desired results, or it can be a poor one that would not produce the intended effects even if implemented well. One aspect of evaluating a program, therefore, is to assess how good the program theory is—in particular, how well it is formulated and whether it presents a plausible and feasible plan for improving the target social conditions. For program theory to be assessed, however, it must first be expressed clearly and completely enough to stand for review. Accordingly, this chapter describes how evaluators can describe the program theory and then assess how good it is.

M ario Cuomo, former governor of New York, once described his mother's rules for success as (1) figure out what you want to do and (2) do it. These are pretty much the same rules that social programs must follow if they are to be effective. Given an identified need, program decisionmakers must (1) conceptualize a program capable of alleviating that need and (2) implement it. In this chapter, we review the concepts and procedures an evaluator can apply to the task of assessing the quality of the program conceptualization, which we have called the program theory. In the next chapter, we describe how the evaluator can assess the quality of the program's implementation.

Whether it is expressed in a detailed program plan and rationale or only implicit in the program's structure and activities, the program theory explains why the program does what it does and provides the rationale for expecting that doing so will achieve the desired results. When examining a program's theory, evaluators often find that it is not very convincing. There are many poorly designed social programs with faults that reflect deficiencies in their underlying conception of how the desired social benefits can be attained. This happens in large part because insufficient attention is given during the planning of new programs to careful, explicit conceptualization of a program's objectives and how they are supposed to be achieved. Sometimes the political context within which programs originate does not permit extensive planning but, even when that is not the case, conventional practices for designing programs pay little attention to the underlying theory. The human service professions operate with repertoires of established services and types of intervention associated with their respective specialty areas. As a result, program design is often a matter of configuring a variation of familiar "off the shelf" services into a package that seems appropriate for a social problem without a close analysis of the match between those services and the specific nature of the problem.

For example, many social problems that involve deviant behavior, such as alcohol and drug abuse, criminal behavior, early sexual activity, or teen pregnancy, are addressed by programs that provide the target population with some mix of counseling and educational services. This approach is based on an assumption that is rarely made explicit during the planning of the program, namely, that people will change their problem behavior if given information and interpersonal support for doing so. While this assumption may seem reasonable, experience and research provide ample evidence that such behaviors are resistant to change even when participants are provided with knowledge about how to change and receive strong encouragement from loved ones to do so. Thus, the theory that education and supportive counseling will reduce deviant behavior may not be a sound basis for program design.

A program's rationale and conceptualization, therefore, are just as subject to critical scrutiny within an evaluation as any other important aspect of the program. If the program's goals and objectives do not relate in a reasonable way to the social conditions the program is intended to improve, or the assumptions and expectations embodied in a program's functioning do not represent a credible approach to bringing about that improvement, there is little prospect that the program will be effective.

The first step in assessing program theory is to articulate it, that is, to produce an explicit description of the conceptions, assumptions, and expectations that constitute the rationale for the way the program is structured and operated. Only rarely can a program immediately provide the evaluator with a full statement of its underlying theory. Although the program theory is always implicit in the program's structure and operations, a detailed account of it is seldom written down in program documents. Moreover, even when some write-up of program theory is available, it is often in material that has been prepared for funding proposals or public relations purposes and may not correspond well with actual program practice.

Assessment of program theory, therefore, almost always requires that the evaluator synthesize and articulate the theory in a form amenable to analysis. Accordingly, the discussion in this chapter is organized around two themes: (1) how the evaluator can explicate and express program theory in a form that will be representative of key stakeholders' actual understanding of the program and workable for purposes of evaluation, and (2) how the evaluator can assess the quality of the program theory that has been thus articulated. We begin with a brief description of a perspective that has provided the most fully developed approaches to evaluating program theory.

The Evaluability Assessment Perspective

One of the earliest systematic attempts to describe and assess program theory arose from the experiences of an evaluation research group at the Urban Institute in the 1970s (Wholey, 1979). They found it often difficult, sometimes impossible, to undertake evaluations of public programs and began to analyze the obstacles. This led to the view that a qualitative assessment of whether minimal preconditions for evaluation were met should precede most evaluation efforts. Wholey and his colleagues termed the process **evaluability assessment** (see Exhibit 5-A).

Evaluability assessment involves three primary activities: (1) description of the *program model* with particular attention to defining the program goals and objectives, (2) assessment of how well defined and evaluable that model is, and (3) identification of stakeholder interest in evaluation and the likely use of the findings. Evaluators conducting evaluability assessments operate much like ethnographers in that they seek to describe and understand the program through interviews and observations that will reveal its "social reality" as viewed by program personnel and other significant stakeholders. The evaluators begin with the conception of the program presented in documents and official information, but then try to see the program through the eyes of those closest to it. The intent is to end up with a description of the program as it exists and an understanding of the program issues that really matter to the parties involved. Although this process involves considerable judgment and discretion on the part of the evaluator, various practitioners have attempted to codify its procedures so that evaluability assessments will be reproducible by other evaluators (see Rutman, 1980; Smith, 1989; Wholey, 1994).

A common outcome of evaluability assessments is that program managers and sponsors recognize the need to modify their programs. The evaluability assessment may reveal that there are faults in a program's delivery system, that the program's target population is not well defined, or that the intervention itself needs to be reconceptualized. Or there may be few program objectives that stakeholders agree on or no feasible performance indicators for the objectives. In such cases, the evaluability assessment has uncovered problems with the program's design that program managers must correct before any meaningful performance evaluation can be undertaken.

The aim of evaluability assessment is to create a favorable climate and an agreed-on understanding of the nature and objectives of the program that will facilitate the design of an evaluation. As such, it can be integral to the approach the evaluator employs to tailor an evaluation and formulate evaluation questions (see Chapters 2 and 3). Exhibit 5-B presents an example of an evaluability assessment that illustrates the typical procedure.

If evaluators and intended users fail to agree on program goals, objectives, information priorities, and intended uses of program performance information, those designing evaluations may focus on answering questions that are not relevant to policy and management decisions. If program goals and objectives are unrealistic because insufficient resources have been applied to critical program activities, the program has been poorly implemented, or administrators lack knowledge of how to achieve program goals and objectives, the more fruitful course may be for those in charge of the program to change program resources, activities, or objectives before formal evaluation efforts are undertaken. If relevant data are unavailable and cannot be obtained at reasonable cost, subsequent evaluation work is likely to be inconclusive. If policymakers or managers are unable or unwilling to use the evaluation information to change the program, even the most conclusive evaluations are likely to produce "information in search of a user." Unless these problems can be overcome, the evaluation will probably not contribute to improved program performance.

These four problems, which characterize many public and private programs, can be reduced and often overcome by a qualitative evaluation process, evaluability assessment, that documents the breadth of the four problems and helps programs—and subsequent program evaluation work—to meet the following criteria:

- Program goals, objectives, important side effects, and priority information needs are well defined.

- Program goals and objectives are plausible.

- Relevant performance data can be obtained.

- The intended users of the evaluation results have agreed on how they will use the information.

Evaluability assessment is a process for clarifying program designs, exploring program reality, and—if necessary—helping redesign programs to ensure that they meet these four criteria. Evaluability assessment not only shows whether a program can be meaningfully evaluated (any program can be evaluated) but also whether evaluation is likely to contribute to improved program performance.

SOURCE: Quoted from Joseph S. Wholey, "Assessing the Feasibility and Likely Usefulness of Evaluation," in *Handbook of Practical Program Evaluation*, eds. J. S. Wholey, H. P. Hatry, and K. E. Newcomer (San Francisco: Jossey-Bass, 1994), p. 16.

EXHIBIT 5-B
Evaluability
Assessment for
the Appalachian
Regional
Commission

Evaluators from the Urban Institute worked with managers and policymakers in the Appalachian Regional Commission (ARC) on the design of their health and child development program. In this evaluability assessment, the evaluators:

- Reviewed existing data on each of the 13 state ARC-funded health and child development programs
- Made visits to five states and then selected two states to participate in evaluation design and implementation
- Reviewed documentation related to congressional, commission, state, and project objectives and activities (including the authorizing legislation, congressional hearings and committee reports, state planning documents, project grant applications, ARC contract reports, local planning documents, project materials, and research projects)
- Interviewed approximately 75 people on congressional staffs and in commission headquarters, state ARC and health and child development staffs, local planning units, and local projects
- Participated in workshops with approximately 60 additional health and child development practitioners, ARC state personnel, and outside analysts

Analysis and synthesis of the resulting data yielded a logic model that presented program activities, program objectives, and the assumed causal links between them. The measurability and plausibility of program objectives were then analyzed and new program designs more likely to lead to demonstrably effective performance were presented. These included both an overall ARC program model and a series of individual models, each concerned with an identified objective of the program.

In reviewing the report, ARC staff were asked to choose among alternative courses of action. The review process consisted of a series of intensive discussions in which ARC and Urban Institute staff focused on one objective and program model at a time. In each session, the evaluators and staff attempted to reach agreement on the validity of the models presented, the importance of the respective objectives, and the extent to which any of the information options ought to be pursued.

ARC ended up adopting revised project designs and deciding to systematically monitor the performance of all their health and child development projects and evaluate the effectiveness of the "innovative" ones. Twelve of the 13 ARC states have since adopted the performance monitoring system. Representatives of those states report that project designs are now much more clearly articulated and they believe the projects themselves have improved.

SOURCE: Adapted from Joseph S. Wholey, "Using Evaluation to Improve Program Performance," in *Evaluation Research and Practice: Comparative and International Perspectives,* eds. R. A. Levine, M. A. Solomon, G.-M. Hellstern, and H. Wollmann (Beverly Hills, CA: Sage, 1981), pp. 92-106.

Evaluability assessment requires program stakeholders to articulate the program's design and logic (the program model); however, it can also be carried out for the purposes of describing and assessing program theory (Wholey, 1987). Indeed, the evaluability assessment approach represents the most fully developed set of concepts and procedures available in the evaluation literature for describing and assessing a program's conceptualization of what it is supposed to be doing and why. We turn now to a more detailed discussion of procedures for identifying and evaluating program theory, drawing heavily on the writings associated with the practice of evaluability assessment.

Describing Program Theory

Evaluators have long recognized the importance of program theory as a basis for formulating and prioritizing evaluation questions, designing evaluation research, and interpreting evaluation findings (Bickman, 1987; Chen and Rossi, 1980; Weiss, 1972; Wholey, 1979). However, program theory has been described and used under various names, for example, logic model, program model, outcome line, cause map, and action theory. There is no general consensus about how best to describe a program's theory, so we will describe a scheme we have found useful in our own evaluation activities.

For this purpose, we depict a social program as centering on the transactions that take place between a program's operations and the population it serves (Exhibit 5-C). These transactions might involve counseling sessions for women with eating disorders in therapists' offices, recreational activities for high-risk youths at a community center, educational presentations to local citizens' groups, nutrition posters in a clinic, informational pamphlets about empowerment zones and tax law mailed to potential investors, delivery of meals to the front doors of elderly persons, or any such point-of-service contact. On one side of this program-target transaction, we have the program as an organizational entity, with its various facilities, personnel, resources, activities, and so forth. On the other side, we have the target participants in their lifespaces with their various circumstances and experiences in relation to the service delivery system of the program.

This simple scheme highlights three interrelated components of a program theory: the program impact theory, the service utilization plan, and the program's organizational plan. The program's **impact theory** consists of assumptions about the change process actuated by the program and the improved conditions that are expected to result. It is operationalized by the program-target transactions, for they constitute the means by which the program expects to bring about its intended effects. The impact theory may be as simple as presuming that exposure to information about the negative

EXHIBIT 5-C
Overview of Program Theory

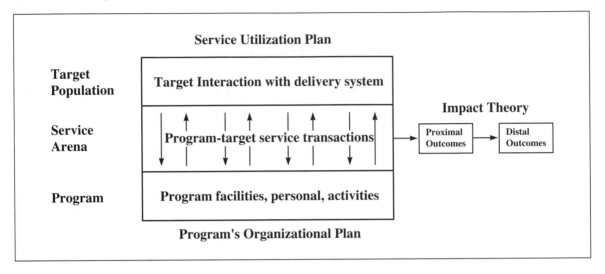

effects of drug abuse will motivate high school students to abstain or as complex as the ways in which an eighth-grade science curriculum will lead to deeper understanding of natural phenomena. It may be as informal as the commonsense presumption that providing hot meals to elderly persons improves their nutrition or as formal as classical conditioning theory adapted to treating phobias. Whatever its nature, however, an impact theory of some sort constitutes the essence of a social program. If the assumptions embodied in that theory about how desired changes are brought about by program action are faulty, or if they are valid but not well operationalized by the program, the intended social benefits will not be achieved.

To instigate the change process posited in the program's impact theory, the intended services must first be provided to the target population. The program's **service utilization plan** is constituted by the program's assumptions and expectations about how to reach the target population, provide and sequence service contacts, and conclude the relationship when services are no longer needed or appropriate. For a program to increase awareness of AIDS risk, for instance, the service utilization plan may be simply that appropriate persons will read informative posters if they are put up in subway cars. A multifaceted AIDS prevention program, on the other hand, may be organized on the assumption that high-risk drug abusers who are referred by outreach workers will go to nearby street-front clinics, where they will receive appropriate testing and information.

The program, of course, must be organized in such a way that it can actually provide the intended services. The third component of program theory, therefore, relates to program resources, personnel, administration, and general organization. We call this component the program's **organizational plan**. The organizational plan can generally be represented as a set of propositions: If the program has such and such resources, facilities, personnel, and so on, if it is organized and administered in such and such a manner, and if it engages in such and such activities and functions, then a viable organization will result that can operate the intended service delivery system. Elements of programs' organizational theories include, for example, assumptions that case managers should have master's degrees in social work and at least five years' experience, that at least 20 case managers should be employed, that the agency should have an advisory board that represents local business owners, that there should be an administrative coordinator assigned to each site, and that working relations should be maintained with the Department of Public Health.

Adequate resources and effective organization, in this scheme, are the factors that make it possible to develop and maintain a service delivery system that enables utilization of the services by the target population. A program's organization and the service delivery system that organization supports are the parts of the program most directly under the control of program administrators and staff. These two aspects together are often referred to as *program process*, and the assumptions and expectations on which that process is based may be called the program **process theory**.

With this overview, we turn now to a more detailed discussion of each of the components of program theory with particular attention to how the evaluator can describe them in a manner that permits analysis and assessment.

Program Impact Theory

Program impact theory is causal theory. It describes a cause-and-effect sequence in which certain program activities are the instigating causes and certain social benefits are the effects they eventually produce. Evaluators, therefore, typically represent program impact theory in the form of a causal diagram showing the cause-and-effect linkages presumed to connect a program's activities with the expected outcomes (Chen, 1990; Lipsey, 1993; Martin and Kettner, 1996). Because programs rarely exercise direct control over the social conditions they are expected to improve, they must generally work indirectly by changing some critical but manageable aspect of the situation, which, in turn, is expected to lead to more far-reaching improvements.

The simplest program impact theory is the basic "two step" in which services affect some intermediate condition that, in turn, improves the social conditions of concern (Lipsey and Pollard, 1989). For instance, a program cannot make it impossible for people to abuse alcohol, but it can attempt to change their attitudes and motivation toward alcohol in ways that help them avoid abuse. More complex program theories may have more steps along the path between program and social benefit and, perhaps, involve more than one distinct path.

The distinctive features of any representation of program impact theory are that each element is either a cause or an effect and that the causal linkages between those elements show a chain of events that begins with program actions and ends with change in the social conditions the program intends to improve (see Exhibit 5-D). The events following directly from the instigating program activities are the most direct outcomes, often called proximal or immediate outcomes (e.g., dietary knowledge and awareness in the first example in Exhibit 5-D). Events further down the chain constitute the more distal or ultimate outcomes (e.g., healthier diet in the first example in Exhibit 5-D). Program impact theory highlights the dependence of the more distal, and generally more important, outcomes on successful attainment of the more proximal ones.

The Service Utilization Plan

An explicit service utilization plan pulls into focus the critical assumptions about how and why the intended recipients of service will actually become engaged with the program and follow through to the point of receiving sufficient services to initiate the change process represented in the program impact theory. It describes the program-target transactions from the perspective of the targets and their lifespaces as they might encounter the program.

A program's service utilization plan can be usefully depicted in a flowchart that tracks the various paths that program targets can follow from some appropriate point prior to first contact with the program through a point where there is no longer any contact. Exhibit 5-E shows an example of a simple service utilization flowchart for a hypothetical aftercare program for released psychiatric patients. One characteristic of such charts is that they identify the possible situations in which the program targets are not engaged with the program as intended. In Exhibit 5-E, for example, we see that formerly hospitalized psychiatric patients may not receive the planned visit from a social worker or referrals to community agencies and, as a consequence, may receive no service at all.

The Program's Organizational Plan

The program's organizational plan is articulated from the perspective of program management. The plan encompasses both the functions and activities the program is expected to perform and the human, financial, and physical resources required for that performance. Central to this scheme are the program services, those specific activities

EXHIBIT 5-D

Diagrams Illustrating Program Impact Theories

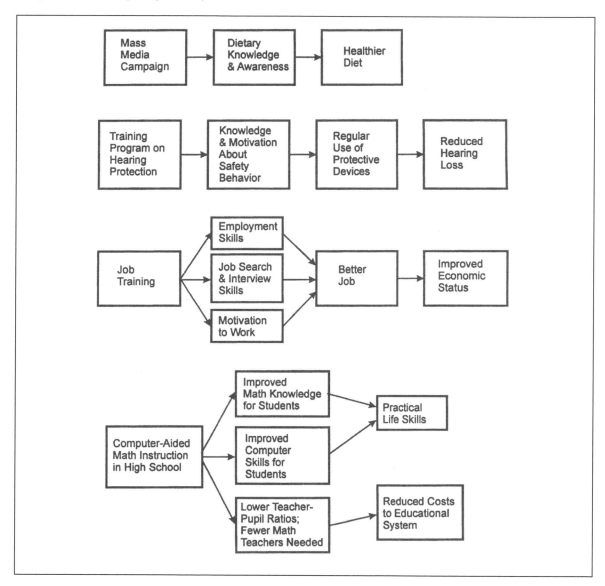

that constitute the program's role in the target-program transactions that are expected to lead to social benefits. However, the organizational plan also must include those functions that provide essential preconditions and ongoing support for the organization's ability to provide its primary services, for instance, fund-raising, personnel management, facilities acquisition and maintenance, political liaison, and the like.

Exhibit 5-E
Service Utilization Flowchart for an Aftercare Program for Psychiatric Patients

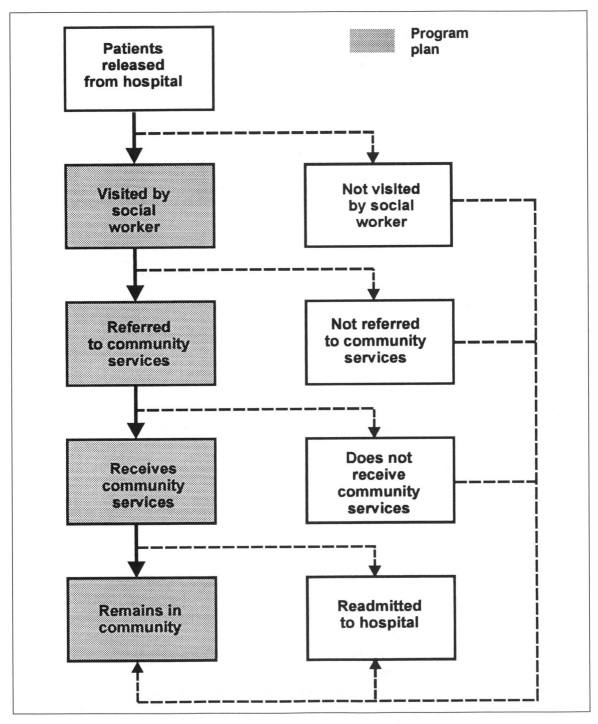

There are many ways to depict a program's organizational plan. If we center it on the target-program transactions, the first element of the organizational plan will be a description of the program's objectives for the services it will provide: what those services are, how much is to be provided, to whom, and on what schedule. The next element might then describe the resources and functions necessary to engage in those service activities. For instance, sufficient personnel with appropriate credentials and skills will be required as will logistical support, proper facilities and equipment, funding, supervision, clerical support, and so forth.

As with the other portions of program theory, it is often useful to describe a program's organizational plan with a diagram. Exhibit 5-F presents an example that depicts the major organizational components of the aftercare program for psychiatric

EXHIBIT 5-F

Organizational Schematic for an Aftercare Program for Psychiatric Patients

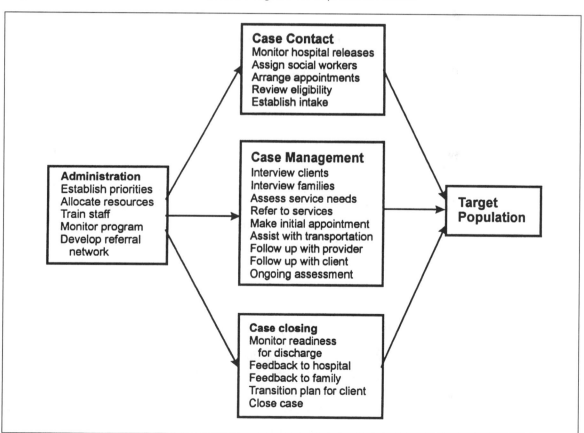

patients whose service utilization scheme is shown in Exhibit 5-E. A common way of representing the organizational plan of a program is in terms of inputs (resources and constraints applicable to the program) and activities (the services the program is expected to provide). In a full logic model of the program, receipt of services (service utilization) is represented as program outputs, which, in turn, are related to the desired outcomes. Exhibit 5-G shows a typical logic model drawn from a widely used workbook prepared by the United Way of America.

Eliciting Program Theory

When a program's theory is spelled out in program documents and well understood by staff and stakeholders, the program is said to be based on an **articulated program theory** (Weiss, 1997). This is most likely to occur when the original design of the program is drawn from social science theory. For instance, a school-based drug use prevention program that features role-playing of refusal behavior in peer groups may be derived from social learning theory and its implications for peer influences on adolescent behavior.

When the underlying assumptions about how program services and practices are presumed to accomplish their purposes have not been fully articulated and recorded, the program has an **implicit program theory** or, as Weiss (1997) put it, a tacit theory. This might be the case for a counseling program to assist couples with marital difficulties. Although it may be reasonable to assume that discussing marital problems with a trained professional would be helpful, the way in which that translates into improvements in the marital relationship is not described by an explicit theory nor would different counselors necessarily agree about the process.

When a program's theory is implicit rather than articulated, the evaluator must extract and describe it before it can be analyzed and assessed. The evaluator's objective is to depict the "program as intended," that is, the actual expectations held by decision-makers about what the program is supposed to do and what results are expected to follow. With this in mind, we now consider the concepts and procedures an evaluator can use to extract and articulate program theory as a prerequisite for assessing it.

Defining the Boundaries of the Program

A crucial early step in articulating program theory is to define the boundaries of the program at issue (Smith, 1989). A human service agency may have many programs and provide multiple services; a regional program may have many agencies and sites. There is usually no one correct definition of a program, and the boundaries

EXHIBIT 5-G

A Logic Model for a Teen Mother Parenting Education Program

| Inputs | Activities | Outputs | Outcomes | | |
			Initial	Intermediate	Longer-Term
Agency provides MSW program manager, part-time RN instructor, nationally certified education manuals, videos, and other teaching tools.	Program provides parenting classes on prenatal-through-infant nutrition, development, safety, and caretaking delivered in high schools twice a week for one hour to teen mothers from 3 months prior, to one year after, delivery of a child.	Pregnant teens attend program.	Teens are knowledgeable about prenatal nutrition and health guidelines.	Teens follow proper nutrition and health guidelines. Teens deliver healthy babies.	Babies achieve appropriate 12-month milestones for physical, motor, verbal, and social development.
Agency and high school identify pregnant teens to participate in program.			Teens are knowledgeable about proper care, feeding, and social interaction with infants.	Teens provide proper care, feeding, and social interaction to their babies.	

SOURCE: Adapted from United Way of America Task Force on Impact, *Measuring Program Outcomes: A Practical Approach.* Alexandria, VA: Author, 1996, p. 42. Used by permission, United Way of America.

the evaluator applies will depend, in large part, on the scope of the evaluation sponsor's concerns and the program domains to which they apply.

One way to define the boundaries of a program for the purpose of articulating the program theory is to work from the perspective of the decisionmakers who are expected to act on the findings of the evaluation. The evaluator's definition of the program should at minimum represent the relevant jurisdiction of those decisionmakers and the organizational structures and activities about which decisions are likely to be made. If, for instance, the sponsor of the evaluation is the director of a local community mental health agency, then the evaluator may define the boundaries of the program around one of the distinct service packages administered by that director, such as outpatient counseling for eating disorders. If the evaluation sponsor is the state director of mental health, however, the relevant program boundaries may be defined around effectiveness questions that relate to the outpatient counseling component of all the local mental health agencies in the state.

Because program theory deals mainly with means-ends relations, the most critical aspect of defining program boundaries is to ensure that they encompass all the important activities, events, and resources linked to one or more outcomes recognized as central to the endeavor. This can be accomplished by starting with the benefits the program intends to produce and working backward to identify all the activities and resources under relevant organizational auspices that are presumed to contribute to attaining those objectives. From this perspective, the eating disorders program at either the local or state level would be defined as the set of activities organized by the respective mental health agency that has an identifiable role in attempting to alleviate eating disorders for the eligible population.

Although these approaches are straightforward in concept, they can be problematic in practice. Not only can programs be complex, with crosscutting resources, activities, and goals, but the characteristics described above as linchpins for program definition can themselves be difficult to establish. Thus, in this matter, as with so many other aspects of evaluation, the evaluator must be prepared to negotiate a program definition agreeable to the evaluation sponsor and key stakeholders and be flexible about modifying the definition as the evaluation progresses.

Explicating the Program Theory

For a program in the early planning stage, program theory might be built by the planners from prior practice and research. At this stage, an evaluator may be able to help develop a plausible and well-articulated theory. For an existing program, however, the appropriate task is to describe the theory that is actually embodied in the program's structure and operation. To accomplish this, the evaluator must work with stakeholders to draw out the theory represented in their actions and assumptions. The general procedure for this involves successive approximation. Draft descriptions of the program theory are generated, usually by the evaluator, and discussed with knowledgeable stakeholder informants to get feedback. The draft is then refined on the basis of their input and shown again to appropriate stakeholders. The theory description developed in this fashion may involve impact theory, process theory, or any components or combination that are deemed relevant to the purposes of the evaluation. Exhibit 5-H presents one evaluator's account of how a program process theory was elicited.

The primary sources of information for developing and differentiating descriptions of program theory are (1) review of program documents; (2) interviews with program stakeholders, and other selected informants; (3) site visits and observation of program functions and circumstances; and (4) the social science literature. Three types of information the evaluator may be able to extract from those sources will be especially useful.

Program Goals and Objectives

Perhaps the most important matter to be determined from program sources relates to the goals and objectives of the program, which are necessarily an integral part of the program theory, especially its impact theory. The goals and objectives that must be represented in program theory, however, are not necessarily the same as those identified in a program's mission statements or in responses to questions asked of stakeholders about the program's goals. To be meaningful for an evaluation, program goals must identify a state of affairs that could realistically be attained as a result of program actions; that is, there must be some reasonable connection between what the program does and what it intends to accomplish. Smith (1989) suggests that, to keep the discussion concrete and specific, the evaluator should use a line of questioning that does not ask about goals directly but asks instead about consequences. For instance, in a review of major program activities, the evaluator might ask about each, "Why do it? What are the expected results? How could you tell if those results actually occurred?"

The resulting set of goal statements must then be integrated into the description of program theory. Goals and objectives that describe the changes the program aims to bring about in social conditions relate to program impact theory. A program goal of reducing unemployment, for instance, identifies a distal outcome in the impact theory. Program goals and objectives related to program activities and service delivery, in turn, help reveal the program process theory. If the program aims to offer afterschool care for latchkey children to working parents, a portion of the service utilization plan is revealed. Similarly, if an objective is to offer literacy classes four times a week, an important element of the organizational plan is identified.

Program Functions, Components, and Activities

To properly describe the program process theory, the evaluator must identify each distinct program component, its functions, and the particular activities and operations associated with those functions. Program functions include such operations as "assess client need," "complete intake," "assign case manager," "recruit referral agencies," "train

EXHIBIT 5-H
Formulating
Program Process
Theory for Adapted
Work Service

Adapted Work Services (AWS) was initiated at the Rochelle Center in Nashville, Tennessee, to provide low-stress, paid work and social interaction to patients in the early stages of Alzheimer's disease. It was based on the belief that the patients would benefit emotionally and cognitively from working in a sheltered environment and their family members would benefit from being occasionally relieved of the burden of caring for them. The evaluator described the procedures for formulating a program process theory for this program as follows:

> The creation of the operational model of the AWS program involved using Post-it notes and butcher paper to provide a wall-size depiction of the program. The first session involved only the researcher and the program director. The first question asked was, "What happens when a prospective participant calls the center for information?" The response was recorded on a Post-it note and placed on the butcher paper. The next step was then identified, and this too was recorded and placed on the butcher paper. The process repeated itself until all (known) activities were identified and placed on the paper. Once the program director could not identify any more activities, the Post-it notes were combined into clusters. The clusters were discussed until potential component labels began to emerge. Since this exercise was the product of only two people, the work was left in an unused room for two weeks so that the executive director and all other members of the management team could react to the work. They were to identify missing, incorrect, or misplaced activities as well as comment on the proposed components. After several feedback sessions from the staff members and discussions with the executive director, the work was typed and prepared for presentation to the Advisory Board. The board members were able to reflect on the content, provide further discussion, and suggest additional changes. Several times during monthly board meetings, the executive director asked that the model be revisited for planning purposes. This helped further clarify the activities as well as sharpen the group's thinking about the program.

SOURCE: Quoted, with permission, from Doris C. Quinn, "Formative Evaluation of Adapted Work Services for Alzheimer's Disease Victims: A Framework for Practical Evaluation in Health Care" (doctoral diss., Vanderbilt University, 1996), pp. 46-47.

field workers," and the like. The evaluator can generally identify such functions by determining the activities and job descriptions of the various program personnel. When clustered into thematic groups, these functions represent the constituent elements of the program process theory.

The Logic or Sequence Linking
Program Functions, Activities, and Components

A critical aspect of program theory is how the various expected outcomes and functions relate to each other. Sometimes these relationships involve only the temporal sequencing of key program activities and their effects; for instance, in a postrelease program for felons, prison officials must notify the program that a convict has been released before the program can initiate contact to arrange services. In other cases, the relationships between outcomes and functions have to do with activities or events that must be coordinated, as when child care and transportation must be arranged in conjunction with job training sessions, or with supportive functions, such as training the instructors who will conduct in-service classes for nurses. Other relationships entail logical or conceptual linkages, especially those represented in the program impact theory. Thus, the connection between mothers' knowledge about how to care for their infants and the actual behavior of providing that care assumes a psychological process through which information influences behavior.

It is because the number and variety of such relationships are often appreciable that evaluators typically construct charts or graphical displays to describe them. These may be configured as lists, flowcharts, or hierarchies, or in any number of creative forms designed to identify the key elements and relationships in a program's theory. Such displays not only portray program theory but also provide a way to make it sufficiently concrete and specific to engage program personnel and stakeholders.

Corroborating the Description of the Program Theory

The description of program theory that results from the procedures we have described will generally represent the program as it was intended more than as it actually is. Program managers and policymakers think of the idealized program as the "real" one with various shortfalls from that ideal as glitches that do not represent what the program is really about. Those further away from the day-to-day operations, on the other hand, may be unaware of such shortfalls and will naturally describe what they presume the program to be even if in actuality it does not quite live up to that image.

Some discrepancy between program theory and reality is therefore natural. Indeed, examination of the nature and magnitude of that discrepancy is the task of process or implementation evaluation, as discussed in the next chapter. However, if the theory is so overblown that it cannot realistically be held up as a depiction of what is supposed to happen, it needs to be revised. Suppose, for instance, that a job training program's service utilization plan calls for monthly contacts between each client and a case manager. If the program resources are insufficient to support case managers, and none are employed, this part of the theory is fanciful and should be restated to more realistically depict what the program might actually be able to accomplish.

Given that the program theory depicts a realistic scenario, confirming it is a matter of demonstrating that pertinent program personnel and stakeholders endorse it as a meaningful account of how the program is intended to work. If it is not possible to generate a theory description that all relevant stakeholders accept as reasonable, this indicates that the program is poorly defined or that it embodies competing philosophies. In such cases, the most appropriate response for the evaluator may be to take on a consultant role and assist the program in clarifying its assumptions and intentions to yield a theory description that will be acceptable to all key stakeholders.

For the evaluator, the end result of the theory description exercise is a detailed and complete statement of the program as intended that can then be analyzed and assessed as a distinct aspect of the evaluation. Note that the agreement of stakeholders serves only to confirm that the theory description does, in fact, represent their understanding of how the program is supposed to work. It does not necessarily mean that the theory is a good one. To determine the soundness of a program theory, the evaluator must not only describe the theory but evaluate it. The procedures evaluators use for that purpose are described in the next section.

Assessing Program Theory

Assessment of some aspect of a program's theory is relatively common in evaluation, often in conjunction with an evaluation of program process or impact. Nonetheless, outside of the modest evaluability assessment literature, remarkably little has been written of a specific nature about how this should be done. Our interpretation of this relative neglect is not that theory assessment is unimportant or unusual, but that it is typically done in an informal manner that relies on commonsense judgments that may not seem to require much explanation. Indeed, when program services are directly related to straightforward objectives, the validity of the program theory may be accepted on the basis of limited evidence or commonsense judgment. An illustration is a meals-on-wheels service that brings hot meals to homebound elderly persons to improve their nutritional intake. In this case, the theory linking the action of the program (providing hot meals) to its intended benefits (improved nutrition) needs little critical evaluation.

Many programs, however, are not based on expectations as simple as the notion that delivering food to elderly persons improves their nutrition. For example, a family preservation program that assigns case managers to coordinate community services for parents deemed at risk of having their children placed in foster care involves many assumptions about exactly what it is supposed to accomplish and how. In such cases, the program theory might easily be faulty, and correspondingly, a rather probing evaluation of it may be warranted.

It is seldom possible or useful to individually appraise each distinct assumption and expectation represented in a program theory. But there are certain critical tests that can be conducted to provide assurance that it is sound. This section summarizes the various approaches and procedures the evaluator might use for conducting that assessment.

Assessment in Relation to Social Needs

The most important framework for assessing program theory builds on the results of needs assessment, as discussed in Chapter 4. Or, more generally, it is based on a thorough understanding of the social problem the program is intended to address and the service needs of the target population. A program theory that does not relate in an appropriate manner to the actual nature and circumstances of the social conditions at issue will result in an ineffective program no matter how well the program is implemented and administered. It is fundamental, therefore, to assess program theory in relationship to the needs of the target population the program is intended to serve.

There is no push-button procedure an evaluator can use to assess whether program theory describes a suitable conceptualization of how social needs should be met. Inevitably, this assessment requires judgment calls. When the assessment is especially critical, its validity is strengthened if those judgments are made collaboratively with relevant experts and stakeholders to broaden the range of perspectives and expertise on which they are based. Such collaborators, for instance, might include social scientists knowledgeable about research and theory related to the intervention, administrators with long experience managing such programs, representatives of advocacy groups associated with the target population, and policymakers or policy advisers highly familiar with the program and problem area.

Whatever the nature of the group that contributes to the assessment, the crucial aspect of the process is specificity. When program theory and social needs are described in general terms, there often appears to be more correspondence than is evident when the details are examined. To illustrate, consider a curfew program prohibiting juveniles under age 18 from being outside their homes after midnight that is initiated in a metropolitan area to address the problem of skyrocketing juvenile crime. The program theory, in general terms, is that the curfew will keep the youths home at night and, if they are at home, they are unlikely to commit crimes. Because the general social problem the program addresses is juvenile crime, the program theory does seem responsive to the social need.

A more detailed problem diagnosis and service needs assessment, however, might show that the bulk of juvenile crimes are residential burglaries committed in the late afternoon when school lets out. Moreover, it might reveal that the offenders represent a relatively small proportion of the juvenile population who have a disproportionately large impact because of their high rates of offending. Furthermore, it might be found that these juveniles are predominantly latchkey youths who have no supervision during afterschool hours. When the program theory is then examined in some detail, it is apparent that it assumes that significant juvenile crime occurs late at night and that potential offenders will both know about and obey the curfew. Furthermore, it depends on enforcement by parents or the police if compliance does not occur voluntarily.

Although even more specificity than this would be desirable, this much detail illustrates how a program theory can be compared with need to discover shortcomings in the theory. In this example, examining the particulars of the program theory and the social problem it is intended to address reveals a large disconnect. The program blankets the whole city rather than targeting the small group of problem juveniles and focuses on activity late at night rather than during the early afternoon, when most of the crimes actually occur. In addition, it makes the questionable assumptions that youths already engaged in more serious lawbreaking will comply with a curfew, that parents who leave their delinquent children unsupervised during the early part of the day will be able to supervise their later behavior, and that the overburdened police force will invest sufficient effort in arresting juveniles who violate the curfew to enforce compliance. Careful review of these particulars alone would raise serious doubts about the validity of this program theory (Exhibit 5-I presents another example).

One useful approach to comparing program theory with what is known (or assumed) about the relevant social needs is to separately assess impact theory and program process theory. Each of these relates to the social problem in a different way and, as each is elaborated, specific questions can be asked about how compatible the assumptions of the theory are with the nature of the social circumstances to which it applies. We will briefly describe the main points of comparison for each of these theory components.

Program impact theory involves the sequence of causal links between program services and outcomes that improve the targeted social conditions. The key point of comparison between program impact theory and social needs, therefore, relates to whether the effects the program is expected to have on the social conditions correspond to what is required to improve those conditions, as revealed by the needs

EXHIBIT 5-1

The Needs of the
Homeless as a
Basis for Assessing
Program Theory

Exhibit 4-J in Chapter 4 described the responses of a sample of homeless men and women to a needs assessment survey. The largest proportions identified a place to live and having a job or steady income as their greatest need. Fewer than half, but significant proportions, also said they needed help with medical, substance abuse, psychological, and legal problems. The evaluators reported that among the service delivery implications of the needs assessment were indications that this population needs interventions that provide ongoing support in a range of domains at varying degrees of intensity. Thus, to be responsive, programs must have the capacity to deliver or broker access to a comprehensive range of services.

These findings offer two lines of analysis for assessment of program theory. First, any program that intends to alleviate homelessness must provide services that address the major problems that homeless persons experience. That is, the expected outcomes of those services (impact theory) must represent improvements in the most problematic domains if the conditions of the homeless are to be appreciably improved. Second, the design of the service delivery system (program process theory) must be such that multiple services can be readily and flexibly provided to homeless individuals in ways that will be accessible to them despite their limited resources and difficult circumstances. Careful, detailed comparison of the program theory embodied in any program for this homeless population with the respective needs assessment data, therefore, will reveal how sound that theory is as a design for effective intervention.

SOURCE: Daniel B. Herman, Elmer L. Struening, and Susan M. Barrow, "Self-Reported Needs for Help Among Homeless Men and Women," *Evaluation and Program Planning,* 1994, 17(3):249-256.

assessment. Consider, for instance, a school-based educational program aimed at getting elementary school children to learn and practice good eating habits. The problem this program attempts to ameliorate is poor nutritional choices among school-age children, especially those in economically disadvantaged areas. The program impact theory would show a sequence of links between the planned instructional exercises and the children's awareness of the nutritional value of foods, culminating in healthier selections and therefore improved nutrition.

Now, suppose a thorough needs assessment shows that the children's eating habits are, indeed, poor but that their nutritional knowledge is not especially deficient. The needs assessment further shows that the foods served at home and even those offered in the school cafeterias provide limited opportunity for healthy selections. Against this background, it is evident that the program impact theory is flawed. Even if the program successfully imparts additional information about healthy eating, the children will not be able to act on it because they have little control over the selection of foods available to them. Thus, the proximal outcomes the program impact theory describes may be achieved, but they are not what is needed to ameliorate the problem at issue.

Program process theory, on the other hand, represents assumptions about the capability of the program to provide services that are accessible to the target population and compatible with their needs. These assumptions, in turn, can be compared with information about the target population's opportunities to obtain service and the barriers that inhibit them from using the service. The process theory for an adult literacy program that offers evening classes at the local high school, for instance, may incorporate instructional and advertising functions and an appropriate selection of courses for the target population. The details of this scheme can be compared with needs assessment data that show what logistical and psychological support the target population requires to make effective use of the program. Child care and transportation may be critical for some potential participants. Also, illiterate adults may be reluctant to enroll in courses without more personal encouragement than they would receive from advertising. Cultural and personal affinity with the instructors may be important factors in attracting and maintaining participation from the target population as well. The intended program process can thus be assessed in terms of how responsive it is to these dimensions of the needs of the target population.

Assessment of Logic and Plausibility

A thorough job of articulating program theory should reveal the critical assumptions and expectations inherent in the program's design. One essential form of assessment is simply a critical review of the logic and plausibility of these aspects of the program theory. Commentators familiar with assessing program theory suggest that a panel of reviewers be organized for that purpose (Chen, 1990; Rutman, 1980; Smith, 1989; Wholey, 1994). Such an expert review panel should include representatives of the program staff and other major stakeholders as well as the evaluator. By definition, however, stakeholders have some direct stake in the program. To balance the assessment and expand the available expertise, it may be advisable to bring in informed persons with no direct relationship to the program. Such outside experts might include experienced administrators of similar programs, social researchers with relevant specialties, representatives of advocacy groups or client organizations, and the like.

A review of the logic and plausibility of program theory will necessarily be a relatively unstructured and open-ended process. Nonetheless, there are some general issues such reviews should address. These are described below in the form of questions reviewers can ask. Additional useful detail can be found in Rutman (1980), Smith (1989), and Wholey (1994). Also see Exhibit 5-J for an example.

- Are the program goals and objectives well defined? The outcomes for which the program is accountable should be stated in sufficiently clear and concrete terms to permit a determination of whether they have been attained. Goals such as "introducing students to computer technology" are not well defined in this sense, whereas "increasing student knowledge of the ways computers can be used" is well defined and measurable.

- Are the program goals and objectives feasible? That is, is it realistic to assume that they can actually be attained as a result of the services the program delivers? A program theory should specify expected outcomes that are of a nature and scope that might reasonably follow from a successful program and that do not represent unrealistically high expectations. Moreover, the stated goals and objectives should involve conditions the program might actually be able to affect in some meaningful fashion, not those largely beyond its influence. "Eliminating poverty" is grandiose for any program, whereas "decreasing the unemployment rate" is not. But even the latter goal might be unrealistic for a program located in a chronically depressed labor market.

- Is the change process presumed in the program theory plausible? The presumption that a program will create benefits for the intended target population depends on the occurrence of some cause-and-effect chain that begins with the targets' interaction with the program and ends with the improved circumstances in the target population that the program expects to bring about. Every step of this causal chain should be plausible. Because the validity of this impact theory is the key to the program's ability to produce the intended effects, it is best if the theory is supported by evidence that the assumed links and relationships actually occur. For example, suppose a program is based on the presumption that exposure to literature about the health hazards of drug abuse will motivate long-term heroin addicts to renounce drug use. In this case, the program theory does not present a plausible change process, nor is it supported by any research evidence.

- Are the procedures for identifying members of the target population, delivering service to them, and sustaining that service through completion well defined and sufficient? The program theory should specify procedures and functions that are both well defined and adequate for the purpose, viewed both from the perspective

EXHIBIT 5-J

Assessing the
Clarity and
Plausibility of the
Program Theory for
Maryland's 4-H
Program

An evaluability assessment of Maryland's 4-H youth program based on program documents and interviews with 96 stakeholder representatives included a review of key facets of the program's theory with the following results:

Question: Are the mission and goals clear?

Conclusion: There is a lack of clarity about the overall mission of 4-H and some lack of agreement among the stakeholders and between persons directly involved in implementing the program and those not. Among the statements of mission were "introduce youth to farm life," develop "sense of responsibility in agriculture and home economics," and "developing life skills."

Question: Is it clear who is to be affected, who the audience is?

Conclusion: There is some lack of agreement between 4-H faculty and the other stakeholders about the audience of 4-H. Written documents identified the audience as youth and adults; any youth between age 8 and 18 was viewed as the traditional audience for the program; recently, 6- and 7-year-olds have been targeted; some informants viewed the adult volunteers who assist with the program as one audience.

Question: Is there agreement about intended effects?

Conclusion: Social, mental, and physical development were listed as the program objectives in the state program direction document. There was agreement among all groups and in written documents that the effects of 4-H are primarily social in nature, for example, self-confidence/self-esteem, leadership, citizenship. There was less agreement about its effects on mental development and no agreement about its impact on physical development.

Question: Is it plausible that the program activities would achieve the intended effects?

Conclusion: Even if all the activities identified in the program model were implemented according to plan, the plausibility of these leading to the intended program effects is questionable. A link appears to be missing from the program logic—something like "Determine the Curriculum." Lack of such a link prevents plausible activities in the initial program events; that is, without a curriculum plan, how can county faculty know what types of leaders to recruit, what to train volunteers to do, and what they and the volunteers should implement?

SOURCE: Adapted from Midge F. Smith, *Evaluability Assessment: A Practical Approach* (Norwell, MA: Kluwer, 1989), p. 91.

of the program's ability to perform them and the target population's likelihood of being engaged by them. Consider, for example, a program to test for high blood pressure among poor and elderly populations to identify those needing medical care. It is relevant to ask whether this service is provided in locations accessible to members of these groups and whether there is an effective means of locating those with uncertain addresses. Absent these characteristics, it is unlikely that many persons from the target groups will receive the intended service.

- Are the constituent components, activities, and functions of the program well defined and sufficient? A program's structure and process should be specific enough to permit orderly operations, effective management control, and monitoring by means of attainable, meaningful performance measures. Most critical, the program components and activities should be sufficient and appropriate to attain the intended goals and objectives. A function such as "client advocacy" has little practical significance if no personnel are assigned to it or there is no common understanding of what it means operationally.

- Are the resources allocated to the program and its various activities adequate? Program resources include not only funding but also personnel, material, equipment, facilities, relationships, reputation, and other such assets. There should be a reasonable correspondence between the program as described in the program theory and the resources available for operating it. A program theory that calls for activities and outcomes that are unrealistic relative to available resources cannot be said to be a good theory. For example, a management training program too short-staffed to initiate more than a few brief workshops cannot expect to have a significant impact on management skills in the organization.

Assessment Through Comparison With Research and Practice

Although every program is distinctive in some ways, few are based entirely on unique assumptions about how to engender change, deliver service, and perform major program functions. Some information applicable to assessing the various components of program theory is likely to exist in the social science and human services research literature. One useful approach to assessing program theory, therefore, is to find out whether it is congruent with research evidence and practical experience elsewhere (Exhibit 5-K summarizes one example of this approach).

There are several ways in which evaluators might compare a program theory with findings from research and practice. The most straightforward is to examine evaluations of programs based on similar concepts. The results will give some indication of the likelihood that a program will be successful and perhaps identify critical problem

EXHIBIT 5-K
GREAT Program
Theory Is Consistent
With Criminological
Research

In 1991 the Phoenix, Arizona, Police Department initiated a program with local educators to provide youths in the elementary grades with the tools necessary to resist becoming gang members. Known as GREAT (Gang Resistance Education and Training), the program has attracted federal funding and is now distributed nationally. The program is taught to seventh graders in schools over nine consecutive weeks by uniformed police officers. It is structured around detailed lesson plans that emphasize teaching youths how to set goals for themselves, how to resist peer pressure, how to resolve conflicts, and how gangs can affect the quality of their lives.

The program has no officially stated theoretical grounding other than Glasser's (1975) reality therapy, but GREAT training officers and others associated with the program make reference to sociological and psychological concepts as they train GREAT instructors. As part of an analysis of the program's impact theory, a team of criminal justice researchers identified two well-researched criminological theories relevant to gang participation: Gottfredson and Hirschi's self-control theory (SCT) and Akers's social learning theory (SLT). They then reviewed the GREAT lesson plans to assess their consistency with the most pertinent aspects of these theories. To illustrate their findings, a summary of Lesson 4 is provided below with the researchers' analysis in italics after the lesson description:

> Lesson 4. Conflict Resolution: Students learn how to create an atmosphere of understanding that would enable all parties to better address problems and work on solutions together. *This lesson includes concepts related to SCT's anger and aggressive coping strategies. SLT ideas are also present: Instructors present peaceful, nonconfrontational means of resolving conflicts. Part of this lesson deals with giving the student a means of dealing with peer pressure to join gangs and a means of avoiding negative peers with a focus on the positive results (reinforcements) of resolving disagreements by means other than violence. Many of these ideas directly reflect constructs used in previous research on social learning and gangs.*

Similar comparisons showed good consistency between the concepts of the criminological theories and the lesson plans for all but one of the eight lessons. The reviewers concluded that the GREAT curriculum contained implicit and explicit linkages both to self-control theory and social learning theory.

SOURCE: Adapted from L. Thomas Winfree, Jr., Finn-Aage Esbensen, and D. Wayne Osgood, "Evaluating a School-Based Gang-Prevention Program: A Theoretical Perspective," *Evaluation Review*, 1996, 20(2):181-203.

areas. Evaluations of very similar programs, of course, will be the most informative in this regard. However, evaluation results for programs that are similar only in terms of general theory, even if different in other regards, might also be instructive.

Consider a mass media campaign in a metropolitan area to encourage women to have mammogram screening for early detection of breast cancer. The impact theory for this program presumes that exposure to TV, radio, and newspaper messages will stimulate a reaction that will eventuate in increased rates of mammogram screening. The credibility of the impact theory assumed to link exposure and increases in testing is enhanced by evidence that similar media campaigns in other cities have resulted in increased mammogram testing. Moreover, the program's process theory also gains some support if the evaluations for other campaigns shows that the program functions and scheme for delivering messages to the target population were similar to that intended for the program at issue. Suppose, however, that no evaluation results are available about media campaigns promoting mammogram screening in other cities. It might still be informative to examine information about analogous media campaigns. For instance, reports may be available about media campaigns to promote immunizations, dental checkups, or other such actions that are health related and require a visit to a provider. So long as these campaigns involve similar principles, their success might well be relevant to assessing the program theory on which the mammogram campaign is based.

In some instances, basic research on the social and psychological processes central to the program may be available as a framework for assessing the program theory, particularly impact theory. Unfortunately for the evaluation field, relatively little basic research has been done on the social dynamics that are common and important to intervention programs. Where such research exists, however, it can be very useful. For instance, a mass media campaign to encourage mammogram screening involves messages intended to change attitudes and behavior. The large body of basic research in social psychology on attitude change and its relationship to behavior provides some basis for assessing the impact theory for such a media campaign. One established finding is that messages designed to raise fears are generally less effective than those providing positive reasons for a behavior. Thus, an impact theory based on the presumption that increasing awareness of the dangers of breast cancer will prompt increased mammogram screening may not be a good one.

There is also a large applied research literature on media campaigns and related approaches in the field of advertising and marketing. Although this literature largely has to do with selling products and services, it too may provide some basis for assessing the program theory for the breast cancer media campaign. Market segmentation studies, for instance, may show what media and what times of the day are best for reaching women with various demographic profiles. The evaluator can then use this information to examine whether the program's service utilization plan is optimal for communicating with women whose age and circumstances put them at risk for breast cancer.

Use of the research literature to help with assessment of program theory is not limited to situations of good overall correspondence between the programs or processes the evaluator is investigating and those represented in the research. An alternate approach is to break the theory down into its component parts and linkages and search for research evidence relevant to each component. Much of program theory can be stated as "if-then" propositions: If case managers are assigned, then more services will be provided; if school performance improves, then delinquent behavior will decrease; if teacher-to-student ratios are higher, then students will receive more individual attention. Research may be available that indicates the plausibility of individual propositions of this sort. The results, in turn, can provide a basis for a broader assessment of the theory with the added advantage of identifying any especially weak links. This approach was pioneered by the Program Evaluation and Methodology Division of the U.S. General Accounting Office as a way to provide rapid review of program proposals arising in the Congress (Cordray, 1993; U.S. General Accounting Office, 1990).

Assessment Via Preliminary Observation

Program theory, of course, is inherently conceptual and cannot be observed directly. Nonetheless, it involves many assumptions about how things are supposed to work that an evaluator can assess by observing the program in operation, talking to staff and service recipients, and making other such inquiries focused specifically on the program theory. Indeed, a thorough assessment of program theory should incorporate some firsthand observation and not rely entirely on logical analysis and armchair reviews. Direct observation provides a reality check on the concordance between program theory and the program it is supposed to describe.

Consider a program for which it is assumed that distributing brochures about good nutrition to senior citizens centers will influence the eating behavior of persons over age 65. Observations revealing that the brochures are rarely read by anyone attending the centers would certainly raise a question about the assumption that the target population will be exposed to the information in the brochures, a precondition for any attitude or behavior change.

To assess a program's impact theory, the evaluator might conduct observations and interviews focusing on the target-program interactions that are expected to produce the intended outcomes. This inquiry would look into whether those outcomes are appropriate for the program circumstances and whether they are realistically attainable. For example, consider the presumption that a welfare-to-work program can enable a large proportion of welfare clients to find and maintain employment. To gauge how realistic the intended program outcomes are, the evaluator might examine the local job market, the work readiness of the welfare population (number physically and mentally fit, skill levels, work histories, motivation), and the economic benefits of working relative to staying on welfare. At the service end of the change process, the evaluator might observe job training activities and conduct interviews with participants to assess the likelihood that the intended changes would occur.

To test the service utilization component of a program's process theory, the evaluator could examine the circumstances of the target population to better understand how and why they might become engaged with the program. This information would permit an assessment of the quality of the program's service delivery plan for locating, recruiting, and serving the intended clientele. To assess the service utilization plan of a midnight basketball program to reduce delinquency among high-risk youths, for instance, the evaluator might observe the program activities and interview participants, program staff, and neighborhood youths about who participates and how regularly. The program's service utilization assumptions would be supported by indications that the most delinquent-prone youths participate regularly in the program.

Finally, the evaluator might assess the plausibility of the organizational component of the program's process theory through observations and interviews relating to program activities and the supporting resources. Critical here is evidence that the program can actually perform the intended functions. Consider, for instance, a program plan that calls for the sixth-grade science teachers throughout a school district to take their classes on two science-related field trips per year. The evaluator could probe the presumption that this would actually be done by interviewing a number of teachers and principals to find out the feasibility of scheduling, the availability of buses and funding, and the like.

Note that any assessment of program theory that involves collection of new data could easily turn into a full-scale investigation of whether what was presumed in the theory actually happened. Indeed, an empirical "theory testing" study is one obvious approach to assessing program theory (see, e.g., Bickman, 1990; Exhibit 5-L gives an example). Here, however, our focus is on the task of assessing the soundness of the program theory description as a plan, that is, as a statement of the program as intended rather than as a statement of what is actually happening (that assessment comes later). In recognizing the role of observation and interview in the process, we are not suggesting that theory assessment necessarily requires a full evaluation of the program. Instead, we are suggesting that some appropriately configured contact with the program activities, target population, and related situations and informants can provide the evaluator with valuable information about how plausible and realistic the program theory is.

EXHIBIT 5-L
Testing a Model of Patient Education for Diabetes

The daily management of diabetes involves a complex interaction of metabolic variables, self-care behaviors, and psychological and social adjustments to having the disease. An important component of treatment for diabetes, therefore, is the instruction of patients so that they have the skills and knowledge required to do their part. A team of university medical researchers with a particular interest in the personal meaning to patients of having diabetes formulated an impact component theory for the effects of patient education, which they diagrammed as follows:

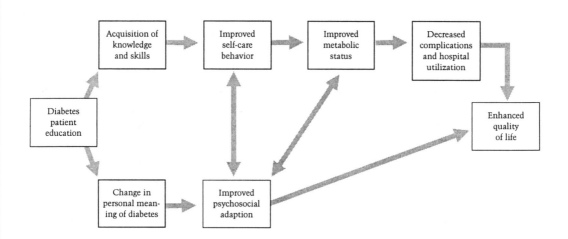

The researchers investigated this model by examining the correlations representing some of the key hypothesized relationships on survey data collected from a sample of 220 people with diabetes recruited from clinics in several states. The data were analyzed using a structural equation analysis which showed only an approximate fit to the model. The relationships between the "personal meaning of diabetes" variables and "psychosocial adaptation" were strong, as were those between knowledge and self-care behavior. However, other relationships in the model were equivocal. The researchers' conclusion was, "While the results showed that the data did not fit the proposed model well enough to allow for definitive conclusions, the results are generally supportive of the original hypothesis that the personal meaning of diabetes is an important element in the daily management of diabetes and the psychosocial adjustment to the disease."

SOURCE: Adapted from George A. Nowacek, Patrick M. O'Malley, Robert A. Anderson, and Fredrick E. Richards, "Testing a Model of Diabetes Self-Care Management: A Causal Model Analysis With LISREL," *Evaluation & the Health Professions*, 1990, 13(3):298-314.

Possible Outcomes of Program Theory Assessment

A program whose conceptualization is weak or faulty has little prospect for success even if it adequately operationalizes that conceptualization. Thus, if the program theory is not sound, there is little reason to assess other evaluation issues, such as the program's implementation, impact, or efficiency. Within the framework of evaluability assessment, finding that the program theory is poorly defined or seriously flawed indicates that the program simply is not evaluable.

When assessment of program theory reveals deficiencies in the program theory, one appropriate response is for the responsible parties to redesign the program. Such program reconceptualization may include (1) clarifying goals and objectives; (2) restructuring program components for which the intended activities are not happening, needed, or reasonable; and (3) working with stakeholders to obtain consensus about the logic that connects program activities with the desired outcomes. The evaluator may help in this process as a consultant.

If an evaluation of program process or impact goes forward without articulation of a credible program theory, then a certain amount of ambiguity will be inherent in the results. This ambiguity is potentially twofold. First, if program process theory is not well defined, there is ambiguity about what the program is expected to be doing operationally. This complicates the identification of criteria for judging how well the program is implemented. Such criteria must then be established individually for the various key program functions through some piecemeal process. For instance, administrative criteria may be stipulated regarding the number of clients to serve, the amount of service to provide, and the like, but they will not be integrated into an overall plan for the program.

Second, if there is no adequate specification of the program impact theory, an impact evaluation may be able to determine whether certain outcomes were produced (see Chapters 7-10), but it will be difficult to explain why or—often more important—why not. Poorly specified impact theory limits the ability to identify or measure the intervening variables on which the outcomes may depend and correspondingly, the ability to explain what went right or wrong in producing the expected outcomes. If program process theory is also poorly specified, it will not even be possible to adequately describe the nature of the program that produced, or failed to produce, the outcomes of interest. Evaluation under these circumstances is often referred to as **black box evaluation** to indicate that assessment of outcomes is made without much insight into what is causing those outcomes.

Only a well-defined and well-justified program theory permits ready identification of critical program functions and what is supposed to happen as a result. This structure provides meaningful benchmarks against which both managers and evaluators can compare actual program performance. The framework of program theory, therefore, gives the program a blueprint for effective management and gives the evaluator guidance for designing the process, impact, and efficiency evaluations described in subsequent chapters.

Summary

- Program theory is an aspect of a program that can be evaluated in its own right. Such assessment is important because a program based on weak or faulty conceptualization has little prospect of achieving the intended results.

- The most fully developed approaches to evaluating program theory have been described in the context of evaluability assessment, an appraisal of whether a program's performance can be evaluated and, if so, whether it should be. Evaluability assessment involves describing program goals and objectives, assessing whether the program is well enough conceptualized to be evaluable, and identifying stakeholder interest in evaluation findings. Evaluability assessment may result in efforts by program managers to better conceptualize their program. It may indicate that the program is too poorly defined for evaluation or that there is little likelihood that the findings will be used. Alternatively, it could find that the program theory is well defined and plausible, that evaluation findings will likely be used, and that a meaningful evaluation could be done.

- To assess program theory, it is first necessary for the evaluator to describe the theory in a clear, explicit form acceptable to stakeholders. The aim of this effort is to describe the "program as intended" and its rationale, not the program as it actually is. Three key components that should be included in this description are the program impact theory, the service utilization plan, and the program's organizational plan.

- The assumptions and expectations that make up a program theory may be well formulated and explicitly stated (thus constituting an articulated program theory), or they may be inherent in the program but not overtly stated (thus constituting an implicit program theory). When a program theory is implicit, the evaluator must extract and articulate the theory by collating and integrating information from program documents, interviews with program personnel and other stakeholders, and observations of program activities. It is especially important to formulate clear, concrete statements of the program's goals and objectives as well as an account of how the desired outcomes are expected to result from program action. The evaluator should seek corroboration from stakeholders that the resulting description meaningfully and accurately describes the "program as intended."

- There are several approaches to assessing program theory. The most important assessment the evaluator can make is based on a comparison of the intervention specified in the program theory with the social needs the program is expected to address. Examining critical details of the program conceptualization in relation to the social problem indicates whether the program represents a reasonable plan for ameliorating that problem. This analysis is facilitated when a needs assessment has been conducted to systematically diagnose the problematic social conditions (Chapter 4).

■ A complementary approach to assessing program theory uses stakeholders and other informants to appraise the clarity, plausibility, feasibility, and appropriateness of the program theory as formulated.

■ Program theory also can be assessed in relation to the support for its critical assumptions found in research or documented practice elsewhere. Sometimes findings are available for similar programs, or programs based on similar theory, so that the evaluator can make an overall comparison between a program's theory and relevant evidence. If the research and practice literature does not support overall comparisons, however, evidence bearing on specific key relationships assumed in the program theory may still be obtainable.

■ Evaluators can often usefully supplement other approaches to assessment with direct observations to further probe critical assumptions in the program theory.

■ Assessment of program theory may indicate that the program is not evaluable because of basic flaws in its theory. Such findings are an important evaluation product in their own right and can be informative for program stakeholders. In such cases, one appropriate response is to redesign the program, a process in which the evaluator may serve as a consultant. If evaluation proceeds without articulation of a credible program theory, the results will be ambiguous. In contrast, a sound program theory provides a basis for evaluation of how well that theory is implemented, what outcomes are produced, and how efficiently they are produced, topics to be discussed in subsequent chapters.

KEY CONCEPTS

Articulated program theory

An explicitly stated version of program theory that is spelled out in some detail as part of a program's documentation and identity or as a result of efforts by the evaluator and stakeholders to formulate the theory.

Black box evaluation

Evaluation of program outcomes without the benefit of an articulated program theory to provide insight into what is presumed to be causing those outcomes and why.

Evaluability assessment

Negotiation and investigation undertaken jointly by the evaluator, the evaluation sponsor, and possibly other stakeholders to determine whether a program meets the preconditions for evaluation and, if so, how the evaluation should be designed to ensure maximum utility.

Impact theory

A causal theory describing cause-and-effect sequences in which certain program activities are the instigating causes and certain social benefits are the effects they eventually produce.

Implicit program theory

Assumptions and expectations inherent in a program's services and practices that have not been fully articulated and recorded.

Organizational plan

Assumptions and expectations about what the program must do to bring about the transactions between the target population and the program that will produce the intended changes in social conditions. The program's organizational plan is articulated from the perspective of program management and encompasses both the functions and activities the program is expected to perform and the human, financial, and physical resources required for that performance.

Process theory

The combination of the program's organizational plan and its service utilization plan into an overall description of the assumptions and expectations about how the program is supposed to operate.

Service utilization plan

Assumptions and expectations about how the target population will make initial contact with the program and be engaged with it through the completion of the intended services. In its simplest form, a service utilization plan describes the sequence of events through which the intended clients are expected to interact with the intended services.

6

Assessing and Monitoring Program Process

Chapter Outline

What Is Program Process Evaluation and Monitoring?
Setting Criteria for Judging Program Process
Common Forms of Program Process Evaluations
Process or Implementation Evaluation
Continuous Program Process Evaluation (Monitoring) and Management Information Systems

Perspectives on Program Process Monitoring
Process Monitoring From the Evaluator's Perspective
Process Monitoring From an Accountability Perspective
Process Monitoring From a Management Perspective

Monitoring Service Utilization
Coverage and Bias
Measuring and Monitoring Coverage
Program Records
Surveys
Assessing Bias: Program Users, Eligibles, and Dropouts

Monitoring Organizational Functions
Service Delivery Is Fundamental
"Nonprograms" and Incomplete Intervention
Wrong Intervention
Unstandardized Intervention
The Delivery System
Specification of Services
Accessibility
Program Support Functions

Analysis of Program Process Monitoring Data
 Description of the Program Operation
 Comparison Between Sites
 Conformity of the Program to Its Design

———————————————

To be effective in bringing about the desired improvements in social conditions, a program needs more than a good plan of attack. Most important, the program must implement its plan; that is, it must actually carry out its intended functions in the intended way.

Although implementing a program concept may seem straightforward, in practice it is often very difficult. Social programs typically must contend with many adverse influences that can compromise even well-intentioned attempts to conduct program business appropriately. The result can easily be substantial discrepancies between the program as intended and the program as actually implemented.

The implementation of a program is reflected in concrete form in the program processes that it puts in place. An important evaluation function, therefore, is to assess the adequacy of program process: the program activities that actually take place and the services that are actually delivered in routine program operation. This chapter introduces the procedures evaluators use to investigate these issues.

After signing a new bill, President John F. Kennedy is reputed to have said to his aides, "Now that this bill is the law of the land, let's hope we can get our government to carry it out." Both those in high places and those on the front lines are often justified in being skeptical about the chances that a social program will be appropriately implemented. Many steps are required to take a program from concept to full operation, and much effort is needed to keep it true to its original design and purposes. Thus, whether any program is fully carried out as envisioned by its sponsors and managers is always problematic.

Ascertaining how well a program is operating, therefore, is an important and useful form of evaluation, known as *program process evaluation*. (A widely used alternative label is *implementation evaluation*.) It does not represent a single distinct evaluation procedure but, rather, a family of approaches, concepts, and methods. The defining theme of program process evaluation (or simply process evaluation) is a focus on the enacted program itself—its operations, activities, functions, performance, component parts, resources, and so forth. When process evaluation involves an ongoing effort to measure and record information about the program's operation, we will refer to it as *program process monitoring.*

What Is Program Process Evaluation and Monitoring?

As was suggested in Chapter 2, evaluators often distinguish between process (or implementation) evaluation and outcome (or impact) evaluation. Process evaluation, in Scheirer's (1994) words, "verifies what the program is and whether or not it is delivered as intended to the targeted recipients." It does not, however, attempt to assess the effects of the program on those recipients. Such assessment is the province of impact evaluation, which we consider in later chapters.

Where process evaluation is an ongoing function involving repeated measurements over time, it is referred to as program monitoring. Corresponding to the distinction between process and outcome evaluation, **program process monitoring** is the systematic and continual documentation of key aspects of program performance that assesses whether the program is operating as intended or according to some appropriate standard, whereas **outcome monitoring** is the continual measurement of intended outcomes of the program, usually of the social conditions it is intended to improve. We discuss outcome monitoring in conjunction with impact evaluations later in this book.

Program process evaluation generally involves assessments of program performance in the domains of service utilization and program organization. Assessing service utilization consists of examining the extent to which the intended target population receives the intended services. Assessing program organization requires comparing the plan for what the program should be doing with what is actually done, especially with regard to providing services. Usually, program process evaluation is directed at one or both of two key questions: (1) whether a program is reaching the appropriate target population and (2) whether its service delivery and support functions are consistent with program design specifications or other appropriate standards. Process evaluation may also examine what resources are being or have been expended in the conduct of the program.

More specifically, program process evaluation schemes are designed to answer such evaluation questions as these:

- How many persons are receiving services?

- Are those receiving services the intended targets?

- Are they receiving the proper amount, type, and quality of services?

- Are there targets who are not receiving services or subgroups within the target population who are underrepresented among those receiving services?

- Are members of the target population aware of the program?

- Are necessary program functions being performed adequately?

- Is staffing sufficient in numbers and competencies for the functions that must be performed?

- Is the program well organized? Do staff work well with each other?

- Does the program coordinate effectively with the other programs and agencies with which it must interact?

- Are resources, facilities, and funding adequate to support important program functions?

- Are resources used effectively and efficiently?

- Is the program in compliance with requirements imposed by its governing board, funding agencies, and higher-level administration?

- Is the program in compliance with applicable professional and legal standards?

- Is performance at some program sites or locales significantly better or poorer than at others?

- Are participants satisfied with their interactions with program personnel and procedures?

- Are participants satisfied with the services they receive?

- Do participants engage in appropriate follow-up behavior after service?

Setting Criteria for Judging Program Process

It is important to recognize the evaluative themes in process evaluation questions such as those listed above. Virtually all involve words such as *appropriate, adequate, sufficient, satisfactory, reasonable, intended,* and other phrasing indicating that an evaluative judgment is required. To answer these questions, therefore, the evaluator or other responsible parties must not only describe the program's performance but also assess whether it is satisfactory. This, in turn, requires that there be some bases for making judgments, that is, some defensible criteria or standards to apply. Where such criteria are not already articulated and endorsed, the evaluator may find that establishing workable criteria is as difficult as determining program performance on the pertinent dimensions.

There are several approaches to the matter of setting criteria for program performance. Moreover, different approaches will likely apply to different dimensions of program performance because the considerations that go into defining, say, what constitutes an appropriate number of clients served are quite different from those pertinent to deciding what constitutes an adequate level of resources. This said, the approach to the criterion issue that has the broadest scope and most general utility in program process evaluation is the application of program theory as described in Chapter 5.

Recall that program theory, as we presented it, is divided into program process theory and program impact theory. Program process theory is formulated to describe the program as intended in a form that virtually constitutes a plan or blueprint for what the program is expected to do and how. As such, it is particularly relevant to program process evaluation. Recall also that program theory builds on needs assessment (whether systematic or informal) and thus connects the program design with the social conditions the program is intended to ameliorate. And, of course, the process through which theory is derived and adopted usually involves input from the major stakeholders and, ultimately, their endorsement. Program theory thus has a certain authority in delineating what a program "should" be doing and, correspondingly, what constitutes adequate performance.

Program process evaluation, therefore, can be built on the scaffolding of program process theory. Process theory identifies the aspects of program performance that are most important to describe and also provides some indication of what level of performance is intended, thereby providing the basis for assessing whether actual performance measures up. Exhibit 5-E in the previous chapter, for instance, illustrates the service utilization component of the program process theory for an aftercare program for released psychiatric patients. This flowchart depicts, step by step, the interactions and experiences patients released from the hospital are supposed to have as a result of program service. A thorough monitoring procedure would systematically document what actually happened at each step. In particular, it would report how many patients were released from the hospital each month, what proportion were visited by a social worker, how many were referred to services and which services, how many actually received those services, and so forth.

If the program processes that are supposed to happen do not happen, then we would judge the program's performance to be poor. In actuality, of course, the situation is rarely so simple. Most often, critical events will not occur in an all-or-none fashion but will be attained to some higher or lower degree. Thus, some, but not all, of the released patients will receive visits from social workers, some will be referred to services, and so forth. Moreover, there may be important quality dimensions. For instance, it would not represent good program performance if a released patient was referred to several community services, but these services were inappropriate to the patient's needs. To determine how much must be done, or how well, we need additional criteria that parallel the information the monitoring procedure provides. If the monitoring procedure reports that 63% of the released patients are visited by a social worker within two weeks of release, we cannot evaluate that performance without some standard that tells us what percentage is "good." Is 63% a poor performance, given that we might expect 100% to be desirable, or is it a very impressive performance with a clientele that is difficult to locate and serve?

The most common and widely applicable criteria for such situations are simply **administrative standards** or objectives, that is, stipulated achievement levels set by program administrators or other responsible parties. For example, the director and staff of a job training program may commit to attaining 80% completion rates for the training or to having 60% of the participants permanently employed six months after receiving training. For the aftercare program above, the administrative target might be to have 75% of the patients visited within two weeks of release from the hospital. By this standard, the 63% found with program monitoring is a subpar performance that, nonetheless, is not too far below the mark.

Administrative standards and objectives for program process performance may be set on the basis of past experience, the performance of comparable programs, or simply the professional judgment of program managers or advisers. If they are reasonably justified, they can provide meaningful standards against which to assess observed program performance. In a related vein, some aspects of program performance may fall under applicable legal, ethical, or professional standards. The "standards of care" adopted in medical practice for treating common ailments, for instance, provide a set of criteria against which to assess program performance in health care settings. Similarly, state children's protective services almost always have legal requirements to meet concerning handling cases of possible child abuse or neglect.

In practice, the assessment of particular dimensions of program process performance is often not based on specific, predetermined criteria but represents an after-the-fact judgment call. This is the "I'll know it when I see it" school of thought on what constitutes good program performance. An evaluator who collects process data on, say, the proportion of high-risk adolescents who recall seeing program-sponsored antidrug media messages may find program staff and other key stakeholders resistant to stating what an acceptable proportion would be. If the results come in at 50%, however, a consensus may arise that this is rather good considering the nature of the population, even though some stakeholders might have reported much higher expectations prior to seeing the data. Other findings, such as 40% or 60%, might also be considered rather good. Only extreme findings, say 10%, might strike all stakeholders as distressingly low. In short, without specific before-measurement criteria a wide range of performance might be regarded as acceptable. Of course, assessment procedures that are too flexible and that lead to a "pass" for all tend to be useless.

Very similar considerations apply to the organizational component of the process theory. A depiction of the organizational plan for the aftercare program was presented in Exhibit 5-F in Chapter 5. Looking back at it will reveal that it, too, identifies dimensions of program performance that can be described and assessed against appropriate standards. Under that plan, for instance, case managers are expected to interview clients and families, assess service needs, make referrals to services, and so forth. A program process evaluation would document and assess what was done under each of those categories.

Common Forms of Program Process Evaluations

Description and assessment of program process are quite common in program evaluation, but the approaches used are varied, as is the terminology they employ. Such assessments may be conducted as a one-shot endeavor or may be continuous so that information is produced regularly over an extended period of time, as in program process monitoring. They may be conducted by "outside" or "inside" evaluators or be set up as management tools with little involvement by professional evaluators. Moreover, their purpose may be to provide feedback for managerial purposes, to demonstrate accountability to sponsors and decisionmakers, to provide a freestanding process evaluation, or to augment an impact evaluation. Amid this variety, we distinguish two principal forms of program process studies, process or implementation evaluation and continuous program monitoring.

Process or Implementation Evaluation

Process or implementation evaluation is typically conducted by evaluation specialists as a separate project that may involve program personnel but is not integrated into their daily routine. When completed and, often, while under way, process evaluation generally provides information about program performance to program managers and other stakeholders, but is not a regular and continuing part of a program's operation. Exhibit 6-A describes a process evaluation of an integrated services program for children.

As an evaluation approach, process evaluation plays two major roles. First, it can stand alone as an evaluation of a program in circumstances where the only questions at issue are about the integrity of program operations, service delivery, and other such matters. There are several kinds of situations that fit this description. A stand-alone process evaluation might be appropriate for a relatively new program, for instance, to answer questions about how well it has established its intended operations and

EXHIBIT 6-A
Process Evaluation to Assess Integrated Services for Children

Many analysts have observed that the traditional system of categorical funding for children's services, with funds allocated to respond to specific problems under strict rules regarding eligibility and expenditures, has not served children's needs well. The critics argue that this system fragments services and inhibits collaboration between programs that might otherwise lead to more effective services. In 1991, the Robert Wood Johnson Foundation launched the Child Health Initiative to test the feasibility of achieving systemic changes through the integration of children's services and finances. Specifically, the initiative called for the development of the following components:

- A decategorization mechanism that would pool existing categorical program funds and create a single children's health fund

- A care coordination procedure using case management that would use the pooled funds to provide comprehensive and continuous care for needy children

- A monitoring system that would identify the health and related needs of children in the community and the gaps in existing services

Nine sites across the country were selected to launch demonstration programs. The Institute for Health Policy Studies, University of California, San Francisco, conducted an evaluation of these programs with two major goals: (1) to gauge the degree to which the implementation of the projects was consistent with the original planning objectives (fidelity to the model) and (2) to assess the extent to which each of the major program components was implemented. In the first year, the evaluation focused on the political, organizational, and design phase of program development. During subsequent years, the focus turned to implementation and preliminary outcomes. A combination of methods was used, including site visits, written surveys completed by the program managers, in-depth interviews of key participants, focus groups of service providers and clients, and reviews of project-related documents.

The evaluation found that most of the nine sites experienced some degree of success in implementing the monitoring and care coordination components, but none was able to implement decategorization. The general findings for each component were as follows:

- Decategorization: Several sites successfully created small pools of flexible funds, but these were from sources other than categorical program funds. No site was able to fully implement decategorization under the definitions originally adopted.

- Care coordination: This was implemented successfully by most of the sites at the client level through case management, but there was generally less coordination at the system level.

- Monitoring: The sites encountered a number of barriers in successfully completing this task, but most instituted some appropriate process.

SOURCE: Adapted from Claire Brindis, Dana C. Hughes, Neal Halfon, and Paul W. Newacheck, "The Use of Formative Evaluation to Assess Integrated Services for Children," *Evaluation & the Health Professions*, 1998, 21(1):66-90.

services. Program process is often the focus of formative evaluation designed to provide useful feedback to managers and sponsors of new programs. In the case of a more established program, a process evaluation might be called for when questions arise about how well the program is organized, the quality of its services, or the success with which it is reaching the target population. A process evaluation may also constitute the major evaluation approach to a program charged with delivering a service known or presumed effective, so that the most significant performance issue is whether that service is being delivered properly. In a managed care environment, for instance, process evaluation may be employed to assess whether the prescribed medical treatment protocols are being followed for patients in different diagnostic categories.

The second major role of process or implementation evaluation is as a complement to an impact evaluation. Indeed, it is generally not advisable to conduct an impact evaluation without including at least a minimal process evaluation. Because maintaining an operational program and delivering appropriate services on an ongoing basis are formidable challenges, it is not generally wise to take program implementation for granted. A full impact evaluation, therefore, includes a process component to determine what quality and quantity of services the program provides so that this information can be integrated with findings on what impact those services have.

Continuous Program Process Evaluation (Monitoring) and Management Information Systems

The second broad form of program process evaluation consists of continuous monitoring of indicators of selected aspects of program process. Such process monitoring can be a useful tool for facilitating effective management of social programs by providing regular feedback about how well the program is performing its critical functions. This type of feedback allows managers to take corrective action when problems arise and can also provide stakeholders with regular assessments of program performance. For these reasons, a form of process assessment is often integrated into the routine information systems of social programs so that appropriate data are obtained, compiled, and periodically summarized. In such cases, process evaluation becomes coextensive with the **management information system (MIS)** in a human service program. Exhibit 6-B describes an MIS that was developed for a marital and family counseling program.

MISs routinely provide information on a client-by-client basis about services provided, staff providing the services, diagnosis or reasons for program participation, sociodemographic data, treatments and their costs, outcome status, and so on. Some of the systems bill clients (or funders), issue payments for services, and store other information, such as a client's treatment history and current participation in other programs. MISs have become the major data source in many instances because much

EXHIBIT 6-B
An Integrated Information System for a Family and Marriage Counseling Agency in Israel

The Marital and Family Counselling Agency is run under the joint auspices of the Tel Aviv Welfare Department and the School of Social Work at Tel Aviv University. The agency provides marital and family counseling and community services for the Jewish, Muslim, and Christian residents of one of the poorest sections of Tel Aviv.

The integrated information system developed for the agency is designed to follow up clients from the moment they request help to the end of treatment. It is intended to serve the agency and the individual counselors by monitoring the process and outcomes of treatment and providing the data needed to make organizational and clinical decisions. To accomplish this, data are collected on three forms and then programmed into the computerized information system. The data elements include the following:

- Background data provided by the client, for example, sociodemographic characteristics, medical and psychological treatment history, the problems for which they are seeking help, the urgency of those problems, their expectations from treatment, and how they found out about the clinic.

- The McMaster Clinical Rating Scale, a standardized scale that monitors families on the basis of six dimensions of family functioning and overall family health; the counselors fill out this form once a month for each client.

- Retrospective evaluation forms filled out after treatment is completed, one by the counselors and another by the clients. This includes, for example, factual questions about the treatment such as its duration, the problems dealt with, the degree to which the client and counselor agreed on the problems, whether there were issues not addressed and why. It also includes retrospective assessments of the process, evaluations of improvement in the presented problems and the McMaster areas of functioning, and client and counselor satisfaction with the process and outcomes.

The counselors can enter and retrieve data from this system whenever they wish and are given a graph of each client's status every three months to support clinical decisions. Also, reports are generated for the clinic's management. For example, a report of the distribution of clients by ethnic group led to the development of a program located within Arab community centers to better reach that population. Other management reports describe the ways and times at which treatment is terminated, the problems that brought clients to the agency, and the percentage of people who applied for treatment but did not show up for the first session. The information system has also been used for research purposes. For example, studies were conducted on the predictors of treatment success, the comparative perceptions by clients and counselors of the treatment process and outcomes, and gender differences in presenting problems.

SOURCE: Adapted from Rivka Savaya, "The Potential and Utilization of an Integrated Information System at a Family and Marriage Counselling Agency in Israel," *Evaluation and Program Planning,* 1998, 21(1):11-20.

of the information that otherwise would have to be gathered in data collection for process monitoring is available in the program's MIS. Even when a program's MIS is not configured to completely fulfill the requirements of a thoroughgoing process evaluation, it may nonetheless provide a large portion of the information an evaluator needs for such purposes. MISs can thus supply data that can be used by both managers and evaluators.

Perspectives on Program Process Monitoring

There is and should be considerable overlap in the purposes of process monitoring whether they are driven by the information needs of evaluators, program managers and staff, or policymakers, sponsors, and stakeholders. Ideally, the monitoring activities undertaken as part of evaluation should meet the information needs of all these groups. In practice, however, limitations on time and resources may require giving priority to one set of information needs over another. Although there are many exceptions, the perspectives of the three key "consumer groups" on the purposes of program monitoring typically vary. These differences in perspective apply generally to outcome monitoring as well.

Process Monitoring From the Evaluator's Perspective

A number of practical considerations underlie the need for evaluation researchers to monitor program process. All too often a program's impact is sharply diminished and, indeed, sometimes reduced to zero because the appropriate intervention was not delivered, was not delivered to the right targets, or both. We believe that more program failures are due to such implementation problems than to lack of potentially effective services. Process monitoring studies, therefore, are essential to understanding and interpreting impact findings. Knowing what took place is a prerequisite for explaining or hypothesizing why a program did or did not work. Without process monitoring, the evaluator is engaged in "black box" research with no basis for deciding whether a larger dose of the program or a different means of delivering the intervention would have changed the impact results.

Process Monitoring From an Accountability Perspective

Process monitoring information is also critical for those who sponsor and fund programs. Program managers have a responsibility to inform their sponsors and funders of the activities undertaken, the degree of implementation of programs, the problems encountered, and what the future holds (see Exhibit 6-C for one perspective

EXHIBIT 6-C

Program and Service
Utilization Studies

Any service organization, especially in an era of shrinking resources, needs to evaluate its services and activities. Through these evaluative activities, an organization can develop and maintain the flexibility needed to respond to an ever-changing environment. It has been suggested that, even in an ideal world, an organization needs to be self-evaluating. Self-evaluation requires an organization to continually review its own activities and goals and to use the results to modify, if necessary, its programs, goals, and directions.

Within an agency, the essential function of evaluation is to provide data on goal achievement and program effectiveness to a primary audience consisting of administration, middle management, and the governing board. This primary audience, especially the administration and board, is frequently confronted with inquiries from important sources in the external environment, such as legislators and funding agencies. These inquiries often focus on issues of client utilization, accessibility, continuity, comprehension, outcome or effectiveness, and cost. The building block of this information is the patterns of use or client utilization study. The patterns of use study, whether it consists of simple inquiries or highly detailed, sophisticated investigations, is basically a description. It describes who uses services and how. It becomes evaluative when it is related to the requirements or purposes of the organization.

SOURCE: Adapted from G. Landsberg, "Program Utilization and Service Utilization Studies: A Key Tool for Evaluation," *New Directions for Program Evaluation*, no. 20 (San Francisco: Jossey-Bass, December 1983), pp. 93-103.

on this matter). However, evaluators frequently are mandated to provide the same or similar information. Indeed, in some cases the sponsors and funders of programs perceive program evaluators as "their eyes and ears," as a second line of information on what is going on in a particular program.

Government sponsors and funding groups, including Congress, operate in the glare of the mass media. Their actions are also visible to the legislative groups who authorize programs and to government "watchdog" organizations. For example, at the federal level, the Office of Management and Budget, part of the executive branch, wields considerable authority over program development, funding, and expenditures. The U.S. General Accounting Office, an arm of Congress, advises members of the House and Senate on the utility of programs and in some cases conducts evaluations. Both state governments and those of large cities have analogous oversight groups. No social program that receives outside funding, whether public or private, can expect to avoid scrutiny and escape demand for **accountability.**

In addition to funders and sponsors, other stakeholders may press for program accountability. In the face of taxpayers' reservations about spending for social programs, together with the increased competition for resources often resulting from cuts in available funding, all stakeholders are scrutinizing both the programs they support and those they do not. Concerned parties use process monitoring information to lobby for the expansion of programs they advocate or find congenial with their self-interests and the curtailment or abandonment of those programs they disdain. Stakeholders, it should be noted, include the targets themselves. A dramatic illustration of their perspective occurred when President Ronald Reagan telephoned an artificial heart recipient patient to wish him well and, with all of the country listening, the patient complained about not receiving his Social Security check.

Clearly, social programs operate in a political world. It could hardly be otherwise, given the stakes involved. The human and social service industry is not only huge in dollar volume and number of persons employed but is also laden with ideological and emotional baggage. Programs are often supported or opposed by armies of vocal community members; indeed, the social program sector is comparable only to the defense industry in its lobbying efforts, and the stands that politicians take with respect to particular programs often determine their fates in elections. Accountability information is a major weapon that stakeholders use in their battles as advocates and antagonists.

Process Monitoring From a Management Perspective

Management-oriented process monitoring (including use of MISs) often is concerned with the same questions as program process or accountability studies; the differences lie in the purposes to which the findings are to be put. Evaluators' interest in monitoring data generally centers on determining how a program's potential impact is related to its implementation. Accountability studies primarily provide information that decisionmakers, sponsors, and other stakeholders need to judge the appropriateness of program activities and to decide whether a program should be continued, expanded, or contracted. Such studies may use the same information base employed by program management staff, but they are usually conducted in a critical spirit. In contrast, management-oriented monitoring activities are concerned less with making decisive judgments and more with incorporating corrective measures as a regular part of program operations.

Process monitoring from a management perspective is particularly vital during the implementation and pilot testing of new programs, especially innovative ones. No matter how well planned such programs may be, unexpected results and unwanted side effects often surface early in the course of implementation. Program designers and managers need to know rapidly and fully about these problems so that changes can be made as soon as possible in the program design. Suppose, for example, that a medical clinic intended to help working mothers is open only during daylight hours. Monitoring may disclose that, however great the demand is for clinic services, the clinic's hours of operation effectively screen out most of the target population. Or suppose that a program is predicated on the assumption that severe psychological problems are prevalent among children who act out in school. If it is found early on that most such children do not in fact have serious disorders, the program can be modified accordingly.

For programs that have moved beyond the development stage to actual operation, program process monitoring serves management needs by providing information on process and coverage (the extent to which a program reaches its intended targets), and hence feedback on whether the program is meeting specifications. Fine-tuning of the program may be necessary when monitoring information indicates that targets are not being reached, that the implementation of the program costs more than initially projected, or that staff workloads are either too heavy or too light. Managers who neglect to monitor a program fully and systematically risk the danger of administering a program that is markedly different from its mandate.

Where monitoring information is to be used for both managerial and evaluation purposes, some problems must be anticipated. How much information is sensible to collect and report, in what forms, at what frequency, with what reliability, and with what degree of confidentiality are among the major issues on which evaluators and managers may disagree. For example, the experienced manager of a nonprofit children's recreational program may feel that the highest priority is weekly information on attendance. The evaluator, however, may be comfortable with aggregating the data monthly or even quarterly, but may believe that before being reported they should be adjusted to take into account variations in the weather, occurrence of holidays, and so on—even though the necessary adjustments require the use of sophisticated statistical procedures.

A second concern is the matter of proprietary claims on the data. For the manager, monitoring data on, say, the results of a program innovation should be kept confidential until discussed with the research committee of the board of directors and presented at the board meeting. The evaluator may wish immediately to write a paper for publication in the *American Journal of Evaluation.* Or a serious drop in clients from a particular ethnic group may result in the administrator of a program immediately replacing the director of professional services, whereas the evaluator's reaction may be to do a study to determine why the drop occurred. As with all relations between program staff and evaluators in general, negotiation of these matters is essential.

A warning: There are many aspects of program management and administration (such as complying with tax regulations and employment laws or negotiating union contracts) that few evaluators have any special competence to assess. In fact, evaluators trained in social science disciplines and (especially) those primarily involved in academic careers may be unqualified to manage anything. It is wise to keep in mind that the evaluator's role, even when sharing information from an MIS, is not to join the administrators in the running of the organization.

In the remainder of this chapter, we concentrate on the concepts and methods pertinent to monitoring program process in the domains of service utilization and program organization. It is in this area that the competencies of persons trained in social research are most relevant.

Monitoring Service Utilization

A critical issue in program process monitoring is ascertaining the extent to which the intended targets actually receive program services. Target participation concerns both program managers and sponsors. Managing a project effectively requires that target participation be kept at an acceptable level and corrective action be taken if it falls below that level.

Monitoring of service utilization is particularly critical for interventions in which program participation is voluntary or in which participants must learn new procedures, change their habits, or take instruction. For example, community mental health centers designed to provide a broad range of services often fail to attract a significant proportion of those who could benefit from their services. Even homeless patients who had been recently discharged from psychiatric hospitals and encouraged to make use of the services of community mental health centers often failed to contact the centers (Rossi, Fisher, and Willis, 1986). Similarly, a program designed to provide information to prospective home buyers might find that few persons seek the services offered. Hence, program developers need to be concerned with how best to motivate potential targets to seek out the program and participate in it. Depending on the particular case, they might, for example, need to build outreach efforts into the program or pay special attention to the geographic placement of program sites (Boruch, Dennis, and Carter-Greer, 1988).

Coverage and Bias

Service utilization issues typically break down into questions about coverage and bias. Whereas **coverage** refers to the extent to which participation by the target population achieves the levels specified in the program design, **bias** is the degree to which some subgroups participate in greater proportions than others. Clearly, coverage and bias are related. A program that reaches all projected participants and no others is obviously not biased in its coverage. But because few social programs ever achieve total coverage, bias is typically an issue.

Bias can arise out of self-selection; that is, some subgroups may voluntarily participate more frequently than others. It can also derive from program actions. For instance, a program's personnel may react favorably to some clients while rejecting or discouraging others. One temptation commonly faced by programs is to select the most "success prone" targets. Such "creaming" frequently occurs because of the self-interests of one or more stakeholders (a dramatic example is described in Exhibit 6-D). Finally, bias may result from such unforeseen influences as the location of a program office, which may encourage greater participation by a subgroup that enjoys more convenient access to program activities.

Although there are many social programs, such as food stamps, that aspire to serve all or a very large proportion of a defined target population, typically programs do not have the resources to provide services to more than a portion of potential targets. In the latter case, the target definition established during the planning and development of the program frequently is not specific enough. Program staff and sponsors can correct this problem by defining the characteristics of the target population more sharply and by using resources more effectively. For example, establishing a health center to provide medical services to persons in a defined community who do not have regular sources of care may result in such an overwhelming demand that many of those who want services cannot be accommodated. The solution might be to add eligibility criteria that weight such factors as severity of the health problem, family size, age, and income to reduce the size of the target population to manageable proportions while still serving the neediest persons. In some programs, such as WIC (Women's, Infants and Children Nutrition Program) or housing vouchers for the poor, undercoverage is a systemic problem; Congress has never provided sufficient funding to cover all who were eligible, perhaps hoping that budgets could be expanded in the future.

The opposite effect, overcoverage, also occurs. For instance, the TV program *Sesame Street* has consistently captured audiences far exceeding the intended targets (disadvantaged preschoolers), including children who are not at all disadvantaged and even adults. Because these additional audiences are reached at no additional cost, this overcoverage is not a financial drain. It does, however, thwart one of *Sesame Street's* original goals, which was to lessen the gap in learning between advantaged and disadvantaged children.

In other instances, overcoverage can be costly and problematic. Bilingual programs in schools, for instance, have often been found to include many students whose primary language is English. Some school systems whose funding from the program depends on the number of children enrolled in bilingual classes have inflated attendance figures by registering inappropriate students. In other cases, schools have used assignment to

EXHIBIT 6-D

"Creaming" the
Unemployed

When administrators who provide public services choose to provide a disproportionate share of program benefits to the most advantaged segment of the population they serve, they provide grist for the mill of service utilization research. The U.S. Employment Service (USES) offers a clear and significant example of creaming, a practice that has survived half a century of USES expansion, contraction, and reorganization. The USES has as its major aim to provide employers with workers, downplaying the purpose of providing workers with work. This leads the USES to send out the best prospects among the unemployed and to slight the less promising.

It is hardly surprising that USES administrators, a generation after the establishment of the program, stressed the necessity rather than the desirability of an employer-centered service. Its success, by design, depended on serving employers, not the "hard-core" unemployed. As President Lyndon Johnson's task force on urban employment problems noted some two weeks before the 1965 Watts riots, "We have yet to make any significant progress in reaching and helping the truly 'hard-core' disadvantaged."

SOURCE: Adapted from David B. Robertson, "Program Implementation Versus Program Design," *Policy Study Review,* 1984, 3:391-405.

bilingual instruction as a means of ridding classes of "problem children," thus saturating bilingual classes with disciplinary cases.

The most common coverage problem in social interventions, however, is the failure to achieve high target participation, either because of bias in the way targets are recruited or retained or because potential clients are unaware of the program, are unable to use it, or reject it. For example, in most employment training programs only small minorities of those eligible by reason of unemployment ever attempt to participate. Similar situations occur in mental health, substance abuse, and numerous other programs (see Exhibit 6-E). We turn now to the question of how program coverage and bias might be measured as a part of program process monitoring.

Measuring and Monitoring Coverage

Program managers and sponsors alike need to be concerned with both undercoverage and overcoverage. Undercoverage is measured by the proportion of the targets in need of a program that actually participates in it. Overcoverage is often expressed as

EXHIBIT 6-E

The Coverage of the
Food Stamp Program
for the Homeless

Based upon a rigorously designed survey of homeless persons sampled from shelters and food kitchens in American cities with a population of 100,000 and over, Burt and Cohen gave some precise dimensions to what we know is true virtually by definition: The homeless live on food intakes that are inadequate both in quantity and in nutritional content. There is no way that a demographic group whose incomes hover slightly above zero can have adequate diets. That the homeless do not starve is largely a tribute to the food kitchens and shelters that provide them with meals at no cost.

Because most homeless persons are eligible by income for food stamps, their participation rates in that program should be high. But they are not: Burt and Cohen reported that only 18% of the persons sampled were receiving food stamps and almost half had never used them. This is largely because certification for food stamps requires passing a means test, a procedure that requires some documentation. This is not easy for many homeless, who may not have the required documents, an address to receive the stamps, or the capability to fill out the forms.

Moreover, the food stamp program is based on implicit assumptions that participants can readily acquire their foodstuffs in a local food store, prepare servings on a stove, and store food supplies in their dwellings. These assumptions do not apply to the homeless. Of course, food stores do sell some food items that can be consumed without preparation and, with some ingenuity, a full meal of such foods can be assembled. So some benefit can be obtained by the homeless from food stamps, but for most homeless persons food stamps are relatively useless.

Legislation passed in 1986 allowed homeless persons to exchange food stamps for meals offered by nonprofit organizations and made shelter residents in places where meals were served eligible for food stamps. By surveying food providers, shelters, and food kitchens, however, Burt and Cohen found that few meal providers had applied for certification as receivers of food stamps. Of the roughly 3,000 food providers in the sample, only 40 had become authorized.

Furthermore, among those authorized to receive food stamps, the majority had never started to collect food stamps or had started and then abandoned the practice. It made little sense to collect food stamps as payment for meals that otherwise were provided free so that, on the same food lines, food stamp participants were asked to pay for their food with stamps while nonparticipants paid nothing. The only food provider who was able to use the system was one that required either cash payment or labor for meals; for this program, food stamps became a substitute for these payments.

SOURCE: Based on Martha Burt and Barbara Cohen, *Feeding the Homeless: Does the Prepared Meals Provision Help?* Report to Congress on the Prepared Meal Provision, vols. I and II (Washington, DC: Urban Institute, 1988). Reprinted with permission.

the number of program participants who are not in need, compared with the total number of participants in the program. Efficient use of program resources requires both maximizing the number served who are in need and minimizing the number served who are not in need.

The problem in measuring coverage is almost always the inability to specify the number in need, that is, the magnitude of the target population. The needs assessment procedures described in Chapter 4, if carried out as an integral part of program planning, usually minimize this problem. In addition, three sources of information can be used to assess the extent to which a program is serving the appropriate target population: program records, surveys of program participants, and community surveys.

Program Records

Almost all programs keep records on targets served. Data from well-maintained record systems—particularly from MISs—can often be used to estimate program bias or overcoverage. For instance, information on the various screening criteria for program intake may be tabulated to determine whether the units served are the ones specified in the program's design. Suppose the targets of a family planning program are women less than 50 years of age who have been residents of the community for at least six months and who have two or more children under age ten. Records of program participants can be examined to see whether the women actually served are within the eligibility limits and the degree to which particular age or parity groups are under- or overrepresented. Such an analysis might also disclose bias in program participation in terms of the eligibility characteristics or combinations of them. Another example, involving public shelter utilization by the homeless, is described in Exhibit 6-F.

However, programs differ widely in the quality and extensiveness of their records and in the sophistication involved in storing and maintaining them. Moreover, the feasibility of maintaining complete, ongoing record systems for all program participants varies with the nature of the intervention and the available resources. In the case of medical and mental health systems, for example, sophisticated, computerized management and client information systems have been developed for managed care purposes that would be impractical for many other types of programs.

In measuring target participation, the main concerns are that the data are accurate and reliable. It should be noted that all record systems are subject to some degree of error. Some records will contain incorrect or outdated information, and others will be incomplete. The extent to which unreliable records can be used for decision making depends on the kind and degree of their unreliability and the nature of the decisions in question. Clearly, critical decisions involving significant outcomes require better records than do less weighty decisions. Whereas a decision on whether

Exhibit 6-F
Public Shelter
Utilization Among
Homeless Adults in
New York and
Philadelphia

The cities of Philadelphia and New York have standardized admission procedures for persons requesting services from city-funded or -operated shelters. All persons admitted to the public shelter system must provide intake information for a computerized registry that includes the client's name, race, date of birth, and gender, and must also be assessed for substance abuse and mental health problems, medical conditions, and disabilities. A service utilization study conducted by researchers from the University of Pennsylvania analyzed data from this registry for New York City for 1987-1994 (110,604 men and 26,053 women) and Philadelphia for 1991-1994 (12,843 men and 3,592 women).

They found three predominant types of users: (1) the chronically homeless, characterized by very few shelter episodes, but episodes that might last as long as several years; (2) the episodically homeless, characterized by multiple, increasingly shorter stays over a long period; and (3) the transitionally homeless, who had one or two stays of short duration within a relatively brief period of time.

The most notable finding was the size and relative resource consumption of the chronically homeless. In New York, for instance, 18% of the shelter users stayed 180 days or more in their first year, consuming 53% of the total number of system days for first-time shelter users, triple the days for their proportionate representation in the shelter population. These long-stay users tended to be older people and to have mental health, substance abuse, and, in some cases, medical problems.

SOURCE: Adapted by permission from Dennis P. Culhane and Randall Kuhn, "Patterns and Determinants of Public Shelter Utilization Among Homeless Adults in New York City and Philadelphia," *Journal of Policy Analysis and Management,* 1998, 17(1):23-43. Copyright © 1998, John Wiley & Sons, Inc.

to continue a project should not be made on the basis of data derived from partly unreliable records, data from the same records may suffice for a decision to change an administrative procedure.

If program records are to serve an important role in decision making on far-reaching issues, it is usually desirable to conduct regular audits of the records. Such audits are similar in intent to those that outside accountants conduct on fiscal records. For example, records might be sampled to determine whether each target has a record, whether records are complete, and whether rules for completing them have been followed.

Surveys

An alternative to using program records to assess target participation is to conduct special surveys of program participants. Sample surveys may be desirable when the required data cannot be obtained as a routine part of program activities or when the size of the target group is large and it is more economical and efficient to undertake a sample survey than to obtain data on all the participants.

For example, a special tutoring project conducted primarily by parents may be set up in only a few schools in a community. Children in all schools may be referred, but the project staff may not have the time or the training to administer appropriate educational skills tests and other such instruments that would document the characteristics of the children referred and enrolled. Lacking such complete records, an evaluation group could administer tests on a sampling basis to estimate the appropriateness of the selection procedures and assess whether the project is serving the designated target population.

When projects are not limited to selected, narrowly defined groups of individuals but instead take in entire communities, the most efficient and sometimes the only way to examine whether the presumed population at need is being reached is to conduct a community survey. Various types of health, educational, recreational, and other human service programs are often community-wide, although their intended target populations may be selected groups, such as delinquent youths, the aged, or women of childbearing age. In such cases, surveys are the major means of assessing whether targets have been reached.

The evaluation of the *Feeling Good* television program illustrates the use of surveys to provide data on a project with a national audience. The program, an experimental production of the Children's Television Workshop (the producer of *Sesame Street*), was designed to motivate adults to engage in preventive health practices. Although it was accessible to homes of all income levels, its primary purpose was to motivate low-income families to improve their health practices. The Gallup organization conducted four national surveys, each of approximately 1,500 adults, at different times during the weeks *Feeling Good* was televised. The data provided estimates of the size of the viewing audiences as well as of the viewers' demographic, socioeconomic, and attitudinal characteristics (Mielke and Swinehart, 1976). The major finding was that the program largely failed to reach the target group, and the program was discontinued.

To measure coverage of Department of Labor programs, such as training and public employment, the department started a periodic national sample survey. The Survey of Income and Program Participation is now carried out by the Bureau of the Census and measures participation in social programs conducted by many federal departments. This large survey, now a three-year panel covering 21,000 households, ascertains through personal interviews whether each adult member of the sampled households has ever participated or is currently participating in any of a number of federal programs. By contrasting program participants with nonparticipants, the survey provides information on the programs' biases in coverage. In addition, it generates information on the uncovered but eligible target populations.

Assessing Bias: Program Users, Eligibles, and Dropouts

An assessment of bias in program participation can be undertaken by examining differences between individuals who participate in a program and either those who drop out or those who are eligible but do not participate at all. In part, the drop-out rate, or attrition, from a project may be an indicator of clients' dissatisfaction with intervention activities. It also may indicate conditions in the community that militate against full participation. For example, in certain areas lack of adequate transportation may prevent those who are otherwise willing and eligible from participating in a program.

It is important to be able to identify the particular subgroups within the target population who either do not participate at all or do not follow through to full participation. Such information not only is valuable in judging the worth of the effort but also is needed to develop hypotheses about how a project can be modified to attract and retain a larger proportion of the target population. Thus, the qualitative aspects of participation may be important not only for monitoring purposes but also for subsequent program planning.

Data about dropouts may come either from service records or from surveys designed to find nonparticipants. However, community surveys usually are the only feasible means of identifying eligible persons who have not participated in a program. The exception, of course, is when adequate information is available about the entire eligible population prior to the implementation of a project (as in the case of data from a census or screening interview). Comparisons with either data gathered for project planning purposes or community surveys undertaken during and subsequent to the intervention may employ a variety of analytical approaches, from purely descriptive methods to highly complex models.

In Chapter 11, we describe methods of analyzing the costs and benefits of programs to arrive at measures of economic efficiency. Clearly, for calculating costs it is important to have estimates of the size of populations at need or risk, the groups who start a program but drop out, and the ones who participate to completion. The same data may also be used in estimating benefits. In addition, they are highly useful in judging whether a project should be continued and whether it should be expanded in either the same community or other locations. Furthermore, project staff require this kind of information to meet their managerial and accountability responsibilities. Although data on project participation cannot substitute for knowledge of impact in judging either the efficiency or the effectiveness of projects, there is little point in moving ahead with an impact analysis without an adequate description of the extent of participation by the target population.

Monitoring Organizational Functions

Monitoring of the critical organizational functions and activities of a program focuses on whether the program is performing well in managing its efforts and using its resources to accomplish its essential tasks. Chief among those tasks, of course, is delivering the intended services to the target population. In addition, programs have various support functions that must be carried out to maintain the viability and effectiveness of the organization, for example, fund-raising, promotion advocacy, and governance and management. Program process monitoring seeks to determine whether a program's actual activities and arrangements sufficiently approximate the intended ones.

Once again, program process theory as described in Chapter 5 is a useful tool in designing monitoring procedures. In this instance, what we called the organizational plan is the relevant component. A fully articulated process theory will identify the major program functions, activities, and outputs and show how they are related to each other and to the organizational structures, staffing patterns, and resources of the program. This depiction provides a map to guide the evaluator in identifying the significant program functions and the preconditions for accomplishing them. Program process monitoring then becomes a matter of identifying and measuring those activities and conditions most essential to a program's effective performance of its duties.

Service Delivery Is Fundamental

As mentioned earlier in this chapter, for many programs that fail to show impacts, the problem is a failure to deliver the interventions specified in the program design, a problem generally known as *implementation failure.* There are three kinds of implementation failures: First, no intervention, or not enough, is delivered; second, the wrong intervention is delivered; and third, the intervention is unstandardized or uncontrolled and varies excessively across the target population.

"Nonprograms" and Incomplete Intervention

Consider first the problem of the "nonprogram" (Rossi, 1978). McLaughlin (1975) reviewed the evidence on the implementation of Title I of the Elementary and Secondary Education Act, which allocated billions of dollars yearly to aid local schools in overcoming students' poverty-associated educational deprivations. Even though schools had expended the funds, local school authorities were unable to describe their

Title I activities in any detail, and few activities could even be identified as educational services delivered to schoolchildren. In short, little evidence could be found that school programs existed that were directed toward the goal of helping disadvantaged children.

The failure of numerous other programs to deliver services has been documented as well. Datta (1977), for example, reviewed the evaluations on career education programs and found that the designated targets rarely participated in the planned program activities. Similarly, an attempt to evaluate PUSH-EXCEL, a program designed to motivate disadvantaged high school students toward higher levels of academic achievement, disclosed that the program consisted mainly of the distribution of buttons and hortative literature and little else (Murray, 1980).

A delivery system may dilute the intervention so that an insufficient amount reaches the target population. Here the problem may be a lack of commitment on the part of a front-line delivery system, resulting in minimal delivery or "ritual compliance," to the point that the program does not exist. Exhibit 6-G, for instance, expands on an exhibit presented in Chapter 2 to describe the implementation of welfare reform in which welfare workers communicated little to clients about the new policies.

Wrong Intervention

The second category of program failure—namely, delivery of the wrong intervention—can occur in several ways. One is that the mode of delivery negates the intervention. An example is the Performance Contracting experiment, in which private firms that contracted to teach mathematics and reading were paid in proportion to pupils' gains in achievement. The companies faced extensive difficulties in delivering the program at school sites. In some sites the school system sabotaged the experiments, and in others the companies were confronted with equipment failures and teacher hostility (Gramlich and Koshel, 1975).

Another way in which wrong intervention can result is when it requires a delivery system that is too sophisticated. There can be a considerable difference between pilot projects and full-scale implementation of sophisticated programs. Interventions that work well in the hands of highly motivated and trained deliverers may end up as failures when administered by staff of a mass delivery system whose training and motivation are less. The field of education again provides an illustration: Teaching methods such as computer-assisted learning or individualized instruction that have worked well within experimental development centers have not fared as well in ordinary school systems because teachers did not have sufficient computer skills.

The distinction made here between an intervention and its mode of delivery is not always clear-cut. The difference is quite clear in income maintenance programs, in which the "intervention" is the money given to beneficiaries and the delivery modes vary from automatic deposits in savings or checking accounts to hand

EXHIBIT 6-G

On the Front Lines:
Are Welfare Workers
Implementing Policy
Reforms?

In the early 1990s, the state of California initiated the Work Pays demonstration project, which expanded the state job preparation program (JOBS) and modified Aid to Families with Dependent Children (AFDC) welfare policies to increase the incentives and support for finding employment. The Work Pays demonstration was designed to "substantially change the focus of the AFDC program to promote work over welfare and self-sufficiency over welfare dependence."

The workers in the local welfare offices were a vital link in the implementation of Work Pays. The intake and redetermination interviews they conducted represented virtually the only in-person contact that most clients had with the welfare system. This fact prompted a team of evaluators to study how welfare workers were communicating the Work Pays policies during their interactions with clients.

The evaluators reasoned that worker-client transactions appropriate to the policy would involve certain "information content" and "use of positive discretion." Information content refers to the explicit messages delivered to clients; it was expected that workers would notify clients about the new program rules for work and earnings, explain opportunities to combine work and welfare to achieve greater self-sufficiency, and inform them about available training and supportive services. Positive discretion relates to the discretion workers have in teaching, socializing, and signaling clients about the expectations and opportunities associated with welfare receipt. Workers were expected to emphasize the new employment rules and benefits during client interviews and communicate the expectation that welfare should serve only as temporary assistance while recipients prepared for work.

To assess the welfare workers' implementation of the new policies, the evaluators observed and analyzed the content of 66 intake or redetermination interviews between workers and clients in four counties included in the Work Pays demonstration. A structured observation form was used to record the frequency with which various topics were discussed and to collect information about the characteristics of the case. These observations were coded on the two dimensions of interest: (1) information content and (2) positive discretion.

The results, in the words of the evaluators:

> In over 80% of intake and redetermination interviews workers did not provide and interpret information about welfare reforms. Most workers continued a pattern of instrumental transactions that emphasized workers'

(Continued)

EXHIBIT 6-G
(Continued)

needs to collect and verify eligibility information. Some workers coped with the new demand by providing information about work-related policies, but routinizing the information and adding it to their standardized, scripted recitations of welfare rules. Others were coping by particularizing their interactions, giving some of their clients some information some of the time, on an ad hoc basis.

These findings suggest that welfare reforms were not fully implemented at the street level in these California counties. Worker-client transactions were consistent with the processing of welfare claims, the enforcement of eligibility rules, and the rationing of scarce resources such as JOBS services; they were poorly aligned with new program objectives emphasizing transitional assistance, work, and self-sufficiency outside the welfare system. (pp. 18-19)

SOURCE: Adapted by permission from Marcia K. Meyers, Bonnie Glaser, and Karin MacDonald, "On the Front Lines of Welfare Delivery: Are Workers Implementing Policy Reforms?" *Journal of Policy Analysis and Management,* 1998, 17(1):1-22. Copyright © 1998, John Wiley & Sons, Inc.

delivery of cash to recipients. Here the intent of the program is to place money in the hands of recipients; the delivery, whether by electronic transfer or by hand, has little effect on the intervention. In contrast, a counseling program may be handled by retraining existing personnel, hiring counselors, or employing certified psychotherapists. In this case, the distinction between treatment and mode of delivery is fuzzy, because it is generally acknowledged that counseling treatments vary by counselor.

Unstandardized Intervention

The final category of implementation failures includes those that result from unstandardized or uncontrolled interventions. This problem can arise when the design of the program leaves too much discretion in implementation to the delivery system, so that the intervention can vary significantly across sites. Early programs of the Office of Economic Opportunity provide examples. The Community Action Program (CAP) gave local communities considerable discretion in choosing among a variety of actions, requiring only "maximum feasible participation" on the part of the poor. Because of the resulting disparities in the programs of different cities, it is almost impossible to document what CAP programs accomplished (Vanecko and Jacobs, 1970).

Similarly, Project Head Start gave local communities funds to set up preschool teaching projects for underprivileged children. In its first decade, Head Start centers varied by sponsoring agencies, coverage, content, staff qualifications, objectives, and a host of other characteristics (Cicirelli, Cooper, and Granger, 1969). Because there was no specified Head Start design, it was not possible to conclude from an evaluation of a sample of projects whether the Head Start concept worked. The only generalization that could be made was that some projects were effective, some were ineffective, and, among the effective ones, some were more successful than others. Only in the past decade has a degree of standardization been achieved to the point that in 2001 it was possible to design and start an evaluation that promises to provide estimates of the program's effectiveness (Advisory Committee on Head Start Research and Evaluation, 1999).

The Delivery System

A program's delivery system can be thought of as a combination of pathways and actions undertaken to provide an intervention. It usually consists of a number of separate functions and relationships. As a general rule, it is wise to assess all the elements unless previous experience with certain aspects of the delivery system makes their assessment unnecessary. Two concepts are especially useful for monitoring the performance of a program's delivery system: specification of services and accessibility.

Specification of Services

A specification of services is desirable for both planning and monitoring purposes. This consists of specifying the actual services provided by the program in operational (measurable) terms. The first task is to define each kind of service in terms of the activities that take place and the providers who participate. When possible, it is best to separate the various aspects of a program into separate, distinct services. For example, if a project providing technical education for school dropouts includes literacy training, carpentry skills, and a period of on-the-job apprenticeship work, it is advisable to separate these into three services for monitoring purposes. Moreover, for estimating program costs in cost-benefit analyses and for fiscal accountability, it is often important to attach monetary values to different services. This step is important when the costs of several programs will be compared or when the programs receive reimbursement on the basis of the number of units of different services that are provided.

For program process monitoring, simple, specific services are easier to identify, count, and record. However, complex elements often are required to design an implementation that is consistent with a program's objectives. For example, a clinic for children may require a physical exam on admission, but the scope of the exam and the tests ordered may depend on the characteristics of each child. Thus, the item "exam" is a service but its components cannot be broken out further without creating a different definition of the service for each child examined. The strategic question is how to strike a balance, defining services so that distinct activities can be identified and counted reliably while, at the same time, the distinctions are meaningful in terms of the program's objectives.

In situations where the nature of the intervention allows a wide range of actions that might be performed, it may be possible to describe services primarily in terms of the general characteristics of the service providers and the time they spend in service activities. For example, if a project places master craftspersons in a low-income community to instruct community members in ways to improve their dwelling units, the craftspersons' specific activities will probably vary greatly from one household to another. They may advise one family on how to frame windows and another on how to shore up the foundation of a house. Any monitoring scheme attempting to document such services could describe the service activities only in general terms and by means of examples. It is possible, however, to specify the characteristics of the providers—for example, that they should have five years of experience in home construction and repair and knowledge of carpentry, electrical wiring, foundations, and exterior construction—and the amount of time they spend with each service recipient.

Indeed, services are often defined in terms of units of time, costs, procedures, or products. In a vocational training project, service units may refer to hours of counseling time provided; in a program to foster housing improvement, they may be defined in terms of amounts of building materials provided; in a cottage industry project, service units may refer to activities, such as training sessions on how to operate sewing machines; and in an educational program, the units may be instances of the use of specific curricular materials in classrooms. All these examples require an explicit definition of what constitutes a service and, for that service, what units are appropriate for describing the amount of service.

Accessibility

Accessibility is the extent to which structural and organizational arrangements facilitate participation in the program. All programs have a strategy of some sort for providing services to the appropriate target population. In some instances, being accessible may simply mean opening an office and operating under the assumption that the designated participants will "naturally" come and make use of the services provided at the site. In other instances, however, ensuring accessibility requires outreach campaigns to recruit participants, transportation to bring persons to the intervention site, and efforts during the intervention to minimize dropouts. For example, in many large cities, special teams are sent out into the streets on very cold nights to persuade homeless persons sleeping in exposed places to spend the night in shelters.

A number of evaluation questions arise in connection with accessibility, some of which relate only to the delivery of services and some of which have parallels to the previously discussed topic of service utilization. The primary issue is whether program actions are consistent with the design and intent of the program with regard to facilitating access. For example, is there a Spanish-speaking staff member always available in a mental health center located in an area with a large Hispanic population?

Also, are potential targets matched with the appropriate services? It has been observed, for example, that community members who originally make use of emergency medical care for appropriate purposes may subsequently use them for general medical care. Such misuse of emergency services may be costly and reduce their availability to other community members. A related issue is whether the access strategy encourages differential use by targets from certain social, cultural, and ethnic groups, or whether there is equal access for all potential targets.

Program Support Functions

Although providing the intended services is presumed to be a program's main function, and one essential to monitor, most programs also perform important support functions that are critical to their ability to maintain themselves and continue to provide service. These functions are of interest to program administrators, of course, but often they are also relevant to monitoring by evaluators or outside decisionmakers. Vital support functions may include such activities as fund-raising; public relations to enhance the program's image with potential sponsors, decisionmakers, or the general public; staff training, including the training of the direct service staff; recruiting and retention of key personnel; developing and maintaining relationships with affiliated programs, referral sources, and the like; obtaining materials required for services; and general advocacy on behalf of the target population served.

Program process monitoring schemes can, and often should, incorporate indicators of vital program support functions along with indicators relating to service activities. In form, such indicators and the process for identifying them are no different than for program services. The critical activities first must be identified and described in specific, concrete terms resembling service units, for example, units of fund-raising activity and dollars raised, training sessions, advocacy events, and the like. Measures are then developed that are capable of differentiating good from poor performance and that can be regularly collected. These measures are then included in the program monitoring procedures along with those dealing with other aspects of program performance.

Analysis of Program Process Monitoring Data

Data, of course, are useful only when they have been appropriately analyzed. In general, the analysis of program process monitoring data addresses the following three issues: description of the program operation, comparison between sites, and conformity of the program to its design.

Description of the Program Operation

Assessing the extent to which a program as implemented resembles the program as designed depends on having a full and accurate description of how the program actually operates. A description derived from program process monitoring data would cover the following topics: estimates of coverage and bias in participation, the types of services delivered, the intensity of services given to participants of significant kinds, and the reactions of participants to the services delivered. Descriptive statements might take the form of narrative accounts, especially when monitoring data are derived from qualitative sources, or quantitative summaries in the form of tables, graphs, and the like.

Comparison Between Sites

When a program includes more than one site, a second question concerns differences in program implementation between the sites. Comparison of sites permits an understanding of the sources of diversity in program implementation and, ultimately, outcomes, such as differences in staff, administration, targets, or surrounding environments, and it also can facilitate efforts to achieve standardization.

Conformity of the Program to Its Design

The third issue is the one with which we began: the degree of conformity between a program's design and its implementation. Shortfalls may occur because the program is not performing functions it is expected to or because it is not performing them as well as expected. Such discrepancies may lead to efforts to move the implementation of a project closer to the original design or to a respecification of the design itself. Such analysis also provides an opportunity to judge the appropriateness of performing an impact evaluation and, if necessary, to opt for more formative evaluation to develop the desired convergence of design and implementation.

Summary

- Program process evaluation is a form of evaluation designed to describe how a program is operating and assess how well it performs its intended functions. It builds on program process theory, which identifies the critical components, functions, and relationships assumed necessary for the program to be effective. Where process evaluation is an ongoing function involving repeated measurements over time, it is referred to as program process monitoring.

- The criteria for assessing program process performance may include stipulations of the program theory, administrative standards, applicable legal, ethical, or professional standards, and after-the-fact judgment calls.

- The common forms of program process evaluation include process (or implementation) evaluation and program process monitoring.

- Process evaluation assesses whether the program is delivered as intended to the targeted recipients and is typically conducted as a separate project by evaluation specialists. It may constitute a stand-alone evaluation when the only questions are about implementation of program operations, service delivery, and other such matters. Process evaluation is also often carried out in conjunction with an impact evaluation to determine what services the program provides to complement findings about what impact those services have.

- When a program has a well-developed MIS, program process monitoring can be integrated into a program's routine information collection and reporting.

- Program process monitoring takes somewhat different forms and serves different purposes when undertaken from the perspectives of evaluation, accountability, and program management, but the types of data required and the data collection procedures used generally are the same or overlap considerably. In particular, program process monitoring generally involves one or both of two domains of program performance: service utilization and organizational functions.

- Service utilization issues typically break down into questions about coverage and bias. The sources of data useful for assessing coverage are program records, surveys of program participants, and community surveys. Bias in program coverage can be revealed through comparisons of program users, eligible nonparticipants, and dropouts.

- Monitoring of a program's organizational functions focuses on how well the program is organizing its efforts and using its resources to accomplish its essential tasks. Particular attention is given to identifying shortcomings in program implementation that prevent a program from delivering the intended services to the target population. Three sources of such implementation failures are incomplete interventions, delivery of the wrong intervention, and unstandardized or uncontrolled interventions.

■ Monitoring of organizational functions also includes attention to the delivery system and program support functions.

■ The analysis of monitoring data typically addresses such issues as description of program operations, comparison of sites, and conformity of a program to its design.

KEY CONCEPTS

Accessibility

The extent to which the structural and organizational arrangements facilitate participation in the program.

Accountability

The responsibility of program staff to provide evidence to stakeholders and sponsors that a program is effective and in conformity with its coverage, service, legal, and fiscal requirements.

Administrative standards

Stipulated achievement levels set by program administrators or other responsible parties, for example, intake for 90% of the referrals within one month. These levels may be set on the basis of past experience, the performance of comparable programs, or professional judgment.

Bias

As applied to program coverage, the extent to which subgroups of a target population are reached unequally by a program.

Coverage

The extent to which a program reaches its intended target population.

Management information system (MIS)

A data system, usually computerized, that routinely collects and reports information about the delivery of services to clients and, often, billing, costs, diagnostic and demographic information, and outcome status.

Outcome monitoring

The continual measurement and reporting of indicators of the status of the social conditions a program is accountable for improving.

Program process monitoring

Process evaluation that is done repeatedly over time.

7

Measuring and Monitoring Program Outcomes

Chapter Outline

The previous chapter discussed how a program's process and performance can be monitored. The ultimate goal of all programs, however, is not merely to function well, but to bring about change—to affect some problem or social condition in beneficial ways. The changed conditions are the intended outcomes or products of the programs. Assessing the degree to which a program produces these outcomes is a core function of evaluators.

A program's intended outcomes are ordinarily identified in the program's impact theory. Sensitive and valid measurement of those outcomes is technically challenging but essential to assessing a program's success. In addition, ongoing monitoring of outcomes can be critical to effective program management. Interpreting the results of outcome measurement and monitoring, however, presents a challenge to stakeholders because a given set of outcomes can be produced by factors other than program processes. This chapter describes how program outcomes can be identified, how they can be measured and monitored, and how the results can be properly interpreted.

Assessing a program's effects on the clients it serves and the social conditions it aims to improve is the most critical evaluation task because it deals with the "bottom line" issue for social programs. No matter how well a program addresses target needs, embodies a good plan of attack, reaches its target population and delivers apparently appropriate services, it cannot be judged successful unless it actually brings about some measure of beneficial change in its given social arena. Measuring that beneficial change, therefore, is not only a core evaluation function but also a high-stakes activity for the program. For these reasons, it is a function that evaluators must accomplish with great care to ensure that the findings are valid and properly interpreted. For these same reasons, it is one of the most difficult and, often, politically charged tasks the evaluator undertakes.

Beginning in this chapter and continuing through Chapter 10, we consider how best to identify the changes a program should be expected to produce, how to devise measures of these changes, and how to interpret such measures. Consideration of program effects begins with the concept of a program *outcome,* so we first discuss that pivotal concept.

Program Outcomes

An **outcome** is the state of the target population or the social conditions that a program is expected to have changed. For example, the amount of smoking among teenagers after exposure to an antismoking campaign in their high school is an outcome. The attitudes toward smoking of those who had not yet started to smoke is also an outcome. Similarly, the "school readiness" of children after attending a preschool program would be an outcome, as would the body weight of people who completed a weight-loss program, the management skills of business personnel after a management training program, and the amount of pollutants in the local river after a crackdown by the local environmental protection agency.

Notice two things about these examples. First, outcomes are observed characteristics of the target population or social conditions, not of the program, and the definition of an outcome makes no direct reference to program actions. Although the services delivered to program participants are often described as program "outputs," *outcomes,* as defined here, must relate to the *benefits* those products or services might have for the participants, not simply their receipt. Thus, "receiving supportive family therapy" is not a program outcome in our terms but, rather, the delivery of a program service. Similarly, providing meals to 100 housebound elderly persons is not a program outcome; it is service delivery, an aspect of program process. The nutritional benefits of those meals for the health of the elderly, on the other hand, are outcomes, as are any improvements in their morale, perceived quality of life, and risk of injury from attempting to cook for themselves. Put another way, outcomes always refer to characteristics that, in principle, could be observed for individuals or situations that have not received program services. For instance, we could assess the amount of smoking, the school readiness, the body weight, the management skills, and the water pollution in relevant situations where there was no program intervention. Indeed, as we will discuss later, we might measure outcomes in these situations to compare with those where the program was delivered.

Second, the concept of an outcome, as we define it, does not necessarily mean that the program targets have actually changed or that the program has caused them to change in any way. The amount of smoking by the high school teenagers may not have changed since the antismoking campaign began, and nobody may have lost any weight during their participation in the weight-loss program. Alternatively, there may be change but in the opposite of the expected direction—the teenagers may have increased their smoking, and program participants may have gained weight. Furthermore, whatever happened may have resulted from something other than the influence of the program. Perhaps the weight-loss program ran during a holiday season when people were prone to overindulge in sweets. Or perhaps the teenagers decreased their smoking in reaction to news of the smoking-related death of a popular rock music celebrity. The challenge for evaluators, then, is to assess not only the outcomes that actually obtain but also the degree to which any change in outcomes is attributable to the program itself.

Outcome Level, Outcome Change, and Net Effect

The foregoing considerations lead to important distinctions in the use of the term *outcome:*

- **Outcome level** is the status of an outcome at some point in time (e.g., the amount of smoking among teenagers).

- **Outcome change** is the difference between outcome levels at different points in time.

- **Program effect** is that portion of an outcome change that can be attributed uniquely to a program as opposed to the influence of some other factor.

Consider the graph in Exhibit 7-A, which plots the levels of an outcome measure over time. The vertical axis represents an *outcome variable* relevant to a program we wish to evaluate. An outcome variable is a measurable characteristic or condition of a program's target population that could be affected by the actions of the program. It might be amount of smoking, body weight, school readiness, extent of water pollution, or any other outcome falling under the definition above. The horizontal axis represents time, specifically, a period ranging from before the program was delivered to its target population until some time afterward. The solid line in the graph shows the average outcome level of a group of individuals who received program services. Note that their status over time is not depicted as a straight horizontal line but, rather, as a line that wiggles around. This is to indicate that smoking, school readiness, management skills, and other such outcome dimensions are not expected to stay constant—they change as a result of many natural causes and circumstances quite extraneous to the program. Smoking, for instance, tends to increase from the preteen to the teenage years. Water pollution levels may fluctuate according to the industrial activity in the region and weather conditions, for example, heavy rain that dilutes the concentrations.

If we measure the outcome variable (more on this shortly), we can determine how high or low the target group is with respect to that variable, for example, how much smoking or school readiness they display. This tells us the *outcome level,* often simply called the outcome. When measured after the target population has received program services, it tells us something about how that population is doing—how many teenagers are smoking, the average level of school readiness among the preschool children, how many pollutants there are in the water. If all the teenagers are smoking, we may be disappointed, and, conversely, if none are smoking, we may be pleased. All by themselves, however, these outcome levels do not tell us much about how effective the program was, though they may constrain the possibilities. If all the teens are smoking, for instance, we can be fairly sure that the antismoking program was not a great

EXHIBIT 7-A
Outcome Level,
Outcome Change,
and Program Effect

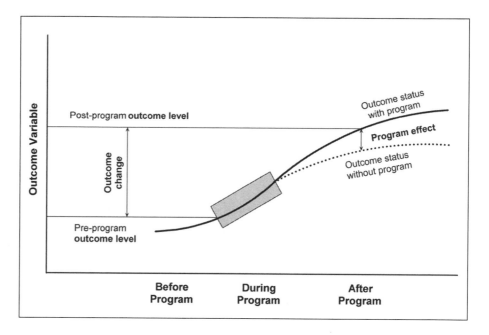

success and possibly was even counterproductive. If none of the teenagers are smoking, that finding is a strong hint that the program has worked because we would not expect them all to spontaneously stop on their own. Of course, such extreme outcomes are rarely found and, in most cases, outcome levels alone cannot be interpreted with any confidence as indicators of a program's success or failure.

If we measure outcomes on our target population before and after they participate in the program, we can describe more than the outcome level, we can also discern outcome *change*. If the graph in Exhibit 7-A plotted the school readiness of children in a preschool program, it would show that the children show less readiness before participating in the program and greater readiness afterward, a positive change. Even if their school readiness after the program was not as high as the preschool teachers hoped it would be, the direction of before-after change shows that there was improvement. Of course, from this information alone, we do not actually know that the preschool program had anything to do with the children's improvement in school readiness. Preschool-aged children are in a developmental period when their cognitive and motor skills increase rather rapidly through normal maturational processes. Other factors may also be at work; for example, their parents may be reading to them and otherwise supporting their intellectual development and preparation for entering school, and that may account for at least part of their gain.

The dashed line in Exhibit 7-A shows the trajectory on the outcome variable that would have been observed if the program participants had not received the program. For the preschool children, for example, the dashed line shows how their school readiness would have increased if they had not been in the preschool program. The solid line shows how school readiness developed when they were in the program. A comparison of the two lines indicates that school readiness would have improved even without exposure to the program, but not quite as much.

The difference between the outcome level attained with participation in the program and that which the same individuals would have attained had they not participated is the part of the change in outcome that the program produced. This is the value added or net gain part of the outcome that would not have occurred without the program. We refer to that increment as the program effect or, alternatively, the program impact. It is the only part of the outcome for which the program can honestly take credit.

Estimation of the program effect, or impact assessment, is the most demanding evaluation research task. The difficulties are highlighted in Exhibit 7-A, where the program effect is shown as the difference between the outcome that actually occurred and the outcome that would have occurred in the absence of the program. It is, of course, impossible to simultaneously observe outcomes for the same people (or other entities) under conditions when they both receive and do not receive a program. We must, therefore, observe the outcome after program participation and then somehow estimate what that outcome would have been without the program. Because the latter outcome is hypothetical for individuals who, in fact, did receive the program, it must be inferred rather than measured or observed. Developing valid inferences under these circumstances can be difficult and costly. Chapters 8 and 9 describe the methodological tools evaluators have available for this challenging task.

Although outcome levels and outcome changes have quite limited uses for determining program effects, they are of some value to managers and sponsors for monitoring program performance. This application will be discussed later in this chapter. For now we continue our exploration of the concept of an outcome by discussing how outcomes can be identified, defined, and measured for the purposes of evaluation.

Identifying Relevant Outcomes

The first step in developing measures of program outcomes is to identify very specifically what outcomes are relevant candidates for measurement. To do this, the evaluator must consider the perspectives of stakeholders on expected outcomes, the outcomes that are specified in the program's impact theory, and relevant prior research. The evaluator will also need to give attention to unintended outcomes that may be produced by the program.

Stakeholder Perspectives

Various program stakeholders have their own understanding of what the program is supposed to accomplish and, correspondingly, what outcomes they expect it to affect. The most direct sources of information about these expected outcomes usually are the stated objectives, goals, and mission of the program. Funding proposals and grants or contracts for services from outside sponsors also often identify outcomes that the program is expected to influence.

A common difficulty with information from these sources is a lack of the specificity and concreteness necessary to clearly identify specific outcome measures. It thus often falls to the evaluator to translate input from stakeholders into workable form and negotiate with the stakeholders to ensure that the resulting outcome measures capture their expectations.

For the evaluator's purposes, an outcome description must indicate the pertinent characteristic, behavior, or condition that the program is expected to change. However, as we discuss shortly, further specification and differentiation may be required as the evaluator moves from this description to selecting or developing measures of this outcome. Exhibit 7-B presents examples of outcome descriptions that would usually be serviceable for evaluation purposes.

Program Impact Theory

A full articulation of the program impact theory, as described in Chapter 5, is especially useful for identifying and organizing program outcomes. An impact theory expresses the outcomes of social programs as part of a logic model that connects the program's activities to proximal (immediate) outcomes that, in turn, are expected to lead to other, more distal outcomes. If correctly described, this series of linked relationships among outcomes represents the program's assumptions about the critical steps between program services and the ultimate social benefits the program is intended to produce. It is thus especially important for the evaluator to draw on this portion of program theory when identifying those outcomes that should be considered for measurement.

Exhibit 7-C shows several examples of the portion of program logic models that describes the impact theory (additional examples are found in Chapter 5). For the purposes of outcome assessment, it is useful to recognize the different character of the more proximal and more distal outcomes in these sequences. Proximal outcomes are those that the program services are expected to affect most directly and immediately. These can be thought of as the "take away" outcomes—those the program participants experience as a direct result of their participation and take with them out the door as they leave. For most social programs, these proximal outcomes are

EXHIBIT 7-B
Examples of
Outcomes Described
Specifically Enough
to Be Measured

Juvenile delinquency
Behavior of youths under the age of 18 that constitute chargeable offenses under applicable laws irrespective of whether the offenses are detected by authorities or the youth is apprehended for the offense.

Contact with antisocial peers
Friendly interactions and spending time with one or more youths of about the same age who regularly engage in behavior that is illegal and/or harmful to others.

Constructive use of leisure time
Engaging in behavior that has educational, social, or personal value during discretionary time outside of school and work.

Water quality
The absence of substances in the water that are harmful to people and other living organisms that drink the water or have contact with it.

Toxic waste discharge
The release of substances known to be harmful into the environment from an industrial facility in a manner that is likely to expose people and other living organisms to those substances.

Cognitive ability
Performance on tasks that involve thinking, problem solving, information processing, language, mental imagery, memory, and overall intelligence.

School readiness
Children's ability to learn at the time they enter school; specifically, the health and physical development, social and emotional development, language and communication skills, and cognitive skills and general knowledge that enable a child to benefit from participation in formal schooling.

Positive attitudes toward school
A child's liking for school, positive feelings about attending, and willingness to participate in school activities.

psychological—attitudes, knowledge, awareness, skills, motivation, behavioral intentions, and other such conditions that are susceptible to relatively direct influence by a program's processes and services.

Proximal outcomes are rarely the ultimate outcomes the program intends to generate, as can be seen in the examples in Exhibit 7-C. In this regard, they are not the most important outcomes from a social or policy perspective. This does not mean, however,

EXHIBIT 7-C

Examples of Program Impact Theories Showing Expected Program Effects on Proximal and Distal Outcomes

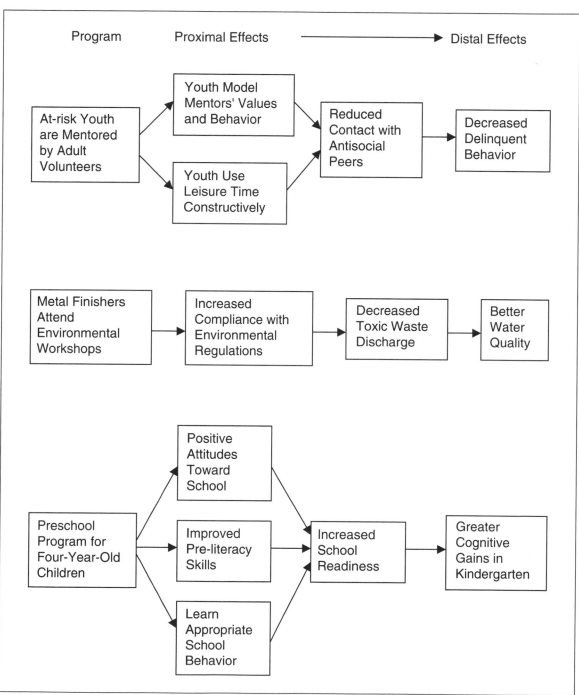

that they should be overlooked in the evaluation. These outcomes are the ones the program has the greatest capability to affect, so it can be very informative to know whether they are attained. If the program fails to produce these most immediate and direct outcomes, and the program theory is correct, then the more distal outcomes in the sequence are unlikely to occur. In addition, the proximal outcomes are generally the easiest to measure and to attribute to the program's efforts. If the program is successful at generating these outcomes, it is appropriate for it to receive credit for doing so. The more distal outcomes, which are more difficult to measure and attribute, may yield ambiguous results. Such results will be more balanced and interpretable if information is available about whether the proximal outcomes were attained.

Nonetheless, it is the more distal outcomes that are typically the ones of greatest practical and political importance. It is thus especially important to clearly identify and describe those that can reasonably be expected to result from the program activities. The value of careful development of the impact theory for these purposes is that it provides the basis for assessing what outcomes are actually reasonable, given the nature of the program.

Generally, however, a program has less direct influence on the distal outcomes in its impact theory. In addition, distal outcomes are also influenced by many other factors outside of the program's control. This circumstance makes it especially important to define the expected distal outcomes in a way that aligns as closely as possible with the aspects of the social conditions that the program activities can affect. Consider, for instance, a tutoring program for elementary school children that focuses mainly on reading, with the intent of increasing educational achievement. The educational achievement outcomes defined for an evaluation of this program should distinguish between those closely related to reading skills and those areas, such as mathematics, that are less likely to be influenced by what the program is actually doing.

Prior Research

In identifying and defining outcomes, the evaluator should thoroughly examine prior research on issues related to the program being evaluated, especially evaluation research on similar programs. Learning which outcomes have been examined in other studies may call attention to relevant outcomes that might otherwise have been overlooked. It will also be useful to determine how various outcomes have been defined and measured in prior research. In some cases, there are relatively standard definitions and measures that have an established policy significance. In other cases, there may be known problems with certain definitions or measures that the evaluator will need to know about.

Unintended Outcomes

So far, we have been considering how to identify and define those outcomes the stakeholders expect the program to produce and those that are evident in the program's impact theory. There may be significant unintended outcomes of a program, however, that will not be identified through these means. These outcomes may be positive or negative, but their distinctive character is that they emerge through some process that is not part of the program's design and direct intent. That feature, of course, makes them very difficult to anticipate. Accordingly, the evaluator must often make a special effort to identify any potential unintended outcomes that could be significant for assessing the program's effects on the social conditions it addresses.

Prior research can often be especially useful on this topic. There may be outcomes that other researchers have discovered in similar circumstances that can alert the evaluator to possible unanticipated program effects. In this regard, it is not only other evaluation research that is relevant but also any research on the dynamics of the social conditions in which the program intervenes. Research about the development of drug use and the lives of users, for instance, may provide clues about possible responses to a program intervention that the program plan has not taken into consideration.

Often, good information about possible unintended outcomes can be found in the firsthand accounts of persons in a position to observe those outcomes. For this reason, as well as others we have mentioned elsewhere in this text, it is important for the evaluator to have substantial contact with program personnel at all levels, program participants, and other key informants with a perspective on the program and its effects. If unintended outcomes are at all consequential, there should be someone in the system who is aware of them and who, if asked, can alert the evaluator to them. These individuals may not present this information in the language of unintended outcomes, but their descriptions of what they see and experience in relation to the program will be interpretable if the evaluator is alert to the possibility that there could be important program effects not articulated in the program logic or intended by the core stakeholders.

Measuring Program Outcomes

Not every outcome identified through the procedures we have described will be of equal importance or relevance, so the evaluator does not necessarily need to measure all of them in order to conduct an evaluation. Instead, some selection may be appropriate. In addition, some important outcomes—for example, very long-term ones—may be quite difficult or expensive to measure and, consequently, may not be feasible to include in the evaluation.

Once the relevant outcomes have been chosen and a full and careful description of each is in hand, the evaluator must next face the issue of how to measure them. Outcome measurement is a matter of representing the circumstances defined as the outcome by means of observable indicators that vary systematically with changes or differences in those circumstances. Some program outcomes have to do with relatively simple and easily observed circumstances that are virtually one-dimensional. One intended outcome of an industrial safety program, for instance, might be that workers wear their safety goggles in the workplace. An evaluator can capture this outcome quite well for each worker at any given time with a simple observation and recording of whether or not the goggles are being worn—and, by making periodic observations, extend the observation to indicate how frequently they are worn.

Many important program outcomes, however, are not as simple as whether a worker is wearing safety goggles. To fully represent an outcome, it may be necessary to view it as multidimensional and differentiate multiple aspects of it that are relevant to the effects the program is attempting to produce. Exhibit 7-B, for instance, provides a description of juvenile delinquency in terms of legally chargeable offenses committed. The chargeable delinquent offenses committed by juveniles, however, have several distinct dimensions that could be affected by a program attempting to reduce delinquency. To begin with, both the frequency of offenses and the seriousness of those offenses are likely to be relevant. Program personnel would not be happy to discover that they had reduced the frequency of offenses but that those still committed were now much more serious. Similarly, the type of offense may require consideration. A program focusing on drug abuse, for example, may expect drug offenses to be the most relevant outcome, but it may also be sensible to examine property offenses, because drug abusers may commit these to support their drug purchases. Other offense categories may be relevant, but less so, and it would obscure important distinctions to lump all offense types together as a single outcome measure.

Most outcomes are multidimensional in this way; that is, they have various facets or components that the evaluator may need to take into account. The evaluator generally should think about outcomes as comprehensively as possible to ensure that no important dimensions are overlooked. This does not mean that all must receive equal attention or even that all must be included in the coverage of the outcome measures selected. The point is, rather, that the evaluator should consider the full range of potentially relevant dimensions before determining the final measures to be used. Exhibit 7-D presents several examples of outcomes with various aspects and dimensions broken out.

One implication of the multiple dimensions of program outcomes is that a single outcome measure may not be sufficient to represent their full character. In the case of

EXHIBIT 7-D
Examples of the
Multiple Dimensions
and Aspects That
Constitute Outcomes

Juvenile delinquency

- Number of chargeable offenses committed during a given period
- Severity of offenses
- Type of offense: violent, property crime, drug offenses, other
- Time to first offense from an index date
- Official response to offense: police contact or arrest; court adjudication, conviction, or disposition

Toxic waste discharge

- Type of waste: chemical, biological; presence of specific toxins
- Toxicity, harmfulness of waste substances
- Amount of waste discharged during a given period
- Frequency of discharge
- Proximity of discharge to populated areas
- Rate of dispersion of toxins through aquifers, atmosphere, food chains, and the like

Positive attitudes toward school

- Liking for teacher
- Liking for classmates
- Liking for school activities
- Willingness to go to school
- Voluntary participation in school activities

juveniles' delinquent offenses, for instance, the evaluation might use measures of offense frequency, severity, time to first offense after intervention, and type of offense as a battery of outcome measures that would attempt to fully represent this outcome. Indeed, multiple measures of important program outcomes help the evaluator guard against missing an important program accomplishment because of a narrow measurement strategy that leaves out relevant outcome dimensions.

Diversifying measures can also safeguard against the possibility that poorly performing measures will underrepresent outcomes and, by not measuring the aspects of the outcome a program most affects, make the program look less effective than it actually is. For outcomes that depend on observation, for instance, having more than one observer may be useful to avoid the biases associated with any one of them. For instance, an evaluator who was assessing children's aggressive behavior with their peers might want the parents' observations, the teacher's observations, and those of any other person in a position to see a significant portion of the child's behavior. An example of multiple measures is presented in Exhibit 7-E.

EXHIBIT 7-E

Multiple Measures of Outcomes

A community intervention to prevent adolescent tobacco use in Oregon included youth anti-tobacco activities (e.g., poster and T-shirt giveaways) and family communication activities (e.g., pamphlets to parents). In the impact assessment the outcomes were measured in a variety of ways:

Outcomes for youths

- Attitudes toward tobacco use
- Knowledge about tobacco
- Reports of conversations about tobacco with parents
- Rated intentions to smoke or chew tobacco
- Whether smoked or chewed tobacco in last month and, if so, how much

Outcomes for parents

- Knowledge about tobacco
- Attitudes toward community prevention of tobacco use
- Attitudes toward tobacco use
- Intentions to talk to children about not using tobacco
- Reports of talks with their children about not using tobacco

SOURCE: Adapted from A. Biglan, D. Ary, H. Yudelson, T. E. Duncan, D. Hood, L. James, V. Koehn, Z. Wright, C. Black, D. Levings, S. Smith, and E. Gaiser, "Experimental Evaluation of a Modular Approach to Mobilizing Antitobacco Influences of Peers and Parents," *American Journal of Community Psychology*, 1996, 24(3):311-339.

Multiple measurement of important outcomes thus can provide for broader coverage of the concept and allow the strengths of one measure to compensate for the weaknesses of another. It may also be possible to statistically combine multiple measures into a single, more robust and valid composite measure that is better than any of the individual measures taken alone. In a program to reduce family fertility, for instance, changes in desired family size, adoption of contraceptive practices, and average desired number of children might all be measured and used in combination to assess the program outcome. Even when measures must be limited to a smaller number than comprehensive coverage might require, it is useful for the evaluator to elaborate all the dimensions and variations in order to make a thoughtful selection from the feasible alternatives.

Measurement Procedures and Properties

Data on program outcomes have relatively few basic sources—observations, records, responses to interviews and questionnaires, standardized tests, physical measurement apparatus, and the like. The information from such sources becomes measurement when it is operationalized, that is, generated through a set of specified, systematic operations or procedures. The measurement of many outcome variables in evaluation uses procedures and instruments that are already established and accepted for those purposes in the respective program areas. This is especially true for the more distal and policy- relevant outcomes. In health care, for instance, morbidity and mortality rates and the incidence of disease or health problems are measured in relatively standardized ways that differ mainly according the nature of the health problem at issue. Academic performance is conventionally measured with standardized achievement tests and grade point average. Occupations and employment status ordinarily are assessed by means of measures developed by the Bureau of the Census.

For other outcomes, various ready-made measurement instruments or procedures may be available, but with little consensus about which are most appropriate for evaluation purposes. This is especially true for psychological outcomes such as depression, self-esteem, attitudes, cognitive abilities, and anxiety. In these situations, the task for the evaluator is generally to make an appropriate selection from the options available. Practical considerations, such as how the instrument is administered and how long it takes, must be weighed in this decision. The most important consideration, however, is how well a ready-made measure matches what the evaluator wants to measure. Having a careful description of the outcome to be measured, as illustrated in Exhibit 7-B, will be helpful in making this determination. It will also be helpful if the evaluator has differentiated the distinct dimensions of the outcome that are relevant, as illustrated in Exhibit 7-D.

When ready-made measurement instruments are used, it is especially important to ensure that they are suitable for adequately representing the outcome of interest. A measure is not necessarily appropriate just because the name of the instrument, or the label given for the construct it measures, is similar to the label given the outcome of interest. Different measurement instruments for the "same" construct (e.g., self-esteem, environmental attitudes) often have rather different content and theoretical orientations that give them a character that may or may not match the program outcome of interest once that outcome is carefully described.

For many of the outcomes of interest to evaluators, there are neither established measures nor a range of ready-made measures from which to choose. In these cases, the evaluator must develop the measures. Unfortunately, there is rarely sufficient time and resources to do this properly. Some ad hoc measurement procedures, such as extracting specific relevant information from official records of known quality, are sufficiently straightforward to qualify as acceptable measurement practice without further demonstration. Other measurement procedures, however, such as questionnaires, attitude scales, knowledge tests, and systematic observational coding schemes, are not so straightforward. Constructing such measures so that they measure what they are supposed to in a consistent fashion is often not easy. Because of this, there are well-established measurement development procedures for doing so that involve a number of technical considerations and generally require a significant amount of pilot testing, analysis, revision, and validation before a newly developed measure can be used with confidence (see, e.g., DeVellis, 2003; Nunnally and Bernstein, 1994). When an evaluator must develop a measure without going through these steps and checks, the resulting measure may be reasonable on the surface but will not necessarily perform well for purposes of accurately assessing program outcomes.

When ad hoc measures must be developed for an evaluation without the opportunity for that development to be done in a systematic and technically proper manner, it is especially important that their basic measurement properties be checked before weight is put on them in an evaluation. Indeed, even in the case of ready-made measures and accepted procedures for assessing certain outcomes, it is wise to confirm that the respective measures perform well for the specific situation to which they will be applied. There are three measurement properties of particular concern: reliability, validity, and sensitivity.

Reliability

The **reliability** of a measure is the extent to which the measure produces the same results when used repeatedly to measure the same thing. Variation in those results constitutes measurement error. So, for example, a postal scale is reliable to the extent that it reports the same "score" (weight) for the same envelope on different occasions. No measuring instrument, classification scheme, or counting procedure is perfectly reliable, but different types of measures have reliability problems to varying degrees.

Measurements of physical characteristics for which standard measurement devices are available, such as height and weight, will generally be more consistent than measurements of psychological characteristics, such as intelligence measured with an IQ test. Performance measures, such as standardized IQ tests, in turn, have been found to be more reliable than measures relying on recall, such as reports of household expenditures for consumer goods. For evaluators, a major source of unreliability lies in the nature of measurement instruments that are based on participants' responses to written or oral questions posed by researchers. Differences in the testing or measuring situation, observer or interviewer differences in the administration of the measure, and even respondents' mood swings contribute to unreliability.

The effect of unreliability in measures is to dilute and obscure real differences. A truly effective intervention, the outcome of which is measured unreliably, will appear to be less effective than it actually is. The most straightforward way for the evaluator to check the reliability of a candidate outcome measure is to administer it at least twice under circumstances when the outcome being measured should not change between administrations of the measure. Technically, the conventional index of this *test-retest* reliability is a statistic known as the product moment correlation between the two sets of scores, which varies between .00 and 1.00. For many outcomes, however, this check is difficult to make because the outcome may change between measurement applications that are not closely spaced. For example, questionnaire items asking students how well they like school may be answered differently a month later, not because the measurement is unreliable but because intervening events have made the students feel differently about school. When the measure involves responses from people, on the other hand, closely spaced measures are contaminated because respondents remember their prior response rather than generating it anew. When the measurement cannot be repeated before the outcome can change, reliability is usually checked by examining the consistency among similar items in a multi-item measure administered at the same time (referred to as internal consistency reliability).

For many of the ready-made measures that evaluators use, reliability information will already be available from other research or from reports of the original development of the measure. Reliability can vary according to the sample of respondents and the circumstances of measurement, however, so it is not always safe to assume that a measure that has been shown to be reliable in other applications will be reliable when used in the evaluation.

There are no hard-and-fast rules about acceptable levels of reliability. The extent to which measurement error can obscure a meaningful program outcome depends in large part on the magnitude of that outcome. We will discuss this issue further in Chapter 10. As a rule of thumb, however, researchers generally prefer that their measures have reliability coefficients of .90 or above, a range that keeps measurement error small relative to all but the smallest outcomes. For many outcome measures applied under the circumstances characteristic of program evaluation, however, this is a relatively high standard.

Validity

The issue of measurement validity is more difficult than the problem of reliability. The **validity** of a measure is the extent to which it measures what it is intended to measure. For example, juvenile arrest records provide a valid measure of delinquency only to the extent that they accurately reflect how much the juveniles have engaged in chargeable offenses. To the extent that they also reflect police arrest practices, they are not valid measures of the delinquent behavior of the juveniles subject to arrest.

Although the concept of validity and its importance are easy to comprehend, it is usually difficult to test whether a particular measure is valid for the characteristic of interest. With outcome measures used for evaluation, validity turns out to depend very much on whether a measure is accepted as valid by the appropriate stakeholders. Confirming that it represents the outcome intended by the program when that outcome is fully and carefully described (as discussed earlier) can provide some assurance of validity for the purposes of the evaluation. Using multiple measures of the outcome in combination can also provide some protection against the possibility that any one of those measures does not tap into the actual outcome of interest.

Empirical demonstrations of the validity of a measure depend on some comparison that shows that the measure yields the results that would be expected if it were, indeed, valid. For instance, when the measure is applied along with alternative measures of the same outcome, such as those used by other evaluators, the results should be roughly the same. Similarly, when the measure is applied to situations recognized to differ on the outcome at issue, the results should differ. Thus, a measure of environmental attitudes should sharply differentiate members of the local Sierra Club from members of an off-road dirt bike association. Validity is also demonstrated by showing that results on the measure relate to or "predict" other characteristics expected to be related to the outcome. For example, a measure of environmental attitudes should be related to how favorably respondents feel toward political candidates with different positions on environmental issues.

Sensitivity

The principal function of outcome measures is to detect changes or differences in outcomes that represent program effects. To accomplish this well, outcome measures should be sensitive to such effects. The **sensitivity** of a measure is the extent to which the values on the measure change when there is a change or difference in the thing being measured. Suppose, for instance, that we are measuring body weight as an outcome for a weight-loss program. A finely calibrated scale of the sort used in physicians' offices might measure weight to within a few ounces and, correspondingly, be able to detect weight loss in that range. In contrast, the scales used to weigh trucks on interstate highways are also valid and reliable measures of weight, but they are not sensitive to differences smaller than a few hundred pounds. A scale that was not sensitive to meaningful fluctuations in the weight of the dieters in the weight-loss program would be a poor choice to measure that outcome.

There are two main ways in which the kinds of outcome measures frequently used in program evaluation can be insensitive to changes or differences of the magnitude the program might produce. First, the measure may include elements that relate to something other than what the program could reasonably be expected to change. These dilute the concentration of elements that are responsive and mute the overall response of the measure. Consider, for example, a math tutoring program for elementary school children that has concentrated on fractions and long division problems for most of the school year. The evaluator might choose an off-the-shelf math achievement test as a reasonable outcome measure. Such a test, however, will include items that cover a wider range of math problems than fractions and long division. Large gains the children have made in these latter areas might be obscured by the items on other topics that are averaged into the final score. A more sensitive measure, clearly, would be one that covered only the math topics that the program actually taught.

Second, outcome measures may be insensitive to the kinds of changes or differences induced by programs when they have been developed largely for diagnostic purposes, that is, to detect individual differences. The objective of measures of this sort is to spread the scores in a way that differentiates individuals who have more or less of the characteristic being measured. Most standardized psychological measures are of this sort, including, for example, personality measures, measures of clinical symptoms (depression, anxiety, etc.), measures of cognitive abilities, and attitude scales. These measures are generally good for determining who is high or low on the characteristic measured, which is their purpose, and thus are helpful for, say, assessing needs or problem severity. However, when applied to a group of individuals who differ widely on the measured characteristic before participating in a program, they may yield such a wide variation in scores after participation that any increment of improvement experienced by each individual will be lost amid the differences between individuals. From a measurement standpoint, the individual differences to which these measures respond so well constitute irrelevant noise for purposes of detecting change or group differences and tend to obscure those effects. Chapter 10 discusses some ways the evaluator can compensate for the insensitivity of measures of this sort.

The best way to determine whether a candidate outcome measure is sufficiently sensitive for use in an evaluation is to find research in which it was used successfully to detect change or difference on the order of magnitude the evaluator expects from the program being evaluated. The clearest form of this evidence, of course, comes from evaluations of very similar programs in which significant change or differences were found using the outcome measure. Appraising this evidence must also take the sample size of the prior evaluation studies into consideration, because the size of the sample affects the ability to detect effects.

An analogous approach to investigating the sensitivity of an outcome measure is to apply it to groups of known difference, or situations of known change, and determine how responsive it is. Consider the example of the math tutoring program mentioned earlier. The evaluator may want to know whether the standardized math achievement tests administered by the school system every year will be sufficiently sensitive to use as an outcome measure. This may be a matter of some doubt, given that the tutoring focuses on only a few math topics, while the achievement test covers a wide range. To check sensitivity before using this test to evaluate the program, the evaluator might first administer the test to a classroom of children before and after they study fractions and long division. If the test proves sufficiently sensitive to detect changes over the period when only these topics are taught, it provides some assurance that it will be responsive to the effects of the math tutoring program when used in the evaluation.

Choice of Outcome Measures

As the discussion so far has implied, selecting the best measures for assessing outcomes is a critical measurement problem in evaluations (Rossi, 1997). We recommend that evaluators invest the necessary time and resources to develop and test appropriate outcome measures (Exhibit 7-F provides an instructive example). A poorly conceptualized outcome measure may not properly represent the goals and objectives of the program being evaluated, leading to questions about the validity of the measure. An unreliable or insufficiently sensitive outcome measure is likely to underestimate the effectiveness of a program and could lead to incorrect inferences about the program's impact. In short, a measure that is poorly chosen or poorly conceived can completely undermine the worth of an impact assessment by producing misleading estimates. Only if outcome measures are valid, reliable, and appropriately sensitive can impact estimates be regarded as credible.

Monitoring Program Outcomes

With procedures for adequate measurement of significant program outcomes formulated, various approaches to learning something about those outcomes can be undertaken by the evaluator or program managers. The simplest approach is outcome monitoring, which we defined in Chapter 6 as the continual measurement and reporting

EXHIBIT 7-F

Reliability and Validity
of Self-Report
Measures With
Homeless Mentally
Ill Persons

Evaluations of programs for homeless mentally ill people typically rely heavily on self-report measures. But how reliable and valid are such measures, particularly with persons who have psychiatric problems? One group of evaluators built a measurement study into their evaluation of case management services for homeless mentally ill clients. They focused on self-report measures of psychiatric symptoms, substance abuse, and service utilization.

Psychiatric symptoms. Self-report on the Brief Symptom Inventory (BSI) was the primary measure used in the evaluation to assess psychiatric symptoms. Internal consistency reliability was examined for five waves of data collection and showed generally high reliabilities (.76-.86) on the scales for anxiety, depression, hostility, and somatization but lower reliability for psychoticism (.65-.67). To obtain evidence for the validity of these scales, correlations were obtained between them and comparable scales from the Brief Psychiatric Rating Schedule (BPRS), rated for clients by master's-level psychologists and social workers. Across the five waves of data collection, these correlations showed modest agreement (.40-.60) for anxiety, depression, hostility, and somatization. However, there was little agreement regarding psychotic symptoms (−.01 to .22).

Substance abuse. The evaluation measure was clients' estimation of how much they needed treatment for alcohol and other substance abuse using scales from the Addiction Severity Index (ASI). For validation, interviewers rated the clients' need for alcohol and other substance abuse treatment on the same ASI scales. The correlations over the five waves of measurement showed moderate agreement, ranging from .44 to .66 for alcohol and .47 to .63 for drugs. Clients generally reported less need for service than the interviewers.

Program contact and service utilization. Clients reported how often they had contact with their assigned program and whether they had received any of 14 specific services. The validity of these reports was tested by comparing them with case managers' reports at two of the waves of measurement. Agreement varied substantially with content area. The highest correlations (.40-.70) were found for contact with the program, supportive services, and specific resource areas (legal, housing, financial, employment, health care, medication). Agreement was considerably lower for mental health, substance abuse, and life skills training services. The majority of the disagreements involved a case manager reporting service and the client reporting none.

(Continued)

EXHIBIT 7-F
Reliability and Validity
of Self-Report
Measures With
Homeless Mentally
Ill Persons (continued)

The evaluators concluded that the use of self-report measures with homeless mentally ill persons was justified but with caveats: Evaluators should not rely solely on self-report measures for assessing psychotic symptoms, nor for information concerning the utilization of mental health and substance abuse services, since clients provide significant underestimates in these areas.

SOURCE: Adapted from Robert J. Calsyn, Gary A. Morse, W. Dean Klinkenberg, and Michael L. Trusty, "Reliability and Validity of Self-Report Data of Homeless Mentally Ill Individuals," *Evaluation and Program Planning*, 1997, 20(1): 47-54.

of indicators of the status of the social conditions the program is accountable for improving. It is similar to program monitoring, as described in Chapter 6, with the difference that the information that is regularly collected and reviewed relates to program outcomes rather than to only program process and performance. Outcome monitoring for a job training program, for instance, might involve routinely telephoning participants six months after completion of the program to ask whether they are employed and, if so, what job they have and what wages they are paid. Detailed discussions of outcome monitoring can be found in Affholter (1994) and Hatry (1999).

Outcome monitoring requires that indicators be identified for important program outcomes that are practical to collect routinely and that are informative with regard to the effectiveness of the program. The latter requirement is particularly difficult. As discussed earlier in this chapter, simple measurement of outcomes provides information only about the status or level of the outcome, such as the number of children in poverty, the prevalence of drug abuse, the unemployment rate, or the reading skills of elementary school students. The difficulty is in identifying *change* in that status and, especially, linking that change specifically with the efforts of the program in order to assess the program's effects or impact.

The source of this difficulty, as mentioned earlier, is that there are usually many influences on a social condition that are not under the program's control. Thus, poverty rates, drug use, unemployment, reading scores, and so forth may change for any number of reasons related to the economy, social trends, and the effects of other programs and policies. Under these circumstances, finding outcome indicators that do a reasonable job of isolating the results attributable to the program in question is not an easy matter. Isolating program effects in a convincing manner from other influences that might have similar effects requires the special techniques of impact evaluation discussed in Chapters 8 and 9.

All that said, outcome monitoring provides useful and relatively inexpensive information about program effects, usually in a reasonable time frame. Whereas an impact assessment may take years to complete, the results of outcome monitoring may be available within months. Furthermore, impact assessments typically require expenditures that are magnitudes greater than those needed for outcome monitoring systems. Because of its limitations, however, outcome monitoring is mainly a technique for generating feedback to help program managers better administer and improve their programs, not one for assessing the program's effects on the social conditions it is intended to benefit. As an illustration, consider the outcome monitoring of a treatment program for alcoholism. A result showing that 80% of the program's clients no longer drink several months after the program ends would present evidence more consistent with effectiveness than one showing only 20% abstaining. Of course, neither result is sufficient to establish real program effects, because the measured level of abstinence will also be affected by the severity of the clients' cases and by other influences on drinking that may override that of the program itself. A good monitoring scheme, however, will also include indicators of the severity of the initial problem, exposure to other important influences, and other relevant factors. While falling short of formal impact assessment, reasonable interpretation and comparison of patterns of such indicators and, especially, of trends in those indicators as programs attempt to improve their effectiveness, can provide useful indications of a program's effectiveness.

Indicators for Outcome Monitoring

Indicators that are to be used for outcome monitoring should be as responsive as possible to program effects. For instance, the outcome indicators should be measured only on the members of the target population who actually receive the program services. This means that readily available social indicators for the geographic areas served by the program, such as census tracts, zip codes, or municipalities, are not good choices for outcome monitoring if they include an appreciable number of persons not actually served by the program. It also means that those initial program participants who do not actually complete the full, prescribed service package should be excluded from the indicator. This is not to say that dropout rates are unimportant as a measure of program performance, but only that they should be assessed as a service utilization issue, not as an outcome issue.

The most interpretable outcome indicators, absent an impact evaluation, are those that involve variables that only the program can affect to any appreciable degree. When these variables also represent outcomes central to the program's mission, they make for an especially informative outcome monitoring system. Consider, for instance, a city street-cleaning program aimed at picking up litter, leaves, and the like from the municipal streets. Photographs of the streets that independent observers rate for cleanliness would be informative for assessing the effectiveness of this program. Short of a small hurricane blowing all the litter into the next county, there simply is not much else likely to happen that will clean the streets.

The outcome indicator easiest to link directly to the program's actions is client satisfaction, increasingly called customer satisfaction even in human service programs. Direct ratings by recipients of the benefits they believe the program provided to them are one form of assessment of outcomes. In addition, creating feelings of satisfaction about the interaction with the program among the participants is a form of outcome, though not one that, in itself, necessarily improves participants' lives. The more pertinent information comes from participants' reports of whether very specific benefits resulted from the service delivered by the program (see Exhibit 7-G). The limitation of such indicators is that program participants may not always be in a position to recognize or acknowledge program benefits, as in the case of drug addicts who are encouraged to use sterile needles. Alternatively, participants may be able to report on benefits but be reluctant to appear critical and thus overrate them, as in the case of elderly persons who are asked about the visiting nurses who come to their homes.

EXHIBIT 7-G

Client Satisfaction Survey Items That Relate to Specific Benefits

Client satisfaction surveys typically focus on satisfaction with program services. While a satisfied customer is one sort of program outcome, this alone says little about the specific program benefits the client may have found satisfactory. For client satisfaction surveys to go beyond service issues, they must ask about satisfaction with the results of service, that is, satisfaction with particular changes the service might have brought about. Martin and Kettner suggest adding items such as the following to routine client satisfaction surveys:

Service: Information and Referral
Question: Has the information and referral program been helpful to you in accessing needed services?

Service: Home-Delivered Meals
Question: Has the home-delivered meals program been helpful to you in maintaining your health and nutrition?

Service: Counseling
Question: Has the counseling program been helpful to you in coping with the stress in your life?

SOURCE: Adapted from Lawrence L. Martin and Peter M. Kettner, *Measuring the Performance of Human Service Programs* (Thousand Oaks, CA: Sage, 1996), p. 97.

Pitfalls in Outcome Monitoring

Because of the dynamic nature of the social conditions that typical programs attempt to affect, the limitations of outcome indicators, and the pressures on program agencies, there are many pitfalls associated with program outcome monitoring. Thus, while outcome indicators can be a valuable source of information for program decisionmakers, they must be developed and used carefully.

One important consideration is that any outcome indicator to which program funders or other influential decision makers give serious attention will also inevitably receive emphasis from program staff and managers. If the outcome indicators are not appropriate or fail to cover all the important outcomes, efforts to improve the performance they reflect may distort program activities. Affholter (1994), for instance, describes a situation in which a state used the number of new foster homes licensed as an indicator of increased placements for children with multiple problems. Workers responded by vigorously recruiting and licensing new homes even when the foster parents lacked the skills needed to work with these children. As a result, the indicator continued to move upward, but the actual placement of children in appropriate foster homes did not improve. In education, this response is called "teaching to the test." Good outcome indicators, by contrast, must "test to the teaching."

A related problem is the "corruptibility of indicators." This refers to the natural tendency for those whose performance is being evaluated to fudge and pad the indicator whenever possible to make their performance look better than it is. In a program for which the rate of postprogram employment among participants is a major outcome indicator, for instance, consider the pressure on the program staff assigned the task of telephoning participants after completion of the program to ascertain their job status. Even with a reasonable effort at honesty, ambiguous cases will more likely than not be recorded as employment. It is usually best for such information to be collected by persons independent from the program. If it is collected internal to the program, it is especially important that careful procedures be used and that the results be verified in some convincing manner.

Another potential problem area has to do with the interpretation of results on outcome indicators. Given a range of factors other than program performance that may influence those indicators, interpretations made out of context can be misleading and, even with proper context, they can be difficult. To provide suitable context for interpretation, outcome indicators must generally be accompanied by other information that provides a relevant basis for comparison or explanation of the results found on those indicators. We consider the kinds of information that can be helpful in the following discussion of the interpretation of outcome data.

Interpreting Outcome Data

Outcome data collected as part of routine outcome monitoring can be especially difficult to interpret if they are not accompanied by information about changes in client mix, relevant demographic and economic trends, and the like. Job placement rates, for instance, are more accurately interpreted as a program performance indicator in the light of information about the seriousness of the unemployment problems of the program participants and the extent of job vacancies in the local economy. A low placement rate may be no reflection on program performance when the program is working with clients with few job skills and long unemployment histories who are confronting an economy with few job vacancies.

Similarly, outcome data usually are more interpretable when accompanied by information about program process and service utilization. The job placement rate for clients completing training may look favorable but, nonetheless, be a matter for concern if, at the same time, the rate of training completion is low. The favorable placement rate may have resulted because all the clients with serious problems dropped out, leaving only the "cream of the crop" for the program to place. It is especially important to incorporate process and utilization information in the interpretation of outcome indicators when comparing different units, sites, or programs. It would be neither accurate nor fair to form a negative judgment of one program unit that was lower on an outcome indicator than other program units without considering whether it was dealing with more difficult cases, maintaining lower dropout rates, or coping with other extenuating factors.

Equally important for interpretation of outcome monitoring data is development of a framework that provides some standard for judging what constitutes better or worse outcomes within the inherent limitations of the data for which these judgments must be made. One useful framework, when it is applicable, is a comparison of outcome status with the preprogram status on the outcome measure to reveal the amount of change that has taken place. For example, it is less informative to know that 40% of the participants in a job training program are employed six months afterward than to know that this represents a change from a preprogram status in which 90% had not held a job for the previous year. One approach to outcome indicators is to define a "success threshold" for program participants and report how many moved from below that threshold to above it after receiving service. Thus, if the threshold is defined as "holding a full-time job continuously for six months," a program might report the proportion of participants falling below that threshold for the year prior to program intake and the proportion of those who were above that threshold during the year after completion of services.

A simple pre-post (before and after) comparison of this sort need not be part of routine outcome monitoring. It can also be done by the evaluator as part of an outcome assessment. As we have noted, the main drawback to this design is that the differences between before and after measures cannot be confidently ascribed to program effects because other processes at work in the intervening period may affect the pre-post differences. One of the main reasons people choose to enter job training programs, for instance, is that they are unemployed and experiencing difficulties obtaining employment. Hence, they are at a low point at the time of entry into the program and, from there, some are likely to locate jobs irrespective of their participation in the program. Pre-post comparisons of employment for such a program will thus always show some upward trend that has little to do with program effects.

Other trends between the two times can also influence pre-post change. A program to reduce crime may appear more effective if it coincides with, say, efforts to increase policing. Confounding factors can also skew a pre-post comparison in the other direction: An employment training program will appear ineffective if it is accompanied by a prolonged period of rising unemployment and depressed economic conditions. In general, then, pre-post comparisons may provide useful feedback to program administrators as part of outcome monitoring, but they do not usually provide credible findings about a program's impact. The rare exception is when there are virtually no intervening events or trends that might plausibly account for a pre-post difference. Exhibit 7-H provides an example of such a situation.

The information that results from measuring program outcome variables, or change in those variables, generally must be interpreted on the basis of the judgments of program administrators, stakeholders, or experts in relation to their expectations for good and poor performance. These judgments are easiest at the extremes—when outcomes are more positive than likely to occur for reasons unrelated to the program, or so negative that little but program failure can explain them.

For instance, suppose that, after a two-month vocational program to train tractor-trailer truck drivers, more than 90% of the participants (selected from among persons without such skills) qualified for the appropriate driver's license. Such a finding suggests that the program has been quite successful in imparting vocational skills—it seems rather unlikely that so large a proportion of previously unskilled persons who wanted to become tractor-trailer truck drivers would be able to qualify for licenses on their own in a two-month period. By the same token, we could draw a relatively firm judgment that the program was ineffective if all the participants failed the license examination.

In reality, of course, the observed outcome would probably be more ambiguous—say, only 30% passing the first time. This more typical finding is difficult to judge and raises the question of whether a comparable group receiving no training would have done as well. Expert judgments might be called on in such circumstances. For instance, persons familiar with adult vocational education and the typical outcomes of intervention programs in that field might be asked to draw on their background to

EXHIBIT 7-H

A Convincing
Pre-Post Outcome
Design for a
Program to Reduce
Residential Lead
Levels in Low-Income
Housing

The toxic effects of lead are especially harmful to children and can impede their behavioral development, reduce their intelligence, cause hearing loss, and interfere with important biological functions. Poor children are at disproportionate risk for lead poisoning because the homes available to low-income tenants are generally older homes, which are more likely to be painted with lead paint and to be located near other sources of lead contamination. Interior lead paint deteriorates to produce microscopic quantities of lead that children may ingest through hand-to-mouth activity. Moreover, blown or tracked-in dust may be contaminated by deteriorating exterior lead paint or roadside soil containing a cumulation of lead from the leaded gasoline used prior to 1980.

To reduce lead dust levels in low-income urban housing, the Community Lead Education and Reduction Corps (CLEARCorps) was initiated in Baltimore as a joint public-private effort. CLEARCorps members clean, repair, and make homes lead safe, educate residents on lead-poisoning prevention techniques, and encourage the residents to maintain low levels of lead dust through specialized cleaning efforts. To determine the extent to which CLEARCorps was successful in reducing the lead dust levels in treated urban housing units, CLEARCorps members collected lead dust wipe samples immediately before, immediately after, and six months following their lead hazard control efforts. In each of 43 treated houses, four samples were collected from each of four locations—floors, window sills, window wells, and carpets—and sent to laboratories for analysis.

Statistically significant differences were found between pre and post lead dust levels for floors, window sills, and window wells. At the six-month follow-up, further significant declines were found for floors and window wells, with a marginally significant decrease for window sills.

Since no control group was used, it is possible that factors other than the CLEARCorps program contributed to the decline in lead dust levels found in the evaluation. Other than relevant, but modest, seasonal effects relating to the follow-up period and the small possibility that another intervention program treated these same households, for which no evidence was available, there are few plausible alternative explanations for the decline. The evaluators concluded, therefore, that the CLEARCorps program was effective in reducing residential lead levels.

SOURCE: Adapted from Jonathan P. Duckart, "An Evaluation of the Baltimore Community Lead Education and Reduction Corps (CLEARCorps) Program," *Evaluation Review*, 1998, 22(3):373-402.

judge whether a 30% outcome represents a success given the nature of the targets. Clearly, the usefulness and validity of such judgments, and hence the worth of an evaluation using them, depend heavily on the judges' expertise and knowledge of the program area.

Where possible, outcome values such as these might be compared with those from similar programs. This process is often referred to as "benchmarking" (Keehley et al., 1996), particularly when program performance on a particular outcome is compared with that of an especially effective program. As in all such comparisons, of course, the results are meaningful for evaluation purposes only when all other things are equal between the programs being compared, a difficult standard to meet in most instances.

Summary

■ Programs are designed to affect some problem or need in positive ways. Evaluators assess the extent to which a program produces a particular improvement by measuring the outcome, the state of the target population or social condition that the program is expected to have changed.

■ Because outcomes are affected by events and experiences that are independent of a program, changes in the levels of outcomes cannot be directly interpreted as program effects.

■ Identifying outcomes relevant to a program requires information from stakeholders, review of program documents, and articulation of the impact theory embodied in the program's logic. Evaluators should also consider relevant prior research and consider possible unintended outcomes.

■ To produce credible results, outcome measures need to be reliable, valid, and sufficiently sensitive to detect changes in outcome level of the order of magnitude that the program might be expected to produce. In addition, it is often advisable to use multiple measures or outcome variables to reflect multidimensional outcomes and to correct for possible weaknesses in one or more of the measures.

■ Outcome monitoring can serve program managers and other stakeholders by providing timely and relatively inexpensive findings that can guide the fine-tuning and improvement of programs. Effective outcome monitoring requires a careful choice of indicators as well as careful interpretation of the resulting data.

■ The interpretation of outcome measures and changes in such measures is difficult. Responsible interpretation requires consideration of a program's environment, events taking place during a program, and the natural changes undergone by targets over time. Interpretation generally must rely on expert judgments of what constitutes good performance, though comparisons with other programs (benchmarking) can also be useful.

KEY CONCEPTS

Impact

See *program effect*.

Outcome

The state of the target population or the social conditions that a program is expected to have changed.

Outcome change

The difference between outcome levels at different points in time. See also *outcome level*.

Outcome level

The status of an outcome at some point in time. See also *outcome*.

Program effect

That portion of an outcome change that can be attributed uniquely to a program, that is, with the influence of other sources controlled or removed; also termed the program's impact. See also *outcome change*.

Reliability

The extent to which a measure produces the same results when used repeatedly to measure the same thing.

Sensitivity

The extent to which the values on a measure change when there is a change or difference in the thing being measured.

Validity

The extent to which a measure actually measures what it is intended to measure.

8

Assessing Program Impact
Randomized Field Experiments

Chapter Outline

Impact assessments are undertaken to find out whether programs actually produce the intended effects. Such assessments cannot be made with certainty but only with varying degrees of confidence. A general principle applies: The more rigorous the research design, the more confident we can be about the validity of the resulting estimate of intervention effects.

The design of impact evaluations needs to take into account two competing pressures. On one hand, evaluations should be undertaken with sufficient rigor that relatively firm conclusions can be reached. On the other hand, practical considerations of time, money, cooperation, and protection of human subjects limit the design options and methodological procedures that can be employed.

Evaluators assess the effects of social programs by comparing information about outcomes for program participants with estimates of what their outcomes would have been had they not participated. This chapter discusses the strongest research design for accomplishing this objective—the randomized field experiment. Randomized experiments compare groups of targets that have been randomly assigned to either experience some intervention or not. Although practical considerations may limit the use of randomized field experiments in some program situations, evaluators need to be familiar with them. The logic of the randomized experiment is the basis for the design of all types of impact assessments and the analysis of the data from them.

Impact assessments are designed to determine what effects programs have on their intended outcomes and whether perhaps there are important unintended effects. As described in Chapter 7, a program effect, or impact, refers to a change in the target population or social conditions that has been brought about by the program, that is, a change that would not have occurred had the program been absent. The problem of establishing a program's impact, therefore, is identical to the problem of establishing that the program is a cause of some specified effect.

In the social sciences, causal relationships are ordinarily stated in terms of probabilities. Thus, the statement "*A* causes *B*" usually means that if we introduce *A*, *B* is more likely to result than if we do not introduce *A*. This statement does not imply that *B* always results from *A*, nor does it mean that *B* occurs only if *A* happens first. To illustrate, consider a job training program designed to reduce unemployment. If successful, it will increase the probability that participants will subsequently be employed. Even a very successful program, however, will not result in employment for every participant. The likelihood of finding a job is related to many factors that have nothing to do with the effectiveness of the training program, such as economic conditions in the community. Correspondingly, some of the program participants would have found jobs even without the assistance of the program.

The critical issue in impact evaluation, therefore, is whether a program produces desired effects over and above what would have occurred without the intervention or, in some cases, with an alternative intervention. In this chapter, we consider the strongest research design available for addressing this issue, the randomized field experiment. We begin with some general considerations about doing impact assessments.

When Is an Impact Assessment Appropriate?

Impact assessment can be relevant at many points in the life course of a social program. At the stage of policy formulation, a pilot demonstration program may be commissioned with an impact assessment to determine whether the proposed program would actually have the intended effects. When a new program is authorized, it is often started initially in a limited number of sites. Impact assessment may be appropriate at that point to show that the program has the expected effects before it is extended to broader coverage. In many cases, the sponsors of innovative programs, such as private foundations, implement programs on a limited scale and conduct impact evaluations with a view to promoting adoption of the program by government agencies if the effects can be demonstrated.

Ongoing programs are also often subject to impact assessments. In some cases, programs are modified and refined to enhance their effectiveness or to accommodate revised program goals. When the changes made are major, the modified program may warrant impact assessment because it is virtually a new program. It is also appropriate, however, to subject many stable, established programs to periodic impact assessment. For example, the high costs of certain medical treatments make it essential to continually evaluate their efficacy and compare it with other means of dealing with the same problem. In other cases, long-established programs are evaluated at regular intervals either because of "sunset" legislation requiring demonstration of effectiveness if funding is to be renewed or as a means of defending the programs against attack by supporters of alternative interventions or other uses for the public funds involved.

In whatever circumstances impact assessments are conducted, there are certain prerequisite conditions that need to be met for the assessment to be meaningful. To begin with, impact assessments build on earlier forms of evaluation. Before undertaking an assessment of a program's impact, the evaluator should assess both the program theory and the program process. Assessment of the program theory should indicate that the program's objectives are sufficiently well articulated to make it possible to specify the expected effects—a necessary prerequisite to an evaluation of those effects. Moreover, the presumption that those effects can be produced by the program's actions should be plausible. Assessment of program process should show that the intervention is sufficiently well implemented to have a reasonable chance of producing the intended effects. It would be a waste of time, effort, and resources to attempt to estimate the impact of a program that lacks plausible, measurable outcomes or that has not been adequately implemented. An important implication of this last consideration is that interventions should be evaluated for impact only when they have been in place long enough to have ironed out implementation problems.

It is important to recognize that the more rigorous forms of impact evaluation involve significant technical and managerial challenges. The targets of social programs are often persons and households who are difficult to reach or from whom it is hard to obtain outcome and follow-up data. In addition, the more credible impact designs are demanding in both their technical and practical dimensions. Finally, as we discuss in detail in Chapter 12, evaluation research has its political dimensions as well. The evaluator must constantly cultivate the cooperation of program staff and target participants in order to conduct impact assessment while contending with inherent pressures to produce timely and unambiguous findings. Before undertaking an impact assessment, therefore, evaluators should give some consideration to whether it is sufficiently justified by the program circumstances, available resources, and the need for information. Program stakeholders often ask for impact assessment because they are interested in knowing if the program produces the intended benefits, but they may not appreciate the prerequisite program conditions and research resources necessary to accomplish it in a credible manner.

Key Concepts in Impact Assessment

All impact assessments are inherently comparative. Determining the impact of a program requires comparing the condition of targets that have experienced an intervention with an estimate of what their condition would have been had they not experienced the intervention. In practice, this is usually accomplished by comparing outcomes for program participants with those of equivalent persons who have experienced something else. There may be one or more groups of targets receiving "something else," which may mean receiving alternative services or simply going untreated. The "equivalent" targets for comparison may be selected in a variety of ways, or comparisons may be made between information about the outcome being examined and similar information from the same targets taken at an earlier time.

Ideally, the conditions being compared should be identical in all respects except for the intervention. There are several alternative (but not mutually exclusive) approaches to approximating this ideal that vary in effectiveness. All involve establishing *control conditions*, groups of targets in circumstances such that they do not receive the intervention being assessed. The available options are not equal: Some characteristically produce more credible estimates of impact than others. The options also vary in cost and level of technical skill required. As in other matters, the approaches to impact assessment that produce the most valid results generally require more skills, more time to complete, and more cost. Broadly, there are two classes of approaches, which we consider next.

Experimental Versus Quasi-Experimental Research Designs

Our discussion of the available options for impact assessment is rooted in the view that the most valid way to establish the effects of an intervention is a **randomized field experiment**, often called the "gold standard" research design for assessing causal effects. The basic laboratory version of a randomized experiment is no doubt familiar. Participants are randomly sorted into at least two groups. One group is designated the **control group** and receives no intervention or an innocuous one; the other group, called the **intervention group**, is given the intervention being tested. Outcomes are then observed for both the intervention and the control groups, with any differences being attributed to the intervention.

The control conditions for a randomized field experiment are established in similar fashion. Targets are randomly assigned to an intervention group, to which the intervention is administered, and a control group, from which the intervention is withheld. There may be several intervention groups, each receiving a different intervention or variation of an intervention, and sometimes several control groups, each also receiving a different variant, for instance, no intervention, a placebo intervention, and the treatment normally available to targets in the circumstances to which the program intervention applies.

All the remaining impact assessment designs consist of nonrandomized **quasi-experiments** in which targets who participate in a program (the "intervention" group) are compared with nonparticipants (the "controls") who are presumed to be similar to participants in critical ways. These techniques are called quasi-experimental because they lack the random assignment to conditions that is essential for true experiments. The main approaches to establishing nonrandomized control groups in impact assessment designs are discussed in the next chapter.

Designs using nonrandomized controls universally yield less convincing results than well-executed randomized field experiments. From the standpoint of validity in the estimation of program effects, therefore, the randomized field experiment is always the optimal choice for impact assessment. Nevertheless, quasi-experiments are useful for impact assessment when it is impractical or impossible to conduct a true randomized experiment.

The strengths and weaknesses of different research designs for assessing program effects, and the technical details of implementing them and analyzing the resulting data, are major topics in evaluation. The classic texts are Campbell and Stanley (1966) and Cook and Campbell (1979). More recent accounts that evaluators may find useful are Shadish, Cook, and Campbell (2002) and Mohr (1995).

"Perfect" Versus "Good Enough" Impact Assessments

For several reasons, evaluators are confronted all too frequently with situations where it is difficult to implement the "very best" impact evaluation design. First, the designs that are best in technical terms sometimes cannot be applied because the intervention or target coverage does not lend itself to that sort of design. For example, the circumstances in which randomized experiments can be ethically and practicably carried out with human subjects are limited, and evaluators must often use less rigorous designs. Second, time and resource constraints always limit design options. Third, the justification for using the best design, which often is the most costly one, varies with the importance of the intervention being tested and the intended use of the results. Other things being equal, an important program—one that is of interest because it attempts to remedy a very serious condition or employs a controversial intervention—should be evaluated more rigorously than other programs. At the other extreme, some trivial programs probably should not have impact assessments at all.

Our position is that evaluators must review the range of design options in order to determine the most appropriate one for a particular evaluation. The choice always involves trade-offs; there is no single, always-best design that can be used universally in all impact assessments. Rather, we advocate using what we call the "good enough" rule in formulating research designs. Stated simply, the evaluator should choose the strongest possible design from a methodological standpoint after having taken into account the potential importance of the results, the practicality and feasibility of each design, and the probability that the design chosen will produce useful and credible results. For the remainder of this chapter, we will focus on randomized field experiments as the most methodologically rigorous design and, therefore, the starting point for considering the best possible design that can be applied for impact assessment.

Randomized Field Experiments

As noted earlier, a program effect or impact can be conceptualized as the difference in outcome between targets that have received a particular intervention and "equivalent" units that have not. If these two groups were perfectly equivalent, both would be subject to the same degree of change induced by factors outside of the program. Any difference in outcome between them, therefore, should represent the effect of the program. The purpose of impact assessments, and of randomized field experiments in particular, is to isolate and measure any such difference.

The critical element in estimating program effects by this method is configuring a control group that does not participate in the program but is equivalent to the group that does. Equivalence, for these purposes, means the following:

- *Identical composition.* Intervention and control groups contain the same mixes of persons or other units in terms of their program-related and outcome-related characteristics.

- *Identical predispositions.* Intervention and control groups are equally disposed toward the project and equally likely, without intervention, to attain any given outcome status.

- *Identical experiences.* Over the time of observation, intervention and control groups experience the same time-related processes—maturation, secular drifts, interfering events, and so forth.

Although perfect equivalence could theoretically be achieved by matching each target in an intervention group with an identical target that is then included in a control group, this is clearly impossible in program evaluations. No two individuals, families, or other units are identical in all respects. Fortunately, one-to-one equivalence on all characteristics is not necessary. It is only necessary for intervention and control groups to be identical in aggregate terms and in respects that are relevant to the program outcomes being evaluated. It may not matter at all for an impact evaluation that intervention and control group members differ in place of birth or vary slightly in age, as long as such differences do not influence the outcome variables. On the other hand, differences between intervention and control groups that are related in any way to the outcomes under investigation will cause errors in estimates of program effects.

Using Randomization to Establish Equivalence

The best way to achieve equivalence between intervention and control groups is to use **randomization** to allocate members of a target population to the two groups.

Randomization is a procedure that allows chance to decide whether a person (or other unit) receives the program or the control condition alternative. It is important to note that "random" in this sense does not mean haphazard or capricious. On the contrary, randomly allocating targets to intervention and control groups requires considerable care to ensure that every unit in a target population has the same probability as any other to be selected for either group.

To create a true random assignment, an evaluator must use an explicit chance-based procedure such as a random number table, roulette wheel, roll of dice, or the ike. For convenience, researchers typically use random number sequences. Tables of random numbers are included in most elementary statistics or sampling textbooks, and many computer statistical packages contain subroutines that generate random numbers. The essential step is that the decision about the group assignment for each participant in the impact evaluation is made solely on the basis of the next random result, for instance, the next number in the random number table (e.g., odd or even). (See Boruch, 1997, and Boruch and Wothke, 1985, for discussions of how to implement randomization.)

Because the resulting intervention and control groups differ from one another only by chance, whatever influences may be competing with an intervention to produce outcomes are present in both groups to the same extent, except for chance fluctuations. This follows from the same chance processes that tend to produce equal numbers of heads and tails when a handful of coins is tossed into the air. For example, with randomization, persons whose characteristics make them more responsive to program services are as likely to be in the intervention as the control group. Hence, both groups should have the same proportion of persons favorably predisposed to benefit from the intervention.

Of course, even though target units are assigned randomly, the intervention and control groups will never be exactly equivalent. For example, more women may end up in the control group than in the intervention group simply by chance. But if the random assignment were made over and over, those fluctuations would average out to zero. The expected proportion of times that a difference of any given size on any given characteristic will be found in a series of randomizations can be calculated from statistical probability models. Any given difference in outcome among randomized intervention and control groups, therefore, can be compared to what is expected on the basis of chance (i.e., the randomization process). Statistical significance testing can then be used to guide a judgment about whether a specific difference is likely to have occurred simply by chance or more likely represents the effect of the intervention. Since the intervention in a well-run experiment is the only difference other than chance between intervention and control groups, such judgments become the basis for discerning the existence of a program effect. The statistical procedures for making such calculations are quite straightforward and may be found in any text dealing with statistical inference in experimental design.

One implication of the role of chance and statistical significance testing is that impact assessments require more than just a few cases. The larger the number of units randomly assigned to intervention and control groups, the more likely those groups are to be statistically equivalent. This occurs for the same reason that tossing 1,000 coins is less likely to deviate from a 50-50 split between heads and tails than tossing 2 coins. Studies in which only one or a few units are in each group rarely, if ever, suffice for impact assessments, since the odds are that any division of a small number of units will result in differences between them. This and related matters are discussed more fully in Chapter 10.

Units of Analysis

The units on which outcome measures are taken in an impact assessment are called the **units of analysis**. The units of analysis in an experimental impact assessment are not necessarily persons. Social programs may be designed to affect a wide variety of targets, including individuals, families, neighborhoods and communities, organizations such as schools and business firms, and political jurisdictions from counties to whole nations. The logic of impact assessment remains constant as one moves from one kind of unit to another, although the costs and difficulties of conducting a field experiment may increase with the size and complexity of units. Implementing a field experiment and gathering data on 200 students, for instance, will almost certainly be easier and less costly than conducting a comparable evaluation with 200 classrooms or 200 schools.

The choice of the units of analysis should be based on the nature of the intervention and the target units to which it is delivered. A program designed to affect communities through block grants to local municipalities requires that the units studied be municipalities. Notice that, in this case, each municipality would constitute one unit for the purposes of the analysis. Thus, an impact assessment of block grants that is conducted by contrasting two municipalities has a sample size of two—quite inadequate for statistical analysis even though observations may be made on large numbers of individuals within each of the two communities.

The evaluator attempting to design an impact assessment should begin by identifying the units that are designated as the targets of the intervention in question and that, therefore, should be specified as the units of analysis. In most cases, defining the units of analysis presents no ambiguity; in other cases, the evaluator may need to carefully appraise the intentions of the program's designers. In still other cases, interventions may be addressed to more than one type of target: A housing subsidy program, for example, may be designed to upgrade both the dwellings of individual poor families and the housing stocks of local communities. Here the evaluator may wish to design an impact assessment that consists of samples of individual households within samples of local communities. Such a design would incorporate two types of units of analysis in order to estimate the impact of the program on individual households and also on the housing stocks of local communities. Such multilevel designs follow the same logic as field experiments with a single type of unit but involve more complex statistical analysis (Murray, 1998; Raudenbush and Bryk, 2002).

The Logic of Randomized Experiments

The logic whereby randomized experiments produce estimates of program effects is illustrated in Exhibit 8-A, which presents a schematic view of a simple before-and-after randomized experiment. As shown there, the mean change on an outcome variable from before to after the period of program exposure is calculated separately for the intervention and control groups. If the assumption of equivalence between the groups (except for program participation) is correct, the amount of change in the control group represents what would have happened to the members of the intervention group had they not received the program. When that amount is subtracted from the change on the outcome variable for the intervention group, the change that is left over directly estimates the mean program effect on that outcome.

This difference between the intervention and control groups (I minus C in Exhibit 8-A), however, also reflects some element of chance stemming from the original random assignment, as described above. Consequently, the exact numerical difference between the mean outcome scores for the intervention and control group cannot simply be interpreted as the program effect. Instead, we must apply an appropriate test of statistical significance to judge whether a difference of that size is likely to have resulted merely by chance. There are conventional statistical tests for this situation, including the t-test, analysis of variance, and analysis of covariance (with the pretest as the covariate).

The schematic presentation in Exhibit 8-A shows the program effect in terms of before-after change on some outcome variable. For some types of outcomes, a preintervention measure is not possible. In a prevention program, for example, there would typically be no instances of the outcome to be prevented before the delivery of the program services. Consider a program to prevent teen pregnancy; it would, of course, be provided to teens who had not yet created a pregnancy, but pregnancy would be the main program outcome of interest. Similarly, the primary outcome of a program designed to help impoverished high school students go to college can be observed only after the

EXHIBIT 8-A
Schematic
Representation of a
Randomized
Experiment

	Outcome Measures		
	Before Program	**After Program**	**Difference**
Intervention group	I1	I2	$I = I2 - I1$
Control group	C1	C2	$C = C2 - C1$

Program effect $= I - C$, where:

    I1, C1   = measures of outcome variable before the program is instituted, for intervention and control groups, respectively

    I2, C2   = measures of outcome variable after program is completed, for intervention and control groups, respectively

    I, C   = outcomes for intervention and control groups, respectively

intervention. There are statistical advantages to having both before and after measures when it is possible, however. For instance, estimates of program effects can be more precise when before measures are available to identify each individual target's starting point prior to the intervention.

Examples of Randomized Experiments in Impact Assessment

Several examples can serve to illustrate the logic of randomized field experiments as applied to actual impact assessments as well as some of the difficulties encountered in real-life evaluations. Exhibit 8-B describes a randomized experiment to test the effectiveness of an intervention to improve the nutritional composition of the food eaten by schoolchildren. Several of the experiment's features are relevant here. First, note that the units of analysis were schools and not, for example, individual students. Correspondingly, entire schools were assigned to either the intervention or control condition. Second, note that a number of outcome measures were employed, covering the multiple nutritional objectives of the intervention. It is also appropriate that statistical tests were used to judge whether the effects (the intervention group's lower intake of overall calories and calories from fat) were simply chance differences.

EXHIBIT 8-B

CATCH: A Field
Experiment on a
Demonstration
Program to Change
the Dietary Habits of
Schoolchildren

According to the recommended dietary allowances, Americans on average consume too many calories derived from fats, especially unsaturated fats, and have diets too high in sodium. These dietary patterns are related to high incidences of coronary diseases and obesity. The Heart, Lung and Blood Institute, therefore, sponsored a randomized field experiment of an intervention designed to bring about better nutritional intake among schoolchildren, the Child and Adolescent Trial for Cardiovascular Health (CATCH).

CATCH was a randomized controlled field trial in which the basic units were 96 elementary schools in California, Louisiana, Minnesota, and Texas, with 56 randomly assigned to be intervention sites and 40 to be controls. The intervention program included training sessions for the food service staffs informing them of the rationale for nutritionally balanced school menus and providing recipes and menus that would achieve that goal. Training sessions on nutrition and exercise were given to teachers, and school administrations were persuaded to make changes in the physical education curriculum for students. In addition, efforts were made to reach the parents of participating students with nutritional information.

Measured by 24-hour dietary intake interviews with children at baseline and at follow-up, children in the intervention schools were significantly lower than children in control schools in total food intake and in calories derived from fat and saturated fat, but no different with respect to intake of cholesterol or sodium. Because these measures include all food over a 24-hour period, they demonstrate changes in food patterns in other meals as well as school lunches. On the negative side, there was no significant lowering of the cholesterol levels in the blood of the students in intervention schools. Importantly, the researchers found that participation in the school lunch program did not decline in the intervention schools, nor was participation lower than in the control schools.

SOURCE: Adapted from R. V. Luepker, C. L. Perry, S. M. McKinlay, P. R. Nader, G. S. Parcel, E. J. Stone, L. S. Webber, J. P. Elder, H. A. Feldman, C. C. Johnson, S. H. Kelder, and M. Wu. "Outcomes of a Field Trial to Improve Children's Dietary Patterns and Physical Activity: The Child and Adolescent Trial for Cardiovascular Health (CATCH)." *Journal of the American Medical Association*, 1996, 275 (March): 768-776.

Exhibit 8-C describes a randomized experiment assessing the effects of case management provided by former mental health patients relative to that provided by mental health personnel. This example illustrates the use of experimental design to compare the effects of a service innovation with the customary type of service. It thus does not

EXHIBIT 8-C
Assessing the Effects of a Service Innovation

A community mental health center in Philadelphia customarily provides intensive case management to clients diagnosed with a major mental illness or having a significant treatment history. Case managers employ an assertive community treatment (ACT) model and assist clients with various problems and services, including housing, rehabilitation, and social activities. The case management teams are composed of trained mental health personnel working under the direction of a case manager supervisor.

In light of recent trends toward consumer-delivered mental health services, that is, services provided by persons who have themselves been mentally ill and received treatment, the community mental health center became interested in the possibility that consumers might be more effective case managers than nonconsumers. Former patients might have a deeper understanding of mental illness because of their own experience and may establish a better empathic bond with patients, both of which could result in more appropriate service plans.

To investigate the effects of consumer case management relative to the mental health center's customary case management, a team of evaluators conducted a randomized field experiment. Initially, 128 eligible clients were recruited to participate in the study; 32 declined and the remaining 96 gave written consent and were randomly assigned to either the usual case management or the intervention team. The intervention team consisted of mental health service consumers operating as part of a local consumer-run advocacy and service organization.

Data were collected through interviews and standardized scales at baseline and one month and then one year after assignment to case management. The measures included social outcomes (housing, arrests, income, employment, social networks) and clinical outcomes (symptoms, level of functioning, hospitalizations, emergency room visits, medication attitudes and compliance, satisfaction with treatment, quality of life). The sample size and statistical analysis were planned to have sufficient statistical power to detect meaningful differences, with special attention to the possibility that there would be no meaningful differences, which would be an important finding for a comparison of this sort. Of the 96 participants, 94 continued receiving services for the duration of study and 91 of them were located and interviewed at the one-year follow-up.

No statistically significant differences were found on any outcome measures except that the consumer case management team clients reported somewhat less satisfaction with treatment and less contact with their families. While these two unfavorable findings were judged to warrant further investigation, the evaluators concluded on the basis of the similarity in the major outcomes that mental health consumers were capable of being equally competent case managers as nonconsumers in this particular service model. Moreover, this approach would provide relevant employment opportunities for former mental patients.

SOURCE: Adapted from Phyllis Solomon and Jeffrey Draine, "One-Year Outcomes of a Randomized Trial of Consumer Case Management." *Evaluation and Program Planning*, 1995, 18(2):117-127.

address the question of whether case management has effects relative to no case management but, rather, evaluates whether a different approach would have better effects than current practice. Another interesting aspect of this impact assessment is the sample of clients who participated. While a representative group of clients eligible for case management was recruited, 25% declined to participate (which, of course, is their right), leaving some question as to whether the results can be generalized to all eligible clients. This is rather typical of service settings: Almost always there is a variety of reasons why some appropriate participants in an impact assessment cannot or will not be included. Even for those who are included, there may be other reasons why final outcome measures cannot be obtained. In the experiment described in Exhibit 8-C, the evaluators were fortunate that only 2 of 96 original participants were lost to the evaluation because they failed to complete service and only 3 were lost because they could not be located at the one-year follow-up.

Exhibit 8-D describes one of the largest and best-known field experiments relating to national policy ever conducted. It was designed to determine whether income support payments to poor, intact (i.e., two-spouse) families would cause them to reduce the amount of their paid employment, that is, create a work disincentive. The study was the first of a series of five sponsored by government agencies, each varying slightly from the others, to test different forms of guaranteed income and their effects on the work efforts of poor and near-poor persons. All five experiments were run over relatively long periods, the longest for more than five years, and all had difficulties maintaining the cooperation of the initial groups of families involved. The results showed that income payments created a slight work disincentive, especially for teenagers and mothers with young children—those in the secondary labor force (Mathematica Policy Research, 1983; Robins et al., 1980; Rossi and Lyall, 1976; SRI International, 1983).

Prerequisites for Conducting Randomized Field Experiments

The desirability of randomized evaluation designs for impact assessment is widely recognized, and there is a growing literature on how to enhance the chances of success (Boruch, 1997; Dennis, 1990; Dunford, 1990). Moreover, many examples of the application of experimental design to impact assessment, such as those cited in this chapter, demonstrate their feasibility under appropriate circumstances.

Despite their power to sustain the most valid conclusions about the effects of interventions, however, randomized experiments account for a relatively small proportion of impact assessments. Political and ethical considerations may rule out randomization, particularly when program services cannot be withheld without violating ethical or legal rules (although the idea of experimentation does not preclude

Exhibit 8-D

The New Jersey-Pennsylvania Income Maintenance Experiment

In the late 1960s, when federal officials concerned with poverty began to consider shifting welfare policy to provide some sort of guaranteed annual income for all families, the Office of Economic Opportunity (OEO) launched a large-scale field experiment to test one of the crucial issues in such a program: the prediction of economic theory that such supplementary income payments to poor families would be a work disincentive.

The experiment was started in 1968 and carried on for three years, administered by Mathematica, Inc., a research firm in Princeton, New Jersey, and the Institute for Research on Poverty of the University of Wisconsin. The target population was two-parent families with income below 150% of the poverty level and male heads whose age was between 18 and 58. The eight intervention conditions consisted of various combinations of income guarantees and the rates at which payments were taxed in relation to the earnings received by the families. For example, in one of the conditions a family received a guaranteed income of 125% of the then-current poverty level, if no one in the family had any earnings. Their plan then had a tax rate of 50% so that if someone in the family earned income, their payments were reduced 50 cents for each dollar earned. Other conditions consisted of tax rates that ranged from 30% to 70% and guarantee levels that varied from 50% to 125% of the poverty line. A control group consisted of families who did not receive any payments.

The experiment was conducted in four communities in New Jersey and one in Pennsylvania. A large household survey was first undertaken to identify eligible families, then those families were invited to participate. If they agreed, the families were randomly allocated to one of the intervention groups or to the control group. The participating families were interviewed prior to enrollment in the program and at the end of each quarter over the three years of the experiment. Among other things, these interviews collected data on employment, earnings, consumption, health, and various social-psychological indicators. The researchers then analyzed the data along with the monthly earnings reports to determine whether those receiving payments diminished their work efforts (as measured in hours of work) in relation to the comparable families in the control groups.

Although about 1,300 families were initially recruited, by the end of the experiment 22% had discontinued their cooperation. Others had missed one or more interviews or had dropped out of the experiment for varying periods. Fewer than 700 remained for analysis of the continuous participants. The overall finding was that families in the intervention groups decreased their work effort by about 5%.

SOURCE: Summary based on D. Kershaw and J. Fair, *The New Jersey Income-Maintenance Experiment*, vol. 1. New York: Academic Press, 1976.

delivering some alternative intervention to a control group). Even when randomization is both possible and permissible, randomized field experiments are challenging to implement, costly if done on a large scale, and demanding with regard to the time, expertise, and cooperation of participants and service providers that are required. They are thus generally conducted only when circumstances are especially favorable, for instance, when a scarce service can be allocated by a lottery or equally attractive program variations can be randomly assigned, or when the impact question has special importance for policy. Dennis and Boruch (1989) identified five threshold conditions that should be met before a randomized field experiment is undertaken (summarized by Dennis, 1990):

- The present practice must need improvement.

- The efficacy of the proposed intervention must be uncertain under field conditions.

- There should be no simpler alternatives for evaluating the intervention.

- The results must be potentially important for policy.

- The design must be able to meet the ethical standards of both the researchers and the service providers.

Some of the conditions that facilitate or impede the utilization of randomized experiments to assess impact are discussed later in this chapter.

Approximations to Random Assignment

The desirable feature of randomization is that the allocation of eligible targets to the intervention and control groups is unbiased; that is, the probabilities of ending up in the intervention or control groups are identical for all participants in the study. There are several alternatives to randomization as a way of obtaining intervention and control groups that may also be relatively unbiased under favorable circumstances and thus constitute acceptable approximations to randomization. In addition, in some cases it can be argued that, although the groups differ, those differences do not produce bias in relation to the outcomes of interest. For instance, a relatively common substitute for randomization is systematic assignment from serialized lists, a procedure that can accomplish the same end as randomization if the lists are not ordered in some way that results in bias. To allocate high school students to intervention and control groups, it might be convenient to place all those with odd ID numbers into the intervention group and all those with even ID numbers into a control group. Under circumstances where the odd and even numbers do not differentiate students on some relevant characteristic, such as odd numbers being assigned to female students and even ones to males, the result will be statistically the same as random assignment. Before using such procedures, therefore, the evaluator must establish how the list was generated and whether the numbering process could bias any allocation that uses it.

Sometimes ordered lists of targets have subtle biases that are difficult to detect. An alphabetized list might tempt an evaluator to assign, say, all persons whose last names begin with "D" to the intervention group and those whose last names begin with "H" to the control group. In a New England city, this procedure would result in an ethnically biased selection, because many names of French Canadian origin begin with "D" (e.g., DeFleur), while very few Hispanic names begin with "H." Similarly, numbered lists may contain age biases if numbers are assigned sequentially. The federal government assigns Social Security numbers sequentially, for instance, so that individuals with lower numbers are generally older than those with higher numbers.

There are also circumstances in which biased allocation may be judged as "ignorable" (Rog, 1994; Rosenbaum and Rubin, 1983). For example, in a Minneapolis test of the effectiveness of a family counseling program to keep children who might be placed in foster care in their families, those children who could not be served by the program because the agency was at full capacity at the time of referral were used as a control group (AuClaire and Schwartz, 1986). The assumption made was that when a child was referred had little or nothing to do with the outcome of interest, namely, a child's prospects for reconciliation with his or her family. Thus, if the circumstances that allocate a target to service or denial of service (or, perhaps, a waiting list for service) are unrelated to the characteristics of the target, the result may be an acceptable approximation to randomization.

Whether events that divide targets into those receiving and not receiving program services operate to make an unbiased allocation, or have biases that can be safely ignored, must be judged through close scrutiny of the circumstances. If there is any reason to suspect that the events in question affect targets with certain characteristics more than others, then the results will not be an acceptable approximation to randomization unless those characteristics can be confidently declared irrelevant to the outcomes at issue. For example, communities that have fluoridated their water supplies cannot be regarded as an intervention group to be contrasted with those who have not for purposes of assessing the effects of fluoridation on dental health. Those communities that adopt fluoridation are quite likely to have distinctive characteristics (e.g., lower average age and more service-oriented government) that cannot be regarded as irrelevant to dental health and thus represent bias in the sense used here.

Data Collection Strategies for Randomized Experiments

Two strategies for data collection can improve the estimates of program effects that result from randomized experiments. The first is to make multiple measurements of the outcome variable, preferably both before and after the intervention that is being assessed. As mentioned earlier, sometimes the outcome variable can be measured only after the intervention, so that no pretest is possible. Such cases aside, the general rule is that the more measurements of the outcome variables made before and after the intervention, the better the estimates of program effect. Measures taken before an intervention indicate the preintervention states of the intervention and control groups and are useful for making statistical adjustments for any preexisting differences that are not fully balanced by the randomization. They are also helpful for determining just how much gain an intervention produced. For example, in the assessment of a vocational retraining project, preintervention measures of earnings for individuals in intervention and control groups would enable the researchers to better estimate the amount by which earnings improved as a result of the training.

The second strategy is to collect data periodically during the course of an intervention. Such periodic measurements allow evaluators to construct useful accounts of how an intervention works over time. For instance, if the vocational retraining effort is found to produce most of its effects during the first four weeks of a six-week program, shortening the training period might be a reasonable option for cutting costs without seriously impairing the program's effectiveness. Likewise, periodic measurements can lead to a fuller understanding of how targets react to services. Some reactions may start slowly and then accelerate; others may be strong initially but trail off as time goes on.

Complex Randomized Experiments

An impact assessment may examine several variants of an intervention or several distinct interventions in a complex design. The New Jersey-Pennsylvania Income Maintenance Experiment (Exhibit 8-D), for example, tested eight variations that differed from one another in the amount of income guaranteed and the tax penalties on family earnings. These variations were included to examine the extent to which different payment schemes might have produced different work disincentives. Critical evaluation questions were whether the effects of payments on employment would vary with (1) the amount of payment offered and (2) the extent to which earnings from work reduced those payments.

Complex experiments along these lines are especially appropriate for exploring potential new policies when it is not clear in advance exactly what form the new policy will take. A range of feasible program variations provides more opportunity to cover the particular policy that might be adopted and hence increases the generalizability of the impact assessment. In addition, testing variations can provide information that helps guide program construction to optimize the effects.

Exhibit 8-E, for example, describes a field experiment conducted on welfare policy in Minnesota. Two program variants were involved in the intervention conditions, both with continuing financial benefits to welfare clients who became employed. One variant included mandatory employment and training activities, while the other did not. If these two versions of the program had proved equally effective, it would clearly be more cost-effective to implement the program without the mandatory employment and training activities. However, the largest effects were found for the combination of financial benefits and mandatory training. This information allows policymakers to

EXHIBIT 8-E

Making Welfare Work and Work Pay: The Minnesota Family Investment Program

---

A frequent criticism of the Aid to Families with Dependent Children (AFDC) program is that it does not encourage recipients to leave the welfare rolls and seek employment because AFDC payments were typically more than could be earned in low-wage employment. The state of Minnesota received a waiver from the federal Department of Health and Human Services to conduct an experiment that would encourage AFDC clients to seek employment and allow them to receive greater income than AFDC would allow if they succeeded. The main modification embodied in the Minnesota Family Investment Program (MFIP) increased AFDC benefits by 20% if participants became employed and reduced their benefits by only $1 for every $3 earned through employment. A child care allowance was also provided so that those employed could obtain child care while working. This meant that AFDC recipients who became employed under this program had more income than they would have received under AFDC.

Over the period 1991 to 1994, some 15,000 AFDC recipients in a number of Minnesota counties were randomly assigned to one of three conditions: (1) an MFIP intervention group receiving more generous benefits and mandatory participation in employment and training activities; (2) an MFIP intervention group receiving only the more generous benefits and not the mandatory employment and training; and (3) a control group that continued to receive the old AFDC benefits and services. All three groups were monitored through administrative data and repeated surveys. The outcome measures included employment, earnings, and satisfaction with the program.

An analysis covering 18 months and the first 9,000 participants in the experiment found that the demonstration was successful. MFIP intervention families were more likely to be employed and, when employed, had larger incomes than control families. Furthermore, those in the intervention group receiving both MFIP benefits and mandatory employment and training activities were more often employed and earned more than the intervention group receiving only the MFIP benefits.

SOURCE: Adapted from Cynthia Miller, Virginia Knox, Patricia Auspos, Jo Anna Hunter-Manns, and Alan Prenstein, *Making Welfare Work and Work Pay: Implementation and 18 Month Impacts of the Minnesota Family Investment Program.* New York: Manpower Demonstration Research Corporation, 1997.

consider the trade-off between the incrementally greater effects on income and employment of the more expensive version of the program and the smaller, but still positive effects of the lower-cost version.

Analyzing Randomized Experiments

The analysis of simple randomized experiments can be quite straightforward. Because the intervention and control groups are statistically equivalent with proper randomization, a comparison of their outcomes constitutes an estimate of the program effect. As noted earlier, a statistical significance test applied to that estimate indicates whether it is larger than the chance fluctuations that are likely to appear when there really is no intervention effect. Exhibit 8-F provides an example of an analysis conducted on a simple randomized experiment. The results are analyzed first by a simple comparison between the mean outcome values for the intervention and control groups, and then with a multiple regression model that provides better statistical control of those variables other than the intervention that might also affect the outcome.

As might be expected, complex randomized experiments require correspondingly complex forms of analysis. Although a simple analysis of variance may be sufficient to obtain an estimate of overall effects, more elaborate analysis techniques will generally be more revealing. Sophisticated multivariate analysis, for instance, can provide greater precision in estimates of intervention effects and permit evaluators to pursue questions that cannot ordinarily be addressed in simple randomized experiments. Exhibit 8-G provides an illustration of how a complex randomized experiment was analyzed through analysis of variance and causal modeling.

Limitations on the Use of Randomized Experiments

Randomized experiments were initially formulated for laboratory and agricultural field research. While their inherent logic is quite appropriate to the task of assessing the impact of social programs, these research designs are nonetheless not applicable to all program situations. In this section, we review some of the limitations on their use in evaluations.

Programs in Early Stages of Implementation

As some of the examples in this chapter have shown, randomized experiments on demonstration programs can yield useful information for purposes of policy and program design. However, once a program design has been adopted and implementation is under way, the impact questions that randomized experiments

EXHIBIT 8-F
Analysis of Randomized Experiments: The Baltimore LIFE Program

The Baltimore LIFE experiment was funded by the Department of Labor to test whether small amounts of financial aid to persons released from prison would help them make the transition to civilian life and reduce the probability of their being arrested and returned to prison. The financial aid was configured to simulate unemployment insurance payments, for which most prisoners are ineligible since they cannot accumulate work credits while imprisoned.

Persons released from Maryland state prisons to return to Baltimore were randomly assigned to either an intervention or control group. Those in the intervention group were eligible for 13 weekly payments of $60 as long as they were unemployed. Those in the control group were told that they were participating in a research project but were not offered payment. Researchers periodically interviewed the participants and monitored their arrest records for a year beyond each prisoner's release date. The arrest records yielded the results over the postrelease year shown in Table 8-F1.

Table 8-F1: Arrest Rates in the First Year After Release

Arrest Charge	Intervention Group (*n* = 216)	Control Group (*n* = 216)	Difference
Theft crimes (e.g., robbery, burglary, larceny)	22.2%	30.6%	−8.4
Other serious crimes (e.g., murder, rape, assault)	19.4%	16.2%	+3.2
Minor crimes (e.g., disorderly conduct, public drinking)	7.9%	10.2%	−2.3

The findings shown in the table are known as main effects and constitute the simplest representation of experimental results. Since randomization has made the intervention and control groups statistically equivalent except for the intervention, the arrest rate differences between them are assumed to be due only to the intervention plus any chance variability.

The substantive import of the findings is summarized in the last column on the right of the table, where the differences between the intervention and control groups in arrest rates are shown for various types of crimes. For theft crimes in the postrelease year the difference of −8.4 percentage points indicated a potential intervention effect in the desired direction. The issue then became whether 8.4 was within the range of expected chance differences, given the sample

(Continued)

Evaluation

EXHIBIT 8-F
(Continued)

sizes (*n*). A variety of statistical tests are applicable to this situation, including chi-square, *t*-tests, and analysis of variance. The researcher used a one-tailed *t*-test, because the direction of the differences between the groups was given by the expected effects of the intervention. The results showed that a difference of –8.4 percentage points or larger would occur by chance less than five times in every hundred experiments of the same sample size (statistically significant at $p \leq .05$). The researchers concluded that the difference was large enough to be taken seriously as an indication that the intervention had its desired effect, at least for theft crimes.

The remaining types of crimes did not show differences large enough to survive the *t*-test criterion. In other words, the differences between the intervention and control groups were within the range where chance fluctuations were sufficient to explain them according to the conventional statistical standards ($p > .05$).

Given these results, the next question is a practical one: Are the differences large enough in a policy sense? In other words, would a reduction of 8.4 percentage points in theft crimes justify the costs of the program? To answer this last question, the Department of Labor conducted a cost-benefit analysis (an approach discussed in Chapter 11) that showed that the benefits far outweighed the costs.

A more complex and informative way of analyzing the theft crime data using multiple regression is shown in Table 8-F2. The question posed is exactly the same as in the previous analysis, but in addition, the multiple regression model takesinto account some of the factors other than the payments that might also affect arrests. The multiple regression analysis statistically controls those other factors while comparing the proportions arrested in the control and intervention groups.

In effect, comparisons are made between intervention and control groups within each level of the other variables used in the analysis. For example, the unemployment rate in Baltimore fluctuated over the two years of the experiment: Some prisoners were released at times when it was easy to get jobs, whereas others were released at less fortunate times. Adding the unemployment rate at time of release to the analysis reduces the variation among individuals due to that factor and thereby purifies estimates of the intervention effect.

Table 8-F2: Multiple Regression Analysis of Arrests for Theft Crimes

Independent Variable	Regression Coefficient (b)	Standard Error of b
Membership in intervention group	–.083*	.041
Unemployment rate when released	.041*	.022

(Continued)

EXHIBIT 8-F

(Continued)

Weeks worked the quarter after release	−.006	.005
Age at release	−.009*	.004
Age at first arrest	−.010*	.006
Prior theft arrests	.028*	.008
Race	.056	.064
Education	−.025	.022
Prior work experience	−.009	.008
Married	−.074	.065
Paroled	−.025	.051
Intercept	.263	.185

$R^2 = .094$*; $N = 432$; *Indicates significance at $p \leq .05$.

Note that all the variables added to the multiple regression analysis of Table 8-F2 were ones that were known from previous research to affect recidivism or chances of finding employment. The addition of these variables strengthened the findings considerably. Each coefficient indicates the change in the probability of postrelease arrest associated with each unit of the independent variable in question. Thus, the −.083 associated with being in the intervention group means that the intervention reduced the arrest rate for theft crimes by 8.3 percentage points. This corresponds closely to what was shown in Table 8-F1, above. However, because of the statistical control of the other variables in the analysis, the chance expectation of a coefficient that large or larger is much reduced, to only two times in every hundred experiments. Hence, the multiple regression results provide more precise estimates of intervention effects. They also tell us that the unemployment rate at time of release, ages at release and first arrest, and prior theft arrests are factors that have a significant influence on the rate of arrest for these ex-prisoners and, hence, affect program outcome.

SOURCE: Adapted from P. H. Rossi, R. A. Berk, and K. J. Lenihan, *Money, Work and Crime: Some Experimental Evidence.*, New York: Academic Press, 1980.

EXHIBIT 8-G
Analyzing a Complex Randomized Experiment: The TARP Study

Based on the encouraging findings of the Baltimore LIFE experiment described in Exhibit 8-F, the Department of Labor decided to embark on a large-scale experiment that would use existing agencies in Texas and Georgia to administer unemployment insurance payments to ex-felons. The objectives of the proposed new program were the same—making ex-felons eligible for unemployment insurance was intended to reduce the need for them to engage in crime to obtain income. However, the new set of experiments, called Transitional Aid to Released Prisoners (TARP), was more differentiated in that they included varying periods of eligibility for benefits and varying rate schedules by which payments were reduced for every dollar earned in employment ("tax rates").

The main effects of the interventions are shown in the analyses of variance in Table 8-G. (For the sake of simplicity, only results from the Texas TARP experiment are shown.) The interventions had no effect on property arrests: The intervention and control groups differed by no more than would be expected by chance. However, the interventions had a very strong effect on the number of weeks worked during the postrelease year: Ex-felons receiving payments worked fewer weeks on the average than those in the control groups, and the differences were statistically significant. In short, it seems that the payments did not compete well with crime but competed quite successfully with employment.

Table 8-G: Analysis of Variance of Property-Related Arrests (Texas data)

A. Property-Related Arrests During Postrelease Year

Intervention Group	Mean Number of Arrests	Percentage Arrested	n
26 weeks payment, 100% tax	.27	22.3	176
13 weeks payment, 25% tax	.43	27.5	200
13 weeks payment, 100% tax	.30	23.5	200
No payments, job placement[a]	.30	20.0	200
Interviewed controls	.33	22.0	200
Uninterviewed controls[b]	.33	23.2	1,000
ANOVA F value	1.15 (p = .33)	.70 (p = .63)	

B. Weeks Worked During Postrelease Year

Intervention Group	Average Number of Weeks Worked	n
26 weeks payment, 100% tax	20.8	169
13 weeks payment, 25% tax	24.6	181

(Continued)

EXHIBIT 8-G

(Continued)

Intervention Group	Average Number of Weeks Worked	n
13 weeks payment, 100% tax	27.1	191
No payments, job placement	29.3	197
Interviewed controls	28.3	189
ANOVA *F* value =	6.98 (*p* < .0001)	

a. Ex-felons in this intervention group were offered special job placement services (which few took) and some help in buying tools or uniforms if required for jobs. Few payments were made.
b. Control observations made through arrest records only; hence, no information on weeks worked.

In short, these results seem to indicate that the experimental interventions did not work in the ways expected and indeed produced undesirable effects. However, an analysis of this sort is only the beginning. The results suggested to the evaluators that a set of counterbalancing processes may have been at work. It is known from the criminological literature that unemployment for ex-felons is related to an increased probability of rearrest. Hence, the researchers postulated that the unemployment benefits created a work disincentive represented in the fewer weeks worked by participants receiving more weeks of benefits or a lower "tax rate" and that this should have the effect of increasing criminal behavior. On the other hand, the payments should have reduced the need to engage in criminal behavior to produce income. Thus, a positive effect of payments in reducing criminal activity may have been offset by the negative effects of less employment over the period of the payments so that the total effect on arrests was virtually zero.

To examine the plausibility of this "counterbalancing effects" interpretation, a causal model was constructed, as shown in Figure 8-G. In that model, negative coefficients are expected for the effects of payments on employment (the work disincentive) and for their effects on arrests (the expected intervention effect). The counterbalancing effect of unemployment, in turn, should show up as a negative coefficient between employment and arrest, indicating that fewer weeks of employment are associated with more arrests. The coefficients shown in Figure 8-G were derived empirically from the data using a statistical technique known as structural equation modeling. As shown there, the hypothesized relationships appear in both the Texas and Georgia data.

This complex experiment, combined with sophisticated multivariate analysis, therefore, shows that the effects of the intervention were negligible but also provides some explanation of that result. In particular, the evidence indicates that the payments functioned as expected to reduce criminal behavior but that a successful program would have to find a way to counteract the accompanying work disincentive with its negative effects.

(Continued)

FIGURE 8-G

(Continued)

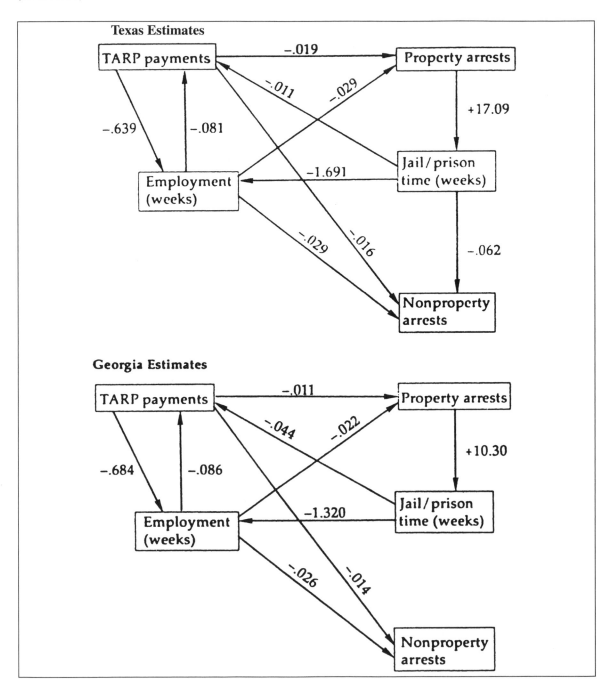

SOURCE: Adapted from P. H. Rossi, R. A. Berk, and K. J. Lenihan, *Money, Work and Crime: Some Experimental Evidence*. New York: Academic Press, 1980.

are so good at answering may not be appropriate until the program is stable and operationally mature. In the early stages of program implementation, various program features often need to be revised for the sake of perfecting the intervention or its delivery. Although a randomized experiment can contrast program outcomes with those for untreated targets, the results will not be very informative if the program has changed during the course of the experiment. If the program has changed appreciably before outcomes are measured, the effects of the different variants of the intervention will all be mixed together in the results with no easy way to determine what program version produced what effects. Expensive field experiments, therefore, are best reserved for tests of firmly designed interventions that will be consistently implemented during the course of the experiment.

Ethical Considerations

A frequent obstacle to the use of randomized experiments is that some stake-holders have ethical qualms about randomization, seeing it as arbitrarily and capriciously depriving control groups of positive benefits. The reasoning of such critics generally runs as follows: If it is worth experimenting with a program (i.e., if the project seems likely to help targets), it is a positive harm to withhold potentially helpful services from those who need them. To do so is therefore unethical. The coun-terargument is obvious: Ordinarily, it is not known whether an intervention is effective; indeed, that is the reason for an experiment. Since researchers cannot know in advance whether or not an intervention will be helpful, they are not depriving the controls of something known to be beneficial and, indeed, may be sparing them from wasting time with an ineffective program.

Sometimes an intervention may present some possibility of harm, and decision-makers might be reluctant to authorize randomization on those grounds alone. In some utility-pricing experiments, for instance, household utility bills had the potential to increase for some intervention groups. The researchers countered this argument by promising intervention households that any such overages would be reimbursed after the study was over. Of course, this promise of reimbursement changes the character of the intervention, possibly fostering irresponsible usage of utilities.

The most compelling ethical objections generally involve the conditions of control groups. If conventional services are known to be effective for their problems, it would generally be unethical to withhold those services for the purposes of testing alternative services. We would not, for instance, deprive schoolchildren of mathematics instruction so that they could constitute a control group in an experiment testing a new math curriculum. In such cases, however, the important question usually is not whether the new curriculum is better than no instruction but, rather, whether it is better than current practices. The appropriate experimental comparison, therefore, is between the new curriculum and a control condition representing current instructional practice.

When program resources are scarce and fall well short of demand, random assignment to control conditions can present an especially difficult ethical dilemma. This procedure amounts to randomly selecting those relatively few eligible targets that will receive the program services. However, if the intervention cannot be given to all who qualify, it can be argued that randomization is the most equitable method of deciding who is to get it, since all targets have an equal chance. And, indeed, if there is great uncertainty about the efficacy of the intervention, this may be quite acceptable. However, when service providers are convinced that the intervention is efficacious, as they often are despite the lack of experimental evidence, they may object strongly to allocating service by chance and insist that the most needy targets receive priority. As will be discussed in the next chapter, this is a situation to which the regression-discontinuity quasi-experimental design is well adapted as an alternative to a randomized experiment.

Differences Between Experimental and Actual Intervention Delivery

Another limitation on the use of randomized experiments in evaluation is that the delivery of an intervention in an experimental impact assessment may differ in critical ways from how it would be delivered in routine practice. With standardized and easily delivered interventions, such as welfare payments, the experimental intervention is quite likely to be representative of what would happen in a fully implemented program—there are only a limited number of ways checks can be delivered. More labor-intensive, high-skill interventions (e.g., job placement services, counseling, and teaching), on the other hand, are likely to be delivered with greater care and consistency in a field experiment than when routinely provided by the program. Indeed, as we saw in Chapter 6, the very real danger that the implementation of an intervention will deteriorate is one of the principal reasons for monitoring program process.

One approach to this problem, when the significance of the policy decision warrants it, is to conduct two rounds of experiments. In the first, interventions are implemented in their purest form as part of the research protocol, and, in the second, they are delivered through public agencies. The evaluation of the Department of Labor's program to provide unemployment insurance benefits to released prisoners described in Exhibits 8-F and 8-G used this strategy. The first stage consisted of the small-scale experiment in Baltimore with 432 prisoners released from the Maryland state prisons. The researchers selected the prisoners before release, provided them with payments, and observed their work and arrest patterns for a year. As described in Exhibit 8-F, the results showed a reduction in theft arrests over the postrelease period for intervention groups receiving unemployment insurance payments for 13 weeks.

The larger second-stage experiment was undertaken in Georgia and Texas with 2,000 released prisoners in each state (Exhibit 8-G). Payments were administered through the Employment Security Agencies in each of the states and they worked with the state prison systems to track the prisoners for a year after release. This second-stage experiment involved conditions close to those that would have been put into place if the program had been enacted through federal legislation. The second-stage experiment, however, found that the payments were not effective when administered under the Employment Security Agency rules and procedures.

Time and Cost

A major obstacle to randomized field experiments is that they are usually costly and time- consuming, especially large-scale multisite experiments. For this reason, they should ordinarily not be undertaken to assess program concepts that are very unlikely to be adopted by decisionmakers or to assess established programs when there is not significant stakeholder interest in evidence about impact. Moreover, experiments should not be undertaken when information is needed in a hurry. To underscore this last point, it should be noted that the New Jersey-Pennsylvania Income Maintenance Experiment (Exhibit 8-D) cost $34 million (in 1968 dollars) and took more than seven years from design to published findings. The Seattle and Denver income maintenance experiments took even longer, with their results appearing in final form long after income maintenance as a policy had disappeared from the national agenda (Mathematica Policy Research, 1983; Office of Income Security, 1983; SRI International, 1983).

Integrity of Experiments

Finally, we should note that the integrity of a randomized experiment is easily threatened. Although randomly formed intervention and control groups are expected to be statistically equivalent at the beginning of an experiment, nonrandom processes may undermine that equivalence as the experiment progresses. Differential attrition may introduce differences between intervention and control participants. In the income maintenance experiments, for example, those families in the intervention groups who received the less generous payment plans and those in the control groups were the ones most likely to stop cooperating with the research. With no reason to believe that the smaller numbers dropping out of the other conditions were at all equivalent, the comparability of the intervention and control groups was compromised with corresponding potential for bias in the estimates of program effects.

Also, it is difficult to deliver a "pure program." Although an evaluator may design an experiment to test the effects of a given intervention, everything that is done to the intervention group becomes part of the intervention. For example, the TARP experiments (Exhibit 8-G) were designed to test the effects of modest amounts of postprison financial aid, but the aid was administered by a state agency and hence the agency's procedures became part of the intervention. Indeed, there are few, if any, large-scale randomized social experiments that have not been compromised in some manner or left with uncertainty about what aspect of the experimental conditions was responsible for any effects found. Even with such problems, however, a randomized field experiment will generally yield estimates of program effects that are more credible than the alternatives, including the nonrandomized designs discussed in the next chapter.

Summary

- The purpose of impact assessments is to determine the effects that programs have on their intended outcomes. Randomized field experiments are the flagships of impact assessment because, when well conducted, they provide the most credible conclusions about program effects.

- Impact assessments may be conducted at various stages in the life of a program. But because rigorous impact assessments involve significant resources, evaluators should consider whether a requested impact assessment is justified by the circumstances.

- The methodological concepts that underlie all research designs for impact assessment are based on the logic of the randomized experiment. An essential feature of this logic is the division of the targets under study into intervention and control groups by random assignment. In quasi-experiments, assignment to groups is accomplished by some means other than true randomization. Evaluators must judge in each set of circumstances what constitutes a "good enough" research design.

- The principal advantage of the randomized experiment is that it isolates the effect of the intervention being evaluated by ensuring that intervention and control groups are statistically equivalent except for the intervention received. Strictly equivalent groups are identical in composition, experiences over the period of observation, and predispositions toward the program under study. In practice, it is sufficient that the groups, as aggregates, are comparable with respect to any characteristics that could be relevant to the outcome.

- Although chance fluctuations will create some differences between any two groups formed through randomization, statistical significance tests allow researchers to estimate the likelihood that observed outcome differences are due to chance rather than the intervention being evaluated.

■ The choice of units of analysis in impact assessments is determined by the nature of the intervention and the targets to which the intervention is directed.

■ Some procedures or circumstances may produce acceptable approximations to randomization, such as assigning every other name on a list or selection into service according to the program's capacity to take additional clients at any given time. However, these alternatives can substitute adequately for randomization only if they generate intervention and control groups that do not differ on any characteristics relevant to the intervention or the expected outcomes.

■ Although postintervention measures of outcome are essential for impact assessment, measures taken before and during an intervention, as well as repeated measurement afterward, can increase the precision with which effects are estimated and enable evaluators to examine how the intervention worked over time.

■ Complex impact assessments may examine several interventions, or variants of a single intervention. The analysis of such experiments requires sophisticated statistical techniques.

■ Despite their rigor, randomized experiments may not be appropriate or feasible for some impact assessments. Their results may be ambiguous when applied to programs in the early stages of implementation, when interventions may change in ways experiments cannot easily capture. Furthermore, stakeholders may be unwilling to permit randomization if they believe it is unfair or unethical to withhold the program services from a control group.

■ Experiments are resource intensive, requiring technical expertise, research resources, time, and tolerance from programs for disruption of their normal procedures for delivering services. They also can create somewhat artificial situations such that the delivery of the program in the intervention condition may differ from the intervention as it is routinely delivered in practice.

KEY CONCEPTS

Control group

A group of targets that do not receive the program intervention and that is compared on outcome measures with one or more groups that do receive the intervention. Compare *intervention group*.

Intervention group

A group of targets that receive an intervention and whose outcome measures are compared with those of one or more control groups. Compare *control group.*

Quasi-experiment

An impact research design in which intervention and control groups are formed by a procedure other than random assignment.

Randomization

Assignment of potential targets to intervention and control groups on the basis of chance so that every unit in a target population has the same probability as any other to be selected for either group.

Randomized field experiment

A research design conducted in a program setting in which intervention and control groups are formed by random assignment and compared on outcome measures to determine the effects of the intervention. See also *control group; intervention group.*

Units of analysis

The units on which outcome measures are taken in an impact assessment and, correspondingly, the units on which data are available for analysis. The units of analysis may be individual persons but can also be families, neighborhoods, communities, organizations, political jurisdictions, geographic areas, or any other such entities.

9

Assessing Program Impact

Alternative Designs

Although well-implemented randomized field experiments are the preferred designs for impact assessments because they yield unbiased estimates of program effects, evaluators must frequently rely on nonrandomized designs for practical reasons. In this chapter, we discuss designs for assessing program outcomes in which control groups are constructed by nonrandom means. These designs are commonly used when it is not possible to randomize targets into groups that participate and do not participate in the program. We also discuss another family of designs that use reflexive controls (comparison of targets with themselves). None of these alternative designs provides the level of certainty that the resulting estimates of program effects are unbiased that randomized field experiments do.

A s we discussed in Chapter 8, a randomized field experiment is the strongest research design for assessing program impact. When implemented well, it yields estimates of impact that are unbiased; that is, there is no built-in tendency for the results to either over- or underestimate the magnitude of program effects. The objective of an evaluator conducting an impact assessment, of course, should be a fair and accurate estimate of the program's actual effects, which is why the randomized field experiment is generally the design of choice when it is feasible.

When a randomized design is not feasible, there are alternative research designs that an evaluator can use. They all share one problematic characteristic, however: Even when well crafted and implemented, they may still yield biased estimates of program effects. Such biases systematically exaggerate or diminish program effects, and the direction the bias may take cannot usually be known in advance. Such biases, of course, can affect stakeholders' interests. Program participants can be disadvantaged if the bias is such that it makes an ineffective or harmful program appear effective. Funders and policymakers concerned about wasting resources also are not helped by that circumstance. On the other hand, a bias that makes a truly effective program appear ineffective or harmful would unfairly belittle the accomplishments of program personnel and possibly cause the program's sponsors to reduce or eliminate the funding for the program.

A major concern of evaluators using any impact assessment design, therefore, should be to minimize bias in the estimate of program effects. Correspondingly, the major issue of concern when nonrandomized designs are used is how to minimize the potential for bias. Because there is no way to accomplish this with certainty, the validity of the results of impact assessments using nonrandomized designs is always at least somewhat questionable. To understand why this is so and the ways researchers try to deal with it, we must understand where bias comes from. With this understanding in hand, we will then turn to the various forms of nonrandomized designs and how they may be used to estimate program effects when a randomized design is not feasible.

Bias in Estimation of Program Effects

After targets have been exposed to a program, evaluators can observe their outcome status and, with valid and reliable measurement, expect to describe it with acceptable accuracy and precision. As discussed in Chapter 7, a program effect is the difference between that observed outcome and the outcome that would have occurred for those same targets, all other things being equal, had they not been exposed to the program. Bias comes into the picture when either the measurement of the outcome with program exposure or the estimate of what the outcome would have been without program exposure is higher or lower than the corresponding "true" value. When the level of either of these outcomes is misrepresented in the evaluation data, the estimate of the program effect, in turn, will be smaller or larger than the actual program effect; that is, it will be biased.

The first problem is bias in measuring the observed outcome for targets exposed to an intervention. This type of bias is relatively easy to avoid by using measures that are valid and responsive to the full range of outcome levels likely to appear among the targets. As a result, bias in impact assessments most often results from research designs that systematically underestimate or overestimate the unobserved outcome that would have occurred without exposure to the intervention. This sort of bias is illustrated in Exhibit 9-A using the graph from Chapter 7 (Exhibit 7-A) that illustrates a program effect. Because the actual outcome-without-intervention cannot be observed for the targets that do, in fact, receive the intervention, we have no ready means to determine when there is this kind of bias in an estimate of the program effect. This inherent uncertainty is what makes the potential for bias so problematic in impact assessment. Note that the advantage of a randomized design is that, though it may misestimate the outcome-without-intervention in any given instance, the randomization makes that happen only by chance so that over- and underestimation are equally likely and there is no systematic bias.

Consider, for example, a simple case of fairly obvious bias. Suppose we are evaluating a reading program for young children that emphasizes vocabulary development, and we have an appropriate vocabulary test for measuring outcome. We use this test to measure the children's vocabulary before and after the program. The test is valid, reliable, and sensitive to the areas of vocabulary development the program stresses, so we are fairly confident we can obtain a valid description of the vocabulary level the children have after participating in the program. To estimate the program's effect on vocabulary, we must then compare that postprogram level with some estimate of what those children's vocabulary level would have been had they not participated in the program. We decide to use the results of the vocabulary test administered before the program began for that purpose. Thus, we assume that, without the program, the

EXHIBIT 9-A
Illustration of Bias
in the Estimate of a
Program Effect

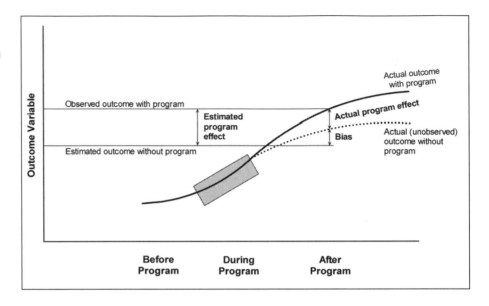

children's vocabulary would not change over the period of interest. We then subtract the mean value of the vocabulary pretest from the posttest to get our estimate of program effect. This situation is illustrated in Exhibit 9-B.

The bias in this estimate of the program effect comes in because the vocabulary of young children is not, in fact, static but rather tends to increase over time (and virtually never decreases under ordinary circumstances). This means that, had the children not been in the program, their vocabulary would have increased anyway, though perhaps not as much as with the help of the program. The amount by which it would have increased on its own is included in our estimate along with the actual program effect. This is the source of the bias in our estimate (as shown in Exhibit 9-B). It is because of such natural changes over time in so many aspects of human behavior that before-after measures almost always produce biased estimates of program effects. Unfortunately for the evaluator engaged in impact assessment, not all forms of bias that may compromise impact assessment are as obvious as this one, as we are about to discuss.

Selection Bias

As we described in the preceding chapter, the most common form of impact assessment design involves comparing two groups of individuals or other units, an

EXHIBIT 9-B

Bias in the Estimate of the Effect of a Reading Program on Children's Vocabulary Based on Before-After Change

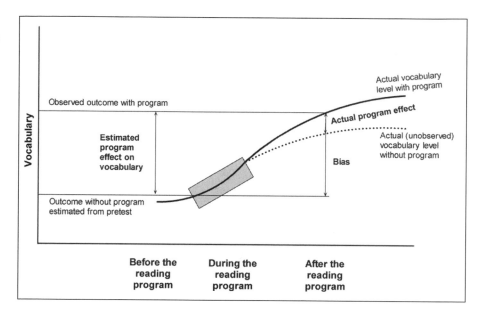

intervention group that receives the program and a control group that does not. The estimate of program effect is then based on the difference between the groups on a suitable outcome measure (e.g., mean outcome score for the intervention group minus the mean outcome score of the control group). That simple difference is an unbiased estimate of the program effect only on the assumption that, if neither group received the program, their mean outcome scores would be the same over the pertinent pre-post time interval. If that assumption can be made, then any actual difference in their scores must be a program effect. The beauty of random assignment of individuals to program and control groups is that we can indeed make this assumption of continuing equivalence, within the bounds of chance fluctuations that can be assessed with statistical significance tests.

If the groups have not been randomly assigned, however, this critical assumption will be questionable. A group comparison design for which the groups have not been formed through randomization is known as a **nonequivalent comparison design** irrespective of how equivalent the groups may appear. This label emphasizes the fact that equivalence on outcome, absent program exposure, cannot necessarily be assumed.

When the equivalence assumption does not hold, the difference in outcome between the groups that would have occurred anyway produces a form of bias in the estimate of program effects that is known as **selection bias.** This type of bias is an inherent threat to the validity of the program effect estimate in any impact assessment using a nonequivalent (i.e., nonrandomized) group comparison design.

Selection bias gets its name because it appears in situations when some process that has influences that are not fully known selects which individuals will be in which group, as opposed to the assignment to groups being determined by pure chance (which has known influences). Imagine, for instance, that we administer the program to a group of individuals who volunteer to participate and use those who do not volunteer as the control group. By volunteering, individuals have self-selected which group they will be in. The selection bias is any difference between volunteers and nonvolunteers that would show up on the outcome measure if neither group got the program. Because we are unlikely to know what all the relevant differences are between volunteers and nonvolunteers, we have limited ability to determine the nature and extent of that bias.

Selection bias, however, does not refer only to bias that results from a deliberate selection into the program or not, as with the volunteers and nonvolunteers. It often has much more subtle forms. Suppose, for example, that an evaluator assessing the impact of a schoolwide drug prevention program finds another nearby school that does not have the program but is otherwise similar. The evaluator could use the children in that school as a control group for the children in the school with the program by comparing the two groups' levels of drug use at the end of the school year. Even if drug use was the same for the children in both schools at the beginning of the school year, however, how does the evaluator know that it would be the same at the end of the year if neither received the program? There are many personal, cultural, and economic factors that influence where a child lives and what school he or she attends. These factors operate to "select" some children to attend the one school and some to attend the other. Whatever differences these children have that influence their school attendance may also influence the likelihood that they will use drugs over the course of the school year at issue. To the extent that happens, there will be selection bias in any estimate of the effects of the drug prevention program made by comparing drug use at the two schools.

Selection bias can also occur through natural or deliberate processes that cause a loss of outcome data for members of intervention and control groups that have already been formed, a circumstance known as **attrition.** Attrition can occur in two ways: (1) targets drop out of the intervention or control group and cannot be reached, or (2) targets refuse to cooperate in outcome measurement. Because the critical issue is whether the groups would be equivalent except for program effects at the time of the postprogram outcome measurement, any missing outcome data from cases originally assigned to intervention or control groups select individuals out of the research design. Whenever attrition occurs as a result of something other than an explicit chance process (e.g., using a random number table or coin flip), which is virtually always, differential attrition has to be assumed. That is, those from the intervention group whose outcome data are missing cannot be assumed to have the same outcome-relevant characteristics as those from the control group whose outcome data are missing. It follows that the comparability of those left in the groups after any attrition will have changed as well, with all the implications for selection bias.

It should be apparent that random assignment designs are not immune from selection bias induced by attrition. Random assignment produces groups that are statistically equivalent at the time of the initial assignment, but it is equivalence at the time of postprogram outcome measurement that protects against selection bias. Consequently, selection bias is produced by any attrition from either the intervention or the control group, or both, such that outcome data are not collected for every unit that was initially randomized. To maintain the validity of a randomized field experiment, therefore, the evaluator must prevent or, at least, minimize attrition on outcome measures, else the design quickly degrades to a nonequivalent comparison group.

Note that the kind of attrition that degrades the research design is a loss of cases from outcome measurement. Targets that drop out of the program do not create selection bias if they still cooperate in outcome measurement. When these targets do not complete the program, it degrades the program implementation but not the research design for assessing the impact of the program at whatever degree of implementation results. The evaluator should thus attempt to obtain outcome measures for everyone in the intervention group whether or not they actually received the full program. Similarly, outcome data should be obtained for everyone in the control group even if some ended up receiving the program or some other relevant service. If full outcome data are obtained, the validity of the design for comparing the two groups is retained. What suffers when there is not full service to the intervention group and the absence of such service to the control group is the sharpness of the comparison and the meaning of the resulting estimates of program effect. Whatever program effects are found represent the effects of the program as delivered to the intended group, which may be less than the full program. If the control group receives services, the effect estimates represent what is gained by providing whatever fuller implementation the intervention group receives relative to the control group.

In sum, selection bias applies not only to the initial assignment of targets to intervention and control groups but also to the data available for the groups at the time of the outcome measurement. That is, selection bias includes all situations in which the units that contribute outcome measures to a comparison between those receiving and not receiving the program differ on some inherent characteristics that influence their status on those outcome measures, aside from those related directly to program participation.

Other Sources of Bias

Apart from selection bias, the other factors that can bias the results of an impact assessment generally have to do with events or experiences other than receiving the program that occur during the period of the intervention. Estimation of program effects by comparing outcomes for intervention and control groups requires not only that the units in both groups be equivalent on outcome-related characteristics but that their outcome-related experiences during the course of the study be equivalent except for the difference in program exposure. To the extent that one group has experiences other than program participation that the other group does not have and that also affect the outcome, the difference between the outcomes for the two groups will reflect the program effect plus the effects of that other experience. Those latter effects, of course, will make the program effect appear larger or smaller than it actually is and thus constitute bias.

Intervening events or experiences are potential problems even when the units that receive the program are compared with those same units prior to receiving the program in a before-and-after design. To the extent that the units have experiences or are subjected to extraneous events during the program period that are unrelated to the program but influence the outcomes, before-and-after comparisons yield biased estimates of program effects. We have already seen an example in the case of the natural growth in vocabulary that would occur for young children over the period of participation in a reading program (Exhibit 9-B).

The difficulty for evaluators is that social programs operate in environments in which ordinary or natural sequences of events inevitably influence the outcomes of interest. For example, many persons who recover from acute illnesses do so naturally because ordinary body defenses are typically sufficient to overcome such illnesses. Thus, medical experiments testing a treatment for some pathological condition—influenza, say—must distinguish the effects of the intervention from the changes that would have occurred without the treatment or the estimates of treatment effects will be quite biased. The situation is similar for social interventions. A program for training young people in particular occupational skills must contend with the fact that some people will obtain the same skills in ways that do not involve the program. Likewise, assessments of a program to reduce poverty must consider that some families and individuals will become better off economically without outside help.

The experiences and events that may produce bias in impact assessments generally fall into three categories: secular trends, interfering events, and maturation.

Secular Trends

Relatively long-term trends in the community, region, or country, sometimes termed *secular drift,* may produce changes that enhance or mask the apparent effects of a program. In a period when a community's birth rate is declining, a program to reduce fertility may appear effective because of bias stemming from that downward trend. Similarly, a program to upgrade the quality of housing occupied by poor families may appear to be more effective than it actually is because of upward national trends in real income that enable everyone to put more resources into their housing. Secular trends can also produce bias that masks the real impact of programs. An effective project to increase crop yields, for example, may appear to have no impact if the estimates of program effects are biased by the influence of unfavorable weather during the program period. Similarly, the effects of a program to provide employment opportunities to released prisoners may be obscured if the program coincides with a depressed period in the labor market.

Interfering Events

Like secular trends, short-term events can produce changes that may introduce bias into estimates of program effect. A power outage that disrupts communications and hampers the delivery of food supplements may interfere with a nutritional program. A natural disaster may make it appear that a program to increase community cooperation has been effective, when in reality it is the crisis situation that has brought community members together.

Maturation

As noted earlier, impact evaluations must often cope with the fact that natural maturational and developmental processes can produce considerable change independently of the program. If those changes are included in estimates of program effects, then those estimates will be biased. For example, the effectiveness of a campaign to increase interest in sports among young adults may be masked by a general decline in such interest that occurs when they enter the labor force. Maturational trends can affect older adults as well: A program to improve preventive health practices among adults may seem ineffective because health generally declines with age.

Bias in Nonrandomized Designs

This discussion of bias in impact assessment has been motivated by the fact that it is the pivotal issue in the design and analysis of all impact assessments that are not conducted as well-implemented randomized field experiments. Indeed, in some circumstances bias can be highly relevant to randomized experiments as well. In the randomized experiment, a proper randomization with no attrition from outcome measurement should prevent selection bias. Careful maintenance of comparable circumstances for program and control groups between random assignment and outcome measurement should prevent bias from the influence of other differential experiences or events on the groups. If either of these conditions is absent from the design, however, there is potential for bias in the estimates of program effect.

Minimizing bias in these estimates is the crucial research design issue with which the evaluator must contend when using any nonrandomized impact assessment design, and any randomized one with relatively high attrition or differential extraneous events or experiences between intervention and control groups. For this reason, we will organize our discussion of the alternatives to the randomized field experiment around consideration of their potential for bias in the resulting estimates of program effect and the ways the evaluator can attempt to reduce it.

Quasi-Experimental Impact Assessment

As noted in Chapter 8, the term *quasi-experiment* is used to describe impact designs that do not involve randomly assigned intervention and control groups. In quasi-experimental designs, targets receiving the intervention are compared to a control group of selected, nonrandomly assigned targets or potential targets that do not receive the intervention. To the extent that the latter resemble the intervention group on relevant characteristics and experiences, or can be statistically adjusted to resemble it, then program effects can be assessed with a reasonable degree of confidence.

A quasi-experimental design may also result when an evaluation that starts as a randomized experiment does not end up that way. Consider, for example, the impact assessment of the New Orleans Homeless Substance Abusers Project, a residential adult resocialization project for homeless alcohol and drug abusers (Devine, Wright, and Brody, 1995). The impact assessment was designed as a randomized experiment but less than one-third of the eligible clients were actually assigned randomly. Program staff subverted the randomization procedure by using an assignment to treatment generated by the procedure only when the person involved was one they viewed as a "good" client for the program; otherwise, the staff assigned that person to the control group. In addition, attrition from the outcome data collection further undermined the intended randomized design. Because the intervention and control groups that resulted did not fulfill the requirements of a randomized experiment, the evaluators were obligated to treat this situation as a quasi-experimental design.

Whether a specific quasi-experiment will yield unbiased estimates of program effects depends largely on the extent to which the design minimizes critical differences between the intervention and control groups. When there is a possibility of relevant differences between the groups, as there typically is in quasi-experiments, there is also a possibility that these differences will bias the estimates of the program effects. Suppose, for instance, that a state program to increase agricultural productivity uses an intensive educational campaign to instruct farmers how to increase production by using fertilizers properly. The evaluators choose a number of agricultural districts as the targets to be exposed to the campaign by asking district agricultural agencies to volunteer to run the educational campaign in their districts. They then select a control group of agricultural districts from among the nonvolunteering districts that match the participating districts with respect to a number of characteristics that might affect agricultural productivity (e.g., average rainfall, average size of farm holdings, crops planted, and average amount of capital equipment per holding). The difficulty is that there might be other, perhaps unknown, differences between the two groups that are strongly related to crop yield. Perhaps the districts in which officials volunteer for the project are more progressive in relation to innovations or more inclined to take risks. To the extent that such districts have also adopted other practices that influence crop yields, a selection bias is at work that will lead to erroneous estimates of program effects.

The use of quasi-experiments, therefore, requires extreme care to ensure as much equivalence as possible between the groups that will be compared. The quasi-experimental techniques to be reviewed here include constructing control groups by matching, equating groups by statistical procedures, regression-discontinuity designs, and the use of reflexive controls (in which targets are compared with themselves).

Constructing Control Groups by Matching

One procedure for constructing control groups in a quasi-experiment is the use of **matching.** In a matched design, the intervention group is typically specified first and the evaluator then constructs a control group by selecting targets unexposed to the intervention that match those in the intervention group on selected characteristics. The logic of this design requires that the groups be matched on any characteristics that would cause them to differ on the outcome of interest under conditions when neither of them received the intervention. To the extent that the matching falls short of equating the groups on characteristics that will influence the outcome, selection bias will be introduced into the resulting program effect estimate.

Choosing Variables to Match

The first difficulty for the evaluator attempting to use a matched design is knowing which characteristics are the essential ones to match. The evaluator should make this determination on the basis of prior knowledge and a theoretical understanding of the social processes in question. Relevant information will often be available from the research literature in substantive areas related to the program. For a program designed to reduce pregnancy among unmarried adolescents, for instance, research on teens' proclivity to bear children would be consulted to identify their motivations for engaging in sexual behavior, becoming pregnant, and so on. The objective in constructing a matched control group would be to select youths that match the treated ones as closely as possible on all the important determinants of teen pregnancy.

Special attention should be paid to identifying variables that are potentially related to the selection processes that divide targets into program participants and nonparticipants. For example, in studying a job training program for unemployed youths, it might be important to match intervention and control groups with regard to the youths' attitudes toward training and their assessments of its value in obtaining employment (Chen, 1990). When the groups cannot be matched on variables related to selection, the evaluator should still identify and measure those variables. This allows them to be incorporated into the data analysis to explore and, perhaps, statistically adjust for any remaining selection bias.

Fortunately, it is not usually necessary to match the groups on every factor mentioned in the relevant research literature that may relate to the outcomes of interest. The pertinent characteristics will often be correlated and, therefore, somewhat redundant. For example, if an evaluator of an educational intervention matches students on the basis of intelligence measures, the individuals will also be fairly well matched on their grade point averages, since intelligence test scores and grades are rather strongly related. The evaluator should be aware of those intercorrelations, however, and attempt to match the groups on all influential, nonredundant factors. If the groups end up differing much on any characteristic that influences the outcome, the result will be a biased estimate of the program effect.

Matching Procedures

Matched control groups may be constructed through either individual or aggregate matching. In individual matching, the effort is to draw a "partner" for each target who receives the intervention from the pool of potential targets unexposed to the program. For children in a school drug prevention program, for example, the evaluator might deem the relevant matching variables to be age, sex, number of siblings, and father's occupation. In this case, the evaluator might scrutinize the roster of unexposed children at, say, a nearby school without the program in the light of these variables in order to locate the closest equivalent child for pairing with each given child in the intervention group. In such a procedure, the criteria of closeness may be adjusted to make matching possible—for example, matching so the exposed and unexposed children are within six months of age. Exhibit 9-C provides an illustration of individual matching.

EXHIBIT 9-C

Studying the Effects of Inclusive Education Using Individually Matched Controls

Students with severe disabilities have traditionally been taught in self-contained special education classrooms, but current policy debates focus on whether more "inclusive" arrangements in general education settings might be preferable. One particular interest is whether inclusive schools facilitate the social development of students with severe disabilities. An important part of the rationale for inclusive education has come from research showing poor social relationships between students with and without disabilities in traditional special education arrangements.

To assess the effects of inclusive education on the social relationships of intermediate students with severe disabilities, a team of researchers devised an impact assessment using students in junior high classrooms on the island of Oahu in Hawaii. In Oahu, disabled students in some schools receive special education support within general education classrooms, while, in other schools, they are taught in self-contained classrooms on the school campus with special education supports provided within those classrooms.

Each of the eight disabled students in regular junior high classrooms was matched with a student in a special education classroom on age, gender, level of disability, adaptive communication behavior, and adaptive social behavior. Statistical analyses for matched pairs revealed no significant differences between students in the two groups. These groups were then compared on outcome measures relating to the students' friendship networks and the character of their interaction with peers without disabilities. The results showed that the students in general education classrooms interacted more frequently with peers without disabilities across a greater range of activities and settings, received and provided higher levels of social support, and had larger friendship networks and more durable relationships with peers without disabilities.

SOURCE: Adapted from Craig H. Kennedy, Smita Shikla, and Dale Fryxell, "Comparing the Effects of Educational Placement on the Social Relationships of Intermediate School Students With Severe Disabilities." *Exceptional Children*, 1997, 64(1):31-47.

With aggregate matching, individuals are not matched case by case, but the overall distributions in the intervention and control groups on each matching variable are made comparable. For instance, the same proportions of children by sex and age would be found in each group, but this result may have been obtained by including a 12-year-old girl and an 8-year-old boy in the control group to balance the aggregate distribution of the intervention group, which included a 9-year-old girl and an 11-year-old boy. Exhibit 9-D gives an example of aggregate matching.

Exhibit 9-D
Evaluation of a
Family Development
Program Using
Aggregate-Matched
Controls

A program was started in Baltimore to serve poor families living in public housing by providing integrated services with the hope of helping families escape from long-term poverty. Services included access to special educational programs for children and adults, job training programs, teenage programs, special health care access, and child care facilities. To the extent possible, these services were delivered within the LaFayette Courts public housing project. Case managers assigned to the housing project helped families choose services appropriate to them. The special feature of this program was its emphasis on serving families rather than individuals. In all, 125 families were enrolled.

To constitute a control group, 125 families were chosen from a comparable public housing project, Murphy Homes. The impact of the Family Development program was then assessed by contrasting the enrolled families with the Murphy Homes sample. After a year of enrollment, the participating families were shown to be higher in self-esteem and sense of control over their fates, but positive impacts on employment and earnings had not yet occurred.

SOURCE: Adapted from Anne B. Shlay and C. Scott Holupka, *Steps Toward Independence: The Early Effects of the LaFayette Courts Family Development Center.* Baltimore, MD: Institute for Policy Studies, Johns Hopkins University, 1991.

Individual matching is usually preferable to aggregate matching, especially when several characteristics are used simultaneously as matching variables. The drawbacks to individual matching are that it is more time-consuming and difficult to execute for a large number of matched variables. Also, matching by individuals can sometimes result in a drastic loss of cases. If matching persons cannot be found for some individuals in the intervention group, those unmatched individuals have to be discarded as data sources. In some situations, the proportion of unmatched individuals can become so large that the exposed targets for which matches are available are no longer representative of the population to which the intervention is applied.

In addition, if the variables on which the matching is done have low reliability, there are circumstances in which serious statistical artifacts may be produced. This is especially likely to occur when the individuals selected for the matches come from different tails of their respective distributions on those variables. Suppose, for instance, that students are being matched on teachers' ratings of scholastic aptitude and that those ratings have modest reliability. If the intervention group for a remedial program comes from schools that have lower scores than those schools from which the control group is to be selected, most matches will be found for the higher-scoring intervention targets and the lower-scoring members of the control schools. Under these circumstances, comparisons between these groups on subsequently measured outcome variables may show spurious differences unrelated to program effects (an artifact called *regression to the mean;* further discussion can be found in Campbell, 1996; Campbell and Boruch, 1975; Hsu, 1995).

However carefully matching is done, there is always the possibility that some critical difference remains between the intervention group and the selected controls. If the relevant variables are known and measured, they can be used as statistical controls (discussed in the next section) even if they cannot be matched. Indeed, a useful variation on the matched control group design is to match on some important variables while controlling others statistically.

In fact, statistical controls have supplanted and supplemented matching to a considerable extent in recent decades. In many applications, they are the functional equivalent of matching. However, matching on at least some variables continues to be relatively common in impact assessments that involve comparison of small numbers of aggregate units, such as schools or communities. They can also be useful when targets are drawn from specialized populations with distinctive clinical, personal, or situational characteristics, such as in the evaluation of medical and health-related interventions (where matching is often referred to as a *case control* design).

Equating Groups by Statistical Procedures

In the most common nonequivalent comparison group design, outcomes for an intervention group are compared with those for a control group that is selected on the basis of relevance and convenience and that must be assumed to differ from the intervention group in outcome-related ways. For example, an evaluator might draw a control group for a community-wide intervention involving senior citizens from a similar community that is convenient to access. Any program effect estimate based on a simple comparison of the outcomes for such intervention and control groups must be presumed to include selection bias. If the relevant differences between the groups can be measured, statistical techniques can be used to attempt to statistically control for the differences between groups that would otherwise lead to biased program effect estimates.

To explain the logic of **statistical controls,** we will rely on a simple example. Exhibit 9-E presents the outcomes of a hypothetical impact assessment of a large vocational training program for unemployed men between the ages of 35 and 40 that was designed to upgrade their skills and enable them to obtain higher-paying jobs. A sample of 1,000 participants was interviewed before they completed the program and again one year afterward. Another 1,000 men in the same age group who did not participate in the

I. Outcome comparison between men 35-40 who completed the training program and a sample of men 35-40 who did not attend the program

	Participants	Nonparticipants
Average wage rate	$7.75	$8.20
n =	1,000	1,000

II. Comparison after adjusting for educational attainment

	Participants		Nonparticipants	
	Less Than High School	High School	Less Than High School	HighSchool
Average wage rate	$7.60	$8.10	$7.75	$8.50
n =	700	300	400	600

III. Comparison adjusting for educational attainment and employment at the start of the training program (or equivalent data for nonparticipants)

	Participants		Nonparticipants			
	Less Than High School Unemployed	High School Unemployed	Less Than High School Unemployed	Employed	High School Unemployed	Employed
Average wage rate	$7.60	$8.10	$7.50	$7.83	$8.00	$8.60
n =	700	300	100	300	100	500

program were sampled from the same metropolitan area and also interviewed at the time the program started and one year after it ended. The men in both samples were asked about their current earnings, and hourly wage rates were computed.

In Panel I of Exhibit 9-E, the average posttraining wage rates of the two groups are compared without application of any statistical controls. Those who had participated in the project were earning an average of $7.75 per hour; those who had not participated, $8.20. Clearly, participants were earning less than nonparticipants; had this been the outcome of a randomized experiment, the difference would have been an unbiased estimate of the program effect. To the extent that participants and nonparticipants differed on earnings-related variables other than participation in the project, however, these unadjusted comparisons include selection bias and could be quite misleading.

Panel II of Exhibit 9-E takes one such difference into account by presenting average wage rates separately for men who had not completed high school and those who had. Note that 70% of the program participants had not completed high school, as opposed to 40% of the nonparticipants, a difference between the groups that is almost certainly related to earnings. When we statistically control education by comparing the wage rates of persons of comparable educational attainment, the hourly wages of participants and nonparticipants approach one another: $7.60 and $7.75, respectively, for those who had not completed high school, $8.10 and $8.50 for those who had. Correcting for the selection bias associated with the education difference diminishes the differences between the wage rates of participants and nonparticipants and yields better estimates of the program effects.

Panel III takes still another difference between the intervention and control groups into account. Since all the program participants were unemployed at the time of enrollment in the training program, it is appropriate to compare participants with those nonparticipants who were also unemployed at the time the program started. In panel III, nonparticipants are divided into those who were unemployed and those who were not at the start of the program. This comparison showed that program participants in the project subsequently earned more at each educational level than comparable nonparticipants: $7.60 and $7.50, respectively, for those who had not completed high school, $8.10 and $8.00 for those who had. Thus, when we statistically control the selection bias associated with differences between the groups on education and unemployment, the vocational training program shows a positive program effect, amounting to a $0.10/hour increment in the wage rates of those who participated.

In any real evaluation, additional control variables would be entered into the analysis, perhaps for previous employment experience, marital status, number of dependents, and race—all factors known to be related to wage rates. Even so, we would have no assurance that statistical control of all these variables would completely remove selection bias from the estimates of program effects, because influential differences between the intervention and control groups might still remain. For instance, those who participated in the program might have had higher levels of motivation to find a job, a factor that is difficult to measure and introduce into the analysis.

Multivariate Statistical Techniques

The adjustments shown in Exhibit 9-E were accomplished in a very simple way to illustrate the logic of statistical controls. In actual application, the evaluator would generally use multivariate statistical methods to control for a number of group differences simultaneously. These methods create a statistical model that represents the overall set of relationships among the control variables and outcome variables. The object of the analysis is to account for the initial measured differences between the intervention and control groups and adjust the outcome difference between those groups by subtracting the portion attributable entirely to those initial differences. Whatever difference on outcomes remains after this subtraction, if any, is interpreted as the program effect. Of course, if there is some influential difference between the groups that is not measured and included in the model, its effect is not subtracted and the remaining program effect estimate will still include selection bias. This is why it is important to identify and measure all those variables on which the groups initially differ that are likely to be related to the outcome variable.

Multivariate statistical models for nonequivalent comparison group designs generally involve one or both of two different types of control variables. One type has to do with the initial characteristics of the group members that are related to the outcome variable. If we imagine that the intervention has no effect (or that there is no intervention), these variables would "predict" the outcome. For instance, in Exhibit 9-E, educational level is such a variable. Other things being equal, those participants with higher education at the beginning of the study are expected to have higher wages at the end. Similarly, absent any intervention effect, those with more job experience, privileged social status, or location in favorable labor markets would be expected to have higher wages at the time of the outcome measurement.

The other type of control variable has to do with the selection of individuals into the intervention versus the control group. This type of control variable relates directly to selection bias, the critical problem of nonequivalent comparison group designs. Control variables of this type might include, for instance, how close individuals lived to the program site, how motivated they were to enroll in the program, whether they had the characteristics that program personnel used to select participants, and so forth. The importance of these variables lies in the fact that, if we could fully account for the characteristics that caused an individual to be selected for one group versus the other, we could statistically control on those characteristics and perfectly offset the selection bias.

In the two sections that follow, we will discuss multivariate statistical analysis using control variables presumed related to outcome, then those presumed related to selection. The latter are essentially a special case of the former, but are sufficiently distinct procedurally to warrant separate discussion.

Modeling the Determinants of Outcome

The objective of multivariate analysis of data from nonequivalent comparison groups is to construct a statistical model that predicts each individual's value on the outcome variable from the control variables measured at the beginning of the study.

If the average outcome for the intervention group is better than predicted from initial status while that of the control group is not, then the difference is interpreted as the program effect. An alternate phrasing is that the analysis tries to establish whether or not receiving the intervention is itself a significant predictor of outcome when the predictive relationship of the control variables has already been taken into account.

The statistical procedures and models used for these purposes depend on the characteristics of the measures, the form of the relationships assumed among the variables in the model, the statistical assumptions deemed realistic, and the technical know-how and proclivities of the analyst. Most commonly, a variant of multiple regression analysis is used (Mohr, 1995; Reichardt and Bormann, 1994) or, sometimes, structural equation modeling (Loehlin, 1992; Wu and Campbell, 1996).

Exhibit 9-F shows an application of multiple regression analysis to data from an assessment of the effects of attendance at Alcoholics Anonymous (AA) meetings on the amount of drinking among problem drinkers. The table in Exhibit 9-F presents summary statistics from a regression analysis predicting the postprogram scores on the Drinking Pattern scale from preprogram variables believed to be related to the probability of drinking. The intervention variable, AA attendance, is included in the regression equation with the control variables to determine whether it makes a significant contribution to predicting outcome above and beyond the influence of the control variables.

The values shown in the Coefficient column are unstandardized regression coefficients expressing the increment on the Drinking Patterns outcome scores associated with each unit of each of the predictor variables. The coefficient for having attended AA meetings is –2.82, meaning that, at the time of outcome measurement, the problem drinkers who attended the AA meetings scored 2.82 points lower on the Drinking Pattern scale than those who did not attend, holding constant all the other variables in the equation. The regression coefficient for AA attendance is thus the estimated program effect, and it indicates that problem drinkers who attended AA drank less afterward than those who did not attend.

The control variables in the multiple regression analysis were selected because prior research indicated that they were related to participation in treatment programs or drinking behavior. Thus, participants' sex, information seeking, perceived seriousness of drinking, baseline drinking, and marital status were expected to affect the amount they drank irrespective of any effect of AA attendance. As it turned out in the analysis in Exhibit 9-F, only one of these variables was significantly related to the drinking outcome—those who drank more at baseline were more likely to be drinking more at the time of outcome measurement.

The worth of the analysis presented in Exhibit 9-F depends largely on how thoroughly the control variables used in the regression model capture the factors involved

EXHIBIT 9-F
Estimating the Effect of AA Attendance Using Regression Modeling

Does attendance at Alcoholics Anonymous (AA) meetings affect the drinking of individuals who have problems with alcohol? It is part of the AA philosophy that the problem drinker must make a voluntary commitment to participation, so self-selection becomes part of the intervention. Thus, any attempt to assess impact by comparing problem drinkers who attend AA with those who do not must deal with selection bias related to the natural differences between these groups. To attempt to equate the groups through statistical controls, researchers in the Palo Alto Veterans Affairs Health Care System used several approaches, one of which was a simple multiple regression model.

First, consideration was given to what variables might be related to AA participation. Based on prior research, three variables were identified—perceived seriousness of drinking, tendency to cope with problems by seeking information and advice, and sex. Two other control variables were selected because of their known relationship to drinking outcomes—baseline drinking scores and marital status. The outcome variable of interest was the amount of drinking measured on a Drinking Pattern scale.

These variables were measured on a sample of 218 individuals with drinking problems and used in a regression model with drinking outcome as the dependent variable and the other variables as independent (predictor) variables. The intervention variable, AA attendance (0 = no, 1 = yes), was also included as a predictor to assess its relation to the outcome when the other predictor variables were statistically controlled.

As shown in the summary below, two of the variables showed significant relationships to outcome, including the intervention variable, AA attendance. The significant negative coefficient for AA attendance indicates that those attending AA drank less at outcome than those not attending, controlling for the other variables in the model. To the extent that those other variables in this statistical model completely controlled for selection bias, the unstandardized regression coefficient shown for AA attendance estimates the program effect on the Drinking Pattern outcome variable.

Regression Results Predicting Drinking Outcome

Predictor Variable	Coefficient	Standard Error
Sex (0 = M, 1 = F)	−1.16	1.09
Information seeking	−.04	.12
Perceived seriousness of drinking	−.44	.57
Baseline drinking	.20*	.09
Married (0 = no, 1 = yes)	−1.69	1.25
AA attendance (0 = no, 1 = yes)	−2.82*	1.15
$R^2 = .079$		

*Statistically significant at $p \leq .05$.

SOURCE: Adapted with permission from Keith Humphreys, Ciaran S. Phibbs, and Rudolf H. Moos, "Addressing Self-Selection Effects in Evaluations of Mutual Help Groups and Professional Mental Health Services: An Introduction to Two-Stage Sample Selection Models." *Evaluation and Program Planning*, 1996, 19(4):301-308.

in problem drinking that differentiated those who attended AA meetings from those who did not. To the extent that all those differences are represented in the model, the additional relationship of AA attendance to the outcome represents a program effect. If the control variables fall short of accounting for selection bias, however, the resulting program effect estimate will still be biased to some unknown degree.

Modeling the Determinants of Selection

A one-stage regression model, such as illustrated in Exhibit 9-F, is configure in terms of the relationships of the control variables to the outcome variable. It may also include variables related to selection into intervention versus control groups. In Exhibit 9-F, for instance, three of the control variables were chosen because the researchers believed they would be related to the likelihood of attending AA meetings—sex, information seeking, and perceived seriousness of drinking. The regression model, nonetheless, incorporates them as outcome predictors, not as predictors of selection into the intervention or control group. Though related to selection, therefore, they are not set up in a way that optimizes the information they carry about selection effects.

An alternate approach that is becoming more commonplace is a two-stage procedure in which the first step is to use relevant control variables to construct a statistical model that predicts selection into the intervention or control group. The second step is to use the results of that analysis to combine all the control variables into a single composite selection variable, or propensity score (for propensity to be selected into one group or the other). The propensity score is then used as a kind of all-in-one selection control variable in an analysis to estimate the program effect on an outcome of interest. This two-stage analysis procedure in which the first stage attempts to statistically describe the differential selection of individuals into nonrandomized intervention and control groups is called **selection modeling.**

Effective selection modeling depends on the evaluator's diligence in identifying and measuring variables related to the process by which individuals select themselves (e.g., by volunteering) or are selected (e.g., administratively) into the intervention versus the control group. Because group membership is a binary variable (e.g., 1 = intervention group, 0 = control group), regression models tailored for dichotomous dependent variables are typically used for selection modeling, for instance, logistic regression. Several variants on selection modeling and two-stage estimation of program effects are available. These include Heckman's econometric approach (Heckman and Hotz, 1989; Heckman and Robb, 1985), Rosenbaum and Rubin's propensity scores (1983, 1984), and instrumental variables (Greene, 1993). Useful general discussion can be found in Humphreys, Phibbs, and Moos (1996) and Stolzenberg and Relles (1997).

Exhibit 9-G shows an application of selection modeling to account for the self-selection of the problem drinkers who attended AA meetings that was described in Exhibit 9-F. The researchers identified three control variables that prior research indicated were likely to be related to AA attendance. As shown in Exhibit 9-G, these variables were used in a stage one analysis to predict AA attendance. The results of that analysis were used to create a new variable, Lambda, which attempts to optimally combine the variables in the stage one model for differentiating the problem drinkers who attended AA from those who did not attend.

The Lambda variable derived from the first-stage analysis was then used as a control variable in a second-stage analysis predicting the outcome of interest, scores on the Drinking Pattern scale. For this purpose, it was entered into a regression analysis with two other control variables also expected to be related to drinking outcome. As shown in Exhibit 9-G, the results of the two-stage selection modeling analysis differ from those of the one-stage analysis shown in Exhibit 9-F. Most notably, by better controlling for selection-related differences between the AA participants and nonparticipants, the second-stage model estimated the program effect to be larger than did the single-stage model in the previous analysis (−6.31 vs. −2.82 on the Drinking Pattern scale).

A composite selection variable resulting from the stage one analysis can, alternatively, be used as a matching variable to create subsets of the intervention and control groups that are equivalent on that composite selection variable. This approach is called *propensity score analysis* (Rosenbaum and Rubin, 1983, 1984). It typically involves dividing the distribution of the propensity score selection variable into quintiles (five groups of equal overall size). Each quintile group includes members of the intervention and control group who all have about the same propensity score (within the quintile range). Estimates of program effect can then be made separately for each of these quintile groups and then combined into an overall estimate.

Propensity-score matching techniques have the advantage of making fewer statistical assumptions than the two-stage multiple regression approach illustrated in Exhibits 9-F and 9-G. As with all selection modeling procedures, however, the ability of this technique to statistically adjust away selection bias is heavily dependent on identification of the variables related to selection into groups and inclusion of them in the statistical model that generates the propensity scores.

Regression-Discontinuity Designs

As the discussion of selection modeling above should make clear, complete and valid data on the variables that are the basis for selection into nonequivalent comparison groups provide the makings for an effective statistical control variable. Suppose,

EXHIBIT 9-G

Estimating the Effect of AA Attendance Using Two-Stage Selection Modeling

By estimating selection effects separately from influences on the outcome variable, two-stage selection modeling has the potential to produce a better estimate of the effects of AA attendance than the one-stage multiple regression analysis presented in Exhibit 9-F. Three of the variables available to the researchers were expected to predict AA participation—perceived seriousness of drinking (those who believe their drinking is a problem are presumed more likely to participate), tendency to cope with problems by seeking information and advice, and sex (women are presumed more likely to seek help than men). These variables were used in the first-stage analysis to predict AA attendance rather than being included in a one-stage model predicting drinking outcome. For this application, the researchers used the Heckman procedure and fit a probit regression model to predict AA participation. As shown in the summary below, two of the variables showed significant independent relationships to attendance.

Stage 1: Probit Regression Predicting AA Attendance

Predictor Variable	Coefficient	Standard Error
Sex (0 = M, 1 = F)	.29	.19
Information seeking	.06*	.02
Perceived seriousness of drinking	.38*	.09
R^2 = .129		

*$p \leq .05$.

This selection model was then used to produce a new variable, Lambda, which estimates the probability that each individual will be in the intervention versus the control group. Lambda is then entered as a control variable in a second-stage regression analysis that attempts to predict the outcome variable, amount of drinking measured on the Drinking Pattern scale. Two outcome-related control variables were also included at this stage—baseline drinking scores and marital status. Finally, inclusion of the intervention variable, AA attendance (0 = no, 1 = yes), allowed assessment of its relation to the outcome when the other predictor variables, including the selection variable, were statistically controlled.

(Continued)

Exhibit 9-G
(Continued)

Stage 2: Least Squares Regression Predicting Drinking Outcome

Predictor Variable	Coefficient	Standard Error
Baseline drinking	.20*	.08
Married (0 = no, 1 = yes)	−1.68	1.23
Lambda	2.10	1.98
AA attendance	−6.31*	3.04
R^2 = .084		

*$p \leq .05$.

The significant coefficient for AA attendance shows that those participating drank less at outcome than those not attending, controlling for baseline drinking and self-selection. Indeed, on the 30-point Drinking Pattern scale, the estimated net effect of AA attendance was a reduction of more than 6 points. Note also that using the two-stage model indicates that the effect of AA attendance is nearly twice as large as the estimate derived in the earlier example using a one-stage regression model.

SOURCE: Adapted with permission from Keith Humphreys, Ciaran S. Phibbs, and Rudolf H. Moos, "Addressing Self-Selection Effects in Evaluations of Mutual Help Groups and Professional Mental Health Services: An Introduction to Two-Stage Sample Selection Models." *Evaluation and Program Planning*, 1996, 19(4):301-308.

now, that instead of trying to figure out what variables were related to selection, the evaluator was given the selection variable up front and could apply it case-by-case to allocate individuals into the intervention or control group according to their scores on that variable. In this circumstance, selection modeling should be a sure thing because there would be no uncertainty about how selection was done and the evaluator would have in hand the measured values that determined it.

A special type of constructed control group design, referred to as a **regression-discontinuity design,** is based on this concept. When this design is applicable, it generally provides less biased estimates of program effects than any of the other quasi-experimental impact assessment designs. Regression-discontinuity designs are appropriate for circumstances when the evaluator cannot randomly assign targets to intervention and control groups but could collaborate with program personnel to divide them systematically on the basis of need, merit, or some other qualifying condition and assign the neediest, most meritorious, and so forth to the intervention condition and those less needy or meritorious to the control condition.

A more descriptive name for the regression-discontinuity design is "cutting-point design" because its key feature is to apply a cutting point to some continuum of need, merit, or other relevant selection variable. Using measured values along that continuum, targets with scores over the cutting point go into one group (e.g., control) and those with scores under the cutting point go into the other group (e.g., intervention). Thus, the selection procedures are explicit and known because the participants are selected into groups according to their scores on a measured variable, which makes the statistical control of selection bias relatively straightforward. To the extent that the known selection process is modeled properly, cutting-point designs approximate randomized experiments with regard to their ability to produce unbiased estimates of program effects.

For example, to estimate the effects of a program providing eligibility for unemployment insurance payments to released prisoners in California (modeled to some degree after the Baltimore LIFE experiment described in Exhibit 8-F), Berk and Rauma (1983) took advantage of the fact that program eligibility was contingent on the number of days a felon worked in prison. Ex-prisoners had to have worked more than 652 days in prison before becoming eligible for any payments, and the amount of payment was made proportional to the number of days worked. The formula applied was explicit and quantitative, the "cutting point" for eligibility was uniformly 652 days of work, and payments were made above that point and not below.

Comparing the rearrest rates of those given payments with those who were not, while using the hours worked in prison as a control variable (modeling selection exactly), provided an estimate of the effect of the payments on rearrest. Regression analysis showed that ex-prisoners who were given payments were estimated to have 13% fewer arrests. This estimate is unbiased insofar as the selection process is known and accurately represented in the statistical analysis by the variable "hours worked in prison."

Despite their advantages, cutting-point designs have not been applied often, partly because not all programs have definite and precise rules for eligibility or are willing to adopt such rules for purposes of impact assessment. However, another reason for their infrequent use seems to be that they are not well understood by evaluators and, therefore, may not be used even when appropriate. Evaluators who conduct impact assessments would profit from an investment in learning more about these designs. Source material can be found in Trochim (1984), Braden and Bryant (1990), Shadish, Cook, and Campbell (2002), and Mohr (1995).

Reflexive Controls

In studies using **reflexive controls**, the estimation of program effects comes entirely from information on the targets at two or more points in time, at least one of which is before exposure to the program. When reflexive controls are used, the presumption must be made that the targets have not changed on the outcome variable during the time between observations except for any change induced by the intervention. Under this assumption, any difference between preintervention and postintervention outcome status is deemed a program effect. For example, suppose that pensioners from a large corporation previously received their checks in the mail but now have them automatically deposited in their bank accounts. Comparison of complaints about late or missing payments before and after this procedure was implemented could be construed as evidence of impact, provided that it was plausible that the rate of burglaries from mailboxes, the level of postal service, and so on had not also changed. This is an example of a simple pre-post study, the procedure we describe next. Then we turn to the strongest type of reflexive control design, time-series designs.

Simple Pre-Post Studies

A simple **pre-post design** (or before-and-after study) is one in which outcomes are measured on the same targets before program participation and again after sufficiently long participation for effects to be expected. Comparing the two sets of measurements produces an estimate of the program effect. As we have noted, the main drawback to this design is that the estimate will be biased if it includes the effects of other influences that occur during the period between the before and measurements. For example, it might be tempting to assess the effects of Medicare by comparing the health status of persons before they became eligible with the same measures taken a few years after participation in Medicare. However, such comparisons would be quite misleading. The effects of aging generally lead to poorer health on their own, which would bias the program effect estimate downward. Other life changes that affect health status may also occur around the time individuals become eligible for Medicare that may also create bias, such as retirement and reduced income.

Sometimes time-related changes are subtle. For example, reflexive controls will be questionable in studies of the effects of clinical treatment for depression. People tend to seek treatment when they are at a low point, after which some remission of their symptoms is likely to occur naturally so that they feel less depressed. Measures of their depression before and after treatment, therefore, will almost automatically show improvement even if the treatment has no positive effects.

In general, simple pre-post reflexive designs provide biased estimates of program effects that have little value for purposes of impact assessment. This is particularly the case when the time elapsed between the two measurements is appreciable—say, a year or more—because over time it becomes more likely that other processes will obscure any effects of the program. The simple pre-post design, therefore, is appropriate mainly for short-term impact assessments of programs attempting to affect conditions that are unlikely to change much on their own. As described in Chapter 7, they may also be useful for purposes of routine outcome monitoring where the purpose is mainly to provide feedback to program administrators, not to generate credible estimates of program effects.

Simple pre-post designs can often be strengthened if it is possible to obtain multiple measures of the outcome that span the preprogram to postprogram periods. The repeated measures in such a series may make it possible to describe ongoing trends that would bias a pre-post effect estimate and adjust them out of that estimate. This is the premise of time-series designs, which we will discuss next.

Time-Series Designs

The strongest reflexive control design is a **time-series design** consisting of a number of observations over a time period spanning the intervention. For example, suppose that instead of just a pre- and postmeasure of pensioners' complaints about late or missing payments, we had monthly information for, say, two years before and one year after the change in payment procedures. In this case, our degree of certainty about the program effects would be higher because we would have more information upon which to base our estimates about what would have happened had there been no change in the mode of check delivery. A second procedure often used is to disaggregate the outcome data by various characteristics of the targets. For example, examining time-series data about pensioners' complaints regarding receipt of checks in high and low crime areas and in rural and urban areas would provide additional insight into the impact of the change in procedure.

Time-series designs may or may not include the same respondents at each time of measurement. Studies using these designs most often draw their data from existing databases that compile periodic information related to the outcomes of interest (e.g., fertility, mortality, and crime). Available databases typically involve aggregated data such as averages or rates computed for one or more political jurisdictions. For example, the Department of Labor maintains an excellent time series that has tracked unemployment rates monthly for the whole country and for major regions since 1948.

When a relatively long time series of preintervention observations exists, it is often possible to model long-standing trends in the target group, projecting those trends through and beyond the time of the intervention and observing whether or not the postintervention period shows significant deviations from the projections. The use of such general time-trend modeling procedures as ARIMA (auto regressive integrated moving average; see Hamilton, 1994; McCleary and Hay, 1980) can identify the best-fitting statistical models by taking into account long-term secular trends and seasonal variations. They also allow for the degree to which any value or score obtained at one point in time is necessarily related to previous ones (technically referred to as *autocorrelation*). The procedures involved are technical and require a fairly high level of statistical sophistication.

Exhibit 9-H illustrates the use of time-series data for assessing the effects of raising the legal drinking age on alcohol-related traffic accidents. This evaluation was made possible by the existence of relatively long series of measures on the outcome variable (more than 200). The analysis used information collected over the eight to ten years prior to the policy changes of interest to establish the expected trends for alcohol-related accident rates for different age groups legally entitled to drink. Comparison of the age- stratified rates experienced after the drinking ages were raised with the expected rates based on the prior trends provided a measure of the program effect.

As noted earlier, the units of analysis in time-series data relevant to social programs are usually highly aggregated. Exhibit 9-H deals essentially with one case, the state of Wisconsin, where accident measures are constructed by aggregating the pertinent data over the entire state and expressing them as accident rates per 1,000 licensed drivers. The statistical models developed to fit such data are vulnerable to bias just like all the other such models we have discussed. For example, if there were significant influences on the alcohol-related accident rates in Wisconsin that were not represented in the trend lines estimated by the model, then the results of the analysis would not be valid.

Simple graphic methods of examining time-series data before and after an intervention can provide crude but useful clues to impact. Indeed, if the confounding influences on an intervention are known and there is considerable certainty that their effects are minimal, simple examination of a time-series plot may identify obvious program effects. Exhibit 9-I presents the primary data for one of the classic applications of time series in program evaluation—the British Breathalyzer crackdown (Ross, Campbell, and Glass, 1970). The graph in that exhibit shows the auto accident rates in Great Britain before and after the enactment and enforcement of drastically changed penalties for driving while under the influence of alcohol. The accompanying chart indicates that the legislation had a discernible impact: Accidents declined after it went into effect, and the decline was especially dramatic for accidents occurring over the weekend, when we would expect higher levels of alcohol consumption. Though the effects are rather evident in the graph, it is wise to confirm them with statistical analysis; the reductions in accidents visible in Exhibit 9-I are, in fact, statistically significant.

Time-series approaches are not necessarily restricted to single cases. When time-series data exist for interventions at different times and in different places, more complex analyses can be undertaken. Parker and Rebhun (1995), for instance, examined the relationship of changes in state laws governing the minimum age of purchase of alcohol with homicide rates using time series covering 1976-1983 for each of the 50 states plus the District of Columbia. They used a pooled cross-section time-series analysis

EXHIBIT 9-H

Estimating the Effects of Raising the Drinking Age From Time-Series Data

During the early 1980s, many states raised the minimum drinking age from 18 to 21, especially after passage of the federal Uniform Drinking Age Act of 1984, which reduced highway construction funds to states that maintained a drinking age less than 21. The general reason for this was the widespread perception that lower drinking ages had led to dramatic increases in the rate of alcohol-related traffic accidents among teenagers. Assessing the impact of raising the drinking age, however, is complicated by downward trends in accidents stemming from the introduction of new automobile safety factors and increased public awareness of the dangers of drinking and driving.

Wisconsin raised its drinking age to 19 in 1984 then to 21 in 1986. To assess the impact of these changes, David Figlio examined an 18-year time series of monthly observations on alcohol-related traffic accidents, stratified by age, that was available from the Wisconsin Department of Transportation for the period from 1976 to 1993. Statistical time-series models were fit to the data for 18-year-olds (who could legally drink prior to 1984), for 19- and 20-year-olds (who could legally drink prior to 1986), and for over-21-year-olds (who could legally drink over the whole time period). The outcome variable in these analyses was the rate of alcohol-related crashes per thousand licensed drivers in the respective age group.

The results showed that, for 18-year-olds, raising the minimum drinking age to 19 reduced the alcohol-related crashes by an estimated 26% from the prior average of 2.2 per month per 1,000 drivers. For 19- and 20-year-olds, raising the minimum to age 21 reduced the monthly crash rate by an estimated 19% from an average of 1.8 per month per 1,000 drivers. By comparison, the estimated effect of the legal changes for the 21-and-older group was only 2.5% and statistically nonsignificant.

The evaluator's conclusion was that the imposition of increased minimum drinking ages in Wisconsin had immediate and conclusive effects on the number of teenagers involved in alcohol-related crashes resulting in substantially fewer than the prelegislation trends would have generated.

SOURCE: Adapted from David N. Figlio, "The Effect of Drinking Age Laws and Alcohol-Related Crashes: Time-Series Evidence From Wisconsin." *Journal of Policy Analysis and Management*, 1995, 14(4):555-566.

with a dummy code (0 or 1) to identify the years before and after the drinking age was raised. Other variables in the model included alcohol consumption (beer sales in barrels per capita), infant mortality (as a poverty index), an index of inequality, racial composition, region, and total state population. This model was applied to homicide

EXHIBIT 9-1
An Analysis of the Impact of Compulsory Breathalyzer Tests on Traffic Accidents

In 1967, the British government enacted a new policy that allowed police to give Breathalyzer tests at the scenes of accidents. The test measured the presence of alcohol in the blood of suspects. At the same time, heavier penalties were instituted for drunken driving convictions. Considerable publicity was given to the provisions of the new law, which went into effect in October 1967.

The chart below plots vehicular accident rates by various periods of the week before and after the new legislation went into effect. Visual inspection of the chart clearly indicates that a decline in accidents occurred after the legislation, which affected most times of the week but had especially dramatic effects for weekend periods. Statistical tests verified that these declines are greater than could be expected from the chance component of these data.

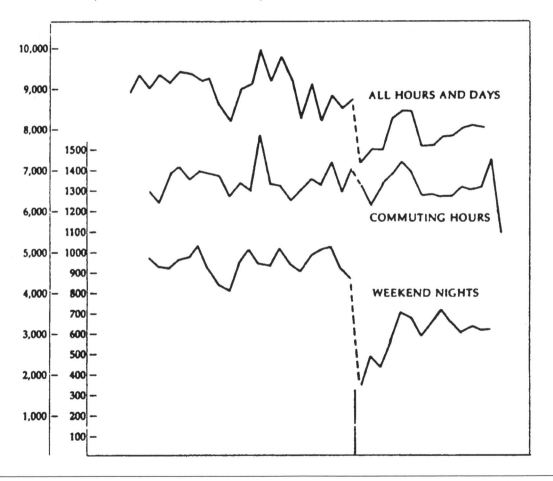

SOURCE: Summary of H. L. Ross, D. T. Campbell, and G. V. Glass, "Determining the Social Effects of a Legal Reform: The British Breathalyzer Crackdown of 1967." *American Behavioral Scientist*, 1970, 13 (March/April): 494-509.

rates for different age groups. Raising the minimum age-of-purchase law was found to be significantly related to reductions in homicide for victims in the age 21-24 category.

Although the time-series analyses we have discussed all use aggregated data, the logic of time-series analyses is also applicable to disaggregated data. An example is the analysis of interventions administered to small groups of persons whose behavior is measured a number of times before, after, and perhaps during program participation. Therapists, for example, have used time-series designs to assess the impact of treatments on individual clients. Thus, a child's performance on some achievement test may be measured periodically before and after a new teaching method is used with the child, or an adult's drinking behavior may be measured before and after therapy for alcohol abuse. The logic of time-series analyses remains the same when applied to a single case, although the statistical methods applied are different because the issues of long-term trends and seasonality usually are not as serious for individual cases (Kazdin, 1982).

Some Cautions About Using
Quasi-Experiments for Impact Assessment

The scientific credibility of well-executed field experiments for producing unbiased estimates of program effects would make them the obvious choice if such designs were typically the easiest, fastest, and least expensive to implement. Unfortunately, the environment of social programs is such that randomized experiments are often difficult to implement well. The value of quasi-experimental designs is that, when carefully done, they offer the prospect of providing credible estimates of program effects while being relatively adaptable to program circumstances that are not inherently compatible with the requirements of more rigorous social research. In short, the advantages of quasi-experimental research designs for program impact assessment rest entirely on their practicality and convenience in situations where randomized field experiments are not feasible.

A critical question is how good quasi-experimental designs typically are in producing valid estimates of program effects. Put another way, how much risk of serious bias in estimating program impact does the evaluator run when using quasi-experimental research designs instead of randomly assigned controls? We would like to be able to answer this question by drawing on a body of research that compares the results of various quasi-experiments with those of randomized experiments in different program situations. Such studies are rare, however, so only a little evidence can be offered along these lines. What the few available comparisons show is what we might expect: Under favorable circumstances and carefully done, quasi-experiments can yield estimates of program effects that are comparable to those derived from randomized designs, but they can also produce wildly erroneous results.

Fraker and Maynard (1984) compared estimates of the effects of an employment program that were derived from control groups constructed by matching with those from a randomized experiment. They used various methods of making individual matches, but none produced results that agreed very closely with those of the randomized experiment. But then Heckman and Hotz (1989) showed that using the appropriate control variables and applying a more sophisticated statistical model to the data did produce effect estimates similar to those from the experiment. A similar comparison for an employment training program was made by LaLonde (1986). In that case, results from statistical controls applied to a nonrandom design were compared with those from a randomized experiment. LaLonde found substantial discrepancies, including a differential bias for female participants (effects overestimated by the quasi-experiment) in comparison to males (effects underestimated).

More recent evidence from different program areas has been somewhat more encouraging. Aiken et al. (1998) compared the results of different impact designs applied to a university-level freshman remedial writing program. They found "highly similar" effect estimates from a nonequivalent (nonrandomized) comparison design with statistical controls, a regression-discontinuity design, and a randomized experiment. A simple pre-post comparison, however, substantially overestimated the program effect.

Broad comparisons of the effect estimates from impact assessments for sets of independent studies within the same program area also shed some light on the validity of the results using constructed controls. Lipsey and Wilson (1993) compared the mean effect size estimates reported for randomized versus nonrandomized designs in 74 meta-analyses of psychological, educational, and behavioral interventions. In many of the sets of studies included in a meta-analysis, the effect estimates from non-randomized comparisons were very similar to those from randomized ones. However, in an equal number of cases there were substantial differences. In some program areas the nonrandomized studies produced much larger effect estimates than the randomized studies, while in other program areas they produced much smaller estimates. Heinsman and Shadish (1996) made a closer examination of the effect estimates in 98 studies over four program areas and also found that nonrandomized designs gave varied results relative to randomized designs—sometimes similar, sometimes appreciably larger or smaller.

What comparative evidence we have, therefore, indicates that, in a given application, impact assessments using quasi-experimental designs can yield effect estimates similar to those that would result from a randomized experiment, but frequently do not. Moreover, the empirical evidence at this point provides little indication of which program circumstances or which variations on quasi-experimental designs are associated with more or less biased estimates. Evaluators using nonrandomized designs for impact assessment, therefore, must rely heavily on a case-by-case analysis of the particular assumptions and requirements of the selected design and the specific characteristics of the program and target population to optimize the likelihood that valid estimates of program effects will result.

Given all the limitations of nonrandomized impact assessment designs pointed out in this chapter, can their use be justified? Clearly, they should not be used if it is possible to use a randomized design. However, when randomized designs cannot be used and the need for an impact assessment is great, then evaluators can proceed with a nonrandomized design provided they do so with an awareness of the limitations and a vigorous attempt to overcome them.

A responsible evaluator faced with an impact assessment task that can be accomplished only using a nonrandomized design has an obligation to advise stakeholders in advance that the resulting estimates of program effect cannot be regarded as definitive. If it is decided to proceed with a nonrandomized design, the evaluator should review relevant research literature to guide the collection of variables that can serve as statistical controls and as the basis for selection modeling. In reporting the findings of nonrandomized impact assessments, the evaluator is also obligated to point out clearly that the effect estimates may be biased.

Summary

■ Impact assessment aims to determine what changes in outcomes can be attributed to the intervention being assessed. While the strongest research design for this purpose is the randomized experiment, there are several potentially valid quasi-experimental impact assessment strategies that can be used when it is not feasible to randomly assign targets to intervention and control conditions.

■ A major concern of evaluators in using any impact assessment design is to minimize bias in the estimate of program effects. Among possible sources of bias that may be especially problematic in quasi-experimental designs are selection bias, secular trends, interfering events, and maturation.

■ In a quasi-experiment, the intervention and control groups are created by ome means other than random assignment. The logic behind quasi-experiments is essentially the same as in randomized experiments, except that the intervention and control groups cannot be assumed to be equivalent. Any difference between them that would eventuate in different outcomes if neither group received the intervention will produce bias in the estimates of program effects. In quasi-experiments, therefore, appropriate procedures must be applied to adjust for those differences in any estimation of program effects.

■ One type of quasi-experimental design involves the use of matched controls. In this design, a control group is constructed by matching program nonparticipants with the participants (individually or as aggregates). To avoid bias in the estimates of program effects resulting from this design, the variables on which the groups are matched must include all those strongly related to outcome on which the groups would otherwise differ.

■ Intervention and control groups may also be equated through statistical procedures (statistical controls). Once again, any outcome-relevant variables on which the groups may differ must be identified and included in the statistical adjustments. In this design, multivariate statistical methods are commonly used to control for a number of group differences simultaneously. Multivariate analysis may use control variables that are presumed to be related to outcome (modeling of the determinants of outcome) or to selection into the control and intervention groups (selection modeling).

■ When it is possible to assign targets to the intervention and control groups on the basis of their scores on a quantitative measure of need, merit, or the like, estimates of program effect from the regression-discontinuity design are generally less susceptible to bias than those from other quasi-experimental designs.

■ Designs using reflexive controls range from simple before-and-after comparisons with one measurement before and one after program participation to time-series designs involving multiple measurements before and after the intervention is in place. Time-series designs are usually much better than simple pre-post designs for estimating program effects.

■ It is appropriate for evaluators to use quasi-experimental designs for impact assessments when randomized designs are not feasible, but only with considered efforts to minimize their potential for bias and acknowledgment of their limitations.

KEY CONCEPTS

Attrition

The loss of outcome data measured on targets assigned to control or intervention groups, usually because targets cannot be located or refuse to contribute data.

Matching

Constructing a control group by selecting targets (individually or as aggregates) that are identical on specified characteristics to those in an intervention group except for receipt of the intervention.

Nonequivalent comparison design

A quasi-experimental design in which intervention and control groups are constructed through some means other than random assignment.

Pre-post design

A reflexive control design in which only one measure is taken before and after the intervention.

Reflexive controls

Measures of an outcome variable taken on participating targets before intervention and used as control observations. See also *pre-post design; time-series design.*

Regression-discontinuity design

A quasi-experimental design in which selection into the intervention or control group is based on the observed value on an appropriate quantitative scale, with targets scoring above a designated cutting point on that scale assigned to one group and those scoring below assigned to the other. Also called a cutting-point design.

Selection bias

Systematic under- or overestimation of program effects that results from uncontrolled differences between the intervention and control groups that would result in differences on the outcome if neither group received the intervention.

Selection modeling

Creation of a multivariate statistical model to "predict" the probability of selection into intervention or control groups in a nonequivalent comparison design. The results of this analysis are used to configure a control variable for selection bias to be incorporated into a second-stage statistical model that estimates the effect of intervention on an outcome.

Statistical controls

The use of statistical techniques to adjust estimates of program effects for bias resulting from differences between intervention and control groups that are related to the outcome. The differences to be controlled by these techniques must be represented in measured variables that can be included in the statistical analysis.

Time-series design

A reflexive control design that relies on a number of repeated measurements of the outcome variable taken before and after an intervention.

10

Detecting, Interpreting, and Analyzing Program Effects

Chapter Outline

The three previous chapters focused on outcome measurement and research design for the purpose of obtaining valid estimates of program effects. Despite good measurement and design, however, the actual effects produced by a program will not necessarily appear in a form that allows the evaluator to be confident about their magnitude or even their existence. Moreover, even when a confident conclusion can be drawn, the evaluator must appraise the practical significance of the program effects.

In this chapter, we discuss considerations related to detecting and interpreting program effects. Attention is also given to ways of representing the magnitude of the effects and analyzing factors that may influence their magnitude. An understanding of these matters will help the evaluator design better impact assessments and contribute to a growing body of knowledge about the effectiveness of social programs.

The end product of an impact assessment is a set of estimates of the effects of the program. Evaluators arrive at these estimates by contrasting outcomes for program participants to estimates of the outcomes that would have resulted if the targets had not participated in the program. As discussed in Chapters 8 and 9, research designs vary in the credibility with which they estimate outcomes absent program participation. However, all effect estimates, including those obtained through randomized experiments, need to be examined carefully to ascertain their significance. How to make such assessments is the major theme of this chapter. We will consider how evaluators can characterize the magnitude of a program effect, how they can detect program effects in a set of data, and how they can assess the practical significance of those effects. We then discuss the more complex issue of analyzing variations in program effects for different subgroups in the target population. At the end of the chapter, we briefly consider how meta-analyses of the effects found in previous impact assessments can help improve the design and analysis of specific evaluations and contribute to the body of knowledge in the evaluation field.

The Magnitude of a Program Effect

The ability of an impact assessment to detect and describe program effects depends in large part on the magnitude of the effects the program produces. Small effects, of course, are more difficult to detect than larger ones, and their practical significance may also be more difficult to describe. Understanding the issues involved in detecting and describing program effects requires that we first consider what is meant by the magnitude of a program effect.

In an impact evaluation, the program effect will appear as the difference between the outcome measured on program targets receiving the intervention and an estimate of what the outcome for those targets would have been had they not received the intervention. The most direct way to characterize the magnitude of the program effect, therefore, is simply as the numerical difference between the means of the two outcome values. For example, a public health campaign might be aimed at persuading elderly persons at risk for hypertension to have their blood pressure tested. If a survey of the target population showed that the proportion tested during the past six months was .17, while the rate among seniors in a control condition was .12, the program effect would be a .05 increase. Similarly, if the mean score on a multi-item outcome measure of knowledge about hypertension was 34.5 for those exposed to the campaign and 27.2 for those in the control condition, the program effect on knowledge would be a gain of 7.3 points on that measurement instrument.

Characterizing the magnitude of a program effect in this manner can be useful for some purposes, but it is very specific to the particular measurement instrument that is being used to assess the outcome. Finding out that knowledge of hypertension as measured on a multi-item scale increased by 7.3 points among seniors exposed to the campaign will mean little to someone who is not very familiar with the scale on which knowledge was measured. To provide a general description of the magnitude of program effects, or to work with them statistically, it is usually more convenient and meaningful to represent them in a form that is not so closely tied to a specific measurement procedure.

One common way to indicate the general magnitude of a program effect is to describe it in terms of a percentage increase or decrease. For the campaign to get more seniors to take blood pressure tests, the increase in the rate from .12 to .17 represents a gain of 41.7% (calculated as .05/.12). The percentage by which a measured value has increased or decreased, however, is only meaningful for measures that have a true zero, that is, a point that represents a zero amount of the thing being measured. The rate at which seniors have their blood pressure checked would be .00 if none of those in the group under study had done so within the six-month period of interest. This is a true zero, and it is thus meaningful to describe the change as a 41.7% increase.

In contrast, the multi-item measure of knowledge about hypertension can only be scaled in arbitrary units. If the knowledge items were very difficult, a person could score zero on that instrument but still be reasonably knowledgeable. Seniors might, for instance, know a lot about hypertension but be unable to give an adequate definition of such terms as *systolic* or *calcium channel inhibitor*. If the measurement instrument contained many items of that sort, it would underestimate the targets' knowledge and possibly obscure real program effects. In addition, the measurement scale might be constructed in such a manner that the lowest possible score was not zero but, maybe, 10.

With this kind of scale, it would not be meaningful to describe the 7.3-point gain shown by the intervention group as a 27% increase in knowledge simply because 34.5 is numerically 27% greater than the control group score of 27.2. Had the scale been constructed differently, the same actual difference in knowledge might have come out as a 10-point increase from a control group score of 75, a 13% change to describe exactly the same gain.

Because many outcome measures are scaled in arbitrary units and lack a true zero, evaluators often use an **effect size statistic** to characterize the magnitude of a program effect rather than a raw difference score or a simple percentage change. An effect size statistic expresses the magnitude of a program effect in a standardized form that makes it comparable across measures that use different units or scales.

The most common effect size statistic that is used to represent effects that vary numerically, such as scores on a test, is the **standardized mean difference.** The standardized mean difference expresses the mean outcome difference between an intervention group and a control group in standard deviation units. The standard deviation is a statistical index of the variation across individuals or other units on a given measure that provides information about the range or spread of the scores. Describing the size of a program effect in standard deviation units, therefore, indicates how large it is relative to the range of scores found between the lowest and highest ones recorded in the study. So, for example, suppose a test of reading readiness is used in the impact assessment of a preschool program and that the mean score for the intervention group is half a standard deviation higher than that for the control group. In this case, the standardized mean difference effect size is .50. The utility of this value is that it can be easily compared to, say, the standardized mean difference for a test of vocabulary that was calculated as .35. The comparison indicates that the preschool program was more effective in advancing reading readiness than in advancing vocabulary.

Some outcomes are binary rather than a matter of degree; that is, a participant either experiences some change or does not. Examples of binary outcomes include committing a delinquent act, becoming pregnant, or graduating from high school. For binary outcomes, an **odds-ratio** effect size is often used to characterize the magnitude of a program effect. An odds ratio indicates how much smaller or larger the odds of an outcome event, say, high school graduation, are for the intervention group compared to the control group. An odds ratio of 1.0 indicates even odds; that is, participants in the intervention group were no more and no less likely than controls to experience the change in question. Odds ratios greater than 1.0 indicate that intervention group members were more likely to experience a change; for instance, an odds ratio of 2.0 means that members of the intervention group were twice as likely to experience the outcome than members of the control group. Odds ratios smaller than 1.0 mean that they were less likely to do so.

These two effect size statistics are described with examples in Exhibit 10-A.

EXHIBIT 10-A
Common Effect Size Statistics

The Standardized Mean Difference

The standardized mean difference effect size statistic is especially appropriate for representing intervention effects found on continuous outcome measures, that is, measures producing values that range over some continuum. Continuous measures include age, income, days of hospitalization, blood pressure readings, scores on achievement tests and other such standardized measurement instruments, and the like. The outcomes on such measures are typically presented in the form of mean values for the intervention and control groups, with the difference between those means indicating the size of the intervention effect. Correspondingly, the standardized mean difference effect size statistic is defined as:

$$\frac{\overline{X}_i - \overline{X}_c}{sd_p}$$

where $\overline{X}_i$ = the mean score for the intervention group,

$\overline{X}_c$ = the mean score for the control group, and

sd_p = the pooled standard deviations of the intervention (sd_i) and control (sd_c) group scores, specifically: $\sqrt{((n_i - 1)sd_i^2 + (n_c - 1)sd_c^2))/(n_i + n_c - 2)}$ n_c with n_i and n_c the sample sizes of the intervention and control groups, respectively.

The standardized mean difference effect size, therefore, represents an intervention effect in standard deviation units. By convention, this effect size is given a positive value when the outcome is more favorable for the intervention group and a negative value if the control group is favored. For example, if the mean score on an environmental attitudes scale was 22.7 for an intervention group (*n* = 25, *sd* = 4.8) and 19.2 for the control group (*n* = 20, *sd* = 4.5), and higher scores represented a more positive outcome, the effect size would be:

$$\frac{22.7 - 19.2}{\sqrt{((24)(4.8^2) + (19)(4.5^2))/(25 + 20 - 2)}} = \frac{3.5}{4.7} = .74$$

That is, the intervention group had attitudes toward the environment that were .74 standard deviations more positive than the control group on the outcome measure.

The Odds Ratio
The odds ratio effect size statistic is designed to represent intervention effects found on binary outcome measures, that is, measures with only two values such as arrested/not arrested, dead/alive, discharged/not discharged, success/failure, and the like. The outcomes on such measures are typically presented as the proportion of individuals in each of the two outcome

(Continued)

EXHIBIT 10-A

(Continued)

categories for the intervention and control groups, respectively. These data can be configured in a 2 × 2 table as follows:

	Positive Outcome	Negative Outcome
Intervention group	p	$1 - p$
Control group	q	$1 - q$

where

p = the proportion of the individuals in the intervention group with a positive outcome,
$1 - p$ = the proportion with a negative outcome,
q = the proportion of the individuals in the control group with a positive outcome,
$1 - q$ = the proportion with a negative outcome,
$p/(1 - p)$ = the odds of a positive outcome for an individual in the intervention group, and
$q/(1 - q)$ = the odds of a positive outcome for an individual in the control group.
The odds ratio is then defined as:

$$\frac{p/(1 - p)}{q/(1 - q)}$$

The odds ratio thus represents an intervention effect in terms of how much greater (or smaller) the odds of a positive outcome are for an individual in the intervention group than for one in the control group. For example, if 58% of the patients in a cognitive-behavioral program were no longer clinically depressed after treatment compared to 44% of those in the control group, the odds ratio would be:

$$\frac{.58/.42}{.44/.56} = \frac{1.38}{.79} = 1.75$$

Thus, the odds of being free of clinical levels of depression for those in the intervention group are 1.75 times greater than those for individuals in the control group.

Detecting Program Effects

Suppose that the real effect of a program on an outcome is exactly zero. In such a case, we would not necessarily expect to find an effect size of exactly zero in an impact evaluation. The outcome values achieved in an impact assessment always include a certain amount of statistical noise stemming from measurement error, the luck of the draw in selecting a research sample and dividing it into intervention and control groups, and other such chance variations. Thus, even when a valid outcome measure is used and there is no real difference between intervention and control groups on the outcome being measured, their mean values on that measure are unlikely to be identical. At the same time, if the actual effect is zero, we would not expect the measured difference to be very large. In other words, if a difference in measured values comes only from statistical noise, we would not want to have so much noise that we are likely to mistake that difference for an actual program effect. In short, we need to be able to assess the chances that an apparent effect is actually statistical noise. This assessment is accomplished through statistical significance testing.

Statistical Significance

If we think of the actual program effect as a signal that we are trying to detect in an impact assessment, the problem of apparent effects that result from statistical noise is one of a low signal-to-noise ratio. Fortunately, statistics provide tools for assessing the level of noise to be expected in the type of data we are working with. If the "signal"—the estimate of program effect that we observe in the data—is large relative to the expected level of statistical noise, we will be relatively confident that we have detected a real effect and not a chance pattern of noise. On the other hand, if the program effect estimate is small relative to the pseudo-effects likely to result from statistical noise, we will have little confidence that we have observed a real program effect.

To assess the signal-to-noise ratio, we must estimate both the program effect signal and the background statistical noise. The best estimate of the program effect is simply the measured mean difference between the outcomes for an intervention and control group, often expressed as an effect size of the sort described in Exhibit 10-A. An estimate of the magnitude of the pseudo-effects likely to result from statistical noise is derived by applying an appropriate statistical probability theory to the data. That estimate is mainly a function of the size of the sample (the number of units in the intervention and control groups being compared) and how widely those units vary on the outcome measure at issue.

This signal-to-noise comparison is routinely accomplished through statistical significance testing. If the difference between the mean outcomes for an intervention and control group is statistically significant, the significance test is telling us that the signal-to-noise ratio, under its assumptions, is such that statistical noise is unlikely to have produced an effect as large as the one observed in the data when the real effect is zero. Conventionally, statistical significance is set at the .05 alpha level. This means that the chance of a pseudo-effect produced by noise being as large as the observed program effect is 5% or less. Given that, we have a 95% confidence level that the observed effect is not simply the result of statistical noise.

Although the .05 significance level has become conventional in the sense that it is used most frequently, there may be good reasons to use a higher or lower level in specific instances. When it is very important for substantive reasons to have very high confidence in the judgment that a program is effective, the evaluator might set a higher threshold for accepting that judgment, say, a significance level of .01, corresponding to a 99% level of confidence that the effect estimate is not purely the result of chance. In other circumstances, for instance, in exploratory work seeking leads to promising interventions, the evaluator might use a lower threshold, such as .10 (corresponding to a 90% level of confidence).

Notice that *statistical significance* does not mean practical significance or importance. A statistically significant finding may or may not be significant theoretically or practically; is it simply a result that is unlikely to be due to chance. Statistical significance is thus a minimum requirement for a meaningful result (we discuss later in this chapter how to assess the practical meaning of a given effect estimate). If a measured program effect is not statistically significant, this means that, by conventional standards, the signal-to-noise ratio is too low for the effect to be accepted as an indication of something that is likely to be a real program effect.

Statistical significance testing is thus the evaluator's first assessment of the magnitude of a measured program effect in an impact assessment. Moreover, it is basically an all-or-nothing test. If the observed effect is statistically significant, it is large enough to be discussed as a program effect. If it is not statistically significant, then no claim that it is a program effect and not simply statistical noise will have credibility in the court of scientific opinion.

Type I and Type II Errors

Statistical significance testing provides a basis for drawing conclusions about whether an effect has been found in the outcome data, but it cannot guarantee that the conclusion will always be correct. The chance variations that constitute statistical noise can sometimes, by happenstance, create a pseudo-effect large enough to be statistically significant even when there is no actual program effect. And, of course, if the statistical noise is large relative to the program effect, those chance variations can easily obscure the effect so that it is not statistically significant even though there really is a program effect. These two types of statistical conclusion error are called **Type I error** and **Type II error,** respectively, and are described more fully in Exhibit 10-B.

EXHIBIT 10-B

Type I and Type II Statistical Inference Errors

Probability of Correct and Incorrect Conclusions in Statistical Significance Testing for Intervention Versus Control Group Differences

Results of Significance Test on Sample Data	Population Circumstances	
	Intervention and Control Means Differ	Intervention and Control Means Do Not Differ
Significant difference	Correct conclusion (probability = $1 - \beta$)	Type I error (probability = α)
Not a significant difference	Type II error (probability = β)	Correct conclusion (probability = $1 - \alpha$)

Statistical Power

Evaluators, of course, should not design impact assessments that are likely to produce erroneous conclusions about program effects, especially at the fundamental level of conclusions about statistical significance. To avoid such mistakes, evaluators must give careful attention to ensuring that the research design has low risks for Type I and Type II errors.

The risk of Type I error (finding statistical significance when there is no program effect) is relatively easy to control. The maximum acceptable chance of that error is set by the researcher when an alpha level for statistical significance is selected for the statistical test to be applied. The conventional alpha level of .05 means that the probability of a Type I error is being held to 5% or less.

Controlling the risk of Type II error (not obtaining statistical significance when there is a program effect) is more difficult. It requires configuring the research design so that it has adequate **statistical power**. Statistical power is the probability that an estimate of the program effect will be statistically significant when, in fact, it represents a real effect of a given magnitude. The likelihood of Type II error is the complementary probability of *not* obtaining statistical significance under these circumstances, or one minus statistical power. So, for example, if statistical power is .80, then the likelihood of Type II error is $1 - .80$, or .20 (20%). An impact assessment design with high statistical power is one that can be counted on to show statistical significance for program effect estimates that are above some threshold the evaluator judges to be too large to overlook.

Statistical power is a function of (1) the effect size to be detected, (2) the sample size, (3) the type of statistical significance test used, and (4) the alpha level set to control Type I error. The alpha probability level is conventionally set at .05 and thus is usually treated as a given. The other three factors require more careful consideration. To design for adequate statistical power, the evaluator must first determine the smallest effect size the design should reliably detect. For this purpose, effect sizes will be represented using an effect size statistic such as the standardized mean difference described in Exhibit 10-A. For instance, the evaluator might select an effect size of .20 in standard deviation units as the threshold for important program effects the research design should detect at a statistically significant level. Determining what numerical effect size corresponds to the minimal meaningful program effect the evaluator wants to detect is rarely straightforward. We will discuss this matter when we take up the topic of the practical significance of program effects later in this chapter.

What Statistical Power Is Appropriate for a Given Impact Assessment?

With a threshold effect size for detection selected, the evaluator must then decide how much risk of Type II error to accept. For instance, the evaluator could decide that the risk of failing to attain statistical significance when an actual effect at the threshold level or higher was present should be held to 5%. This would hold Type II error to the same .05 probability level that is customary for Type I error. Because statistical power is one minus the probability of Type II error, this means that the evaluator wants a research design that has a power of .95 for detecting an effect size at the selected threshold level or larger. Similarly, setting the risk of Type II error at .20 would correspond to a statistical power of .80.

What remains, then, is to design the impact evaluation with a sample size and type of statistical test that will yield the desired level of statistical power. The sample size factor is fairly straightforward—the larger the sample, the higher the power. Planning for the best statistical testing approach is not so straightforward. The most important consideration involves the use of control variables in the statistical model being applied in the analysis. Control variables that are correlated with the outcome measure have the effect of extracting the associated variability in that outcome measure from the analysis of the program effect. Control variables representing nuisance factors can thus reduce the statistical noise and increase the signal-noise ratio in ways that increase statistical power. The most useful control variable for this purpose is generally the preintervention measure of the outcome variable itself. A pretest of this sort taps into preexisting individual differences on the outcome variable that create variation in scores unrelated to the effects of the program. Because any source of irrelevant variation in the scores contributes to the statistical noise, use of well-chosen control variables can greatly enhance statistical power.

To achieve this favorable result, the control variable(s) must have a relatively large correlation with the outcome variable and be integrated into the analysis that assesses the statistical significance of the program effect estimate. The forms of statistical analysis that involve control variables in this way include analysis of covariance, multiple regression, structural equation modeling, and repeated measures analysis of variance.

Deciding about the statistical power of an impact assessment is a substantive issue. If the evaluator expects that the program's effects will be small and that such small effects are worthwhile, then a design powerful enough to detect such small effects will be needed. For example, an intervention that would lower automobile accident deaths by as little as 1% might be judged worthwhile because saving lives is so important. In contrast, when the evaluator judges that an intervention is worthwhile only when its effects are large, then it may be quite acceptable if the design lacks power for detecting smaller effects. An expensive computer programming retraining program may be considered worthwhile implementing, for instance, only if at least half of the trainees subsequently obtain relevant employment, a relatively large effect that may be all the design needs to be able to detect with high power.

It is beyond the scope of this text to discuss the technical details of statistical power estimation, sample size, and statistical analysis with and without control variables. Proficiency in these areas is critical for competent impact assessment, however, and should be represented on any evaluation team undertaking such work. More detailed information on these topics can be found in Cohen (1988), Kraemer and Thiemann (1987), and Lipsey (1990, 1998).

Exhibit 10-C presents a representative example of the relationships among the factors that have the greatest influence on statistical power. It shows statistical power for various combinations of effect sizes and sample sizes for the most common statistical test of the difference between the means of two groups (a *t*-test or, equivalently, a one-way analysis of variance with no control variables and alpha = .05).

Close examination of the chart in Exhibit 10-C will reveal how difficult it can be to achieve adequate statistical power in an impact evaluation. Relatively high power is attained only when either the sample size or the threshold effect size is rather large. Both of these conditions often are unrealistic for impact evaluation.

Suppose, for instance, that the evaluator wants to hold the risk of Type II error to the same 5% level that is customary for Type I error, corresponding to a .95 power level. This is a quite reasonable objective in light of the unjustified damage that might be done to a program if it produces meaningful effects that the impact evaluation fails to detect at a statistically significant level. Suppose, further, that the evaluator determines that a statistical effect size of .20 on the outcome at issue would represent a positive program accomplishment and should be detected. The chart in Exhibit 10-C shows that the usual statistical significance test at the alpha = .05 standard and no control variables would require a sample size of somewhat more than 650 in each group (intervention

Exhibit 10-C
Statistical Power as a Function of Sample Size and Effect Size for a t-Test With Alpha = .05

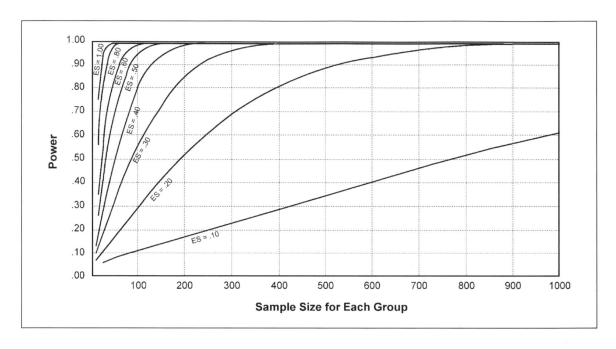

and control), for a total of more than 1,300. While such numbers may be attainable in some evaluation situations, they are far larger than the sample sizes usually reported in impact evaluation studies.

When practical constraints require smaller samples, there is a disproportionate increase in the threshold effect size that can be reliably detected. For a sample of 100 in each of the control and intervention groups, for instance, which is in the range typical of much evaluation work, a power of .95 (i.e., a .05 Type II error risk) is attained only for effect sizes larger than .50. If smaller statistical effects represent important program accomplishments, this evaluation design has only a modest likelihood of detecting them as statistically significant. The value of well-chosen control variables in a situation such as this is that they act to magnify the statistical effect size and thereby allow the same power to be attained with a smaller sample.

When program effects are not statistically significant, this result is generally taken as an indication that the program failed to produce effects. This interpretation of statistically nonsignificant results is technically incorrect and quite unfair if the lack of statistical significance was the result of an underpowered study and not the program's failure to produce meaningful effects. Such findings mean only that the observed effects are not reliably larger than the statistical noise, which itself is very large in an underpowered study, not that the effects are necessarily small or nonexistent. These nuances, however, are not likely to offset the impression of failure given by a report that no significant effects were found in an impact evaluation.

The seriousness of the problem of underpowered impact assessment studies in evaluation practice is illustrated in Exhibit 10-D, which is drawn from a large **meta-analysis** (an analysis of the statistical effects from multiple studies of a topic). The

Exhibit 10-D
Statistical Significance of the Effects of Delinquency Interventions

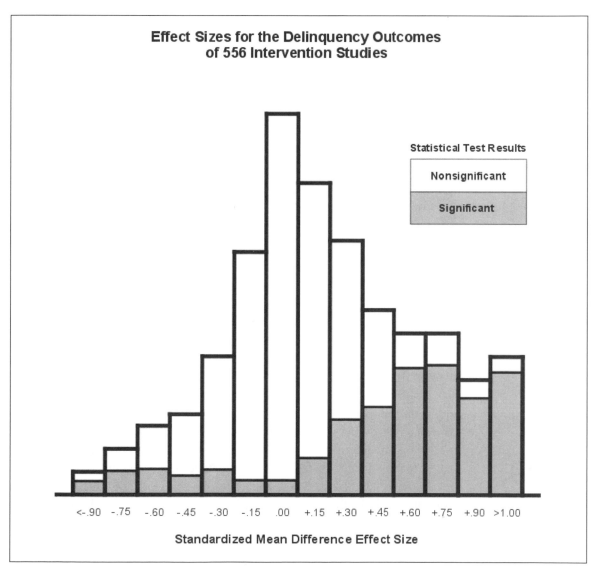

Effect Sizes for the Delinquency Outcomes of 556 Intervention Studies

Statistical Test Results: Nonsignificant, Significant

Standardized Mean Difference Effect Size

graph in this exhibit shows the distribution of effect sizes (represented as standardized mean differences; see Exhibit 10-A) for all the outcome measures reported in a set of 556 evaluations of the effects of intervention programs for juvenile delinquents. These evaluation studies were located through a vigorous search of published and unpublished sources that attempted to find virtually every qualifying study that had been conducted and reported. It is thus unlikely that it greatly misrepresents practice in this particular evaluation area.

The shaded part of the graph in this exhibit indicates the proportion of the effect estimates at each magnitude level that were found to be statistically significant in the source evaluation study. Note that it is only for the very largest effect sizes that an acceptably high proportion were detected at a statistically significant level. Many effects of a magnitude that might well represent important program benefits were not found to be statistically significant. This is a direct result of low statistical power. Even though the effect estimates were relatively large, the amount of statistical noise in the studies was also large, mainly because of small sample sizes and underutilization of control variables in the statistical analysis.

Consider the portion of the graph in Exhibit 10-D that shows effect size estimates in the range of .30. Many of the outcomes in these studies are the reoffense (recidivism) rates of the juvenile offenders as measured, for instance, by subsequent arrests recorded by the police. An effect size of .30 in standard deviation units for such a measure corresponds to the difference between an intervention group with a 38% recidivism rate in the six months after intervention and a control group with a 50% recidivism rate. This represents a 24% reduction in the number of juveniles reoffending (.12/.50), which certainly seems like a worthwhile program effect. Despite that, effects of this magnitude were not found to be statistically significant for more than half of the instances in which they were reported. Such results reveal more about the failure of evaluators to design adequately powered studies than the failure of the programs to produce meaningful effects.

Assessing the Practical Significance of Program Effects

As we have discussed, impact assessment research designs yield conclusions about the statistical significance of program effects and allow the extraction of statistical effect sizes of the sort described in Exhibit 10-A. Those statistical effect sizes, however, are not necessarily good guides to the *practical* magnitude of the program effects they represent. Nor is their level of statistical significance indicative of their practical significance. A small statistical effect may represent a program effect of considerable practical significance. Conversely, a large statistical effect for a program may be of little practical significance. For example, a very small reduction in the rate at which people with a particular illness must be hospitalized may have very important cost implications for health insurers. But improvements in their satisfaction with their care that are statistically larger may have negligible financial implications for those same stakeholders.

For stakeholders and evaluators to interpret and appraise the program effects found in an impact assessment, therefore, these effects must first be translated into terms that are relevant to the social conditions the program aims to improve. Sometimes this can be accomplished simply by restating the statistical effect size in terms of the original outcome measurement scale, but only if that scale has readily interpretable practical significance. In the example of juvenile delinquency programs, a common outcome measure is the rate of rearrest within a given time period after program participation. If a program reduces rearrest rates by 24%, this amount can readily be interpreted in terms of the number of juveniles affected and the number of delinquent offenses prevented. In a context of familiarity with juvenile delinquency, the practical significance of these effects is also readily interpretable. Effects on other inherently meaningful outcome measures, such as number of lives saved, amount of increase in annual income, and reduced rates of school dropouts, are likewise relatively easy to interpret in a practical sense.

For many other program effects, interpretation is not so easy. Suppose we find that a math tutoring program for low-performing sixth-grade students has raised their scores from 42 to 45 on the mathematics subtest of the Omnibus Test of Basic Skills. We also know that this represents a statistical effect size of .30 standard deviation units and that it is statistically significant. But, in practical terms, how much improvement in math skills does this represent? Is this a big program effect or a small one? Few people are so intimately familiar with the items and scoring of a particular math achievement test that they can interpret statistical effect sizes directly from its scoring scale.

Interpretation of statistical effects on outcome measures with values that are not inherently meaningful requires comparison with some external referent that will put the effect size in practical context. With achievement tests, for instance, we might compare program effects against the test norms. If the national norm on the math test is 50, we see that the math tutoring reduced the gap between the students in the program and the norm by about 38% (from 8 points to 5), but still left them well short of the average skill level.

Another frame of reference might be derived from the average scores for the students in the different grades in the school. Suppose that the mean score for the sixth graders in the school was 47 and that the mean for seventh graders was 50. The 3-point increase found as the effect of the math tutoring can now be seen as the equivalent of a full grade-level increase in performance. If the seventh grade mean were 67, however, we would judge the same 3-point increase to be quite small in grade-level equivalents. A similar referent for interpreting the practical magnitude of program effects might be provided by a suitable threshold value on the outcome measure that is being used. If it is possible to set a reasonable "success" threshold for a particular outcome measure and to determine the proportion of individuals above and below that threshold, then the corresponding program effects can be restated as an increase (or decrease) in the success rate. For example, a mental health program that treats depression might use the Beck Depression Inventory as an outcome measure. Suppose the program effect was assessed as .50 standard deviations and that this corresponded to the difference between a mean score of 14.3 for the treatment group and 17.8 for the control group. On this instrument, scores in the 17-20 range are recognized as the borderline for clinical depression, so one informative index of practical significance is to examine the number of patients in each group with posttest scores under 17, which represents a level of depression below the clinical borderline range. This might reveal, for instance, that 42% of the control group was below the clinical threshold at the end of the treatment period while 77% of the treatment group fell below that level. The practical magnitude of the treatment effect is more readily appraised against this diagnostic threshold than as a statistical effect on an arbitrary scale.

Another basis for comparison that can help the evaluator and program stakeholders interpret the practical significance of program effects is the distribution of effects found in evaluations of similar programs. A review of the program evaluation literature examining the effects of marriage counseling on marital satisfaction or, even better, a meta-analysis of the effects of such programs, might show that their mean effect size was around .46, with most of the effects ranging between .12 and .80. With this information in hand, an evaluator who finds an effect of .34 on marital satisfaction in an impact assessment of a particular marriage counseling program will be able to recognize it as a rather middling performance for a program of this type. Of course, there may be good reasons for lower than average performance if the program serves an atypical clientele or operates under especially difficult circumstances. Nonetheless, this sort of general comparison with the effects of similar programs on comparable outcomes, if available, can serve as a point of departure for appraising the magnitude of program effects.

There is no all-purpose best way to interpret the magnitude of program effects and appraise their practical significance, but approaches such as those we have just described will often be applicable and useful. What is clear is that simple statements of statistical significance or reports of statistical effect sizes are rarely sufficient for describing those effects. The evaluator, therefore, should be prepared to provide one or more translations of the statistical effects into terms that can be more readily interpreted in the practical context within which the program operates. The particular form of the translation and the referents that will be most meaningful in any given context will vary, and the evaluator may need to be resourceful in developing a suitable interpretive framework. The approaches we have described, and others that may be useful in some circumstances, are itemized in Exhibit 10-E, but this list does not exhaust the possibilities.

Examining Variations in Program Effects

So far, our discussion of program effects has focused on the overall mean effect for an intervention group relative to a suitable control group. However, program effects are rarely identical for all the subgroups in a target population or for all the outcomes, and the variations in effects should also be of interest to an evaluator. Examining such variations requires that other variables be brought into the picture in addition to the outcome measure of interest and intervention/control group membership. When attention is directed toward possible differences in program effects for subgroups of the target population, the additional variables define the subgroups to be analyzed and are called moderator variables. For examining how varying program effects on one outcome variable affect another outcome variable, both outcome variables must be included in the analysis with one of them tested as a potential mediator variable. The sections that follow describe how variations in program effects can be related to moderator or mediator variables and how the evaluator can uncover those relationships to better understand the nature of those program effects.

Moderator Variables

A **moderator variable** characterizes subgroups in an impact assessment for which the program effects may differ. For instance, gender would be such a variable when considering whether the program effect for the participants under study varied for males and females. To explore this possibility, the evaluator would divide both the intervention and control groups into male and female subgroups, determine the mean program effect on a particular outcome for each gender, and then compare those effects. The evaluator might discover that the program effect for females was larger (or smaller) than the effect for males and that the difference was statistically significant.

It is relatively common for moderator analysis to reveal variations in program effects for different subgroups of program targets. The major demographic variables of gender, age, ethnicity, and socioeconomic status often characterize groups that respond differently to any given social program. It is, of course, useful for program stakeholders to know which groups the program is more and less effective with as well as its overall average effects. Thus, the investigation of moderator variables is often an important aspect of impact assessment. It may identify subgroups for which program effects are especially large or small, reveal program effects for some types of targets even when the

Difference on the Original Measurement Scale

When the original outcome measure has inherent practical meaning, the effect size may be stated directly as the difference between the outcome for the intervention and control groups on that measure. For example, the dollar value of health services used after a prevention program or the number of days of hospitalization after a program aimed at decreasing time to discharge would generally have inherent practical meaning in their respective contexts.

Comparison With Test Norms or Performance of a Normative Population

For programs that aim to raise the outcomes for a target population to mainstream levels, program effects may be stated in terms of the extent to which the program effect reduced the gap between the preintervention outcomes and the mainstream level. For example, the effects of a program for children who do not read well might be described in terms of how much closer their reading skills at outcome are to the norms for their grade level. Grade-level norms might come from the published test norms, or they might be determined by the reading scores of the other children who are in the same grade and school as the program participants.

Differences Between Criterion Groups

When data on relevant outcome measures are available for groups of recognized differences in the program context, program effects can be compared to their differences on the respective outcome measures. Suppose, for instance, that a mental health facility routinely uses a depression scale at intake to distinguish between patients who can be treated on an outpatient basis and more severe cases that require inpatient treatment. Program effects measured on that depression scale could be compared with the difference between inpatient and outpatient intake scores to reveal if they are small or large relative to that well-understood difference.

Proportion Over a Diagnostic or Other Success Threshold

When a value on an outcome measure can be set as the threshold for success, the proportion of the intervention group with successful outcomes can be compared to the proportion of the control group with such outcomes. For example, the effects of an employment program on income might be expressed in terms of the proportion of the intervention group with household income above the federal poverty level in contrast to the proportion of the control group with income above that level.

Proportion Over an Arbitrary Success Threshold

Expressing a program effect in terms of success rate may help depict its practical significance even if the success rate threshold is relatively arbitrary. For example, the mean outcome value for the control group could be used as a threshold value. Generally, 50% of the control group

(Continued)

EXHIBIT 10-E
(Continued)

will be above that mean. The proportion of the intervention group above that same value will give some indication of the magnitude of the program effect. If, for instance, 55% of the intervention group is above the control group outcome mean, the program has not affected as many individuals as when 75% are above that mean.

Comparison With the Effects of Similar Programs

The evaluation literature may provide information about the statistical effects for similar programs on similar outcomes that can be compiled to identify effects that are small and large relative to what other programs achieve. Meta-analyses that systematically compile and report such effects are especially useful for this purpose. Thus, a standardized mean difference effect size of .22 on the number of consecutive days without smoking after a smoking cessation program could be viewed as having larger practical effects if the average effect size for other programs was around .10 on that outcome measures than if it was .50.

Conventional Guidelines

Cohen (1988) provided guidelines for what are generally "small," "medium," and "large" effect sizes in social science research. Though these were put forward in the context of conducting power analysis, they are widely used as rules of thumb for judging the magnitude of intervention effects. For the standardized mean difference effect size, for instance, Cohen suggested that .20 was a small effect, .50 a medium one, and .80 a large one.

overall mean program effect for all targets is small, and allow the evaluator to probe the outcome data in ways that strengthen the overall conclusions about the program's effectiveness. For example, focusing attention on the groups receiving the least benefit from the program and finding ways to boost the effects for those groups is an obvious way to strengthen a program and increase its overall effectiveness.

Evaluators can most confidently and clearly detect variations in program effects for different subgroups when they define the subgroups at the start of the impact assessment. In that case, there are no selection biases involved. For example, a target obviously does not become a male or a female as a result of selection processes at work during the period of the intervention. However, selection biases can come into play when subgroups are defined that emerge during the course of the intervention. For example, if some members of the control and intervention groups moved away after being assigned to intervention or control conditions, then whatever forces influenced that behavior may also be affecting outcomes. Consequently, the analysis needs to take into account any selection biases in the formation of such emergent subgroups.

If the evaluator has measured relevant moderator variables, it can be particularly informative to examine differential program effects for those targets most in need of the benefits the program attempts to provide. It is not unusual to find that program effects are smallest for those who were most in need when they were recruited into the impact study. An employment training program, for instance, will typically show better job placement outcomes for participants with recent employment experience and some job-related skills than for chronically unemployed persons with little experience and few skills, who are the targets most in need. While that itself is not surprising or necessarily a fault in the program, moderator analysis can reveal whether the neediest cases receive any benefit at all. If positive program effects appear only for the less needy and are zero or trivial for those most in need, the implications for evaluating and improving the program are quite different than if the neediest benefit, but by a smaller amount.

The differential effects of the employment training program in this example could be so strong that the overall mean effect of the program on, say, later earnings might be large despite a null effect on the chronically unemployed subgroup. Without moderator analysis, the overall positive effect would mask the fact that the program was ineffective with a critical subgroup. Such masking can work the other way around as well. The overall program effect may be negligible, suggesting that the program was ineffective. Moderator analysis, however, may reveal large effects for a particular subgroup that are washed out in the overall results by poor outcomes in larger groups. This can happen easily, for instance, with programs that provide "universal" services that cover individuals who do not have the condition the program is attempting to change. A broad drug prevention program in a middle school, for example, will involve many students who do not use drugs and have little risk of ever using them. No matter how good the program is, it cannot improve on the drug-use outcomes these students will have anyway. The important test of program effects may thus be a moderator analysis examining outcomes for the subgroup that is at high risk.

One important role of moderator analysis, therefore, is to avoid premature conclusions about program effectiveness based only on the overall mean program effects. A program with overall positive effects may still not be effective with all types of participants. Similarly, a program that shows no overall effects may be quite effective with some subgroups. Another possibility that is rare but especially important to diagnose with moderator analysis is a mix of positive and negative effects. A program could have systematically harmful effects on one subgroup of participants that would be masked in the overall effect estimates by positive effects in other subgroups. A program that works with juvenile delinquents in a group format, for instance, might successfully reduce the subsequent delinquency of the more serious offenders in the group. The less serious offenders in the mix, on the other hand, may be more influenced by their peer relations with the serious offenders than by the program and actually increase their delinquency rates (cf. Dishion, McCord, and Poulin, 1999). Depending on the proportions of more and less serious offenders, this negative effect may not be evident in the overall mean effect on delinquency for the whole program.

In addition to uncovering differential program effects, evaluators can also use moderator analysis to test their expectations about what differential effects should appear. This can be especially helpful for probing the consistency of the findings of an impact assessment and strengthening the overall conclusions about program effects that are drawn from those findings. Chapters 7, 8, and 9 discuss the many possible sources of bias and ambiguity that can complicate attempts to derive a valid estimate of program effects. While there is no good substitute for methodologically sound measurement and design, selective probing of the patterns of differential program effects can provide another check on the plausibility that the program itself—and not some other uncontrolled influence on outcomes—has produced the effects observed.

One form of useful probing, for instance, is dose-response analysis. This concept derives from medical research and reflects the expectation that, all other things equal, a larger dose of the treatment should produce more benefit, at least up to some optimal dose level. It is difficult to keep all other things equal, of course, but it is still generally informative for the evaluator to conduct moderator analysis when possible on differential amount, quality, or type of service. Suppose, for instance, that a program has two service delivery sites that serve a similar clientele. If the program has been more fully implemented in one site than the other, the program effects would be expected to be larger at that site. If they are not, and especially if they are larger at the weaker site, this inconsistency casts doubt on the presumption that the effects being measured actually stem from the program and not from other sources. Of course, there may be a reasonable explanation for this apparent inconsistency, such as faulty implementation data or an unrecognized difference in the nature of the clientele, but the analysis still has the potential to alert the evaluator to possible problems in the logic supporting the conclusions of the impact assessment.

Another example of similar spirit was presented in the preceding chapter as Exhibit 9-I. That exhibit describes an evaluation classic, the time-series evaluation of the effects of the British Breathalyzer program on traffic accidents. Because the time-series design used in that evaluation is not especially strong for isolating program effects, an important part of the evaluation was a moderator analysis that examined differential effects for weekday commuting hours in comparison to weekend nights. The researchers' expectation was that, if it was the program that produced the observed reduction in accidents, the effects should be larger during the weekend nights when drinking and driving were more likely than during commuter hours. The results confirmed that expectation and thus lent support to the conclusion that the program had been effective. Had the results turned out the other way, with a larger effect during commuter hours, the plausibility of that conclusion would have been greatly weakened.

The logic of moderator analysis aimed at probing conclusions about the program's role in producing the observed effects is thus one of checking whether expectations about differential effects are confirmed. The evaluator reasons that, if the program is operating as expected and truly having effects, those effects should be larger here and smaller there—for example, larger where the behavior targeted for change is most prevalent, where more or better service is delivered, for groups that should be naturally more responsive, and so forth. If appropriate moderator analysis confirms these expectations, it provides supporting evidence about the existence of program effects. Most notably, if such analysis fails to confirm straightforward expectations, it serves as a caution to the evaluator that there may be some influences on the program effect estimates other than the program.

While recognizing the value of using moderator analysis to probe the plausibility of conclusions about program effects, we must also point out the hazards. For example, the amount of services received by program targets is not randomly assigned, so comparisons among subgroups on moderator variables related to amount of service may be biased. The program participants who receive the most service, for instance, may be those with the most serious problems. In this case a simple-dose response analysis will show smaller effects for those receiving the largest service dose. However, if the evaluator looks within groups of equal severity, the expected dose-response relation may appear. Clearly, there are limits to the interpretability of moderator analysis aimed at testing for program effects, which is why we present it as a supplement to good impact assessment design, not as a substitute.

Mediator Variables

Another aspect of variation in program effects that may warrant attention in an impact assessment concerns possible mediator relationships among outcome variables. A **mediator variable** in this context is a proximal outcome that changes as a result of exposure to the program and then, in turn, influences a more distal outcome. A mediator is thus an intervening variable that comes between program exposure and some key outcome and represents a step on the causal pathway by which the program is expected to bring about change in the outcome. The proximal outcomes identified in a program's impact theory, as discussed in Chapters 5 and 7, are all mediator variables.

Like moderator variables, mediator variables are interesting for two reasons. First, exploration of mediator relationships helps the evaluator and the program stakeholders better understand what change processes occur among targets as a result of exposure to the program. This, in turn, can lead to informed consideration of ways to enhance that process and improve the program to attain better effects. Second, testing for the mediator relationships hypothesized in the program logic is another way of probing the evaluation findings to determine if they are fully consistent with what is expected if the program is in fact having the intended effects.

We can illustrate the analysis of mediator relationships using an example from the program impact theories depicted in Chapter 7, repeated here as Exhibit 10-F. The schematic in the exhibit deals with a program in which adult volunteers mentor at-risk youths. The distal outcome the program intends to affect is the youths' delinquent behavior. The causal pathway posited in the impact theory is that contact with mentors will influence the youths to emulate the positive values and behaviors of those mentors and to use their leisure time more constructively. This, in turn, is expected to lead to reduced contact with antisocial peers and then finally to decreased delinquent behavior. In this hypothesized pathway, positive values and behaviors and constructive use of leisure time are mediating variables between program exposure and contact with peers. Contact with peers, similarly, is presumed to mediate the relationship between changes in values, behavior, and leisure time use and decreased delinquency.

To simplify, we will consider for the moment only the hypothesized role of positive values as a mediator of the effects of the mentor on the youths' contact with antisocial peers. A test of whether there are mediator relationships among these variables involves, first, confirming that there are program effects on both the proximal outcome (values) and the distal outcome (contact with antisocial peers). If the proximal outcome is not influenced by the program, it cannot function as a mediator of that influence. If the distal outcome does not show a program effect, there is nothing to mediate. If there are such effects, the critical test of mediation is the relationship between the proximal

EXHIBIT 10-F

An Example of a Program Impact Theory Showing the Expected Proximal and Distal Outcomes

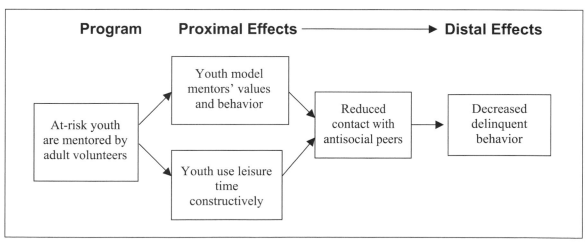

and distal outcomes when the intervention variable is statistically controlled. One appropriate technique for making this test would be multiple regression analysis with control variables, discussed in a different context in Chapter 9. For the case at hand, contact with antisocial peers would be the dependent variable in that analysis. The predictor variables would be positive values and group status (a binary variable with 1 = intervention group, 0 = control group). If positive values showed a significant relationship to contact with antisocial peers while participation in the mentoring program is statistically controlled, a mediator relationship is indicated.

More detailed discussions of the statistical procedures for testing mediator relationships can be found in Baron and Kenny (1986) and MacKinnon and Dwyer (1993). For present purposes, our interest is mainly what can be learned from such analyses. If all the mediator relationships posited in the impact theory for the mentoring program were demonstrated by such analysis, this would add considerably to the plausibility that the program was indeed producing the intended effects. But even if the results of the mediator analysis are different from expectations, they will have diagnostic value for the program. Suppose, for instance, that youths' positive values show an effect of the program but not a mediator relationship to contact with antisocial peers or delinquent behavior. Suppose, further, that use of leisure time does show strong mediator relationships to these variables. This pattern of results suggests that, although positive values are affected by the relationship with the mentors, they do not lead to the other intended outcomes. Thus, the program is likely to achieve better results on contact with antisocial peers and delinquent behavior if it trains the mentors to place more emphasis on constructive use of leisure time.

The Role of Meta-Analysis

Throughout this and the previous chapters on impact assessment we have stressed the advantages of using the findings of impact assessments that have already been conducted when designing and analyzing a new impact assessment. In addition, if each new evaluation builds on those that have gone before, knowledge about programs can become cumulative.

Much can be gained by careful study of reports of individual impact assessments and the traditional literature reviews available in professional journals and on the Internet. For many of the evaluator's purposes, however, the most useful summaries may be the increasing number of meta-analyses that statistically synthesize the findings of scores or even hundreds of prior impact assessments. Unfortunately, this form of research synthesis has limited applicability to situations where there is not a fairly large number of impact assessments of a similar class of programs. For many interventions, especially large-scale programs, there may not be a large enough pool of evaluations for anyone to have undertaken a meta-analysis. Where they exist, however, meta-analyses can provide the evaluator with invaluable information.

It is useful for evaluators to understand how meta-analyses are constructed. In a typical meta-analysis, reports of all available impact assessment studies of a particular intervention or type of program are first collected. The program effects on selected outcomes are then encoded as effect sizes using an effect size statistic of the sort shown in Exhibit 10-A. Other descriptive information about the evaluation methods, program participants, and nature of the intervention is also recorded. All of this is put in a database and various statistical analyses are conducted on the variation in effects and the factors associated with that variation (Cooper and Hedges, 1994; Lipsey and Wilson, 2001). The results can be informative for evaluators designing impact assessments of programs similar to those represented in the meta-analysis. In addition, by summarizing what evaluators collectively have found about the effects of a particular type of program, the results can be informative to the field of evaluation. We turn now to a brief discussion of each of these contributions.

Informing an Impact Assessment

Any meta-analyses conducted and reported for interventions of the same general type as one for which an evaluator is planning an impact assessment will generally provide useful information for the design of that study. Consequently, the evaluator should pay particular attention to locating relevant meta-analysis work as part of the general review of the relevant literature that should precede an impact assessment. Exhibit 10-G summarizes results from a meta-analysis of school-based programs to prevent aggressive behavior that illustrate the kind of information often available.

Meta-analysis focuses mainly on the statistical effect sizes generated by intervention studies and thus can be particularly informative with regard to that aspect of an impact assessment. To give proper consideration to statistical power, for instance, an evaluator must have some idea of the magnitude of the effect size a program might produce and what minimal effect size is worth trying to detect. Meta-analyses will typically provide information about the overall mean effect size for a program area and, often, breakdowns for different program variations. With information on the standard deviation of the effect sizes, the evaluator will also have some idea of the breadth of the effect size distribution and, hence, some estimate of the likely lower and upper range that might be expected from the program to be evaluated.

Program effect sizes, of course, may well be different for different outcomes. Many meta-analyses examine the different categories of outcome variables represented in the available evaluation studies. This information can give an evaluator an idea of what effects other studies have considered and what they found. Of course, the meta-analysis will be of less use if the program to be evaluated is concerned about an outcome that has

EXHIBIT 10-G

An Example of Meta-Analysis Results: Effects of School-Based Intervention Programs on Aggressive Behavior

Many schools have programs aimed at preventing or reducing aggressive and disruptive behavior. To investigate the effects of these programs, a meta-analysis of the findings of 221 impact evaluation studies of such programs was conducted.

A thorough search was made for published and unpublished study reports that involved school-based programs implemented in one or more grades from preschool through the last year of high school. To be eligible for inclusion in the meta-analysis, the study had to report outcome measures of aggressive behavior (e.g., fighting, bullying, person crimes, behavior problems, conduct disorder, and acting out) and meet specified methodological standards.

Standardized mean difference effect sizes were computed for the aggressive behavior outcomes of each study. The mean effect sizes for the most common types of programs were as follows:

In addition, a moderator analysis of the effect sizes showed that program effects were larger when

Therapy or counseling services (therapy-like services such as group or individual counseling and case management)	.33
Social competence training, cognitive-behavioral (training to develop social skills, understand and control anger, resolve conflict, and the like using cognitive-behavioral approaches)	.27
Behavioral and classroom management techniques (use of various behavioral techniques such as rewards, token economies, contingency contracts, to shape behavior)	.22
Social competence training, not cognitive behavioral (training to develop social skills, understand and control anger, resolve conflict, and the like using instructional approaches other than cognitive-behavioral techniques)	.20
Multimodal programs (interventions that include at least three components such as social competence training, counseling, classroom management, parent training, academic services, and the like)	.15

- high-risk children were the target population,
- programs were well implemented,
- programs were administered by teachers, and
- a one-on-one individualized program format was used.

SOURCE: Adapted from Sandra J. Wilson, Mark W. Lipsey, and James H. Derzon, "The Effects of School-Based Intervention Programs on Aggressive Behavior: A Meta-Analysis." *Journal of Consulting and Clinical Psychology*, 2003, 71(1):136-149. Reprinted with permission from the American Psychological Association.

not been examined in evaluations of other similar programs. Even then, however, results for similar types of variables—attitudes, behavior, achievement, and so forth—may help the evaluator anticipate both the likelihood of effects and the expected magnitude of those effects.

Similarly, after completing an impact assessment, the evaluator may be able to use relevant meta-analysis results in appraising the magnitude of the program effects that have been found in the assessment. The effect size data presented by a thorough meta-analysis of impact assessments in a program area constitute a set of norms that describe both typical program effects and the range over which they vary. An evaluator can use this information as a basis for judging whether the various effects discovered for the program being evaluated are representative of what similar programs attain. Of course, this judgment must take into consideration any differences in intervention characteristics, clientele, and circumstances between the program at hand and those represented in the meta-analysis results.

A meta-analysis that systematically explores the relationship between program characteristics and effects on different outcomes not only will make it easier for the evaluator to compare effects but may offer some clues about what features of the program may be most critical to its effectiveness. The meta-analysis summarized in Exhibit 10-G, for instance, found that programs were much less effective if they were delivered by laypersons (parents, volunteers) than by teachers and that better results were produced by a one-on-one than by a group format. An evaluator conducting an impact assessment of a school-based aggression prevention program might, therefore, want to pay particular attention to these characteristics of the program.

Informing the Evaluation Field

Aside from supporting the evaluation of specific programs, a major function of the evaluation field is to summarize what evaluations have found generally about the characteristics of effective programs. Though every program is unique in some ways, this does not mean that we should not aspire to discover some patterns in our evaluation findings that will broaden our understanding of what works, for whom, and under what circumstances. Reliable knowledge of this sort not only will help evaluators to better focus and design each program evaluation they conduct, but it will provide a basis for informing decisionmakers about the best approaches to ameliorating social problems.

Meta-analysis has become one of the principal means for synthesizing what evaluators and other researchers have found about the effects of social intervention in general. To be sure, generalization is difficult because of the complexity of social programs and the variability in the results they produce. Nonetheless, steady progress is being made in many program areas to identify more and less effective intervention models, the nature and magnitude of their effects on different outcomes, and the most critical determinants of their success. As a side benefit, much is also being learned about the role of the methods used for impact assessment in shaping the results obtained.

One important implication for evaluators of the ongoing efforts to synthesize impact evaluation results is the necessity to fully report each impact evaluation so that it will be available for inclusion in meta-analysis studies. In this regard, the evaluation field itself becomes a stakeholder in every evaluation. Like all stakeholders, it has distinctive information needs that the evaluator must take into consideration when designing and reporting an evaluation.

Summary

■ The ability of an impact assessment to detect program effects, and the importance of those effects, will depend in large part on their magnitude. The evaluator must, therefore, be familiar with the considerations relevant to describing both the statistical magnitude and the practical magnitude of program effects.

■ To describe the statistical magnitude of a program effect, evaluators often use effect size statistics such as a standardized mean difference or, for outcomes that are binary, an odds ratio.

■ A small statistical effect can be difficult to detect in an impact assessment against the background statistical noise present in any research study. The signal-to-noise comparison that initially determines if a program's statistical effects are large enough to be reliably distinguished from background noise is accomplished through statistical significance testing. If an effect is not statistically significant, the evaluator has no scientific basis for claiming it exists.

■ In attempting to statistically detect program effects, the evaluator may draw the wrong conclusion from the outcome data. An apparent effect may be statistically significant when there is no actual program effect (a Type I error), or statistical significance may not be attained when there really is a program effect (a Type II error).

■ To avoid erroneous conclusions about statistical effects, evaluators must give careful attention to ensuring that the research design has low risks for Type I and Type II errors. The probability of Type I error is constrained by the alpha level for statistical significance, conventionally set at .05. Keeping the risk of Type II error low, however, is more difficult and requires that the research design have high statistical power.

■ The statistical power of a research design for detecting a specified minimal effect size is mainly determined by the size of the samples in the intervention and control groups and the statistical significance test used, especially the influence of the control variables incorporated into the statistical test.

■ Although the evaluator's ability to detect program effects depends on their statistical magnitude, large statistical effects do not necessarily mean that the effects have practical significance. Interpreting the practical magnitude of statistical effects generally requires that they be translated into terms that are directly relevant to the social conditions the program aims to improve. There is no one, all-purpose best way to accomplish this translation, but there are many options available to a resourceful evaluator.

■ Whatever the overall mean program effect, there are usually variations in effects for different subgroups of the target population. Investigating moderator variables, which characterize distinct subgroups, is an important aspect of impact assessment. The investigation may reveal that program effects are especially large or small for some subgroups, and it allows the evaluator to probe the outcome data in ways that can strengthen the overall conclusions about a program's effectiveness.

■ The investigation of mediator variables probes variation in proximal program effects in relationship to more distal effects to determine if one leads to the other as implied by the program's impact theory. These linkages define mediator relationships that can inform the evaluator and program stakeholders about the change processes that occur among targets as a result of exposure to the program.

■ The results of meta-analyses can be informative for evaluators designing impact assessments. Their findings typically indicate the outcomes affected by the type of program represented and the magnitude and range of effects that might be expected on those outcomes. They also provide a basis for appraising the effects found in an impact assessment in comparison to those found for similar programs.

■ In addition, meta-analysis has become one of the principal means for synthesizing what evaluators and other researchers have found about the effects of social intervention. In this role, it informs the evaluation field about what has been learned collectively from the thousands of impact evaluations that have been conducted over the years.

Key Concepts

Effect size statistic

A statistical formulation of an estimate of program effect that expresses its magnitude in a standardized form that is comparable across outcome measures using different units or scales. Two of the most commonly used effect size statistics are the *standardized mean difference* and the *odds ratio*.

Mediator variable

In an impact assessment, a proximal outcome that changes as a result of exposure to the program and then, in turn, influences a more distal outcome. The mediator is thus an intervening variable that provides a link in the causal sequence through which the program brings about change in the distal outcome.

Meta-analysis

An analysis of effect size statistics derived from the quantitative results of multiple studies of the same or similar interventions for the purpose of summarizing and comparing the findings of that set of studies.

Moderator variable

In an impact assessment, a variable, such as gender or age, that characterizes subgroups for which program effects may differ.

Odds ratio

An effect size statistic that expresses the odds of a successful outcome for the intervention group relative to that of the control group.

Standardized mean difference

An effect size statistic that expresses the mean outcome difference between an intervention and control group in standard deviation units.

Statistical power

The probability that an observed program effect will be statistically significant when, in fact, it represents a real effect. If a real effect is not found to be statistically significant, a Type II error results. Thus, statistical power is one minus the probability of a Type II error. See also *Type II error.*

Type I error

A statistical conclusion error in which a program effect estimate is found to be statistically significant when, in fact, the program has no effect on the target population.

Type II error

A statistical conclusion error in which a program effect estimate is not found to be statistically significant when, in fact, the program does have an effect on the target population.

11

Measuring Efficiency

Chapter Outline

Key Concepts in Efficiency Analysis
Ex Ante and Ex Post Efficiency Analyses
Cost-Benefit and Cost-Effectiveness Analyses
The Uses of Efficiency Analyses

Conducting Cost-Benefit Analyses
Assembling Cost Data
Accounting Perspectives
Measuring Costs and Benefits
Monetizing Outcomes
Shadow Prices
Opportunity Costs
Secondary Effects (Externalities)
Distributional Considerations
Discounting
Comparing Costs to Benefits
When to Do *Ex Post* Cost-Benefit Analysis

Conducting Cost-Effectiveness Analyses

Whether programs have been implemented successfully and the degree to which they are effective are at the heart of evaluation. However, it is just as critical to be informed about the cost of program outcomes and whether the benefits achieved justify those costs. Comparison of the costs and benefits of social programs is one of the most important considerations in deciding whether to expand, continue, or terminate them.

Efficiency assessments—cost-benefit and cost-effectiveness analyses—provide a frame of reference for relating costs to program results. In addition to providing information for making decisions on the allocation of resources, they are often useful in gaining the support of planning groups and political constituencies that determine the fate of social intervention efforts.

The procedures employed in both types of analyses are often highly technical, and their applications will be described only briefly in this chapter. However, because the issue of the cost or effort required to achieve a given magnitude of desired change is implicit in all impact evaluations, all program evaluators must understand the ideas embodied in efficiency analyses, even if the technical procedures are beyond their skills.

E fficiency issues arise frequently in decision making about social interventions, as the following examples illustrate.

- Policymakers must decide how to allocate funding among a variety of adult educational programs, ranging from basic literacy programs for new immigrants to vocational training for displaced workers. All the programs have been shown to have substantial impact in completed evaluations. In this circumstance, an important consideration for policymakers will likely be any evidence on the degree to which each of the programs' **benefits** (positive outcomes, both direct and indirect) exceed their **costs** (direct and indirect inputs required to produce the intervention).

- A government agency is reviewing national disease control programs currently in operation. If additional funds are to be allocated to disease control, which programs would show the biggest payoffs per dollar of expenditure?

- Evaluations in the criminal justice field have established the effectiveness of various alternative programs aimed at reducing recidivism. Which program is most cost-effective to the criminal justice system? Given the policy choices, how would altering the current pattern of expenditures maximize the efficiency of correctional alternatives?

■ Members of a private funding group are debating whether to promote a program of low-interest loans for home construction or a program to give work skills training for married women to increase family income. How should they decide?

These are examples of common resource allocation dilemmas faced by planners, funding groups, and policymakers everywhere. Again and again, decisionmakers must choose how to allocate scarce resources to put them to optimal use. Consider even the fortunate case in which pilot projects of several programs have shown them all to be effective in producing the desired impacts. The decision of which to fund on a larger scale must take into account the relationship between costs and outcomes in each program. Although other factors, including political and value considerations, come into play, the preferred program often is the one that produces the most impact on the most targets for a given level of expenditure. This simple principle is the foundation of cost-benefit and cost-effectiveness analyses, techniques that provide systematic approaches to resource allocation analysis.

Both cost-benefit and cost-effectiveness analyses are means of judging the efficiency of programs. As we will elaborate, the difference between the two types of analyses is the way in which the outcomes of a program are expressed. In *cost-benefit* analyses, the outcomes of programs are expressed in monetary terms; in *cost-effectiveness* analyses, outcomes are expressed in substantive terms. For example, a cost-benefit analysis of a program to reduce cigarette smoking would focus on the difference between the dollars expended on the antismoking program and the dollar savings from reduced medical care for smoking-related diseases, days lost from work, and so on. A cost-effectiveness analysis of the same program would estimate the dollars that had to be expended to convert each smoker into a nonsmoker. (Later in this chapter we discuss the basis for deciding whether to undertake a cost-benefit or cost-effectiveness analysis.)

The basic procedures and concepts underlying resource allocation analysis stem from work undertaken in the 1930s to establish decision-making criteria for public investment activities. Early applications in the United States were to water resource development; in England, to transportation investments. After World War II, organizations such as the World Bank began to apply cost-benefit analysis to both specific project activities and national programs in less developed as well as industrialized countries. (For a review of how efficiency analyses have been applied in the federal government over the years, see Nelson, 1987.)

Cost-benefit and cost-effectiveness analyses in the social program arena have their analogue in the world of business, where costs are constantly compared with sales income. For instance, a computer company may be concerned with assessing the relationship of costs to income before committing to a new line of personal computers for the home market. Or a small-restaurant owner might be concerned with whether it would be more profitable to provide live dinner music or to promote lunchtime specials.

The idea of judging the utility of social intervention efforts in terms of their efficiency (profitability, in business terms) has gained widespread acceptance. However, the question of "correct" procedures for actually conducting cost-benefit and cost-effectiveness analyses of social programs remains an area of considerable controversy (Eddy, 1992; Zerbe, 1998). As we will discuss, this controversy is related to a combination of unfamiliarity with the analytical procedures employed, reluctance to impose monetary values on many social program outcomes, and an unwillingness to forsake initiatives that have been held in esteem for extended periods of time. Evaluators undertaking cost-benefit or cost-effectiveness analyses of social interventions must be aware of the particular issues involved in applying efficiency analyses to their specific field, as well as the limitations that characterize the use of cost-benefit and cost-effectiveness analyses in general. (For comprehensive discussions of efficiency assessment procedures, see Gramblin, 1990; Nas, 1996; Yates, 1996.)

Key Concepts in Efficiency Analysis

Cost-benefit and cost-effectiveness analyses can be viewed both as conceptual perspectives and as sophisticated technical procedures. From a conceptual point of view, perhaps the greatest value of efficiency analysis is that it forces us to think in a disciplined fashion about both costs and benefits. In the case of virtually all social programs, identifying and comparing the actual or anticipated costs with the known or expected benefits can prove invaluable. Most other types of evaluation focus mainly on the benefits. Furthermore, efficiency analyses provide a comparative perspective on the relative utility of interventions. Judgments of the comparative utility of different initiatives are unavoidable, since social programs, almost without exception, are conducted under resource constraints. Almost invariably, maintaining continuing support depends on convincing policymakers and funders that the "bottom line" (i.e., dollar benefits or the equivalent) justifies the program.

An interesting illustration of decision making along these lines is a report of a large bank's support of a day care center for its employees (see Exhibit 11-A). As the report documents, despite the difficulties of undertaking efficiency analyses, and even when they are somewhat crudely done, they can provide evidence whether company-supported social programs are justified in terms of monetary savings to the company. The article from which the excerpt in Exhibit 11-A is taken also discusses preventive health programs, day care centers, and lunchtime educational programs established by various businesses. In each case, knowing the bottom line in terms of company costs relative to benefits to the company was the basis of the company's decisions.

EXHIBIT 11-A

Cost Savings From a
Bank's Child Care
Facilities

In January 1987, Union Bank opened a new profit center in Los Angeles. This one, however, doesn't lend money. It doesn't manage money. It takes care of children.

The profit center is a day-care facility at the bank's Monterey Park operations center. Union Bank provided the facility with a $105,000 subsidy [in 1987]. In return, it saved the bank as much as $232,000. There is, of course, nothing extraordinary about a day-care center. What is extraordinary is the $232,000. That number is part of a growing body of research that tries to tell companies what they are getting—on the bottom line—for the dollars they invest in such benefits and policies as day-care assistance, wellness plans, maternity leaves, and flexible work schedules.

The Union Bank study, designed to cover many questions left out of other evaluations, offers one of the more revealing glimpses of the savings from corporate day-care centers. For one thing, the study was begun a year before the center opened, giving researchers more control over the comparison statistics. Union Bank approved spending $430,000 to build its day-care center only after seeing the savings projections.

Using data provided by the bank's human resource department, Sandra Burud, a child-care consultant in Pasadena, California, compared absenteeism, turnover, and maternity leave time the first year of operation and the year before. She looked at the results for 87 users of the center, a control group of 105 employees with children of similar ages who used other day-care options, and employees as a whole.

Her conclusion: The day-care center saves the bank $138,000 to $232,000 a year—numbers she calls "very conservative." Ms. Burud says savings on turnover total $63,000 to $157,000, based mostly on the fact that turnover among center users was 2.2 percent compared with 9.5 percent in the control group and 18 percent throughout the bank.

She also counted $35,000 in savings on lost days' work. Users of the center were absent an average of 1.7 fewer days than the control group, and their maternity leaves were 1.2 weeks shorter than for other employees. Ms. Burud also added a bonus of $40,000 in free publicity, based on estimates of media coverage of the center.

Despite the complexities of measurement, she says, the study succeeds in contradicting the "simplistic view of child care. This isn't a touchy-feely kind of program. It's as much a management tool as it is an employee benefit."

SOURCE: J. Solomon, "Companies Try Measuring Cost Savings From New Types of Corporate Benefits," *Wall Street Journal*, December 29, 1988, p. B1. Reprinted by permission of *The Wall Street Journal*, Dow Jones & Company, Inc. All rights reserved worldwide.

In spite of their value, however, it bears emphasis that in many evaluations formal, complete efficiency analyses are either impractical or unwise for several reasons. First, efficiency analysis may be unnecessary if the efficacy of the program is either very minimal or extremely high. Conducting an efficiency analysis makes sense primarily when a program is effective but not perfectly so. Second, the required technical procedures may call for methodological sophistication not available to the project's staff. Third, political or moral controversies may result from placing economic values on particular input or outcome measures, controversies that could obscure the relevance and minimize the potential utility of an otherwise useful and rigorous evaluation. Fourth, expressing the results of evaluation studies in efficiency terms may require selectively taking different costs and outcomes into account, depending on the perspectives and values of sponsors, stakeholders, targets, and evaluators themselves (what are referred to as **accounting perspectives**). The dependence of results on the accounting perspective employed may be difficult for at least some of the stakeholders to comprehend, again obscuring the relevance and utility of evaluations. (We discuss accounting perspectives in more detail later in this chapter.)

Furthermore, efficiency analysis may be heavily dependent on untested assumptions, or the requisite data for undertaking cost-benefit or cost-effectiveness calculations may not be fully available. Even the strongest advocates of efficiency analyses acknowledge that there often is no single "right" analysis. Moreover, in some applications, the results may show unacceptable levels of sensitivity to reasonable variations in the analytic and conceptual models used and their underlying assumptions.

Although we want to emphasize that the results of all cost-benefit and cost-effectiveness analyses should be treated with caution, and sometimes with a fair degree of skepticism, such analyses can provide a reproducible and rational way of estimating the efficiency of programs. Even strong advocates of efficiency analyses rarely argue that such studies should be the sole determinant of decisions about programs. Nonetheless, they are a valuable input into the complex mosaic from which decisions emerge.

Ex Ante and Ex Post Efficiency Analyses

Efficiency analyses are most commonly undertaken either (1) prospectively during the planning and design phase of an initiative (***ex ante* efficiency analysis**) or (2) retrospectively, after a program has been in place for a time and has been demonstrated to be effective by an impact evaluation, and there is interest in making the program permanent or possibly expanding it (***ex post* efficiency analysis**).

In the planning and design phases, *ex ante* efficiency analyses may be undertaken on the basis of a program's anticipated costs and outcomes. Such analyses, of course, must assume a given magnitude of positive impact even if this value is only a conjecture. Likewise, the costs of providing and delivering the intervention must be estimated.

In some cases, estimates of both the inputs and the magnitude of impact can be made with considerable confidence, either because there has been a pilot program (or a similar program in another location) or because the program is fairly simple in its implementation. Nevertheless, because *ex ante* analyses cannot be based entirely on empirical information, they run the risk of seriously under- or overestimating net benefits (which may be understood for now as the total benefits minus the total costs). Indeed, the issue of the accuracy of the estimates of both inputs and outputs is one of the controversial areas in *ex ante* analyses.

Ex ante cost-benefit analyses are most important for those programs that will be difficult to abandon once they have been put into place or that require extensive commitments in funding and time to be realized. For example, the decision to increase ocean beach recreational facilities by putting in new jetties along the New Jersey ocean shore would be difficult to overturn once the jetties had been constructed; thus, there is a need to estimate the costs and outcomes of such a program compared with other ways of increasing recreational opportunities, or to judge the wisdom of increasing recreational opportunities compared with the costs and outcomes of allocating the resources to another social program area.

Thus, when a proposed program would require heavy expenditures, decisions whether to proceed can be influenced by an *ex ante* cost-benefit analysis. Exhibit 11-B illustrates such a situation with regard to the testing of health care workers for HIV. Even though the possibility of, say, a surgeon or dentist transmitting HIV/AIDS to a patient is a matter of serious consequences and concern, testing the vast number of health care workers in this country for HIV would surely be quite expensive. Before embarking on such a program, it is wise to develop some estimate, even if crude, of how expensive it is likely to be in relation to the number of patient infections averted. The analysis summarized in Exhibit 11-B showed that under most risk scenarios any reasonable policy option would likely be quite expensive. Moreover, there was considerable uncertainty in the estimates possible from available information. Given the high, but uncertain, cost estimates, policymakers would be wise to move cautiously on this issue until better information could be developed.

Most often, however, *ex ante* efficiency analyses for social programs are not undertaken. As a consequence, many social programs are initiated or markedly modified without attention to the practicality of the action in cost-benefit or cost-effectiveness terms. For example, it might seem worthwhile to expand dental health services for children in Head Start to include a particular dental treatment that has been shown to prevent cavities. However, suppose that, while the treatment can be expected to reduce cavities by an average of one-half cavity per child per year, its annual cost per child is four times what dentists would charge on average for filling a single cavity. An efficiency analysis in such a case might easily dissuade decisionmakers from implementing the program.

A study by Phillips and others in 1994 examined the cost-effectiveness of alternative policies for HIV testing of health care workers, including physicians, surgeons, and dentists. The policy options considered were (a) mandatory and (b) voluntary testing, and for those who test positive, (a) exclusion from patient care, (b) restriction of practice, or (c) a requirement that patients be informed of their HIV status.

The derivation of costs in this study was based on data obtained from reviewing the pertinent literature and consulting with experts. The cost estimates included three components: (a) counseling and testing costs, (b) additional treatment costs because of early detection of HIV-positive cases, and (c) medical care costs averted per patient infection averted. Costs were estimated by subtracting (c) from (a) + (b).

Analyzing all options under high, medium, and low HIV prevalence and transmission risk scenarios, the study concluded that one-time mandatory testing with mandatory restriction of practice for a health care worker found HIV positive was more cost-effective than the other options. While showing the lowest cost of the policies considered, that option nonetheless was estimated to cost $291,000 per infection averted for surgeons and $500,000 for dentists. Given these high costs and the political difficulties associated with adopting and implementing mandatory restrictions on practice, this was not considered a viable policy option.

The analysts also found that the cost-effectiveness estimates were highly sensitive to variations in prevalence and transmission risk and to the different patterns of practice for physicians in contrast to dentists. The incremental cost per infection averted ranged from $447 million for dentists under low prevalence/transmission risk conditions to a savings of $81,000 for surgeons under high prevalence/transmission risk conditions.

Given the high costs estimated for many of the options and the uncertainty of the results, the authors concluded as follows: "Given the ethical, social, and public health implications, mandatory testing policies should not be implemented without greater certainty as to their cost-effectiveness."

SOURCE: Adapted from Tevfik F. Nas, *Cost-Benefit Analysis: Theory and Application* (Thousand Oaks, CA: Sage, 1996), pp. 191-192. Original study was K. A. Phillips, R. A. Lowe, J. G. Kahn, P. Lurie, A. L. Avins, and D. Ciccarone, "The Cost Effectiveness of HIV Testing of Physicians and Dentists in the United States," *Journal of the American Medical Association*, 1994, 271:851-858.

Most commonly, efficiency analyses in the social program field take place after the completion of an impact evaluation, when the impact of a program is known. In such *ex post* cost-benefit and cost-effectiveness assessments, the analysis is undertaken to assess whether the costs of the intervention can be justified by the magnitude of the program effects.

The focus of such assessments may be on examining the efficiency of a program in absolute or comparative terms, or both. In absolute terms, the idea is to judge whether the program is worth what it costs either by comparing costs to the monetary value of benefits or by calculating the money expended to produce some unit of outcome. For example, a cost-benefit analysis may reveal that for each dollar spent to reduce shoplifting in a department store, $2 are saved in terms of stolen goods, an outcome that clearly indicates that the shoplifting program would be economically beneficial. Alternatively, a cost-effectiveness study might show that the program expends $50 to avert each shoplifting.

In comparative terms, the issue is to determine the differential "payoff" of one program versus another—for example, comparing the costs of elevating the reading achievement scores of schoolchildren by one grade level produced by a computerized instruction program with the costs of achieving the same increase through a peer tutorial program. In *ex post* analyses, estimates of costs and outcomes are based on studies of the types described in previous chapters on impact evaluations.

Cost-Benefit and Cost-Effectiveness Analyses

Many considerations besides economic efficiency are brought to bear in policy making, planning, and program implementation, but economic efficiency is almost always critical, given that resources are inevitably scarce. Cost-benefit and cost-effectiveness analyses have the virtue of encouraging evaluators to become knowledgeable about program costs. Surprisingly, many evaluators pay little attention to costs and are unaware of the information sources they need to contact and the complexities of describing program costs. In contrast, program costs are very salient to many of the stakeholder groups important to a program's acceptance and modification. Consequently, attention to costs by evaluation staff often increases cooperation and support from such groups.

A cost-benefit analysis requires estimates of the benefits of a program, both tangible and intangible, and estimates of the costs of undertaking the program, both direct and indirect. Once specified, the benefits and costs are translated into a common measure, usually a monetary unit.

Cost-benefit analysis requires the adoption of a particular economic perspective; in addition, certain assumptions must be made to translate program inputs and outputs into monetary figures. As we have noted, there is considerable controversy in the field regarding the "correct" procedures to use in converting inputs and outputs into monetary values. Clearly, the assumptions underlying the definitions of the measures of costs and benefits strongly influence the resulting conclusions. Consequently, the analyst is required, at the very least, to state the basis for the assumptions that underlie the analysis.

Often, analysts do more than that. They may undertake several sensitivity analyses, which alter important assumptions in order to test how sensitive the findings are to the variations in assumptions. Sensitivity analyses are a central feature of well-conducted efficiency studies. Indeed, an important advantage of formal efficiency studies over impressionistically gathered information about costs in relation to outcomes is that the assumptions and procedures are open to review and checking. For example, in an ex ante cost-benefit analysis of the savings achieved by a program to reduce recidivism, the costs of criminal justice processing of averted arrests must be "guesstimated." The savings achieved by the program change considerably depending on whether those costs are assumed to be $5,000, $10,000, or some other figure.

In general, there is much more controversy about converting outcomes into monetary values than there is about inputs. Cost-benefit analysis is least controversial when applied to technical and industrial projects, where it is relatively easy to place a monetary value on benefits as well as costs. Examples include engineering projects designed to reduce the costs of electricity to consumers, highway construction to facilitate transportation of goods, and irrigation programs to increase crop yields. Estimating benefits in monetary terms is frequently more difficult in social programs, where only a portion of program inputs and outputs may easily be assigned a monetary value. For example, future occupational gains from an educational project can be translated into monetary values (i.e., increased earnings) without incurring too much controversy. The issues are more complex in such social interventions as fertility control programs or health services projects because one must ultimately place a value on human life to fully monetize the program benefits (Jones-Lee, 1994; Mishan, 1988).

The underlying principle is that cost-benefit analysts attempt to value both inputs and outputs at what is referred to as their marginal social values. For many items, such as the cost of providing a certain medicine or the monetary benefit of outfitting new cars with engines that burn less gasoline, market prices perform this task quite well. The situation is most difficult when the good or service is not traded and therefore does not have a market price.

Because of the controversial nature of valuing outcomes, in many cases, especially regarding human services, cost-effectiveness analysis is seen as a more appropriate technique than cost-benefit analysis. Cost-effectiveness analysis requires monetizing only the program's costs; its benefits are expressed in outcome units. For example, the cost-effectiveness of distributing free textbooks to rural primary school children could be expressed in terms of how much each $1,000 in project costs increased the average reading scores of the targeted children.

For cost-effectiveness analysis, then, efficiency is expressed in terms of the costs of achieving a given result. That is, the efficiency of a program in attaining its goals is assessed in relation to the monetary value of the inputs required for a designated unit of outcome. This type of analysis can be especially useful in comparing the efficiency of different programs. For example, alternative educational interventions may be compared by measuring the costs for each alternative of achieving a specific educational gain as measured by test scores. Exhibit 11-C describes such a case. Here, relating costs to gains in mathematics and reading among elementary school children permitted a comparison of the cost-effectiveness of different interventions. The analysis found that counseling by other students provided more impact per $100 than other approaches. Surprisingly, such peer counseling was more cost-effective than a high-tech, computer-assisted instruction program.

Cost-effectiveness studies can be useful both before and after programs are put into place. An *ex ante* cost-effectiveness analysis allows potential programs to be compared and ranked according to the magnitudes of their expected effects relative to their estimated costs. In *ex post* cost-effectiveness analyses, actual program costs and benefits replace, to a considerable extent, estimates and assumptions. Moreover, retrospective analyses can yield useful insights about specific program processes that can be applied to designing more efficient programs. However, comparisons of outcomes in relation to costs require that the programs under consideration have the same types of outcomes. If programs produce different outcomes, such as reduction in number of days in bed in the case of a medical care program and increased reading competence in the instance of an educational program, then one is still left with the difficulty of valuing the two outcomes. That is, how much is an average reduction of two bed days "worth" compared with a mean increase of 10 points on a standard reading test?

The Uses of Efficiency Analyses

Efficiency analyses, at least *ex post* analyses, should be considered an extension of, rather than an alternative to, impact evaluation. Since the estimation of either monetized benefits or substantive effects depends on knowledge of a program's impact, it is impossible to engage in *ex post* cost-benefit or cost-effectiveness calculations for programs whose impacts are unknown and inestimable. It also is senseless to do so for ineffective programs, that is, when impact evaluations discover no significant program effects. When applied to efficacious programs, efficiency analyses are useful to those who must make policy decisions regarding the support of one program over another, or who need to decide in absolute terms whether the outcomes of a program are worth its costs, or who are required to review the utility of programs at different points in time.

EXHIBIT 11-C

Cost-Effectiveness of Computer-Assisted Instruction

To assist decisionmakers in considering different approaches to improving the mathematics and reading performance of elementary school children, a cost-effectiveness study was undertaken of computer-assisted instruction (CAI) compared to three alternative interventions. The findings run counter to some conventional expectations. Although the CAI alternative did relatively well according to the cost-effectiveness criterion, it did not do as well as peer tutoring. It is somewhat surprising that a traditional and a labor-intensive approach (peer tutoring) appears to be far more cost-effective than an electronic intervention, a widely used CAI approach. Moreover, the low ranking for the option of increasing the instructional time in the classroom, the centerpiece of many of the calls for educational reform, makes it a relatively poor choice for both reading and mathematics from a cost-effectiveness perspective (see table).

To estimate the cost-effectiveness of the various alternatives, the researchers first determined the magnitude, in standard deviation units (effect sizes), of the increases on mathematics and reading achievement test scores resulting from each approach. They then determined the cost of each instructional approach and computed the achievement score effect per $100 spent per student for each approach. The results, averaging the mathematics and reading achievement findings, are presented in the table.

Average Cost-Effectiveness Ratios of Four Interventions for Two Subject Areas (average of mathematics and reading effect sizes for each $100 cost per student per subject)

Intervention	Cost-Effectiveness Ratio
Cross-age tutoring	
Combined peer and adult program	.22
Peer component	.34
Adult component	.07
Computer-assisted instruction	.15
Reducing class size	
From 35 to 30	.11
From 30 to 25	.09
From 25 to 20	.08
From 35 to 20	.09
Increasing instructional time	.09

SOURCE: Adapted from H. M. Levin, G. V. Glass, and G. R. Meister, "Cost-Effectiveness of Computer-Assisted Instruction," *Evaluation Review*, 1987, 11(1):50-72.

Moreover, efficiency analysis can be useful in determining the degree to which different levels or "strengths" of interventions produce different levels of benefits and can be used in a formative manner to help improve program performance (Yates, 1996).

Conducting Cost-Benefit Analyses

With the basic concepts of efficiency analysis in hand, we turn now to how such analyses are conducted. Because many of the basic procedures are similar, we discuss cost-benefit analysis in detail and then treat cost-effectiveness analysis more briefly. We begin with a step necessary to both types of studies, the assembling of cost data.

Assembling Cost Data

Cost data are obviously essential to the calculation of efficiency measures. In the case of *ex ante* analyses, program costs must be estimated, based on costs incurred in similar programs or on knowledge of the costs of program processes. For *ex post* efficiency analyses, it is necessary to analyze program financial budgets, segregating out the funds used to finance program processes as well as collecting costs incurred by targets or other agencies.

Useful sources of cost data include the following:

- Agency fiscal records: These include salaries of program personnel, space rental, stipends paid to clients, supplies, maintenance costs, business services, and so on.

- Target cost estimates: These include imputed costs of time spent by clients in program activities, client transportation costs, and so on. (Typically these costs have to be estimated.)

- Cooperating agencies: If a program includes activities of a cooperating agency, such as a school, health clinic, or another government agency, the costs borne can be obtained from the cooperating agency.

Fiscal records, it should be noted, are not always easily comprehended. The evaluator may have to seek help from an accounting professional.

It is often useful to draw up a list of the cost data needed for a program. Exhibit 11-D shows a worksheet representing the various costs for a program that provided high school students with exposure to working academic scientists to heighten students' interest in pursuing scientific careers. Note that the worksheet identifies the several parties to the program who bear program costs.

EXHIBIT 11-D
Worksheet for
Estimating
Annualized Costs for
a Hypothetical
Program

"Saturday Science Scholars" is a program in which a group of high school students gather for two Saturdays a month during the school year to meet with high school science teachers and professors from a local university. Its purpose is to stimulate the student interest in scientific careers and expose them to cutting-edge research. The following worksheet shows how a variety of costs were borne by different levels of government, the university, and participating students and their parents.

Cost Ingredients	Total Cost	Cost to School District	Cost to State Gov't	Cost to University	Cost to Students and Parents
Personnel					
2 high school teachers	9,000	9,000			
2 university professors	14,400			14,400	
2 parent aides (volunteers)	3,600			3,600	
Facilities					
High school science lab and classroom	2,000	2,000			
Materials and equipment					
Photocopies	400	400			
Materials for science experiments	500	250		250	
Laboratory equipment	500			500	
Other					
Maintenance and janitorial services	1,500	1,500			
Insurance	1,800	1,800			
Utilities	900	900			
Required client inputs					
Transportation (time, vehicle costs)	625				625
Total ingredients cost	35,255	15,850	0	15,150	4,225
User fees		−1,000			1,000
Other cash subsidies		−7,500	7,500		
Net costs	35,225	7,350	7,500	15,150	5,225

SOURCE: Adapted from Henry M. Levin and Patrick J. McEwan, *Cost-Effectiveness Analysis*, 2nd ed., Table 5.2. Thousand Oaks, CA: Sage, 2001.

Accounting Perspectives

To carry out a cost-benefit analysis, one must first decide which perspective to take in calculating costs and benefits. What point of view should be the basis for specifying, measuring, and monetizing benefits and costs? In short, costs to and benefits for whom? Benefits and costs must be defined from a single perspective because mixing points of view results in confused specifications and overlapping or double counting. Of course, several cost-benefit analyses for a single program may be undertaken, each from a different perspective. Separate analyses based on different perspectives often provide information on how benefits compare to costs as they affect relevant stakeholders. Generally, three accounting perspectives may be used for the analysis of social projects, those of (1) individual participants or targets, (2) program sponsors, and (3) the communal social unit involved in the program (e.g., municipality, county, state, or nation).

The *individual-target* accounting perspective takes the point of view of the units that are the program targets, that is, the persons, groups, or organizations receiving the intervention or services. Cost-benefit analyses using the individual-target perspective often produce higher benefit-to-cost results (net benefits) than those using other perspectives. In other words, if the sponsor or society bears the cost and subsidizes a successful intervention, then the individual program participant benefits the most. For example, an educational project may impose relatively few costs on participants. Indeed, the cost to targets may primarily be the time spent in participating in the project, since books and materials usually are furnished. Furthermore, if the time required is primarily in the afternoons and evenings, there may be no loss of income involved. The benefits to the participants, meanwhile, may include improvements in earnings as a result of increased education, greater job satisfaction, and increased occupational options, as well as transfer payments (stipends) received while participating in the project.

The *program sponsor* accounting perspective takes the point of view of the funding source in valuing benefits and specifying cost factors. The funding source may be a private agency or foundation, a government agency, or a for-profit firm. From this perspective, the cost-benefit analysis most closely resembles what frequently is termed *private profitability analysis.* That is, analysis from this perspective is designed to reveal what the sponsor pays to provide a program and what benefits (or "profits") should accrue to the sponsor.

The program sponsor accounting perspective is most appropriate when the sponsor is confronted with a fixed budget (i.e., there is no possibility of generating additional funds) and must make decisive choices between alternative programs. A county government, for example, may favor a vocational education initiative that includes student stipends over other programs because this type of program would reduce the costs of public assistance and similar subsidies (since some of the persons in the vocational education program would have been supported by income maintenance funds). Also, if the future incomes of the participants were to increase because of the training received, their direct and indirect tax payments would increase, and these also could be included in calculating benefits from a program sponsor perspective. The costs to the government sponsor include the costs of operation, administration, instruction, supplies, facilities, and any additional subsidies or transfers paid to the participants during the training. Another illustration, Exhibit 11-E, shows a cost-benefit calculation involving the savings to the mental health system that result from providing specialized services to patients with co-occurring mental disorders and substance abuse problems.

The *communal* accounting perspective takes the point of view of the community or society as a whole, usually in terms of total income. It is, therefore, the most comprehensive perspective but also usually the most complex and thus the most difficult to apply. Taking the point of view of society as a whole implies that special efforts are being made to account for **secondary effects,** or *externalities*—indirect project effects, whether beneficial or detrimental, on groups not directly involved with the intervention. A secondary effect of a training program, for example, might be the spillover of the training to relatives, neighbors, and friends of the participants. Among the more commonly discussed negative external effects of industrial and technical projects are pollution, noise, traffic, and destruction of plant and animal life. Moreover, in the current literature, communal cost-benefit analysis has been expanded to include equity considerations, that is, the **distributional effects** of programs among different subgroups. Such effects result in a redistribution of resources in the general population. From a communal standpoint, for example, every dollar earned by a minority member who had been unemployed for six months or more may be seen as a "double benefit" and so entered into the analyses.

Exhibit 11-F illustrates the benefits that need to be taken into account from a communal perspective. In this exhibit, Gray and associates (1991) report on an effort to integrate several quasi-experimental studies to come out with a reasonable cost-to-benefit analysis of the efficiency of different correctional approaches. As shown in the table in Exhibit 11-F, benefits are of several different types. Although, as the article carefully notes, there are serious uncertainties about the precision of the estimates, the results are important to judges and other criminal justice experts concerned with the costs to society of different types of sentences.

The components of a cost-benefit analysis conducted from a communal perspective include most of the costs and benefits that also appear in calculations made from the individual and program sponsor perspectives, but the items are in a sense valued and monetized differently. For example, communal costs for a project include **opportunity costs**, that is, alternative investments forgone by the community to fund the project in question. These are obviously not the same as opportunity costs incurred by

EXHIBIT 11-E

Costs and Savings to
the Mental Health
System of Providing
Specialized Dual
Diagnosis Programs

People with serious mental disorders and co-occurring substance disorders (*dual diagnosis*) are very difficult and costly to treat by means of the
usual mental health or substance abuse services. Providing them with specialized dual diagnosis treatment programs might improve the outcomes
but would add to the cost of services. However, if those improved outcomes decreased the need for subsequent mental health services, they
might result in savings that would offset the costs of the specialized program. Viewed from the perspective of policymakers in the mental health
system, therefore, a crucial question is whether the cost to the mental
health system of specialized programs for this client population will be
recovered in savings to the system through reduced need for subsequent
services.

To address this question, a team of evaluation researchers randomly
assigned 132 patients to three specialized dual diagnosis programs and
assessed both the outcomes and the costs. The "control" program was
based on a 12-step recovery model and was the "usual care" condition for
dual diagnosis patients in this mental health system. It involved referral to
community Alcoholics Anonymous or Narcotics Anonymous meetings
and associated supportive services to help the client manage the recovery
process. A more intensive program option used a behavioral skills model
that relied on cognitive-behavioral treatment focusing on social and independent living skills and prevention of relapses. A less intensive option
featured case management in which reduced caseloads allowed clinicians
to provide individualized assistance in such areas as daily living, housing,
legal problems, and the like.

The behavioral skills model produced the largest positive effects on measures of client functioning and symptoms but was also the most expensive
program to deliver. To further explore the cost considerations, the evaluators examined service utilization and cost data for the clients in each of
the three programs for four time periods: the six months before the dual
diagnosis programs began (baseline), the six months after, the 12 months
after, and the 18 months after.

Mental health service costs were divided into two categories: supportive services and intensive services. Supportive services included case
management, outpatient visits, medication visits, day services, and
other such routine services for mental health patients. Intensive services included the more costly treatments for serious episodes, for
instance, inpatient services, skilled nursing care, residential treatment,
and emergency visits.

(Continued)

EXHIBIT 11-E
(Continued)

The costs of supportive services were expected to show an increase for all of the specialized dual diagnosis programs, corresponding to the extra resources required to provide them. Any significant savings to the mental health system were expected to appear as a result of decreased use of expensive intensive services. Thus, the cost analysis focused on the amount by which the costs of supportive services increased from baseline in comparison to the amount by which the costs of intensive services decreased. The table shows the results for the change in service utilization costs between the six-month baseline period and the 18 months after the program began.

As expected, the cost of supportive services generally increased after the specialized programs were implemented, except for the case management program, which actually showed a reduction in total support cost from the baseline service period. The largest increase in support costs, on the other hand, was associated with the relatively intensive behavioral skills program.

Also, as hoped, the costs for intensive services were reduced from baseline for all of the specialized programs. The greater impacts of the behavioral skills program on client functioning and symptoms, however, did not translate into corresponding decreases in service utilization and associated cost savings. Indeed, the usual-care condition of the 12-step program produced the greatest decreases in subsequent costs for intensive services. However, while the case management program did not yield such large decreases, its lower support costs resulted in a savings-to-costs ratio that was comparable to that of the 12-step program. Additional analyses showed that these programs also generally resulted in savings to the medical system, the criminal justice system, and the families of the clients.

In terms of costs and savings directly to the mental health system, therefore, both the 12-step and the case management programs produced considerably more savings than they cost. Indeed, the cost analysis estimated that for every $1 invested in providing these programs there were about $9 in savings that would accrue over the subsequent 18 months. Moreover, the case management program could actually be implemented with a net reduction in support service costs, thus requiring no additional investment. The behavioral skills program, on the other hand, produced a net loss to the mental health system. For every $1 invested in it, there was only a $0.53 savings to the mental health system.

(Continued)

EXHIBIT 11-E
(Continued)

Average per Client Change in Costs of Services Used From Baseline to 18 Months Later, in Dollars

	12-Step Program	Behavioral Skills	Case Management
Change in mental health supportive costs (a)	+728	+1,146	−370
Change in mental health intensive costs (b)	−6,589	−612	−3,291
Ratio of (b) to (a)	9.05	0.53	8.89

SOURCE: Adapted from Jeanette M. Jerell and Teh-Wei Hu, "Estimating the Cost Impact of Three Dual Diagnosis Treatment Programs," *Evaluation Review*, 1996, 20(2):160-180.

an individual as a consequence of participating in the project. Communal costs also include outlays for facilities, equipment, and personnel, usually valued differently than they would be from the program sponsor perspective. Finally, these costs do not include transfer payments because they would also be entered as benefits to the community and the two entries would simply cancel each other out.

Obviously, the decision about which accounting perspective to use depends on the stakeholders who constitute the audience for the analysis, or who have sponsored it. In this sense, the selection of the accounting perspective is a political choice. An analyst employed by a private foundation interested primarily in containing the costs of hospital care, for example, likely will take the program sponsor's accounting perspective, emphasizing the perspectives of hospitals. The analyst might ignore the issue of whether the cost-containment program that has the highest net benefits from a sponsor accounting perspective might actually show a negative cost-to-benefit value when viewed from the standpoint of the individual. This could be the case if the individual accounting perspective included the opportunity costs involved in having family members stay home from work because the early discharge of patients required them to provide the bedside care ordinarily received in the hospital.

Generally, the communal accounting perspective is the most politically neutral. If analyses using this perspective are done properly, the information gained from an individual or a program sponsor perspective will be included as data about the distribution of costs and benefits. Another approach is to undertake cost-benefit analyses from more than one accounting perspective. The important point, however, is that cost-benefit analyses, like other evaluation activities, have political features.

Exhibit 11-F

Costs to Benefits of
Correctional
Sentences

The control of crime by appropriate sentencing of convicted offenders must take into account not only the costs of implementing each of the three choices typically available to judges—prison, jail, or probation sentences—but also the benefits derived. The major correctional approaches are *incapacitation* through removing the offender from the community by incarceration in a prison or jail, *deterrence* by making visible the consequences of criminal behavior to discourage potential offenders, and *rehabilitation* by resocialization and redirection of criminals' behavior. Each approach generates different types of "benefits" for society. Since jail sentences are usually short, for instance, the incapacitation benefit is very small compared with the benefit from prison sentences, although, since no one likes being in jail, the deterrence benefit of jail is estimated to be about five-sixths that of prison.

Gray and associates attempted to estimate *ex ante* the monetary value of these different social benefits for each sentencing option (see table). On average, probation sentences showed greater net benefits than jail, which, in turn, showed a smaller negative benefit than prison. However, the relative weight given to each benefit varied according to the type and circumstances of the offense. For example, the costs of a burglary (loss to the victim plus costs of the police investigation, arrest, and court proceedings) comes to about $5,000, suggesting that perhaps long prison sentences are called for in the case of recidivist burglars to maximize the incapacitation benefit. In contrast, the cost of apprehending and trying persons for receiving stolen property is less than $2,000, and a short jail sentence or even probation may be the most efficient response.

Estimated Annual Social Costs and Benefits per Offender, in Dollars, for Different Correctional Sentences (average across all offenses)

	Incapacitation Benefit	Rehabilitation Benefit	Deterrence Benefit	Costs	Net Benefits
Prison	+6,732	−10,356	+6,113	−10,435	−7,946
Jail	+774	−5,410	+5,094	−2,772	−2,315
Probation	0	−2,874	+5,725	−1,675	+1,176

SOURCE: Adapted from T. Gray, C. R. Larsen, P. Haynes, and K. W. Olson, "Using Cost-Benefit Analysis to Evaluate Correctional Sentences," *Evaluation Review*, 1991, 15(4):471-481.

Exhibit 11-G shows some of the basic components of cost-benefit analyses for the different accounting perspectives for an employment training program (the program sponsor in this case is a government agency). The list is not to be taken as complete but as an illustration only. Specific items included in real analyses vary.

EXHIBIT 11-G

Components of Cost-Benefit Analyses From Different Perspectives for a Hypothetical Employment Training Program

	Individual (targets)	Program Sponsor (government)	Communal or Societal
Benefits	Increase in net earnings (after taxes)	Increase in tax revenues	Increase in gross earnings (before taxes)
	Additional benefits received (e.g., direct transfers, fringe and noneconomic benefits)	Decrease in expenses of public assistance and other subsidies	Increase in other income (e.g., fringe benefits, excluding direct transfers)
		Value of work done within the project (salary and fringes at market costs)	Decrease in expenses of alternative projects no longer applicable
			Value of work done within the project (salary and fringes at market costs)
Costs	Opportunity costs (net earnings forgone) Loss of direct subsidies no longer applicable (alternative social programs) Costs related to participation (e.g., fees, materials)	Taxes lost Project costs (e.g., capital, administrative, instructional, direct subsidies)	Opportunity costs (gross earnings forgone) Project costs (excluding direct subsidies or transfer payments)

SOURCE: Adapted from Jeanette M. Jerell and Teh-Wei Hu, "Estimating the Cost Impact of Three Dual Diagnosis Treatment Programs," *Evaluation Review*, 1996, 20(2):160-180.

Exhibit 11-H provides a simplified, hypothetical example of cost-benefit calculations for a training program from the three accounting perspectives. Again, the monetary figures are oversimplifications; a real analysis would require far more complex treatment of the measurement issues involved. Note that the same components may enter into the calculation as benefits from one perspective and as costs from another and that the difference between benefits and costs, or net benefit, will vary, depending on the accounting perspective used.

In some cases, it may be necessary to undertake a number of analyses. For example, if a government group and a private foundation jointly sponsor a program, separate analyses may be required for each to judge the return on its investment. Also, the analyst might want to calculate the costs and benefits to different groups of targets, such as the direct and indirect targets of a program. For example, many communities try to provide employment opportunities for residents by offering tax advantages to industrial corporations if they build their plants there. Costs-to-benefits comparisons could be calculated for the employer, the employees, and also the "average" resident of the community, whose taxes may rise to take up the slack resulting from the tax break to the factory owners. Other refinements might be included as well. For example, we excluded direct subsidies from the communal perspective, both as a cost and as a benefit, because they probably would balance each other out; however, under certain conditions it may be that the actual economic benefit of the subsidies is less than the cost.

For a detailed practical guide to calculating efficiency analyses, see Greenberg and Appenzeller (1998). The authors provide a detailed step-by-step manual using employment training programs and welfare-to-work programs as examples.

Measuring Costs and Benefits

The specification, measurement, and valuation of costs and benefits—procedures that are central to cost-benefit analysis—raise two distinct problems. The first is identifying and measuring all program costs and benefits. This problem is most acute for *ex ante* appraisals, where often there are only speculative estimates of costs and impact. However, data often are limited in *ex post* cost-benefit analyses as well. For many social interventions, the information from an evaluation (or even a series of evaluations) may in itself prove insufficient for a retrospective cost-benefit analysis to be carried out. Thus, evaluations often provide only some of the necessary information, and the analyst frequently must use additional sources or judgments.

The second problem in many social programs is the difficulty of expressing all benefits and costs in terms of a common denominator, that is, translating them into monetary units. Social programs frequently do not produce results that can be valued accurately by means of market prices. For example, many would argue that the benefits of a fertility control project, a literacy campaign, or a program providing training in improved health practices cannot be monetized in ways acceptable to the various

EXHIBIT 11-H

Hypothetical Example of Cost-Benefit Calculation From Different Accounting Perspectives for a Typical Employment Training Program

Benefit/Costs	
(1) Earnings improvement of trainees (before taxes)	$100,000
(2) Earnings improvement of trainees (after taxes)	80,000
(3) Value of work done in training period	10,000
(4) Project costs for facility and personnel	50,000
(5) Project costs for equipment and supplies	5,000
(6) Trainee stipends (direct transfer payments)	12,000
(7) Earnings forgone by trainees (before taxes)	11,000
(8) Earnings forgone by trainees (after taxes)	9,000
(9) Taxes lost: (7) − (8)	2,000

	Individual	Program Sponsor	Communal
Benefits	(2) 80,000	(1) − (2) 20,000	(1) 100,000
	(6) 12,000	(3) 10,000	(3) 10,000
	92,000	30,000	110,000
Costs	(8) 9,000	(4) 50,000	(4) 50,000
		(5) 5,000	(5) 5,000
		(6) 12,000	(7) 11,000
		2,000	66,000
		69,000	
Net benefit[a]	83,000	−39,000	44,000

a. Note that net social (communal) benefit can be split into net benefit for trainees plus net benefit for the government; in this case, the latter is negative: 83,000 + (−39,000) = 44,000.

stakeholders. What value should be placed on the embarrassment of an adult who cannot read? In such cases, cost-effectiveness analysis might be a reasonable alternative, because such analysis does not require that benefits be valued in terms of money, but only that they be quantified by outcome measures.

Monetizing Outcomes

Because of the advantages of expressing benefits in monetary terms, especially in cost-benefit analysis, a number of approaches have been specified for monetizing outcomes or benefits (Thompson, 1980). Five frequently used ones are as follows.

1. *Money measurements.* The least controversial approach is to estimate direct monetary benefits. For example, if keeping a health center open for two hours in the

evening reduces targets' absence from work (and thus loss of wages) by an average of 10 hours per year, then, from an individual perspective, the annual benefit can be calculated by multiplying the average wage by 10 hours by the number of employed targets.

2. *Market valuation.* Another relatively noncontroversial approach is to monetize gains or impacts by valuing them at market prices. If crime is reduced in a community by 50%, benefits can be estimated in terms of housing prices through adjustment of current values on the basis of prices in communities with lower crime rates and similar social profiles.

3. *Econometric estimation.* A more complicated approach is to estimate the presumed value of a gain or impact in market terms. For example, the increase in tax receipts from greater business revenue due to a reduced fear of crime could be determined by calculating relevant tax revenues of similar communities with lower crime rates, and then estimating the tax receipts that would ensue for the community in question. Such estimation may require complex analytical efforts and the participation of a highly trained economic analyst.

Econometric analysis, especially when performed with refined contemporary multivariate techniques, is a popular choice because it can account for the other influences on the variable in question (in the preceding example, taxes lost because of fear of crime). The analytical effort required to do quality econometric work is certainly complex, and the assumptions involved are sometimes troublesome. However, econometric analysis, like all good methodological procedures, requires making assumptions explicit, thereby enabling others to evaluate the analytical basis of the claims made.

4. *Hypothetical questions.* A quite problematic approach is to estimate the value of intrinsically nonmonetary benefits by questioning targets directly. For instance, a program to prevent dental disease may decrease participants' cavities by an average of one at age 40; thus, one might conduct a survey on how much people think it is worth to have an additional intact tooth as opposed to a filled tooth. Such estimates presume that the monetary value obtained realistically expresses the worth of an intact tooth. Clearly, hypothetical valuations of this kind are open to considerable skepticism.

5. *Observing political choices.* The most tentative approach is to estimate benefits on the basis of political actions. If state legislatures are consistently willing to appropriate funds for high-risk infant medical programs at a rate of $40,000 per child saved, this figure could be used as an estimate of the monetary benefits of such programs. But given that political choices are complex, shifting, and inconsistent, this approach is generally very risky.

In summary, all relevant components must be included if the results of a cost-benefit analysis are to be valid and reliable and reflect fully the economic effects of a project. When important benefits are disregarded because they cannot be measured or monetized, the project may appear less efficient than it is; if certain costs are omitted, the project will seem more efficient. The results may be just as misleading if estimates of costs or benefits are either too conservative or too generous. As a means of dealing with the problem, analysts often will value everything that can reasonably be valued and then list the things that cannot be valued. They will then estimate the value that would have to be placed on the nonmonetary benefits for the project to be a "go."

Shadow Prices

Benefits and costs need to be defined and valued differently, depending on the accounting perspective used. For many programs, however, the outputs simply do not have market prices (e.g., a reduction in pollution or the work of a homemaker), yet their value must be estimated. The preferred procedure is to use **shadow prices,** also known as *accounting prices,* to reflect better than do actual market prices the real costs and benefits to society. Shadow prices are derived prices for goods and services that are supposed to reflect their true benefits and costs. Sometimes it is more realistic to use shadow prices even when actual prices are available. For example, suppose an experimental program is implemented that requires a director who is knowledgeable about every one of the building trades. For the single site, the sponsors may be fortunate to find a retired person who is very interested in the program and willing to work for, say, $30,000 per year. But if the program was shown to be a success through an impact evaluation and a cost-benefit analysis was undertaken, it might be best to use a shadow price of, say, $50,000 for the director's salary because it is very unlikely that additional persons with the nonmonetary interests of the first director could be found (Nas, 1996).

Opportunity Costs

The concept of opportunity costs reflects the fact that resources generally are limited. Consequently, individuals or organizations choose from existing alternatives the ways these resources are to be allocated, and these choices affect the activities and goals of the decisionmakers. The opportunity cost of each choice can be measured by the worth of the forgone options.

Although this concept is relatively simple, the actual estimation of opportunity costs often is complex. For example, a police department may decide to pay the tuition of police officers who want to go to graduate school in psychology or social work on the grounds that the additional schooling will improve the officers' job performance. To have the money for this program, the department might have to keep its police cars an extra two months each. The opportunity costs in this case could be estimated by calculating the additional repair costs that would be incurred if the department's cars were replaced later. Since in many cases opportunity costs can be estimated only by making assumptions about the consequences of alternative investments, they are one of the controversial areas in efficiency analyses.

Secondary Effects (Externalities)

As we have noted, projects may have secondary or external effects—side effects or unintended consequences that may be either beneficial or detrimental. Because such effects are not deliberate outcomes, they may be inappropriately omitted from cost-benefit calculations if special efforts are not made to include them.

For many social programs, two types of secondary effects are likely: displacement and vacuum effects. For example, an educational or training project may produce a group of newly trained persons who enter the labor market, compete with workers already employed, and displace them (i.e., force them out of their jobs). Participants in the project may also vacate jobs they held previously, leaving a vacuum that other workers might fill.

Secondary effects, or externalities, may be difficult to identify and measure. Once found, however, they should be incorporated into the cost-benefit calculations.

Distributional Considerations

Traditionally, judgments of the effectiveness of social interventions are predicated on the notion that an effective intervention makes at least one person better off and nobody worse off. In economics, this yardstick is called the *Pareto criterion.* Cost-benefit analysis, however does not use the Pareto criterion but, rather, the potential Pareto criterion. Under this criterion, the gains must potentially compensate for the losses, with something left over. That is, it is presumed—although not necessarily tested— that if the program's impact is estimated, more targets will be better off than worse off, or, more accurately, that the "balance" between total gains and total losses will be positive. This criterion may be very difficult to satisfy in social programs, however, particularly those that rely on income transfers. Lowering the minimum wage for teenagers, for instance, may increase their employment at the cost of reducing work opportunities for older adults.

Often the concern is not simply with winners versus losers but with movement toward equity within a target population, that is, with distributional effects. This is particularly true in the case of programs designed to improve the general quality of life of a group or community.

The basic means of incorporating equity and distributional considerations in a cost-benefit analysis involve a system of weights whereby benefits are valued more if they produce the anticipated positive effects. The assumption is that some accomplishments are worth more than others to the community, both for equity reasons and for the increase in human well-being, and should therefore be weighted more heavily. Thus, if a lowered minimum wage for teenagers decreases the family incomes of the moderately disadvantaged, the dollars gained and lost could be weighted differently, depending on the degree of disadvantage to the families.

The weights to be assigned can be determined by the appropriate decision-makers, in which case value judgments will obviously have to be made. They may also be derived through certain economic principles and assumptions. In any case, it is clear that weights cannot be applied indiscriminately. Analysts will undoubtedly develop further refinements as they continue to deal with the issue of distributional effects. An intermediate solution to considerations of equity in cost-benefit analyses is to first test to see whether the costs and benefits of a program meet the potential Pareto criterion. If so, calculations can be undertaken for separate subgroups in the population. Such disaggregation might be done for separate income groups, for instance, or for students with different levels of achievement. Such distributional issues are especially important in analyses of issues where costs are in part borne by taxpayers who do not receive direct benefits, as in the case of the effects of schooling. Publicly supported education yields benefits primarily to those families who have children in school and, disproportionately, to those who are less well off and hence pay lower taxes.

Discounting

Another major element in the methodology of efficiency analyses concerns the treatment of time in valuing program costs and benefits. Intervention programs vary in duration, and successful ones in particular produce benefits that are derived in the future, sometimes long after the intervention has taken place. Indeed, the effects of many programs are expected to persist through the participants' lifetimes. Evaluators, therefore, must often extrapolate into the future to measure costs and benefits, especially when benefits are gauged as projected income changes for program participants. Otherwise, the evaluation would be based only on the restricted period of time for which actual program performance data are available.

Costs and benefits occurring at different points in time must, therefore, be made commensurable by taking into account the time patterns for a program's costs and benefits. The applicable technique, known as **discounting,** consists of reducing costs and benefits that are dispersed through time to a common monetary base by adjusting them to their present values. For example, costs are usually highest at the beginning of an intervention, when many of the resources must be expended; they either taper off or cease when the intervention ends. Even when a cost is fixed or a benefit is constant, increments of expenditures made or benefits derived at different points in time cannot be considered equivalent. Instead of asking, "How much more will my investment be worth in the future?" it is standard economic practice to ask, "How much less are benefits derived in the future worth compared to those received in the present?" The same goes for costs. The answer depends on what we assume to be the rate of interest, or the discount rate, and the time frame chosen. Exhibit 11-I provides an example of discounting.

EXHIBIT 11-I

Discounting Costs and Benefits to Their Present Values

Discounting is based on the simple notion that it is preferable to have a given amount of capital in the present rather than in the future. All else equal, present capital can be saved in a bank to accumulate interest or can be used for some alternative investment. Hence, it will be worth more than its face value in the future. Put differently, a fixed amount payable in the future is worth less than the same amount payable in the present.

Conceptually, discounting is the reverse of compound interest, since it tells us how much we would have to put aside today to yield a fixed amount in the future. Algebraically, discounting is the reciprocal of compound interest and is carried out by means of the simple formula

$$\text{Preset value of an amount} = \frac{\text{Amount}}{(1 + r)^t}$$

where r is the discount rate (e.g., .05) and t is the number of years. The total stream of benefits (and costs) of a program expressed in present values is obtained by adding up the discounted values for each year in the period chosen for study. An example of such a computation follows.

A training program is known to produce increases of $1,000 per year in earnings for each participant. The earnings improvements are discounted to their present values at a 10% discount rate for five years.

Over the five years, total discounted benefits equal $909.09 + $826.45 + . . . + $620.92, or $3,790.79. Thus, increases of $1,000 per year for the next five years are not currently worth $5,000 but only $3,790.79. At a 5% discount rate, the total present value would be $4,329.48. In general, all else being equal, benefits calculated using low discount rates will appear greater than those calculated with high rates.

		Year		
1	**2**	**3**	**4**	**5**
$1,000	$1,000	$1,000	$1,000	$1,000
$(1 + .10)^1$	$(1 + .10)^2$	$(1 + .10)^3$	$(1 + .10)^4$	$(1 + .10)^5$
= $909.09	= $826.45	= $751.32	= $683.01	= $620.92

The choice of time period on which to base the analysis depends on the nature of the program and whether the analysis is *ex ante* or *ex post*. All else being equal, a program will appear more beneficial the longer the time horizon chosen.

There is no authoritative approach for fixing the discount rate. One choice is to fix the rate on the basis of the opportunity costs of capital, that is, the rate of return that could be earned if the funds were invested elsewhere. But there are considerable differences in opportunity costs depending on whether the funds are invested in the private sector, as an individual might do, or in the public sector, as a quasi-government body may decide it must. The length of time involved and the degree of risk associated with the investment are additional considerations.

The results of a cost-benefit analysis are thus particularly sensitive to the choice of discount rate. In practice, evaluators usually resolve this complex and controversial issue by carrying out discounting calculations based on several different rates. Furthermore, instead of applying what may seem to be an arbitrary discount rate or rates, the evaluator may calculate the program's **internal rate of return,** or the value that the discount rate would have to be for program benefits to equal program costs.

A related technique, *inflation adjustment,* is used when changes over time in asset prices should be taken into account in cost-benefit calculations. For example, the prices of houses and equipment may change considerably because of the increased or decreased value of the dollar at different times.

Earlier we referred to the net benefits of a program as the total benefits minus the total costs. The necessity of discounting means that **net benefits** are more precisely defined as the total discounted benefits minus the total discounted costs. This total is also referred to as the *net rate of return.*

It is clear that with the many considerations involved there can be considerable disagreement on the monetary values to be placed on benefits. The disputes that arise in setting these values underlie much of the conflict over whether cost-benefit analysis is a legitimate way of estimating the efficiency of programs.

Comparing Costs to Benefits

The final step in cost-benefit analysis consists of comparing total costs to total benefits. How this comparison is made depends to some extent on the purpose of the analysis and the conventions in the particular program sector. The most direct comparison can be made simply by subtracting costs from benefits, after appropriate discounting. For example, a program may have costs of $185,000 and calculated benefits of $300,000. In this case, the net benefit (or profit, to use the business analogy) is $115,000. Although generally more problematic, sometimes the ratio of benefits to costs is used rather than the net benefit. This measure is generally regarded as more difficult to interpret and should be avoided (Mishan, 1988).

In discussing the comparison of benefits to costs, we have noted the similarity to decision making in business. The analogy is real. In particular, in deciding which programs to support, some large private foundations actually phrase their decisions in investment terms. They may want to balance a high-risk venture (i.e., one that might show a high rate of return but has a low probability of success) with a low-risk program (one that probably has a much lower rate of return but a much higher probability of success). Thus, foundations, community organizations, or government bodies might wish to spread their "investment risks" by developing a portfolio of projects with different likelihoods and prospective amounts of benefit.

Sometimes, of course, the costs of a program are greater than its benefits. In Exhibit 11-J, a cost-to-benefit analysis is presented that documents the negative results of a federal initiative to control noise. In this analysis, the costs of regulatory efforts to control the noise from motorcycles, trucks, and buses were estimated to be considerably higher than the benefits of the program. In the exhibit's table, the findings for truck and bus regulations are reported; note the negative values when benefits are subtracted from costs and the less than 1.0 values resulting when benefits are divided by costs. Of course, one can quarrel over the measure of benefits, which was simply the increase in property values resulting from a decline in decibels (dBAs) of noise. Nevertheless, according to Broder (1988), the analysis was a major reason why the Reagan administration abandoned the program.

It bears noting that sometimes programs that yield negative values are nevertheless important and should be continued. For example, there is a communal responsibility to provide for severely retarded persons, and it is unlikely that any procedure designed to do so will have a positive value (subtracting costs from benefits). In such cases, one may still want to use cost-benefit analysis to compare the efficiency of different programs, such as institutional care and home care.

When to Do Ex Post Cost-Benefit Analysis

Earlier in this chapter, we discussed the importance of undertaking *ex ante* analyses in developing programs that result in irrevocable or almost irrevocable commitments. We also indicated that many more *ex ante* analyses are called for in the social program arena than are currently performed. Too often it is only after programs are put into place that policymakers and sponsors realize that the costs of programs compared to their benefits make them impractical to implement on a permanent basis.

In the case of *ex post* evaluations, it is important to consider a number of factors in determining whether to undertake a cost-benefit analysis. In some evaluation contexts, the technique is feasible, useful, and a logical component of a comprehensive evaluation; in others, its application may rest on dubious assumptions and be of limited utility.

EXHIBIT 11-J

A Study of the Birth and Death of a Regulatory Agenda

It has long been the case that, once funded, government programs are almost impossible to eliminate. Most organizations build up constituencies over the years that can be called on to protect them if threatened. Thus, it was particularly remarkable that the federal Office of Noise Abatement and Control (ONAC) at the Environmental Protection Agency (EPA) was disbanded during the Reagan administration, thus terminating a major social regulatory program without a public outcry.

Although the halt in the spread of inefficient noise regulation is one of few examples of lasting relief from social regulation provided by the Reagan administration, a further irony is that much of the economic analysis that was at least partly instrumental in motivating the change in policy was produced by the prior administration. Specifically, President Carter's Council of Economic Advisors and the Council on Wage and Price Stability, an agency disbanded by the Reagan administration, had produced several economic analyses for the public docket that were highly critical of the regulations, although it was the Reagan administration that acted on these analyses.

Cost-Benefit Analysis of Truck and Bus Noise Regulations

	Truck Noise Regulations		Bus Noise Regulations	
	83 dBAs	80 dBAs	83 dBAs	80 dBAs
Benefits (a)	1,056	1,571	66.2	188.5
Costs (b)	1,241	3,945	358.8	967.3
Net benefits (a) − (b)	−185	−2,374	−292.6	−778.8
Benefit-cost ratio (a)/(b)	.85	.40	.18	.19

NOTE: dBAs = decibels. Costs and benefits are in millions of 1978 dollars except for ratios.

SOURCE: Adapted from I. E. Broder, "A Study of the Birth and Death of a Regulatory Agenda: The Case of the EPA Noise Program," *Evaluation Review,* 1988, 12(3):291-309.

Optimal prerequisites of an *ex post* cost-benefit analysis of a program include the following:

■ The program has independent or separable funding. This means that its costs can be separated from those incurred by other activities.

■ The program is beyond the development state, and it is certain that its effects are significant.

- The program's impact and the magnitude of that impact are known or can be validly estimated.

- Benefits can be translated into monetary terms.

- Decisionmakers are considering alternative programs, rather than simply whether or not to continue the existing project.

Ex post efficiency estimation—both cost-benefit and cost-effectiveness analyses—should be components of many impact evaluations. In Exhibit 11-K, the impact of a program to replace machinery in cotton mills that causes an inordinate amount of dust is reported. Viscusi (1985) provides two sets of figures in the exhibit's table, showing the number of cases of byssinosis (lung disease) and of long-term disabilities that were reduced by the initiative as well as the estimated number of cases that might have been reduced given full compliance with the program. His cost data indicate that even total disabilities are prevented for less than $1,500, clearly an amount that the most conservative factory owner must acknowledge represents a saving compared to the spiraling costs of disability insurance for industrial workers. Merely presenting the information on the number of cases of lung disease that would be reduced by enforcing OSHA's standards—without demonstrating the comparatively low costs of the program—probably would not have had much impact on plant owners.

Conducting Cost-Effectiveness Analyses

Cost-benefit analysis allows evaluators to compare the economic efficiency of program alternatives, even when the interventions are not aimed at common goals. After initial attempts in the early 1970s to use cost-benefit analysis in social fields, however, some evaluators became uneasy about directly comparing cost-benefit calculations for, say, family planning to those for health, housing, or educational programs. As we have noted, sometimes it is simply not possible to obtain agreement on critical values—for example, on the monetary value of a life prevented by a fertility control project, or of a life saved by a health campaign—and them compare the results.

Cost-effectiveness analysis can be viewed as an extension of cost-benefit analysis to projects with commensurable goals. It is based on the same principles and uses the same methods as cost-benefit analysis. The assumptions of the method, as well as the procedures required for measuring costs and discounting, for example, are the same for both approaches. Therefore, the concepts and methodology introduced previously with regard to cost-benefit analysis can also be regarded as a basis for understanding the cost-effectiveness approach.

EXHIBIT 11-K
Cotton Dust
Regulation: An
OSHA Success Story

In the late 1970s, the Occupational Safety and Health Administration (OSHA) took a major step in attempting to promote the health of workers in the textile industry, tightening its standard on cotton dust levels in textile plants. Because the OSHA cotton dust standard was widely believed to be ineffective, it became the target of a major political debate and a fundamental U.S. Supreme Court decision. However, the evidence indicates that the standard has had a significant beneficial effect on worker health, and at a cost much lower than originally anticipated. For instance, data on the relationship between exposure to cotton dust and disease incidence, as well as the disability data and the evidence based on worker turnover, suggest that the risks of byssinosis (lung disease) have been reduced dramatically. The cost of eliminating even cases classified as "totally disabled" is less than $1,500, and thus there is a strong economic basis for the enforcement of OSHA standards.

Estimated Reduction in Byssinosis Cases Associated With the Introduction of the Cotton Dust Standard

Type of Case	No. of Cases Reduced per Year, 1978-1982	Total No. of Cases Reduced per Year If Full Compliance
Byssinosis, Grades ½ and 1	3,517	5,047
Byssinosis over Grade 1	1,634	2,349
Partial disabilities	843	1,210
Total disabilities	339	487

SOURCE: Adapted, with permission, from W. K. Viscusi, "Cotton Dust Regulation: An OSHA Success Story?" *Journal of Policy Analysis and Management*, 1985, 4(3):325-343. Copyright © 1985, John Wiley & Sons, Inc.

In contrast to cost-benefit analysis, however, cost-effectiveness analysis does not require that benefits and costs be reduced to a common denominator. Instead, the effectiveness of a program in reaching given substantive goals is related to the monetary value of the costs. In cost-effectiveness analyses, programs with similar goals are evaluated and their costs compared. Efficiency is judged by comparing costs for units of outcome. Thus, one can compare two or more programs aimed at lowering the fertility rate, or different educational methods for raising achievement levels, or various interventions to reduce infant mortality.

Cost-effectiveness analysis thus allows comparison and rank ordering of programs in terms of the various inputs required for different degrees of goal achievement. But because the benefits are not converted to a common denominator, we cannot ascertain the worth or merit of a given intervention in monetary terms from such analyses. Likewise, we cannot determine which of two or more programs in different areas produces better returns. We can compare the relative efficiency of different programs only if they have the same or roughly similar goals and have the same outcome measures. Cost-effectiveness analysis, then, is a particularly good method for evaluating programs with similar outcomes without having to monetize the outcomes. Moreover, if a service or program is known to produce positive outcomes, or presumed to, cost-effectiveness analysis may be conducted in terms of costs per client served. Identifying such unit costs makes it possible to compare the efficiency of different programs that provide similar services or different service components within a multiservice program. Exhibit 11-L provides an example of a cost analysis of this sort for methadone treatment programs for intravenous drug abusers. Of particular interest to the evaluators was the relative magnitude of the costs per client for an add-on employment training component compared with the costs of the standard program. However, the analysis was also able to reveal differences in costs per client across programs at four separate sites.

EXHIBIT 11-L

Cost Analysis of Training and Employment Services in Methadone Treatment

Prior evaluation research has shown that vocational and employment counseling for drug users has positive effects not only on employment but also on drug use and criminality. Despite these encouraging signs, many drug treatment programs have reduced or eliminated vocational services due to changes in program emphasis or financial pressures. Against this background, a team of evaluators at Research Triangle Institute conducted cost analysis on four methadone maintenance programs with employment services components to help decisionmakers explore the feasibility of a renewed emphasis on vocational services in substance abuse treatment.

The standard treatment in these programs involved methadone maintenance for intravenous drug users for as long as 12 months or more, random urine tests approximately once a month, monthly individual counseling sessions, and one to four group counseling sessions per month.

The Training and Employment Program (TEP) component of these programs included vocational needs assessment, location of existing training and employment programs suitable to the needs of methadone clients, and placement into training and jobs. Each program had an on-site vocational specialist to work with both the drug counselors and the clients to identify and address vocational issues, provide job-related services, and maintain weekly contact with each assigned client.

Findings from a randomized impact assessment of the standard methadone treatment (STD) plus TEP compared with STD only showed that the methadone clients had high rates of unemployment and lacked

(Continued)

EXHIBIT 11-L
(Continued)

vocational services and that TEP helped them access such services, obtain training, and reduce their short-term unemployment.

Given these positive findings, the critical practical question is how much the TEP component added to the cost of the standard treatment program. To assess this, the evaluators examined the total costs and cost per client of TEP in comparison to the analogous costs of the standard program without TEP for each of the four program sites. The main results are summarized in the table.

The results of this analysis indicated that the cost per client of the TEP component ranged from $1,648 to $2,215, amounts corresponding to between 42% and 50% of the cost of the standard methadone treatment without TEP.

Annual Total and per Client Costs of Adding Training and Employment Program (TEP) Services Compared With the Costs of Standard (STD) Services

	Program A	Program B	Program C	Program D
Personnel	$38,402	$41,681	$49,762	$50,981
Support and supplies for vocational specialists	11,969	14,467	17,053	6,443
Travel	1,211	3,035	2,625	1,870
Other overhead	7,736	14,033	2,619	2,728
Total annual TEP costs	59,318	73,217	72,060	62,022
TEP clients served	36	38	43	28
Cost per client served	$1,648	$1,927	$1,676	$2,215
Total annual STD cost	$819,202	$1,552,816	$2,031,698	$1,531,067
STD clients served	210	400	573	300
STD cost per client	$3,901	$3,882	$3,546	$5,104
Total TEP cost/total STD cost	7.2%	4.7%	3.5%	4.1%
TEP per client/STD per client	42.2%	49.6%	47.3%	43.4%

Because many methadone maintenance clients are not appropriate for training and employment services, however, a TEP component will not be applicable to the entire caseload of the standard treatment program. When the incremental costs of adding a TEP component to the total program were figured, therefore, the results showed that the TEP component added only 3.5% to 7.2% to the total program budget. In addition, the analysis showed different degrees of efficiency across programs in providing both TEP and standard services, as indicated in the varying costs per client.

SOURCE: Adapted from M. T. French, C. J. Bradley, B. Calingaert, M. L. Dennis, and G. T. Karuntzos, "Cost Analysis of Training and Employment Services in Methadone Treatment," *Evaluation and Program Planning*, 1994, 17(2):107-120.

Although some sponsors and program staff are prejudiced against efficiency analyses because they deal chiefly with "dollars" and not "people," the approach that underlies them is no different from that of any stakeholder who needs to assess the utility of implementing or maintaining a program. Our world of limited resources, though often decried, nevertheless requires setting one program against another and deciding on resource allocation. Competent efficiency analysis can provide valuable information about a program's economic potential or actual payoff and thus is important for program planning, implementation, and policy decisions, as well as for gaining and maintaining the support of stakeholders.

Summary

- Efficiency analyses provide a framework for relating program costs to outcomes. Whereas cost-benefit analyses directly compare benefits to costs in commensurable (monetary) terms, cost-effectiveness analyses relate costs expressed in monetary terms to units of substantive results achieved.

- Efficiency analyses can require considerable technical sophistication and the use of consultants. As a way of thinking about program results, however, they direct attention to costs as well as benefits and have great value for the evaluation field.

- Efficiency analyses can be useful at all stages of a program, from planning through implementation and modification. Currently, *ex post* analyses are more commonplace than *ex ante* analyses in the social program arena because reasonably sound estimates of costs and benefits prior to program implementation are often lacking. Nevertheless, *ex ante* analyses should be undertaken more often than they are, particularly for programs that are expensive either to implement or to evaluate. Different sets of assumptions can create a range of analyses; one thing these analyses may reveal is the improbability of achieving the desired net benefits under any sensible set of assumptions.

- Efficiency analyses use different assumptions and may produce correspondingly different results depending on which accounting perspective is taken: that of individual targets or participants, program sponsors, or the community or society. Which perspective should be taken depends on the intended consumers of the analysis and thus involves political choice.

- Cost-benefit analysis requires that program costs and benefits be known, quantified, and transformed to a common measurement unit. Options for monetizing outcomes or benefits include money measurements, market valuation, econometric estimation, hypothetical questions asked of participants, and observation of political choices. Shadow, or accounting, prices are used for costs and benefits when market prices are unavailable or, in some circumstances, as substitutes for market prices that may be unrealistic.

- In estimating costs, the concept of opportunity costs allows for a truer estimate but can be complex and controversial in application.

- The true outcomes of projects include secondary and distributional effects, both of which should be taken into account in full cost-benefit analyses.

- In cost-benefit analysis, both costs and benefits must be projected into the future to reflect the long-term effects of a program. In addition, future benefits and costs must be discounted to reflect their present values.

- Cost-effectiveness analysis is a feasible alternative to cost-benefit analysis when benefits cannot be calibrated in monetary units. It permits comparison of programs with similar goals in terms of their relative efficiency and can also be used to analyze the relative efficiency of variations of a program.

KEY CONCEPTS

Accounting perspectives

Perspectives underlying decisions on which categories of goods and services to include as costs or benefits in an efficiency analysis.

Benefits

Positive program outcomes, usually translated into monetary terms in cost-benefit analysis or compared with costs in cost-effectiveness analysis. Benefits may include both direct and indirect outcomes.

Costs

Inputs, both direct and indirect, required to produce an intervention.

Discounting

The treatment of time in valuing costs and benefits of a program in efficiency analyses, that is, the adjustment of costs and benefits to their present values, requiring a choice of discount rate and time frame.

Distributional effects

Effects of programs that result in a redistribution of resources in the general population.

Ex ante efficiency analysis

An efficiency (cost-benefit or cost-effectiveness) analysis undertaken prior to program implementation, usually as part of program planning, to estimate net outcomes in relation to costs.

Ex post efficiency analysis

An efficiency (cost-benefit or cost-effectiveness) analysis undertaken after a program's outcomes are known.

Internal rate of return

The calculated value for the discount rate necessary for total discounted program benefits to equal total discounted program costs.

Net benefits

The total discounted benefits minus the total discounted costs. Also called net rate of return.

Opportunity costs

The value of opportunities forgone because of an intervention program.

Secondary effects

Effects of a program that impose costs on persons or groups who are not targets.

Shadow prices

Imputed or estimated costs of goods and services not valued accurately in the marketplace. Shadow prices also are used when market prices are inappropriate due to regulation or externalities. Also known as accounting prices.

The Social Context
of Evaluation

This chapter is concerned with the social and political context of evaluation activities. Evaluation involves more than simply using appropriate research procedures. It is a purposeful activity, undertaken to affect the development of policy, to shape the design and implementation of social interventions, and to improve the management of social programs. In the broadest sense of politics, evaluation is a political activity.

There are, of course, intrinsic rewards for evaluators, who may derive great pleasure from satisfying themselves that they have done as good a technical job as possible—like artists whose paintings hang in their attics and never see the light of day, and poets whose penciled foolscap is hidden from sight in their desk drawers. But that is not really what it is all about. Evaluations are a real-world activity. In the end, what counts is not the critical acclaim with which an evaluation is judged by peers in the field but the extent to which it leads to modified policies, programs, and practices—ones that, in the short or long term, improve the conditions of human life.

Evaluation practitioners are diverse in their disciplinary outlooks, their ideological and political orientations, and their economic and career aspirations. Despite this diversity, however, nearly all evaluators share a common perspective about the purposefulness of their work. The major rationale for doing applied work is to have an impact on the actions and thinking of the broad classes of persons who affect social change, and who in their policy and action roles use the findings and conclusions provided by evaluators.

In the 21st century, compared with the late 1970s, when the first edition of *Evaluation* was published, evaluators are more sophisticated, not only about technical matters but also about the place of evaluation research in the policy and social program arena. (For an overview of the growth and change in the field, see Chelimsky and Shadish, 1997; Haveman, 1987; Shadish, Cook, and Leviton, 1991. For a different view of change in evaluation, see Guba and Lincoln, 1989.) At the same time, strains and tensions persist about methodological matters, the education of evaluators, and organizational arrangements for the conduct of evaluations. Moreover, there are political and ideological issues concerning the social responsibility of evaluators that continue to confront the field, disagreement on the most effective ways to disseminate findings, and differences of opinion about the best strategies for maximizing the utility of evaluations. With the experience of the past several decades, evaluators have become more humble about the potency of their efforts and have come to realize that social policy cannot be based on evaluation alone. Even the strongest proponents of the evaluation enterprise acknowledge that its potential contributions to social policy are constrained by the range of competencies and interests of both the persons who undertake evaluations and the consumers of them, by diversity in styles of work and organizational arrangements, and by the political considerations and economic constraints that accompany all efforts at planned social change. Most important of all, in a democratic society, social change cannot and should not be determined by the rule of experts but, rather, should be the outcome of processes that take into account the views of the various interests concerned.

In addition, evaluators, most of whom are convinced that social programs might improve the human condition, have been disappointed by finding out that many programs do not produce marked improvements, some are not effective at all, and a few have been shown to have perverse effects. We have learned that designing effective programs and properly implementing them are very difficult. To many, it has not been an uplifting experience to have been the bearer of bad news.

Accordingly, evaluators have experienced the frustrations, feelings of inadequacy, and lack of self-confidence common to all whose efforts often fall short of their hopes and aspirations. And their response has been the same as well: a great amount of introspection, a concerted effort to shift the blame to others, and an outpouring of verbal and written commentaries about the dismal state of social and human affairs, in particular the futility of developing and implementing effective and efficient interventions. Some social commentators have even castigated current evaluation practices as often unable to recognize successful programs as such (Schorr, 1997).

It is evident that simply undertaking well-designed and carefully conducted evaluations of social programs by itself will not eradicate our human and social problems. But the contributions of the evaluation enterprise in moving us in the desired direction should be recognized. There is considerable evidence that the findings of evaluations do often influence policies, program planning and implementation, and the ways social programs are administered, sometimes in the short term and other times in the long term.

Insofar as evaluators aim to influence policy and practice, evaluation activities fall under the general rubric of *applied* social research. Although the boundaries separating applied research from *basic* or *academic* research are not always clear, there are qualitative differences between the two (Freeman and Rossi, 1984). Some of these we have discussed in earlier chapters, as when we noted that evaluations need to be conducted so that they are "good enough" to answer the questions under study. This pragmatic standard contrasts with that used by basic researchers, who typically strive for the "best" methodology that can be used in carrying out their research. Of course, basic research is also constrained by resources, so that compromises are often necessary.

Three additional distinctions between applied and basic research are important to understand. First, basic research typically is initiated to satisfy the intellectual interests of the investigators and their aspirations to contribute to the knowledge base of a substantive area of interest to themselves and their peers. Basic research is often directed to topics that are of central concern to the discipline in question. In contrast, applied work is undertaken because it might contribute to solving a practical problem. In the evaluation field, most often the impetus for undertaking work comes not from the evaluators themselves but from persons and groups who are concerned with a particular social problem. Thus, it is imperative that the evaluator understands the social ecology of the evaluation field. This is the first major topic that we take up in this chapter.

Second, basic researchers generally are trained in a single disciplinary orientation to which they typically remain committed throughout their careers. They draw on a narrow band of methodological procedures, and from one study to the next address a limited substantive domain. For example, an economist may make the costs of health care her area of expertise and consistently apply econometric modeling procedures to her chosen area of study. Similarly, a sociologist might primarily use participant observation as his method of choice and devote most of his career to the study of the professions. In contrast, evaluators sometimes move from one program area to another, confronting diverse questions that typically require familiarity with a range of research methods and a variety of substantive areas. For example, one of the authors has conducted evaluations of programs concerned with nutrition, crime prevention, effects of natural disasters, child abuse and neglect, homelessness, normative consensus, and the income effects of educational attainment, using methods that range from randomized experiments to large-scale cross-sectional studies and the statistical analysis of archived administrative records. The fact that evaluators can often be confronted with widely different subject areas raises a number of issues about the training, outlook, and theoretical perspectives of evaluators in contrast to basic researchers and, more generally, about the profession of evaluation (Shadish and Reichardt, 1987). The evaluation profession is the second major topic in this chapter.

Third, although concerns about ethics and professional standards are important in both basic and applied research, they loom larger and are of greater societal importance in applied work. If basic researchers violate professional standards, their discipline may suffer, but if applied researchers cross the line the effects might be felt by programs, the target populations involved, and the society as a whole. Accordingly, issues of ethics and professional standards in evaluation are the third major topic of this chapter.

Fourth, there is a major difference in the audiences for basic and applied work, and in the criteria for assessing its utilization. Basic researchers are most concerned with their peers' responses to their studies; utilization is judged by the acceptance of their papers in scholarly journals and the extent to which the research stimulates work by others. Applied researchers are concerned not only about peer judgments of their efforts but also about the judgments of the sponsors of their studies. Moreover, the test of utilization is not only how much it advances the field but how great a contribution it makes to the development and implementation of policies and programs and, ultimately, to the resolution of social problems. Utilization of evaluation results, and ways to maximize it, constitutes our final topic.

Every evaluation has its unique features, requiring specially tailored solutions to the problems encountered. For this reason, it is difficult to offer detailed prescriptions about how evaluations should be conducted. Nevertheless, the field is now mature enough that it is possible to offer reasonably sound observations about the state of the evaluation art, as well as general guidelines and advice on the conduct of the work. This chapter is based on an admixture of our own experiences and the writings of colleagues who have addressed the various interpersonal, political, and structural issues that surround doing evaluations.

The Social Ecology of Evaluations

Whether evaluations are used depends largely on forces in the social and political contexts in which the evaluations are undertaken. Consequently, to conduct successful evaluations, evaluators need to continually assess the social ecology of the arena in which they work.

Sometimes the impetus and support for an evaluation come from the highest decision-making levels: Congress or a federal agency may mandate evaluations of innovative programs, as the Department of Health and Human Services did in the case of waivers given to states for innovative reforms in income maintenance programs (Gueron and Pauly, 1991), or the president of a large foundation may insist that the foundation's major social action programs be evaluated, as in the case of the supported-housing programs of the Robert Wood Johnson Foundation (Rog et al., 1995). At other times, evaluation activities are initiated in response to requests from managers and supervisors of various operating agencies and focus on administrative matters specific to those agencies and stakeholders (Oman and Chitwood, 1984). At still other times, evaluations are undertaken in response to the concerns of individuals and groups in the community who have a stake in a particular social problem and the planned or current efforts to deal with it.

Whatever the impetus may be, evaluators' work is conducted in a real-world setting of multiple and often conflicting interests. In this connection, two essential features of the context of evaluation must be recognized: the existence of multiple stakeholders and the related fact that evaluation is usually part of a political process.

Multiple Stakeholders

In undertaking their studies, evaluators usually find that a diversity of individuals and groups have an interest in their work and its outcomes. These stakeholders may hold competing and sometimes combative views about the appropriateness of the evaluation work and about whose interests will be affected by the outcome. To conduct their work effectively and contribute to the resolution of the issues at hand, evaluators must understand their relationships to the stakeholders involved as well as the relationships between stakeholders. The starting point for achieving this understanding is to recognize the range of stakeholders who directly or indirectly can affect the usefulness of evaluation efforts.

The Range of Stakeholders

The existence of a range of stakeholders is as much a fact of life for the lone evaluator situated in a single school, hospital, or social agency as it is for evaluators associated with evaluation groups in large organized research centers, federal and state agencies, universities, or private foundations. In an abstract sense, every citizen who should be concerned with the efficacy and efficiency of efforts to improve social conditions has a stake in the outcome of an evaluation. In practice, of course, the stakeholder groups concerned with any given evaluation effort are more narrowly based, consisting of those who perceive direct and visible interests in the program. Within stakeholder groups, various stakeholders typically have different perspectives on the meaning and importance of an evaluation's findings. These disparate viewpoints are a source of potential conflict not only between stakeholders themselves but also between these persons and the evaluator. No matter how an evaluation comes out, there are some to whom the findings are good news and some to whom they are bad news.

To evaluate is to make judgments; to conduct an evaluation is to provide empirical evidence that can be used to substantiate judgments. The distinction between making judgments and providing information on which judgments can be based is useful and clear in the abstract, but often difficult to make in practice. No matter how well an evaluator's conclusions about the effectiveness of a program are grounded in rigorous research design and sensitively analyzed data, some stakeholders are likely to perceive the results of an evaluation to be arbitrary or capricious judgments and to react accordingly.

Very little is known about how evaluation audiences are formed and activated. Nor is it completely clear how the interests of stakeholder groups are engaged and acted on by a given evaluation outcome. Perhaps the only reliable prediction is that the parties most likely to be attentive to an evaluation, both during its conduct and after a report has been issued, are the evaluation sponsors and the program managers and staff. Of course, these are the groups who usually have the most at stake in the continuation of the program and whose activities are most clearly judged by the evaluation report.

The reactions of beneficiaries or targets of a program are especially problematic. In many cases, beneficiaries may have the strongest stake in an evaluation's outcome, yet they are often the least prepared to make their voices heard. Target beneficiaries tend to be unorganized and scattered in space; often they are poorly educated and unskilled in political communication. Sometimes they are reluctant even to identify themselves. When target beneficiaries do make themselves heard in the course of an evaluation, it is often through organizations that aspire to be their representatives. For example, homeless persons rarely make themselves heard in the discussion of programs directed at relieving their distressing conditions. But the National Coalition for the Homeless, an organization mainly composed of persons who themselves are not homeless, will often act as the spokesperson in policy discussions dealing with homelessness.

Consequences of Multiple Stakeholders

There are two important consequences of the phenomenon of multiple stakeholders. First, evaluators must accept that their efforts are but one input into the complex political processes from which decisions and actions eventuate. Second, strains invariably result from the conflicts in the interests of these stakeholders. In part, these strains can be eliminated or minimized by anticipating and planning for them; in part, they come with the turf and must be dealt with on an ad hoc basis or simply accepted and lived with.

The multiplicity of stakeholders for evaluations generates strains for evaluators in three main ways. First, evaluators are often unsure whose perspective they should take in designing an evaluation. Is the proper perspective that of the society as a whole, the government agency involved, the program staff, the clients, or one or more of the other stakeholder groups? For some evaluators, especially those who aspire to provide help and advice on fine-tuning programs, the primary audience often appears to be the program staff. For those evaluators whose projects have been mandated by a legislative body, the primary audience may appear to be the community, the state, or the nation as a whole.

The issue of which perspective to take in an evaluation should not be understood as an issue of whose bias to accept. Perspective issues are involved in defining the goals of a program and deciding which stakeholder's concerns should be attended to. In contrast, bias in an evaluation usually means distorting an evaluation's design to favor findings that are in accord with some stakeholder's desires. Every evaluation is undertaken from some set of perspectives, but an ethical evaluator tries to avoid biasing evaluation findings in the design or analysis.

Some schools of evaluation strongly emphasize that certain perspectives should dominate in the conduct of evaluations. The "utilization-focused evaluation" approach (e.g., Patton, 1997) asserts that evaluations ought to be designed to reflect the interests of "primary users" and specifies methods for determining in specific cases who they may be. The advocates of "empowerment evaluation" (e.g., Fetterman, Kaftarian, and Wandersman, 1996) claim that the aim of evaluations should be to empower marginalized groups, usually the poor and minorities, and therefore urge evaluators to adopt the perspectives of these groups and to involve them in the design and analysis of evaluations. It must be emphasized that neither of these approaches is biased, in the sense used above. Nevertheless, our own view on the perspectives from which evaluations should be conducted is more agnostic. In discussing the different accounting perspectives for conducting efficiency analyses in Chapter 11, we noted that there is no one proper perspective but, rather, that different perspectives may be equally legitimate. The clients' or targets' perspective cannot claim any more legitimacy than that of the program or the government agency that funds the program. In our judgment, then, the responsibility of the evaluator is not to take one of the many perspectives as the legitimate one but, rather, to be clear about the perspective from which a particular evaluation is being undertaken while explicitly giving recognition to the existence of other perspectives. In reporting the results of an evaluation, an evaluator should state, for example, that the evaluation was conducted from the viewpoint of the program administrators while acknowledging the alternative perspectives of the society as a whole and of the client targets.

In some evaluations, it may be possible to provide several perspectives on a program. Consider, for example, an income maintenance program. From the viewpoint of a target client, a successful program may be one that provides payment levels sufficient to meet basic consumption needs, so from this perspective the program with relatively low levels of payments may be judged as falling short of its aim. But, from the perspective of state legislators, for whom the main purpose of the program is to facilitate the movement of clients off program rolls, the low level of payment may be seen as a desirable incentive. By the same token, a generous income maintenance program that might be judged a success from the perspective of the beneficiaries may be seen by the legislators as fostering welfare dependency. These contrasting views imply that the evaluator must be concerned with both kinds of program outcomes: the adequacy of payment levels and also how dependency is affected by payment levels.

A second way in which the varying interests of stakeholders generate strain for evaluators concerns the responses to the evaluation findings. Regardless of the perspective utilized in the evaluation, there is no guarantee that the outcome will be satisfactory to any particular group of stakeholders. Evaluators must realize, for example, that even the sponsors of evaluations may turn on them when the results do not support the worth of the policies and programs they advocate. Although evaluators often anticipate negative reactions from other stakeholder groups, frequently they are unprepared for the responses of the sponsors to findings that are contrary to what was expected or desired. Evaluators are in a very difficult position when this occurs. Losing the support of the evaluation sponsors may, for example, leave evaluators open to attacks by other stakeholders, attacks they expected would be fended off by the sponsors. Furthermore, sponsors are a major source of referrals for additional work in the case of outside evaluators, and the providers of paychecks for inside ones. An illustration of the problem is provided in Exhibit 12-A, in which the findings of a needs assessment study of the homeless of Chicago were severely challenged by advocacy stakeholders. (For a very different view of the same events, see Hoch, 1990.) The reactions of stakeholders in Chicago should not be taken as universal—there are many instances in which unwelcome findings are accepted and even acted on. Furthermore, reactions to an evaluation in the long term may change; within a few years Rossi's (1989) needs assessment of the homeless became widely regarded as one of the best descriptions of the homeless in the 1980s.

A third source of strain is the misunderstandings that may arise because of difficulties in communicating with different stakeholders. The vocabulary of the evaluation field is no more complicated and esoteric than the vocabularies of the social sciences from which it is derived. But this does not make the vocabulary of evaluation understandable and accessible to lay audiences. For instance, the concept of *random* plays an important role in impact assessment. To evaluation researchers, the random allocation of targets to experimental and control groups means something quite precise, delimited, and indeed valuable, as we discussed in Chapter 8. In lay language, however, "random" often has connotations of *haphazard, careless, aimless, casual,* and so on—all of which have pejorative connotations. Thus, evaluators use the term *random* at their peril if they do not at the same time carefully specify its meaning.

It may be too much to expect an evaluator to master the subtleties of communication relevant to all the widely diverse audiences for evaluations. Yet the problem of communication remains an important obstacle to the understanding of evaluation procedures and the utilization of evaluation results. Evaluators are, therefore, well advised to anticipate the communication barriers in relating to stakeholders, a topic we will discuss more fully later in this chapter.

Disseminating Evaluation Results

For evaluation results to be used, they must be disseminated to and understood by major stakeholders and the general public. For our purposes, *dissemination* refers to the set of activities through which knowledge about evaluation findings is made available to the range of relevant audiences.

Dissemination is a critical responsibility of evaluation researchers. An evaluation that is not made accessible to its audiences is clearly destined to be ignored. Accordingly, evaluators must take care in writing their reports and make provision for ensuring that findings are delivered to major stakeholders.

EXHIBIT 12-A

The Consequences of
Contrary Results

In the middle 1980s, the Robert Wood Johnson Foundation and the Pew Memorial Trust provided a grant to the Social and Demographic Institute at the University of Massachusetts to develop practical methods of undertaking credible enumerations of the homeless. The two foundations had just launched a program funding medical clinics for homeless persons, and an accurate count of the homeless was needed to assess how well the clinics were covering their clients.

Our findings concerning how many homeless were in Chicago quickly became the center of a controversy. The interests of the Chicago homeless were defended and advanced by the Chicago Coalition for the Homeless and by the Mayor's Committee on the Homeless, both composed of persons professionally and ideologically devoted to these ends. These two groups were consistently called on by the media and by public officials to make assessments of the status of the Chicago homeless. Their views about homelessness in essence defined the conventional wisdom and knowledge on this topic. In particular, a widely quoted estimate that between 20,000 and 25,000 persons were homeless in Chicago came from statements made by the Coalition and the Mayor's Committee.

At the outset, the Chicago Coalition for the Homeless maintained a neutral position toward our study. The study, its purposes, and its funding sources were explained to the coalition, and we asked for their cooperation, especially in connection with obtaining consent from shelter operators to interview their clients. The coalition neither endorsed our study nor condemned it, expressing some skepticism concerning our approach and especially about the operational definition of homelessness, arguing for a broader definition of homelessness that would encompass persons in precarious housing situations, persons living double-upped with families, single-room-occupancy renters, and so on.

When the data from Phase I were processed, we were shocked by the findings. The estimate of the size of the homeless population was many magnitudes smaller than the numbers used by the coalition: 2,344, compared to 20,000-25,000. Because we had anticipated a much larger homeless population, our sample of streets was too small to achieve much precision for such small numbers. We began to question whether we had made some egregious error in sample design or execution. Adding to our sense of self-doubt, the two foundations that had supported most of the project also began to have doubts, their queries fueled in part by direct complaints from the advocates for the homeless. To add to our troubles, the

(Continued)

EXHIBIT 12-A
(Continued)

Phase I survey had consumed all the funds that our sponsors had provided, which were originally intended to support three surveys spread over a year. After checking over our Phase I findings, we were convinced that they were derived correctly but that they would be more convincing to outsiders if the study were replicated. We managed to convince our funding sponsors to provide more funds for a second survey that was designed with a larger sample of Chicago blocks than Phase I. The street sample was also supplemented by special purposive samples in places known to contain large numbers of homeless persons (bus, elevated, and subway stations; hospital waiting rooms; etc.) to test whether our dead-of-the-night survey time missed significant numbers of homeless persons who were on the streets during the early evening hours but had found sleeping accommodations by the time our interviewing teams searched sample blocks.

When the data were in from Phase II, our calculated estimate of the average size of the nightly homeless in Chicago was 2,020 with a standard error of 275. Phase II certainly had increased the precision of our estimates but had not resulted in substantially different ones. Using data from our interviews, we also attempted to estimate the numbers of homeless persons we may have missed because they were temporarily housed, in jail, in a hospital, or in prison. In addition, we estimated the number of homeless children accompanying parents (we found no homeless children in our street searches). Adding these additional numbers of homeless persons to the average number who were nightly homeless as estimated from our Phase I and Phase II surveys, we arrived at a total of 2,722. This last estimate was still very far from the 20,000- to 25,000-person estimates of the Chicago Coalition.

Although the final report was distributed to the Chicago newspapers, television stations, and interested parties on the same date, somehow copies of the report had managed to get into the hands of the coalition. Both major Chicago newspapers ran stories on the report, followed the next day by denunciatory comments from members of the coalition. Despite our efforts to direct attention to the findings on the composition of the homeless, the newspapers headlined our numerical estimates. The comments from the coalition were harshly critical, claiming that our study was a serious disservice to the cause of the homeless and an attempt to lull public consciousness by severely (and deliberately) underestimating the number of homeless. Coalition comments included suggestions that the content of the report was dictated by the Illinois Department of Public Aid, that the study was

(Continued)

EXHIBIT 12-A
(Continued)

technically defective, and that our definition of the homeless omitted the thousands of persons forced to live with friends and relatives or in substandard housing conditions, or who negotiated sleeping arrangements every night.

Invited to give a presentation to the Mayor's Committee on the Homeless, I found my talk greeted by a torrent of criticism, ranging from the purely technical to the accusation of having sold out to the conservative forces of the Reagan administration and the Thompson Republican Illinois regime. But the major theme was that our report had seriously damaged the cause of homeless people in Chicago by providing state and local officials with an excuse to dismiss the problem as trivial. (In point of fact, the Illinois Department of Public Aid pledged to multiply its efforts to enroll homeless persons in the income maintenance programs the department administered.) Those two hours were the longest stretch of personal abuse I have suffered since basic training in the Army during World War II. It was particularly galling to have to defend our carefully and responsibly derived estimates against a set of estimates whose empirical footings were located in a filmy cloud of sheer speculation.

Almost overnight, I had become persona non grata in circles of homeless advocates. When I was invited by the Johnson Foundation to give a talk at a Los Angeles meeting of staff members from the medical clinics the foundation financed, no one present would talk to me except for a few outsiders. I became a nonperson wandering through the conference, literally shunned by all.

SOURCE: Adapted from Peter H. Rossi, "No Good Applied Research Goes Unpunished!" *Social Science and Modern Society,* 1987, 25(1):74-79.

Obviously, results must be communicated in ways that make them intelligible to the various stakeholder groups. External evaluators generally provide sponsors with technical reports that include detailed and complete (not to mention honest) descriptions of the evaluation's design, data collection methods, analysis procedures, results, suggestions for further research, and recommendations regarding the program (in the case of monitoring or impact evaluations), as well as a discussion of the limitations of the data and analysis. Technical reports usually are read only by peers, rarely by the stakeholders who count. Many of these stakeholders simply are not accustomed to reading voluminous documents, do not have the time to do so, and might not be able to understand them.

For this reason, every evaluator must learn to be a "secondary disseminator." **Secondary dissemination** refers to the communication of results and recommendations that emerge from evaluations in ways that meet the needs of stakeholders (as opposed to **primary dissemination** to sponsors and technical audiences, which in most cases is the technical report). Secondary dissemination may take many different forms, including abbreviated versions of technical reports (often called executive summaries), special reports in more attractive and accessible formats, oral reports complete with slides, and sometimes even movies and videotapes.

The objective of secondary dissemination is simple: to provide results in ways that can be comprehended by the legendary "intelligent layperson," admittedly a figure sometimes as elusive as Bigfoot. Proper preparation of secondary dissemination documents is an art form unknown to most in the field, because few opportunities for learning are available during one's academic training. The important tactic in secondary communication is to find the appropriate style for presenting research findings, using language and form understandable to audiences who are intelligent but unschooled in the vocabulary and conventions of the field. *Language* implies a reasonable vocabulary level that is as free as possible from esoteric jargon; *form* means that secondary dissemination documents should be succinct and short enough not to be formidable. Useful advice for this process can be found in Torres, Preskill, and Piontek (1996). If the evaluator does not have the talents to disseminate his or her findings in ways that maximize utilization—and few of us do—an investment in expert help is justified. After all, as we have stressed, evaluations are undertaken as purposeful activities; they are useless unless they can get attention from stakeholders.

Evaluation as a Political Process

Throughout this book, we have stressed that evaluation results can be useful in the decision-making process at every point during a program's evolution and operations. In the earliest phases of program design, evaluations can provide basic data about social problems so that sensitive and appropriate services can be designed. While prototype programs are being tested, evaluations of pilot demonstrations may provide estimates of the effects to be expected when the program is fully implemented. After programs have been in operation, evaluations can provide considerable knowledge about accountability issues. But this is not to say that what is useful in principle will automatically be understood, accepted, and used. At every stage, evaluation is only one ingredient in an inherently political process. And this is as it should be: Decisions with important social consequences should be determined in a democratic society by political processes.

In some cases, project sponsors may contract for an evaluation with the strong anticipation that it will critically influence the decision to continue, modify, or terminate a project. In those cases, the evaluator may be under pressure to produce information quickly, so that decisions can be made expeditiously. In short, evaluators may have a receptive audience. In other situations, evaluators may complete their assessments of an intervention only to discover that decisionmakers react slowly to their findings. Even more disconcerting are the occasions when a program is continued, modified, or terminated without regard to an evaluation's valuable and often expensively obtained information.

Although in such circumstances evaluators may feel that their labors have been in vain, they should remember that the results of an evaluation are only one of the elements in a complex decision-making process. This point was clearly illustrated as long ago as 1915 in the controversy over the evaluation of the Gary plan in New York City public schools, described in Exhibit 12-B. The many parties involved in a human service program, including sponsors, managers, operators, and targets, often have very high stakes in the program's continuation, and their frequently unsupportable but enthusiastic claims may count more heavily than the coolly objective results of an evaluation. Moreover, whereas the outcome of an evaluation is simply a single argument on one side or another, the outcome of typical American political processes may be viewed as a balancing of a variety of interests.

In any political system that is sensitive to weighing, assessing, and balancing the conflicting claims and interests of a number of constituencies, the evaluator's role is that of an expert witness, testifying to the degree of a program's effectiveness and bolstering that testimony with empirically based information. A jury of decisionmakers and other stakeholders may give such testimony more weight than uninformed opinion or shrewd guessing, but they, not the expert witness, are the ones who must reach a verdict. There are other considerations to be taken into account.

To imagine otherwise would be to see evaluators as having the power of veto in the political decision-making process, a power that would strip decisionmakers of their prerogatives. Under such circumstances, evaluators would become philosopher-kings whose pronouncements on particular programs would override those of all the other parties involved.

In short, the proper role of evaluation is to contribute the best possible knowledge on evaluation issues to the political process and not to attempt to supplant that process. Exhibit 12-C contains an excerpt from an article by one of the founders of modern evaluation theory, Donald T. Campbell, expounding a view of evaluators as servants of "the Experimenting Society."

EXHIBIT 12-B

Politics and
Evaluation

This exhibit concerns the introduction of a new plan of school organization into the New York City schools in the period around World War I. The so-called Gary plan modeled schools after the new mass production factories, with children being placed on shifts and moved in platoons from subject matter to subject matter. The following account is a description of how evaluation results entered into the political struggle between the new school board and the existing school system administration.

The Gary plan was introduced into the schools by a new school board appointed by a reform mayor, initially on a pilot basis. School Superintendent Maxwell, resentful of interference in his professional domain and suspicious of the intent of the mayor's administration, had already expressed his feelings about the Gary plan as it was operating in one of the pilot schools: "Well, I visited that school the other day, and the only thing I saw was a lot of children digging in a lot." Despite the superintendent's views, the Gary system had been extended to 12 schools in the Bronx, and there were plans to extend it further. The cry for more research before extending the plan was raised by a school board member.

In the summer of 1915, Superintendent Maxwell ordered an evaluative study of the Gary plan as it had been implemented in the New York schools. The job was given to B. R. Buckingham, an educational psychologist in the research department of the New York City schools and a pioneer in the development of academic achievement tests. Buckingham used his newly developed academic achievement tests to compare two Gary-organized schools, six schools organized on a competing plan, and eight traditionally organized schools. The traditionally organized schools came out best on average, while the two Gary-organized schools averaged poorest.

Buckingham's report was highly critical of the eager proponents of the Gary system for making premature statements concerning its superiority. No sooner had the Buckingham report appeared than a veritable storm of rebuttal followed, both in the press and in professional journals. Howard W. Nudd, executive director of the Public Education Association, wrote a detailed critique of the Buckingham report, which was published in the *New York Globe,* the *New York Times, School and Society,* and the *Journal of Education.* Nudd argued that at the time Buckingham conducted his tests, the Gary plan had been in operation in one school for only four months and in the other for less than three weeks. He asserted that much

(Continued)

Exhibit 12-B
(Continued)

of the requested equipment had not been provided and that the work of the Gary schools had been seriously disturbed by the constant stream of visitors who descended to examine the program. In a detailed, school-by-school comparison, Nudd showed that in one of the Gary-organized schools 90% of the pupils came from immigrant homes where Italian was their first tongue while some of the comparison schools were largely populated by middle-class, native-born children. Moreover, pupils in one of the Gary schools had excellent test scores that compared favorably with those from other schools. When scores were averaged with the second Gary school, however, the overall result put the Gary plan well behind.

Buckingham had no answer to the contention of inadequate controls, but he argued that he was dealing, not with two schools, six schools, or eight schools, but with measurements on more than 11,000 children and therefore his study represented a substantial test of the Gary scheme. He justified undertaking his study early on the grounds that the Gary plan, already in operation in 12 Bronx schools, was being pushed on the New York schools and superintendent precipitously. As noted above, there was pressure from the mayor's office to extend the plan throughout the New York City schools and to make any increase in the education budget contingent on wholesale adoption of the Gary system. The president of the Board of Education found it advantageous to cite Nudd's interpretation of the Buckingham report in debate at the Board of Education meeting. Superintendent Maxwell continued to cite the Buckingham study as evidence against the effectiveness of the Gary plan, even a year and a half later.

SOURCE: Adapted from A. Levine and M. Levine, "The Social Context of Evaluation Research: A Case Study," *Evaluation Quarterly*, 1977, 1(4):515-542.

Political Time and Evaluation Time

There are two additional strains involved in doing evaluations, compared with academic social research, that are consequences of the fact that the evaluator is engaged in a political process involving multiple stakeholders. One is the need for evaluations to be relevant and significant in a policy sense, a topic we will take up momentarily; the other is the difference between political time and evaluation time.

Evaluations, especially those directed at assessing program impact, take time. Usually, the tighter and more elegant the study design, the longer the time period required

EXHIBIT 12-C

Social Scientists as Servants of the Experimenting Society

> Societies will continue to use preponderantly unscientific political processes to decide upon ameliorative program innovations. Whether it would be good to increase the role of social science in deciding on the content of the programs tried out is not at issue here. The emphasis is rather more on the passive role for the social scientist as an aid in helping society decide whether or not its innovations have achieved desired goals without damaging side effects. The job of the methodologist for the experimenting society is not to say *what is to be done,* but rather to say *what has been done.* The aspect of social science that is being applied is primarily its research methodology rather than its descriptive theory, with the goal of learning more than we do now from the innovations decided upon by the political process. . . . This emphasis seems to be quite different from the present role as government advisors of most economists, international relations professors, foreign area experts, political scientists, sociologists of poverty and race relations, psychologists of child development and learning, etc. Government asks what to do, and scholars answer with an assurance quite out of keeping with the scientific status of their fields. In the process, the scholar-advisors too fall into the overadvocacy trap and fail to be interested in finding out what happens when their advice is followed. Certainty that one already knows precludes finding out how valid one's theories are. We social scientists could afford more of the modesty of the physical sciences, [and] should more often say that we can't know until we've tried. . . . Perhaps all I am advocating . . . is that social scientists avoid cloaking their recommendations in a specious pseudoscientific certainty, and instead acknowledge their advice as consisting of but wise conjectures that need to be tested in implementation.

SOURCE: Quoted from Donald T. Campbell, "Methods for the Experimenting Society," *Evaluation Practice,* 1991, 12(3):228-229.

to perform the evaluation. Large-scale social experiments that estimate the net effects of major innovative programs may require anywhere from four to eight years to complete and document. The political and program worlds often move at a much faster pace. Policymakers and project sponsors usually are impatient to know whether or not a program is achieving its goals, and often their time frame is a matter of months, not years.

For this reason, evaluators frequently encounter pressure to complete their assessments more quickly than the best methods permit, as well as to release preliminary results. At times, evaluators are asked for their "impressions" of a program's effectiveness, even when they have stressed that such impressions are liable to be useless in the absence of firm results. For example, a major change in public welfare was enacted in the Personal Responsibility and Work Opportunity Act of 1996. In 1997 and 1998, evaluators were being asked by the mass media and legislators how effective the welfare reforms were, although for almost all states the reforms had yet to be worked out in detail, much less been put in place. It was only after three or four years that credible evidence began to appear. In the meantime, so great was the desire for evaluative evidence that the mass media and even legislators turned to anecdotes, usually dramatic, as evidence and were often far off the mark.

In addition, the planning and procedures related to initiating evaluations within organizations that sponsor such work often make it difficult to undertake timely studies. In most cases, procedures must be approved at several levels and by a number of key stakeholders. As a result, it can take considerable time to commission and launch an evaluation, not counting the time it takes to implement and complete it. Although both government and private sector sponsors have tried to develop mechanisms to speed up the planning and procurement processes, these efforts are hindered by the workings of their bureaucracies, by legal requirements related to contracting, and by the need to establish agreement on the evaluation questions and design.

It is not clear what can be done to reduce the pressure resulting from the different time schedules of evaluators and decisionmakers. It is important that evaluators anticipate the time demands of stakeholders, particularly the sponsors of evaluations, and avoid making unrealistic time commitments. Generally, a long-term study should not be undertaken if the information is needed before the evaluation can be completed.

A strategic approach is to confine technically complex evaluations to pilot or prototype projects for interventions that are unlikely to be implemented on a large scale in the immediate future. Thus, randomized controlled experiments may be most appropriate to evaluate the worth of new programs (initially implemented on a relatively small scale) before such programs appear on the agendas of decision-making bodies.

Another strategy for evaluators is to anticipate the direction of programs and policy activities, rather than be forced to undertake work that cannot be accomplished in the time allocated. One proposal that has attracted some attention is to establish independent evaluation institutes dedicated to examining, on a pilot or prototype basis, interventions that might one day be in demand. Evaluation centers could be established that continually assess the worth of alternative programs for dealing with social problems that are of perpetual concern or that have a high probability of emerging in the years ahead. Although this proposal has some attractive features, especially to professional evaluators, it is not at all clear that it is possible to forecast accurately what, say, the next decade's social issues will be. Perhaps the most successful approximation of efforts to maximize the contributions of evaluation activities prior to the implementation of new initiatives is the prospective evaluation synthesis of the Program Evaluation and Methodology Division of the U.S. General Accounting Office (GAO). As Chelimsky (1987) describes in Exhibit 12-D, her division's *ex ante* activities can make important contributions to shaping social legislation. (See also Chelimsky, 1991, for a general view

EXHIBIT 12-D

Using Evaluative Activities in the Analysis of Proposed New Programs

Many of us spend much of our time doing retrospective studies; these are and will continue to be the meat and potatoes of evaluation research. Congress asks us for them and asks the executive branch to do them, and they are needed, but these studies are not the easiest ones to insert into the political process, and they may well be the least propitious from the viewpoint of use. . . . By contrast, before a program has started, evaluators can have an enormous effect in improving the reasoning behind program purposes or goals, in identifying the problems to be addressed, and in selecting the best point of intervention and the type of intervention most likely to succeed. The tempo at which new programs are sometimes introduced presents some difficulty. . . . The pace often becomes so frantic that the lead time necessary to gear up for evaluative work is simply impossible to obtain if results are to be ready soon enough to be useful.

At the General Accounting Office (GAO) we are developing a method I call the Evaluation Planning Review which is specifically intended to be useful in the formulation of new programs. We have just given it a first try by looking at a proposed program focusing on teenage pregnancy. Essentially, the method seeks to gather information on what is known about past, similar programs and apply the experience to the architecture of the new one. Senator Chaffee asked us to look at the bill he was introducing; we managed to secure four good months to do the work, and it has been a major success from both the legislative point of view and our own. From a more general, political perspective, providing understanding ahead of time of how a program might work can render a valuable public service—either by helping to shore up a poorly thought-out program or by validating the basic soundness of what is to be undertaken. True, there are questions that decisionmakers do not pose to evaluators that could usefully be posed, which seems a priori to be a problem for the framework; however, even when evaluators have been free to choose the questions, this particular type of question has not often been asked. Also, evaluators can always influence the next round of policy questions through their products.

SOURCE: Eleanor Chelimsky, "The Politics of Program Evaluation," *Society*, 1987, 25(1):26-27.

of how applied social research intersects with policy making.) As things stand now, however, we believe that the tension caused by the disparities between political and research time will continue to be a problem in the employment of evaluation as a useful tool for policymakers and project managers.

Issues of Policy Significance

Evaluations, we have stressed, are done with a purpose that is practical and political in nature. In addition to the issues we have already reviewed, the fact that evaluations are ultimately conducted to affect the policy-making process introduces several considerations that further distinguish an evaluator's work from that of a basic researcher.

Policy space and policy relevance. The alternatives considered in designing, implementing, and assessing a social program are ordinarily those that are within current **policy space**, the set of alternative policies that can garner political support at any given point in time. A difficulty, however, is that policy space keeps changing in response to the efforts of influential figures to gain support from other policymakers and from ordinary community members. For example, in the 1990s policy space with respect to crime control was dominated by programs of long and sometimes mandatory sentences for selected types of criminals. In contrast, during the 1970s it was centered on the development of community- based treatment centers as an alternative to imprisonment, on the grounds that prisons were breeding places for crime and that criminals would be best helped by being kept in close contact with the normal, civilian world.

The volatility of policy space is illustrated by the Transitional Aid to Released Prisoners (TARP) experiments, discussed in earlier chapters, which were conducted in the late 1970s to evaluate the effectiveness in reducing recidivism of providing short-term financial support to recently released felons. Whatever the merits of the Georgia and Texas TARP experiments, by the time the evaluation findings were available, federal policy space had changed so drastically that the policies emerging from those experiments had no chance of being considered. In particular, the Reagan administration had replaced the Carter administration, changing the agenda dramatically. Thus, evaluators need to be sensitive not only to the policy space that exists when a research program is initiated but also to changes in the social and political context that alter the policy space as the evaluation proceeds.

Too often a prospective program may be tested without sufficient understanding of how the policy issues are seen by those decisionmakers who will have to approve the enactment of the program. Hence, even though the evaluation of the program in question may be flawless, its findings may prove irrelevant. In the New Jersey-Pennsylvania income maintenance experiment, the experiment's designers posed as their central issue the following question: How large is the work disincentive effect of an income maintenance plan? By the time the experiment was completed and congressional committees were considering various income maintenance plans, however, the key issue was no longer the work disincentive effect. Rather, members of Congress were more concerned with how many different forms of welfare could be consolidated into one comprehensive package, without ignoring important needs of the poor and without creating many inequities (Rossi and Lyall, 1976). The policy space had changed.

Because a major purpose of evaluative activities is to help decisionmakers form new social policies and to assess the worth of ongoing programs, evaluation research must be sensitive to the various policy issues involved and the limits of policy space. The goals of a project must resemble those articulated by policymakers in deliberations on the issues of concern. A carefully designed randomized experiment showing that a reduction in certain regressive taxes would lead to an improvement in worker productivity may be irrelevant if decisionmakers are more concerned with motivating entrepreneurs and attracting potential investments.

For these reasons, responsible impact assessment design must necessarily involve, if at all possible, some contact with relevant decisionmakers to ascertain their interests in the project being tested. A sensitive evaluator needs to know what the current and future policy space will allow to be considered. For an innovative project that is not currently being discussed by decisionmakers, but is being tested because it may become the subject of future discussion, the evaluators and sponsors must rely on their informed forecasts about what changes in policy space are likely. For other projects, the processes of obtaining decisionmakers' opinions are quite straightforward. Evaluators can consult the proceedings of deliberative bodies (e.g., government committee hearings or legislative debates), interview decisionmakers' staffs, or consult decisionmakers directly.

Policy significance. The fact that evaluations are conducted according to the canons of social research may make them superior to other modes of judging social programs. But evaluations provide only superfluous information unless they directly address the value issues of persons engaged in policy making, program planning, and management, that is, unless there is **policy significance**. The weaknesses of evaluations, in this regard, tend to center on how research questions are stated and how findings are interpreted (Datta, 1980). The issues here involve considerations that go beyond methodology. To maximize the utility of evaluation findings, evaluators must be sensitive to two levels of policy considerations.

First, programs that address problems perceived as critical require better (i.e., more rigorous) assessments than interventions related to relatively trivial concerns. Technical decisions, such as setting statistical power levels, should be informed by the nature of policy and program considerations. These are always matters of judgment and sensitivity.

Even when formal efficiency analyses are undertaken, the issue remains. For example, the decision to use an individual, program, or community accounting perspective is determined by policy and sponsorship considerations.

Second, evaluation findings have to be assessed according to how far they are generalizable, whether the findings are significant to the policy and to the program, and whether the program clearly fits the need (as expressed by the many factors that are involved in the policy-making process). An evaluation may produce results that all would agree are statistically significant and generalizable and yet be too small to be significant for policy, planning, and managerial action (Lipsey, 1990; Sechrest and Yeaton, 1982). The issues involved have been discussed in detail in Chapter 10 under the rubric of "practical significance."

Basic science models versus policy-oriented models. Social scientists often do not grasp the difference in emphasis required in formulating a model purposefully to *alter* a phenomenon as opposed to developing a causal model to *explain* the phenomenon. For example, much of the criminal behavior of young men can be explained by the extent of such behavior among males in their social network—fathers, brothers, other male relatives, friends, neighbors, schoolmates, and so on. This is a fascinating finding that affords many insights into the geographic and ethnic distributions of crime rates. However, it is not a useful finding in terms of altering the crime rate because it is difficult to envisage an acceptable public policy that would alter the social networks of young men. Short of yanking young males out of their settings and putting them into other environments, it is not at all clear that anything can be done to affect their social networks. Policy space will likely never (we hope) include population redistribution for these purposes.

In contrast, it is easier to envisage a public policy that would attempt to alter the perceived costs of engaging in criminal activities, even though they are a weaker determinant of crime. The willingness to engage in crime is sluggishly and weakly related to subjective probabilities: The more that individuals believe they likely will be caught if they commit a crime, convicted if caught, and imprisoned if convicted, the lower the probability of criminal behavior. Thus, to some extent the incidence of criminal acts will be reduced if the police are effective in arresting criminals, if the prosecution is diligent in obtaining convictions, and if the courts have a harsh sentencing policy. None of these relationships is especially strong, yet these findings are much more significant for public policy that attempts to control crime than the social network explanation of criminal behavior. Mayors and police chiefs can implement programs that increase the proportion of criminals apprehended, prosecutors can work harder at obtaining convictions, and judges can refuse to plea-bargain. Moreover, dissemination of these policy changes in ways that reach the potential offenders would, in itself, have some modest impact on the crime rate. The general point should be clear: Basic social science models often ignore practical policy significance, but for evaluators this must be a central concern.

The missing engineering tradition. Our discussion of policy-relevant and policy-signif-icant research points to a more general lesson: In the long term, evaluators—indeed, all applied researchers—and their stakeholders must develop an "engineering tradition," something that currently is missing in most of the social sciences. Engineers are dis-tinguished from their "pure science" counterparts by their concern with working out the details of how scientific knowledge can be used to grapple with real-life problems. It is one thing to know that gases expand when heated and that each gas has its own expansion coefficient; it is quite another to be able to use that principle to mass-produce economical, high-quality gas turbine engines.

Similar engineering problems exist with respect to social science findings. For example, consider the practical issues confronted by policymakers and other stake-holders in the 1980s when there was much dissatisfaction with the existing welfare pro-grams but also much uncertainty about how they should be changed. In Congress there was a growing consensus that the incentives involved in welfare payments under Aid to Families with Dependent Children (AFDC) fostered dependency and hindered the movement of AFDC clients off the rolls into employment. Well-supported social science theories in economics and in psychological learning theory posited that changing incentives often alters behavior. The engineering issue was how best to change the mix of incentives in welfare programs to reduce dependency and to encourage clients to seek employment. Existing social science knowledge, however, provided no guidance about the relative effectiveness of a variety of incentive changes. Accordingly, the Department of Health and Human Services encouraged states to modify AFDC rules to provide incentives for clients to seek and obtain employment. Several versions of incen-tive packages were tested in randomized experiments (Gueron and Pauly, 1991). The experiments tested programs in which adults on welfare were prepared through train-ing for employment, allowed to retain some proportion of their employment earnings without reduction in welfare payments, and aided to find employment. Had well-developed social science engineering knowledge existed in the 1980s, welfare reform may well have taken place long before the end of the 1990s.

Although we believe that a social science engineering tradition is a worthwhile goal, it is clear that the social sciences are not yet in a position to establish such a tradi-tion. The existing knowledge base is growing, but it may be decades before it is exten-sive enough. In addition, we are not certain how such social science engineers should be trained, and we suspect that training models will have to await the appearance of a sufficient number of exemplars from which to learn.

Our hope is that the foregoing observations about the dynamics of conducting evaluations in the context of the real world of program and social policy sensitize the evaluator to the importance of "scouting" the terrain when embarking on an evaluation and of remaining alert to ecological changes that occur during the evaluation process. Such efforts may be at least as important to the successful conduct of evaluation activities as the technical appropriateness of the procedures employed.

Evaluating Evaluations

As evaluations have become more sophisticated, judging whether some particular evaluation was performed skillfully and the findings were interpreted properly becomes more and more difficult. Especially for laypersons and public officials, assessing the credibility of evaluations may be beyond their reach. In addition, there may often be contradictory research findings arising from several evaluations of the same program. How to reconcile conflicting evaluation claims can present problems even to evaluation experts. To meet the need for validating evaluations and for adequate communication of their findings, several approaches have been tried.

Quite frequently, the contracts or grants funding large-scale evaluations call for the formation of advisory committees composed of evaluation experts and policy analysts to oversee the conduct of the evaluation and provide expert advice to the evaluators and the funders. The advisory committee approach can be viewed as a way to raise the quality of evaluations and at the same time to provide greater legitimacy to their findings.

There also have been intensive reviews of evaluations, including reanalyses of evaluation datasets. For example, the National Academy of Sciences from time to time forms committees to review evaluations and synthesize their findings on topics of policy interest or significant controversy. Coyle, Boruch, and Turner (1991) reviewed AIDS education evaluations with regard to the adequacy of their designs recommending improvements in the quality of such work. Similar critical reviews have been written of evaluations in other substantive areas. For example, Mosteller and Boruch (2002) have edited a set of papers on the use of randomized experiments in the evaluation of educational programs.

Reviews such as those just mentioned, however, typically take several years to complete and hence do not meet the needs of policymakers who require more timely information. More timely commentary on evaluations requires more rapid review and assessment. A promising attempt to be timely was funded in 1997 through a grant from the Smith-Richardson Foundation. The University of Maryland's School of Public Affairs was commissioned to convene a "blue ribbon" commission of prominent evaluators and policy analysts to review and comment on the expected considerable flow of evaluations of the reforms in public welfare undertaken under the Personal Responsibility and Work Opportunity Reconciliation Act of 1996 (Besharov, Germanis, and Rossi, 1998). It was intended that the Committee to Review Welfare Reform Research would issue periodic reports addressed to policymakers assessing the adequacy of the evaluations and drawing out their implications for policy. The first set of reviews has been published (Besharov, 2003) and others are planned for the future. Unfortunately, it does not appear that the reviews can be written within a few months after evaluations are released, as originally planned.

A more ambitious undertaking is the recently formed international Campbell Collaboration, a cooperative undertaking of social scientists concerned with evaluation, whose purpose is to undertake systematic reviews of program evaluations in several substantive domains. The Campbell Collaboration has published several reviews, for example, of "Scared Straight" juvenile delinquency prevention programs, and plans to periodically issue additional reviews (www.campbellcollaboration.org).

Despite these examples, we believe that the typical program evaluation is not ordinarily subject to the judgment of peers in the evaluation community. Some policymakers may have the competence to judge their adequacy, but most may have to rely on the persuasive qualities of evaluation reports. For this reason, as discussed in a later section, evaluation standards are of recurring importance in the professional associations of evaluators.

The Profession of Evaluation

There is no roster of all persons who identify themselves as evaluators and no way of fully describing their backgrounds or the range of activities in which they are engaged. At a minimum, some 50,000-75,000 persons are engaged, full- or part-time, in evaluation activities. We arrived at this estimate by adding together the numbers of federal, state, county, and city government organizations engaged in social program development and implementation, along with the numbers of school districts, hospitals, mental hospitals, and universities and colleges, all of which are usually obligated to undertake one or more types of evaluation activities. We do not know the actual number of persons engaged in evaluation work in these groups, and we have no way of estimating the numbers of university professors and persons affiliated with nonprofit and for-profit applied research firms who do evaluations. Indeed, the actual number of full- and part-time evaluators may be double or triple our minimum estimate.

It is clear that evaluators work in widely disparate social program areas and devote varying amounts of their working time to evaluation activities. At best, the role definition of the evaluator is blurred and fuzzy.

At the one extreme, persons may perform evaluations as an adjunct activity. Sometimes they undertake their evaluation activities simply to conform to legislative or regulatory requirements, as apparently is the case in many local school systems. To comply with some state or federal funding requirements, schools often must have someone designated as an "evaluator," and so name someone on their teaching or management staffs to serve in that capacity. Often the person appointed has no particular qualifications for the assignment either by training or by experience. At the other extreme, within university evaluation institutes and social science departments, and within applied social research firms in the private and nonprofit sectors, there are full-time evaluation specialists, highly trained and with years of experience, who are working at the frontiers of the evaluation field.

Indeed, the labels *evaluators* and *evaluation researchers* conceal the heterogeneity, diversity, and amorphousness of the field. Evaluators are not licensed or certified, so the identification of a person as an evaluator provides no assurance that he or she shares any core knowledge with any other person so identified. The proportion of evaluators who interact and communicate with each other, particularly across social program areas, likely is very small. The American Evaluation Association, the major "general" organization in the field, has only a few thousand members, and the cross-disciplinary journal with the most subscribers, *Evaluation Review,* likewise is read by only a few thousand. Within program areas, there are only weak social networks of evaluators, most of whom are unaffiliated with national and local professional organizations that have organized evaluation "sections."

In brief, evaluation is not a "profession," at least in terms of the formal criteria that sociologists generally use to characterize such groups. Rather, it can best be described as individuals sharing a common label who form a loose aggregate, who are not formally organized, and who may have little in common with one another in terms of the range of tasks they undertake or their competencies, work sites, and outlooks. This feature of the evaluation field underlies much of the discussion that follows.

Intellectual Diversity and Its Consequences

Evaluation has a richly diverse intellectual heritage. All the social science disciplines—economics, psychology, sociology, political science, and anthropology—have contributed to the development of the field. Individuals trained in each of these disciplines have made contributions to the conceptual base of evaluation research and to its methodological repertoire. Persons trained in the various human service professions with close ties to the social sciences, medicine, public health, social welfare, urban planning, public administration, education, and so on have made important methodological contributions and have undertaken landmark evaluations. In addition, the applied mathematics fields of statistics, biometrics, econometrics, and psychometrics have contributed important ideas on measurement and analysis.

Cross-disciplinary borrowing has been extensive. Take the following examples: Although economics traditionally has not been an experimentally based social science, economists have designed and implemented a significant proportion of the federally sponsored large-scale, randomized field experiments of the past several decades, including the highly visible experiments in public welfare, employment training, income maintenance, housing allowance, and national health insurance. Sociologists and psychologists have borrowed heavily from the econometricians, notably in their use of time-series analysis methods and simultaneous equation modeling. Sociologists have contributed many of the conceptual and data collection procedures used in monitoring organizational performance, and psychologists have contributed the idea of regression-discontinuity designs to time-series analyses. Psychometricians have provided some of the basic ideas underlying theories of measurement applicable to all fields, and anthropologists have provided some of the basic approaches used in qualitative fieldwork. Indeed, the vocabulary of evaluation is a mix from all of these disciplines. The list of references at the back of this book is testimony to the multidisciplinary character of the evaluation field.

In the abstract, the diverse roots of the field are one of its attractions. In practice, however, they confront evaluators with the need to be general social scientists and lifelong students if they are even to keep up, let alone broaden their knowledge base. Furthermore, the diversity in the field accounts to a considerable extent for the "improper" selection of research approaches for which evaluators are sometimes criticized. Clearly, it is impossible for every evaluator to be a scholar in all of the social sciences and to be an expert in every methodological procedure.

There is no ready solution to the need to have the broad knowledge base and range of competencies ideally required by the "universal" evaluator. This situation means that evaluators must at times forsake opportunities to undertake work because their knowledge bases may be too narrow, that they may have to use an "almost good enough" method rather than the appropriate one they are unfamiliar with, and that sponsors of evaluations and managers of evaluation staffs must be highly selective in deciding on contractors and in making work assignments. It also means that at times evaluators will need to make heavy use of consultants and solicit advice from peers.

In a profession, a range of opportunities is provided for keeping up with the state of the art and expanding one's repertoire of competencies—for example, the peer learning that occurs at regional and national meetings and the didactic courses provided by these professional associations. At present, only a fraction of the many thousands of evaluation practitioners participate in professional evaluation organizations and can take advantage of the opportunities they provide.

The Education of Evaluators

The diffuse character of the evaluation field is exacerbated by the different ways in which evaluators are educated. Few people in evaluation have achieved responsible posts and rewards by working their way up from lowly jobs within evaluation units. Most evaluators have some sort of formal graduate training either in social science departments or in professional schools. One of the important consequences of the multidisciplinary character of evaluation is that appropriate training for full participation in it cannot be adequately undertaken within any single discipline. In a few universities, interdisciplinary programs have been set up that include graduate instruction across a number of departments. In these programs, a graduate student might be directed to take courses in test construction and measurement in a department of psychology, econometrics in a department of economics, survey design and analysis in a department of sociology, policy analysis in a political science department, and so on.

Interdisciplinary training programs, however, are neither common nor very stable. In the typical research-oriented university where graduate training is usually obtained, the powerful units are the traditional departments. The interdepartmental coalitions of faculty that form interdisciplinary programs tend to have short lives, because departments typically do not reward participation in such ventures very highly and faculty drift back into their departments as a consequence. The result is that too often graduate training of evaluators primarily is unidisciplinary despite the clear need for it to be multidisciplinary.

Moreover, within academic departments, applied work is often regarded less highly than "pure" or "basic" research. As a consequence, training in evaluation-related competencies is often limited. Psychology departments may provide fine courses on experimental design but fail to consider very much the special problems of implementing field experiments in comparison with laboratory studies; sociology departments may teach survey research courses but not deal at all with the special data collection problems involved in interviewing the unique populations that are typically the targets of social programs. Then, too, the low status accorded applied work in graduate departments often is a barrier to undertaking evaluations as dissertations and theses.

If there is any advice to be given in this regard, it is that students who are interested in an evaluation career must be assertive. Often the student must take the lead in hand-tailoring an individual study program that includes course offerings in a range of departments, be insistent about undertaking an applied dissertation or thesis, and seize on any opportunities within university research institutes and in the community to supplement formal instruction with relevant apprenticeship learning.

The other training route is the professional school. Schools of education train evaluators for positions in that field, programs in schools of public health and medical care produce persons who engage in health service evaluations, and so on. In fact, over time these professional schools, as well as MBA programs, have become the training sites for many evaluators.

These programs have their limitations as well. One criticism raised about them is that they are too "trade school" oriented in outlook. Consequently, some of them fail to provide the conceptual breadth and depth that allows graduates to move back and forth across social program areas, and to grasp technical innovations when they occur. Moreover, particularly at a master's level, many professional schools are required to have a number of mandatory courses, because their standing and sometimes their funding depend on accreditation by professional bodies who see the need for common training if graduates are going to leave as MSWs, MPHs, MBAs, and the like. Because many programs therefore leave little time for electives, the amount of technical training that can be obtained in courses is limited. Increasingly, the training of evaluators in professional schools therefore has moved from the master's to the doctoral level.

Also, in many universities both faculty and students in professional schools are viewed as second-class citizens by those located in social science departments. This elitism often isolates students so that they cannot take advantage of course offerings in several social science departments or apprenticeship training in their affiliated social science research institutes. Students trained in professional schools, particularly at the master's level, often trade off opportunities for intensive technical training for substantive knowledge in a particular program area and the benefits of professional certification. The obvious remedy is either undertaking further graduate work or seizing opportunities for additional learning of technical skills while pursuing an evaluation career.

We hold no brief for one route over the other; each has its advantages and liabilities. Increasingly, it appears that professional schools are becoming the major suppliers of evaluators, at least in part because of the reluctance of graduate social science departments to develop appropriate applied research programs. But these professional schools are far from homogeneous in what they teach, particularly in the methods of evaluation they emphasize—thus the continued diversity of the field.

Consequences of Diversity in Origins

The existence of many educational pathways to becoming an evaluator contributes to the lack of coherence in the field. It accounts, at least in part, for the differences in the very definition of evaluation, and the different outlooks regarding the appropriate way to evaluate a particular social program. Of course, other factors contribute to this diversity, including social and political ideologies of evaluators.

Some of the differences are related to whether the evaluator is educated in a professional school or a social science department. For example, evaluators who come out of professional schools such as social work or education are much more likely than those trained in, say, sociology to see themselves as part of the program staff and to give priority to tasks that help program managers. Thus, they are likely to stress formative evaluations that are designed to improve the day-to-day operations of programs, whereas the more social-science minded are more likely to be primarily concerned with effectiveness and efficiency issues.

The diversity is also related to differences among social science departments and among professional schools. Evaluators trained as political scientists frequently are oriented to policy analysis, an activity designed to aid legislators and high-level executives, particularly government administrators. Anthropologists, as one might expect, are predisposed to qualitative approaches and are unusually attentive to target populations' interests in evaluation outcomes. Psychologists, in keeping with their discipline's emphasis on small-scale experiments, often are concerned more with the validity of the causal inference in their evaluations than the generalizability to program practice. In contrast, sociologists are often more concerned with the potential for generalization and are more willing to forsake some degree of rigor in the causal conclusions to achieve it. Economists are likely to work in still different ways, depending on the body of microeconomic theory to guide their evaluation designs.

Similar diversity can be found among those educated in different professional schools. Evaluators trained in schools of education may focus on educational competency tests in measuring the outcome of early-childhood education programs, whereas social work graduates may focus on caseworker ratings of children's emotional status and parental reports of their behavior. Persons coming from schools of public health may be most interested in preventive practices, those from medical care administration programs in frequency of physician encounters and duration of hospitalization, and so on.

It is easy to exaggerate the distinctive outlook that each discipline and profession manifests in approaching the design and conduct of evaluations, and there are many exceptions to the preferences and tendencies just described. Indeed, a favorite game among evaluation buffs is to guess an author's disciplinary background from the content of an article he or she has written. Nevertheless, disciplinary and professional diversity has produced a fair degree of conflict within the field of evaluation. Evaluators hold divided views on topics ranging from epistemology to the choice of methods and the major goals of evaluation. Some of the major divisions are described briefly below.

Orientations to primary stakeholders. As mentioned earlier in this chapter, evaluators differ about whose perspective should be taken in an evaluation. Some evaluators believe that evaluations should be mainly directed toward helping program managers to improve their programs. This view of evaluation sees its purpose primarily as consultation to program management to the point that the difference between technical assistance and evaluation becomes blurred. According to this view, an evaluation succeeds to the extent that programs are improved. These evaluation orientations tend also to avoid making judgments about the worth of programs on the grounds that most programs can be made to work with the help of evaluators. (See Patton, 1997, for a well-articulated argument for utilization-focused evaluation.)

Others hold that the purpose of evaluations should be to help program beneficiaries (targets) to become empowered. This view of evaluation believes that engaging targets in a collaborative effort to define programs and their evaluation leads targets to become more "in charge" of their lives and leads to an increase in the sense of personal efficacy. (Fetterman, Kaftarian, and Wandersman, 1996, contains examples of this approach.)

At the other extreme of this division are the evaluators who believe that evaluators should mainly serve those stakeholders who fund the evaluation. Such evaluations take on the perspective of the funders, adopting their definitions of program goals and program outcomes.

Our own view has been stated earlier in this chapter. We believe that evaluations ought to be sensitive to the perspectives of all the major stakeholders. Ordinarily, contractual requirements require that primary attention be given to the evaluation sponsor's definitions of program goals and outcomes. However, such requirements do not exclude other perspectives. We believe that it is the obligation of evaluators to state clearly the perspective from which the evaluation is undertaken and to point out what other major perspectives are involved. When an evaluation has the resources to accommodate several perspectives, multiple perspectives should be used.

Epistemological differences. The "cultural wars" that are being waged in the humanities and some of the social sciences have touched evaluation as well. Postmodern theories of knowledge are reflected in evaluation with claims that social problems are social constructions and that knowledge is not absolute but, rather, that there are different "truths," each valid for the perspective from which it derives. Postmodernists tend to favor qualitative research methods that produce rich "naturalistic" data and evaluation perspectives favoring those of the program personnel and target populations. (See Guba and Lincoln, 1989, for a foremost exponent of postmodern evaluation.)

Those who oppose the postmodern position are not homogeneous in their beliefs on the nature of knowledge. Nevertheless, among the opponents to postmodernism there is some strong consensus that truth is not entirely relativistic. For example, while most believe that the definition of poverty is a social construction, they are also convinced that the distribution of annual incomes can be described through research operations on which most social scientists can agree. That is, whether a given income level is regarded as poverty is a matter of social judgment, but the number of households at that income level can be estimated with a known sampling error. This position implies that disagreements among researchers on empirical findings are mainly matters of method or measurement error rather than matters involving different truths.

Our own position, as exemplified throughout this book, is clearly not postmodern. We believe that there are close matches between methods and evaluation problems. For given research questions, there are better methods and poorer methods. Indeed, the major concern in this book is how to choose the method for a given research question that is likely to produce the most credible findings.

The qualitative-quantitative division. Coinciding with some of the divisions within the evaluation community is the division between those who advocate qualitative methods and those who argue for quantitative ones. A sometimes pointless literature has developed around this "issue." On one side, the advocates of qualitative approaches stress the need for intimate knowledge and acquaintance with a program's concrete manifestations in attaining valid knowledge about the program's effects. Qualitative evaluators tend to be oriented toward formative evaluation, that is, making a program work better by feeding information on the program to its managers. In contrast, quantitatively oriented evaluators often view the field as being primarily concerned with impact assessments or summative evaluation. They focus on developing measures of program characteristics, processes, and impact that allow program effectiveness to be assessed with relatively high credibility.

Often the polemics obscure the critical point—namely, that each approach has utility, and the choice of approaches depends on the evaluation question at hand. We have tried in this book to identify the appropriate applications of each viewpoint. As we have stressed, qualitative approaches can play critical roles in program design and are important means of monitoring programs. In contrast, quantitative approaches are much more appropriate in estimates of impact as well as in assessments of the efficiency of social program efforts. (For a balanced discussion of the qualitative-quantitative discussion, see Reichardt and Rallis, 1994.)

Thus, it is fruitless to raise the issue of which is the better approach without specifying the evaluation questions to be studied. Fitting the approach to the research purposes is the critical issue; to pit one approach against the other in the abstract results in a pointless dichotomization of the field. Even the most avid proponents of one approach or the other recognize the contribution each makes to social program evaluations (Cronbach, 1982; Patton, 1997). Indeed, the use of multiple methods, often referred to as *triangulation,* can strengthen the validity of findings if results produced by different methods are congruent. Using multiple methods is a means of offsetting different kinds of bias and measurement error (for an extended discussion of this point, see Greene and Caracelli, 1997).

The problem, as we see it, is both philosophical and strategic. Evaluations are undertaken primarily as contributions to policy and program formulation and modification activities, as we have stressed, that have a strong political dimension. As Chelimsky (1987) has observed, "It is rarely prudent to enter a burning political debate armed only with a case study" (p. 27).

Diversity in Working Arrangements

The diversity of the evaluation field is also manifest in the variety of settings and bureaucratic structures in which evaluators work. First, there are two contradictory theses about working arrangements, or what might be called the insider-outsider debate. One position is that evaluators are best off when their positions are as secure and independent as possible from the influence of project management and staff. The other is that sustained contact with the policy and program staff enhances evaluators' work by providing a better understanding of the organization's objectives and activities while inspiring trust and thus increasing the evaluator's influence.

Second, there are ambiguities surrounding the role of the evaluator vis-à-vis program staff and groups of stakeholders regardless of whether the evaluator is an insider or outsider. The extent to which relations between staff members should resemble other structures in corporations or the collegial model that supposedly characterizes academia is an issue. But it is only one dimension to the challenge of structuring appropriate working relationships that confronts the evaluator.

Third, there is the concern on the part of evaluators with the "standing" of the organizations with which they are affiliated. Like universities, the settings in which evaluators work can be ranked and rated along a number of dimensions and a relatively few large evaluation organizations constitute a recognized elite subset of work places. Whether it is better to be a small fish in a big pond or vice versa is an issue in the evaluation field.

The discussion that follows, it bears emphasis, is based more on impressions of the authors of this text than on empirical research findings. Our impressions may be faulty, but it is a fact that debates surrounding these issues are commonplace whenever a critical mass of evaluators congregates.

Inside Versus Outside Evaluations

In the past, some experienced evaluators went so far as to state categorically that evaluations should never be undertaken within the organization responsible for the administration of a project, but should always be conducted by an outside group. One reason "outsider" evaluations may have seemed the desired option is that there were differences in the levels of training and presumed competence of insider and outsider evaluation staffs. These differences have narrowed. The career of an evaluation researcher has typically taken one of three forms. Until the 1960s, a large proportion of evaluation research was done by either university-affiliated researchers or research firms. Since the late 1960s, public service agencies in various program areas have been hiring researchers for staff positions to conduct more in-house evaluations. Also, the proportion of evaluations done by private, for-profit research groups has increased markedly. As research positions in both types of organizations have increased and the academic job market has declined, more persons who are well trained in the social and behavioral sciences have gravitated toward research jobs in public agencies and for-profit firms.

The current evidence is far from clear regarding whether inside or outside evaluations are more likely to be of higher technical quality. But technical quality is not the only criterion; utility may be just as important. A study in the Netherlands of external and internal evaluations suggests that internal evaluations may have a higher rate of impact on organizational decisions. According to van de Vall and Bolas (1981), of more importance than which category of researchers excels at influencing social policy are those variables responsible for the higher rate of utilization of internal researchers' findings. The answer, they suggest, lies partly in a higher rate of communication between inside researchers and policymakers, accompanied by greater consensus, and partly in a balance between standards of epistemological and implemental validity: "In operational terms, this means that social policy researchers should seek equilibrium between time devoted to methodological perfection and translating results into policy measures" (p. 479). Their data suggest that currently in-house social researchers are in a more favorable position than external researchers for achieving these instrumental goals.

Given the increased competence of staff and the visibility and scrutiny of the evaluation enterprise, there is no reason now to favor one organizational arrangement over another. Nevertheless, there remain many critical points during an evaluation when there are opportunities for work to be misdirected and consequently misused irrespective of the locus of the evaluators. The important issue, therefore, is that any evaluation strikes an appropriate balance between technical quality and utility for its purposes, recognizing that those purposes may often be different for internal evaluations than for external ones.

Organizational Roles

Whether evaluators are insiders or outsiders, they need to cultivate clear understandings of their roles with sponsors and program staff. Evaluators' full comprehension of their roles and responsibilities is one major element in the successful conduct of an evaluation effort.

Again, the heterogeneity of the field makes it difficult to generalize on the best ways to develop and maintain the appropriate working relations. One common mechanism is to have in place advisory groups or one or more consultants to oversee evaluations and provide some aura of authenticity to the findings. The ways such advisory groups or consultants work depend on whether an inside or an outside evaluation is involved and on the sophistication of both the evaluator and the program staff. For example, large-scale evaluations undertaken by federal agencies and major foundations often have advisory groups that meet regularly and assess the quality, quantity, and direction of the work. Some public and private health and welfare organizations with small evaluation units have consultants who provide technical advice to the evaluators or advise agency directors on the appropriateness of the evaluation units' activities, or both.

Sometimes advisory groups and consultants are mere window dressing; we do not recommend their use if that is their only function. When members are actively engaged, however, advisory groups can be particularly useful in fostering interdisciplinary evaluation approaches, in adjudicating disputes between program and evaluation staffs, and in defending evaluation findings in the face of concerted attacks by those whose interests are threatened.

The Leadership Role of Evaluation "Elite" Organizations

A small group of evaluators, numbering perhaps no more than 1,000, constitutes an "elite" in the field by virtue of the scale of the evaluations they conduct and the size of the organizations for which they work. They are somewhat akin to those elite physicians who practice in the hospitals of important medical schools. They and their settings are few in number but powerful in establishing the norms for the field. The ways in which they work and the standards of performance in their organizations represent an important version of professionalism that persons in other settings may use as a role model.

The number of organizations that carry out national or otherwise large-scale evaluations with a high degree of technical competence is quite small. But in terms of both visibility and evaluation dollars expended, these organizations occupy a strategic position in the field. Most of the large federal evaluation contracts over the years have been awarded to a small group of profit-making research firms (such as Abt Associates, Mathematica Policy Research, and Westat, to name a few) and not-for-profit research organizations and universities (examples are the RAND Corporation, the Research Triangle Institute, the Urban Institute, and the Manpower Development Research Corporation). A handful of research-oriented universities with affiliated research institutes—the National Opinion Research Center (NORC) at the University of Chicago, the Institute for Research on Poverty at the University of Wisconsin, the Joint Center for Poverty Research (University of Chicago and Northwestern University), and the Institute for Social Research at the University of Michigan, for example—also receive grants and contracts for undertaking large-scale evaluations. In addition, the evaluation units of federal agencies that contract for and fund evaluation research, and a few of the large national foundations, include significant numbers of highly trained evaluators on their staffs. Within the federal government, perhaps the highest concentration of skilled evaluators was to be found until recently in the Program Evaluation and Methodology Division of the GAO, where a large group of evaluation specialists has extended the activities of this key "watchdog" organization from auditing to assessing appropriate program implementation and estimating the impact of federal initiatives.

One of the features of these elite for-profit and nonprofit organizations is a continual concern with the quality of their work. In part, this has come about because of earlier critiques of their efforts, which formerly were not as well conducted technically as those done by persons in academic institutions (Bernstein and Freeman, 1975). But as they came to dominate the field, at least in terms of large-scale evaluations, and as they found sponsors of evaluations increasingly using criteria of technical competence in selecting contractors, their efforts improved markedly from a methodological standpoint. So, too, have the competencies of their staffs, and they now compete for the best-trained persons in applied work. Also, they have found it to be in their self-interest to encourage staff to publish in professional journals, participate actively in professional organizations, and engage in frontier efforts to improve the state of the art. To the extent that there is a general movement toward professionalism, these organizations are its leaders.

Evaluation Standards, Guidelines, and Ethics

If the evaluation field cannot be characterized as an organized profession in the usual sense, it has nevertheless become increasingly professionalized. With the move to professionalization, many evaluators began to pressure their professional associations to formulate and publish standards that could guide them in their evaluation work and in negotiations with evaluation funders and other major stakeholders. For example, it would be useful to evaluators to be able to bolster an argument for the right to freely publish evaluation findings if they could cite a published set of practice standards that included publication rights as standard evaluation practice. In addition, almost every practicing evaluator encounters situations requiring ethical judgments. For example, does an evaluator studying a child abuse prevention program have an obligation to report his observation of child abuse in a family revealed in the course of an interview on parenting practices? Published standards or practice guidelines also provide legitimacy to those who advertise their services as practices in conformity with them.

Two major efforts have been made to provide guidance to evaluators. Under the aegis of the American National Standards Institute (ANSI), the Joint Committee on Standards for Educational Evaluation (1994) has published *The Program Evaluation Standards,* now in its second edition. The Joint Committee is made up of representatives from several professional associations, including, among others, the American Evaluation Association, the American Psychological Association, and the American

Educational Research Association. Originally set up to deal primarily with educational programs, the Joint Committee expanded its coverage to include all kinds of program evaluation. The *Standards* cover a wide variety of topics ranging from what provisions should appear in evaluation contracts through issues in dealing with human subjects to the *Standards* for the analysis of quantitative and qualitative data. Each of the several core *Standards* is illustrated with cases illustrating how the *Standards* can be applied in specific instances.

The second major effort, *Guiding Principles for Evaluators* (American Evaluation Association, Task Force on Guiding Principles for Evaluators, 1995), has been adopted by the American Evaluation Association. Rather than proclaim standard practices, the *Guiding Principles* set out five quite general principles for the guidance of evaluators. The principles follow, and the full statements are presented in Exhibit 12-E.

A. *Systematic inquiry:* Evaluators conduct systematic, data-based inquiries about whatever is being evaluated.

B. *Competence:* Evaluators provide competent performance to stakeholders.

C. *Integrity/honesty:* Evaluators ensure the honesty and integrity of the entire evaluation process.

D. *Respect for people:* Evaluators respect the security, dignity, and self-worth of the respondents, program participants, clients, and other stakeholders with whom they interact.

E. *Responsibilities for general and public welfare:* Evaluators articulate and take into account the diversity of interests and values that may be related to the general and public welfare.

These five principles are elaborated and discussed in the *Guiding Principles*, although not to the detailed extent found in the Joint Committee's work. Just how useful such general principles may be is problematic. An evaluator who has a specific ethical problem will likely find very little guidance in any one of them. (See Shadish, Newman, et al., 1995, for critical appraisals of the *Guiding Principles*.)

We expect that developing a set of practice standards and ethical principles that can provide pointed advice to evaluators will take some time. The diversity of evaluation styles will make it difficult to adopt standards because any practice so designated may contradict what some group may consider good practice. The development of standards would be considerably advanced by the existence of *case law*, the accumulation of adjudicated specific instances in which the principles have been applied. However, neither the Joint Committee's *Standards* nor the American Evaluation Association's *Guiding Principles* have any mode of enforcement, the usual institutional mechanism for the development of case law.

EXHIBIT 12-E

The American
Evaluation
Association's
*Guiding Principles
for Evaluators*

A. *Systematic inquiry: Evaluators conduct systematic, data-based inquiries about whatever is being evaluated.*

1. Evaluators should adhere to the highest appropriate technical standards in conducting their work, whether that work is quantitative or qualitative in nature, so as to increase the accuracy and credibility of the evaluative information they produce.

2. Evaluators should explore with the client the shortcomings and strengths both of the various evaluation questions it might be productive to ask and the various approaches that might be used for answering those questions.

3. When presenting their work, evaluators should communicate their methods and approaches accurately and in sufficient detail to allow others to understand, interpret, and critique their work. They should make clear the limitations of an evaluation and its results. Evaluators should discuss in a contextually appropriate way those values, assumptions, theories, methods, results, and analyses that significantly affect the interpretation of the evaluative findings. These statements apply to all aspects of the evaluation, from its initial conceptualization to the eventual use of findings.

B. *Competence: Evaluators provide competent performance to stakeholders.*

1. Evaluators should possess (or, here and elsewhere as appropriate, ensure that the evaluation team possesses) the education, abilities, skills, and experience appropriate to undertake the tasks proposed in the evaluation.

2. Evaluators should practice within the limits of their professional training and competence and should decline to conduct evaluations that fall substantially outside those limits. When declining the commission or request is not feasible or appropriate, evaluators should make clear any significant limitations on the evaluation that might result. Evaluators should make every effort to gain the competence directly or through the assistance of others who possess the required expertise.

3. Evaluators should continually seek to maintain and improve their competencies, in order to provide the highest level of performance in their evaluations. This continuing professional development might include formal coursework and workshops, self-study, evaluations of one's own practice, and working with other evaluators to learn from their skills and expertise.

C. *Integrity/honesty: Evaluators ensure the honesty and integrity of the entire evaluation process.*

(Continued)

EXHIBIT 12-E
(Continued)

1. Evaluators should negotiate honestly with clients and relevant stakeholders concerning the costs, tasks to be undertaken, limitations of methodology, scope of results likely to be obtained, and uses of data resulting from a specific evaluation. It is primarily the evaluator's responsibility to initiate discussion and clarification of these matters, not the client's.

2. Evaluators should record all changes made in the originally negotiated project plans, and the reasons why the changes were made. If those changes would significantly affect the scope and likely results of the evaluation, the evaluator should inform the client and other important stakeholders in a timely fashion (barring good reason to the contrary, before proceeding with further work) of the changes and their likely impact.

3. Evaluators should seek to determine, and where appropriate be explicit about, their own, their clients,' and other stakeholders' interests concerning the conduct and outcomes of an evaluation (including financial, political, and career interests).

4. Evaluators should disclose any roles or relationships they have concerning whatever is being evaluated that might pose a significant conflict of interest with their role as an evaluator. Any such conflict should be mentioned in reports of the evaluation results.

5. Evaluators should not misrepresent their procedures, data, or findings. Within reasonable limits, they should attempt to prevent or correct any substantial misuses of their work by others.

6. If evaluators determine that certain procedures or activities seem likely to produce misleading evaluative information or conclusions, they have the responsibility to communicate their concerns, and the reasons for them, to the client (the one who funds or requests the evaluation). If discussions with the client do not resolve these concerns, so that a misleading evaluation is then implemented, the evaluator may legitimately decline to conduct the evaluation if that is feasible and appropriate. If not, the evaluator should consult colleagues or relevant stakeholders about other proper ways to proceed (options might include, but are not limited to, discussions at a higher level, a dissenting cover letter or appendix, or refusal to sign the final document).

7. Barring compelling reason to the contrary, evaluators should disclose all sources of financial support for an evaluation, and the source of the request for the evaluation.

D. *Respect for people: Evaluators respect the security, dignity, and self-worth of the respondents, program participants, clients, and other stakeholders with whom they interact.*

(Continued)

EXHIBIT 12-E
(Continued)

1. Where applicable, evaluators must abide by current professional ethics and standards regarding risks, harms, and burdens that might be engendered to those participating in the evaluation; regarding informed consent for participation in evaluation; and regarding informing participants about the scope and limits of confidentiality. Examples of such standards include federal regulations about protection of human subjects or the ethical principles of such associations as the American Anthropological Association, the American Educational Research Association, or the American Psychological Association. Although this principle is not intended to extend the applicability of such ethics and standards beyond their current scope, evaluators should abide by them where it is feasible and desirable to do so.

2. Because justified negative or critical conclusions from an evaluation must be explicitly stated, evaluations sometimes produce results that harm client or stakeholder interests. Under this circumstance, evaluators should seek to maximize the benefits and reduce any unnecessary harms that might occur, provided this will not compromise the integrity of the evaluation findings. Evaluators should carefully judge when the benefits from doing the evaluation or in performing certain evaluation procedures should be forgone because of the risks or harms. Where possible, these issues should be anticipated during the negotiation of the evaluation.

3. Knowing that evaluations often will negatively affect the interests of some stakeholders, evaluators should conduct the evaluation and communicate its results in a way that clearly respects the stakeholders' dignity and self-worth.

4. Where feasible, evaluators should attempt to foster the social equity of the evaluation, so that those who give to the evaluation can receive some benefits in return. For example, evaluators should seek to ensure that those who bear the burdens of contributing data and incurring any risks are doing so willingly and that they have full knowledge of, and maximum feasible opportunity to obtain, any benefits that may be produced from the evaluation. When it would not endanger the integrity of the evaluation, respondents or program participants should be informed if and how they can receive services to which they are otherwise entitled without participating in the evaluation.

5. Evaluators have the responsibility to identify and respect differences among participants, such as differences in their culture, religion, gender, disability, age, sexual orientation, and ethnicity, and to be mindful of potential implications of these differences when planning, conducting, analyzing, and reporting their evaluations.

(Continued)

EXHIBIT 12-E
(Continued)

E. *Responsibilities for general and public welfare: Evaluators articulate and take into account the diversity of interests and values that may be related to the general and public welfare.*

1. When planning and reporting evaluations, evaluators should consider including important perspectives and interests of the full range of stakeholders in the object being evaluated. Evaluators should carefully consider the justification when omitting important value perspectives or the views of important groups.

2. Evaluators should consider not only the immediate operations and outcomes of whatever is being evaluated but also the broad assumptions, implications, and potential side effects of it.

3. Freedom of information is essential in a democracy. Hence, barring compelling reason to the contrary, evaluators should allow all relevant stakeholders to have access to evaluative information and should actively disseminate that information to stakeholders if resources allow, If different evaluation results are communicated in forms that are tailored to the interests of different stakeholders, those communications should ensure that each stakeholder group is aware of the existence of the other communications. Communications that are tailored to a given stakeholder
should always include all important results that may bear on interests of that stakeholder. In all cases, evaluators should strive to present results as clearly and simply as accuracy allows so that clients and other stakeholders can easily understand the evaluation process and results.

4. Evaluators should maintain a balance between client needs and other needs. Evaluators necessarily have a special relationship with the client who funds or requests the evaluation. By virtue of that relationship, evaluators must strive to meet legitimate client needs whenever it is feasible and appropriate to do so. However, that relationship can also place evaluators in difficult dilemmas when client interests conflict with other interests, or when client interests conflict with the obligation of evaluators for systematic inquiry, competence, integrity, and respect for people. In these cases, evaluators should explicitly identify and discuss the conflicts with the client and relevant stakeholders, resolve them when possible, determine whether continued work on the evaluation is advisable if the conflicts cannot be resolved, and make clear any significant limitations on the evaluation that might result if the conflict is not resolved.

5. Evaluators have obligations that encompass the public interest and good. These obligations are especially important when evaluators are supported by publicly generated funds, but clear threats to the public good should never be ignored in any evaluation. Because the

(Continued)

Exhibit 12-E
(Continued)

> public interest and good are rarely the same as the interests of any particular group (including those of the client or funding agency), evaluators will usually have to go beyond an analysis of particular stakeholder interests when considering the welfare of society as a whole.

SOURCE: From American Evaluation Association, "Guiding Principles for Evaluators: A Report from the AEA Task Force on Guiding Principles for Evaluators," by D. Newman, M.A. Scheirer, W. Shadish, & C. Wye. Available from http://eval.org/EvaluationDocuments/ aeaprin6.html. Reprinted with permission.

Until such evaluation standards and ethical rules are established, evaluators will have to rely on such general principles as the profession appears to be currently willing to endorse. A useful discussion of the many issues of applied ethics for program evaluation can be found in Newman and Brown (1996).

Evaluators should understand that the *Guiding Principles* do not supersede ethical standards imposed by most human services agencies and universities. Most social research centers and almost all universities have standing committees that deal with research involving humans, and most require that research plans be submitted in advance for approval. Almost all such reviews focus on *informed consent*, upholding the principle that research subjects in most cases should be informed about a research in which they are asked to participate, the risks to which they may be exposed, and should consent to becoming a research subject. In addition, most professional associations (e.g., the American Sociological Association, the American Psychological Association) also have ethics codes that are applicable as well and may provide useful guides to professional issues such as proper acknowledgment to collaborators, avoiding exploitation of research assistants, and so on.

How to apply such guidelines in pursuing evaluations is both easy and difficult. It is easy in the sense that the guidelines uphold general ethical standards that anyone would follow in all situations but difficult in cases when the demands of the research might appear to conflict with a standard. For example, an evaluator in need of business might be tempted to bid on an evaluation that called for using methods with which he is not familiar, an action that might be in conflict with one of the *Guiding Principles*. In another case, an evaluator might worry whether the procedures she intends to use provide sufficient information for participants to understand that there are risks to participation. In such cases, our advice to the evaluator is to consult other experienced evaluators and in any case avoid taking actions that might appear to conflict with the guidelines.

Utilization of Evaluation Results

In the end, the worth of evaluations must be judged by their utility. For this reason, considerable thought and research have been devoted to the use of evaluation results. As a starting point, the conventional three-way classification of the ways evaluations are used is helpful (Leviton and Hughes, 1981; Rich, 1977; Weiss, 1988).

First, evaluators prize the **direct (instrumental) utilization,** that is, the documented and specific use of evaluation findings by decisionmakers and other stakeholders. For example, in developing medical care programs for the poor, Congress and health policy makers used evaluators' data showing that patients of health maintenance organizations are hospitalized fewer days than patients who are treated in the ambulatory clinics of hospitals (Freeman, Kiecolt, and Allen, 1982). More recently, the excellent field experiments conducted by the Manpower Development Research Corporation on workfare conducted under AFDC waivers (Gueron and Pauly, 1991) are influencing how the states are currently reforming welfare.

Second, evaluators value **conceptual utilization**. As Rich (1977) defined it, *conceptual utilization* refers to the use of evaluations to influence thinking about issues in a general way. An example is the current effort to control the costs of delivering health and welfare services, which was stimulated at least in part by evaluations of the efficacy of these services and their costs-to-benefits ratios. These evaluations did not lead to the adoption of specific programs or policies, but they provided evidence that present ways of delivering health care were costly and inefficient.

A third type of use is *persuasive utilization,* the enlisting of evaluation results in efforts either to support or to refute political positions—in other words, to defend or attack the status quo. For example, one of the frequent rationales used by the Reagan administration in defending the cutting of social programs was the lack of clear findings of positive impact in the evaluations of major programs. Persuasive use is similar to speech writers inserting quotes into political speeches, whether they are applicable or not. For the most part, the persuasive use of evaluations is out of the hands of program evaluators and sponsors alike and will not concern us further.

Do Evaluations Have Direct Utility?

Disappointment about the extent of the utilization of evaluations apparently is due to their limited direct or instrumental use. It is clear that many evaluations initiated for their direct utility fell short of that mark. However, it is only in the past two decades that the extent of direct use has been systematically studied. These recent efforts challenge the previously held belief that evaluations do not have direct utility.

One careful study (Leviton and Boruch, 1983), for example, examined the direct use of evaluations sponsored by the U.S. Department of Education. The authors found numerous instances in which the results of evaluations led to important program changes and even more incidents in which they were influential inputs, though not the sole inputs, in the decision-making process.

Chelimsky (1991) also cites several instances in which social science research provided critical knowledge for the development of public policy. Unfortunately, large-scale evaluations typically dominate the printed literature. Many small-scale evaluations, especially those that are diagnostic and formative, have experienced direct use in improving programs, but these studies do not ordinarily find their way into the printed literature.

In summary, there does seem to be a fair degree of instrumental utilization, although a pessimistic view on this point is still widely held among both evaluators and potential consumers of evaluations. Subsequently, we will suggest means to increase the utilization of evaluations. Most of these suggestions are particularly relevant to increasing the direct use of studies. However, it is also important to appropriately value the conceptual use of evaluations.

Conceptual Use of Evaluations

No doubt every evaluator has had moments of glorious dreams in which a grateful world receives with adulation the findings of his or her evaluation and puts the results immediately and directly to use. Most of our dreams must remain dreams. We would argue, however, that the conceptual utilization of evaluations often provides important inputs into policy and program development and should not be compared with finishing the race in second place. Conceptual utilization may not be as visible to peers or sponsors, yet this use of evaluations deeply affects the community as a whole or critical segments of it.

"Conceptual use" includes the variety of ways in which evaluations indirectly have an impact on policies, programs, and procedures. This impact ranges from sensitizing persons and groups to current and emerging social problems to influencing future program and policy development by contributing to the cumulative results of a series of evaluations.

Evaluations perform a sensitizing role by documenting the incidence, prevalence, and distinguishing features of social problems. Diagnostic evaluation activities, described in Chapter 4, have provided clearer and more precise understanding of changes occurring in the family system, critical information on the location and distribution of unemployed persons, and other meaningful descriptions of the social world.

Impact assessments, too, have conceptual utility. A specific example is the current concern with "notch" groups in the development of medical care policy. Evaluations of programs to provide medical care to the poor have found that the very poor, those who are eligible for public programs such as Medicaid, often are adequately provided with health services. Those just above them—in the "notch" group that is not eligible for public programs—tend to fall in the cracks between public assistance and being able to provide for their own care. They have decidedly more difficulty receiving services, and, when seriously ill, represent a major burden on community hospitals, which cannot turn them away yet receive reimbursement neither from the patients nor from the government. Concern with the near-poor, or notch group, is increasing because of their exclusion from a wide range of health, mental health, and social service programs.

An interesting example of a study that had considerable long-term impact is the now classic Coleman report on educational opportunity (Coleman et al., 1966). The initial impetus for this study was a 1964 congressional mandate to the (then) Office of Education to provide information on the quality of educational opportunities provided to minority students in the United States. Its actual effect was much more far-reaching: The report changed the conventional wisdom about the characteristics of good and bad educational settings, turning policy and program interest away from problems of fiscal support to ways of improving teaching methods (Moynihan, 1991).

The conceptual use of evaluation results creeps into the policy and program worlds by a variety of routes, usually circuitous, that are difficult to trace. For example, Coleman's report did not become a Government Printing Office best-seller; it is unlikely that more than a few hundred people actually read it cover to cover. In 1967, a year after his report had been published by the Government Printing Office, Coleman was convinced that it had been buried in the National Archives and would never emerge again. But journalists wrote about it, essayists summarized its arguments, and major editorial writers mentioned it. Through these communication brokers, the findings became known to policymakers in the education field and to politicians at all levels of government.

Eventually, the findings in one form or another reached a wide and influential audience. Indeed, by the time Caplan and his associates (Caplan and Nelson, 1973) questioned influential political figures in Washington about which social scientists had influenced them, Coleman's name was among the most prominently and consistently mentioned.

Some of the conceptual utilizations of evaluations may be described simply as consciousness-raising. For example, the development of early-childhood education programs was stimulated by the evaluation findings resulting from an impact assessment of *Sesame Street.* The evaluation found that although the program did have an effect on young children's educational skills, the magnitude of the effect was not as large as the program staff and sponsors imagined it would be. Prior to the evaluation, some educators were convinced that the program represented the "ultimate" solution and that they could turn their attention to other educational problems. The evaluation findings led to the conviction that early-childhood education was in need of further research and development.

As in the case of direct utilization, evaluators have an obligation to do their work in ways that maximize conceptual utilization. In a sense, however, efforts at maximizing conceptual utilization are more difficult to devise than ones to optimize direct use. To the extent that evaluators are hired guns and turn to new ventures after completing an evaluation, they may not be around or have the resources to follow through on promoting conceptual utilization. Sponsors of evaluations and other stakeholders who more consistently maintain a commitment to particular social policy and social problem areas must assume at least some of the responsibility, if not the major portion, for maximizing the conceptual use of evaluations. Often these parties are in a position to perform the broker function alluded to earlier.

Variables Affecting Utilization

In studies of the use of social research in general, and evaluations in particular, five conditions appear to affect utilization consistently (Leviton and Hughes, 1981):

- Relevance

- Communication between researchers and users

- Information processing by users

- Plausibility of research results

- User involvement or advocacy

The importance of these conditions and their relative contributions to utilization have been carefully studied by Weiss and Bucuvalas (1980). They examined 155 decisionmakers in the mental health field and their reactions to 50 actual research reports. Decisionmakers, they found, apply both a truth test and a utility test in screening social research reports. Truth is judged on two bases: research quality and conformity to prior knowledge and expectations. Utility refers to feasibility potential and the degree of challenge to current policy. The Weiss and Bucuvalas study provides convincing evidence of the complexity of the utilization process (see Exhibit 12-F).

Guidelines for Maximizing Utilization

Out of the research on utilization and the real-world experiences of evaluators, a number of guidelines for increasing utilization have emerged. These have been summarized by Solomon and Shortell (1981) and are briefly noted here for reference.

EXHIBIT 12-F

Truth Tests and
Utility Tests

In coping with incoming floods of information, decisionmakers invoke three basic frames of reference. One is the relevance of the content of the study to their sphere of responsibility, another is the trustworthiness of the study, and the third is the direction that it provides. The latter two frames, which we have called truth and utility tests, are each composed of two interdependent components:

Truth tests—Is the research trustworthy?
  Can I rely on it? Will it hold up under attack?
  The two specific components are
  1. Research quality: Was the research conducted by proper scientific methods?
  2. Conformity to user expectations: Are the results compatible with my experience, knowledge, and values?

Utility tests—Does the research provide direction? Does it yield guidance either for immediate action or for considering alternative approaches to problems? The two specific components are
  1. Action orientation: Does the research show how to make feasible changes in things that can feasibly be changed?
  2. Challenge to the status quo: Does the research challenge current philosophy, program, or practice? Does it offer new perspectives?

Together with relevance (i.e., the match between the topic of the research and the person's job responsibilities), the four components listed above constitute the frames of reference by which decisionmakers assess social science research. Research quality and conformity to user expectations form a single truth test in that their effects are contingent on each other: Research quality is less important for the usefulness of a study when results are congruent with officials' prior knowledge than when results are unexpected or counterintuitive. Action orientation and challenge to the status quo represent alternative functions that a study can serve. They constitute a utility test, since the kind of explicit and practical direction captured by the action orientation frame is more important for a study's usefulness when the study provides little criticism or reorientation (challenge to the status quo) than it is when challenge is high. Conversely, the criticisms of programs and the new perspectives embedded in challenge to the status quo add more to usefulness when a study lacks prescriptions for implementation.

SOURCE: Adapted, with permission, from C. H. Weiss and M. J. Bucuvalas, "Truth Tests and Utility Tests: Decision-Makers' Frames of Reference for Social Science Research," *American Sociological Review*, April 1980, 45:302-313.

1. *Evaluators must understand the cognitive styles of decisionmakers.* For instance, there is no point in presenting a complex piece of analysis to a politician who cannot or will not consume such material. Thus, reports and oral presentations tailored to a predetermined audience may be more appropriate than, say, academic journal articles.

2. *Evaluation results must be timely and available when needed.* Evaluators must, therefore, balance thoroughness and completeness of analysis with timing and accessibility of findings. In doing so, they may have to risk criticism from some of their academic colleagues, whose concepts of scholarship cannot always be met because of the need for rapid results and crisp reporting.

3. *Evaluations must respect stakeholders' program commitments.* The usefulness of evaluations depends on wide participation in the evaluation design process to ensure sensitivity to various stakeholders' interests. Differences in values and outlooks between clients and evaluators should be explicated at the outset of a study and be a determinant of whether a specific evaluation is undertaken by a particular evaluation team.

4. *Utilization and dissemination plans should be part of the evaluation design.* Evaluation findings are most likely to be used if the evaluation effort includes "teaching" potential users the strengths and limitations of the effort, the degree to which one may expect definitive results, how the information from the evaluation can be effectively communicated by decisionmakers to their constituencies, and what criticisms and other reactions may be anticipated.

5. *Evaluations should include an assessment of utilization.* Evaluators and decisionmakers must not only share an understanding of the purposes for which a study is undertaken but also agree on the criteria by which its successful utilization may be judged. However much informality is necessary, an effort should be made to judge the extent to which the uses of findings meet these expectations.

Although these guidelines are relevant to the utilization of all program evaluations, the roles of evaluation consumers do differ. Clearly, these differing roles affect the uses to which information is put and, consequently, the choice of mechanisms for maximizing utility. For example, if evaluations are to influence federal legislation and policies, they must be conducted and "packaged" in ways that meet the needs of congressional staff. For the case of educational evaluation and legislation, Florio, Behrmann, and Goltz (1979) furnished a useful summary of requirements that rings as true today as when it was compiled (see Exhibit 12-G).

Exhibit 12-G

Educational
Evaluation: The
Unmet Potential

The interviewees (congressional staff involved in developing educational legislation) mentioned more than 90 steps that could be taken to improve the use of educational studies in the formation of legislative policy. The most common themes, which reflect the current barriers to such use, are the ways in which research and assessment reports are presented and the failure to meet the needs demanded by the policy cycles in Congress. Staffers struck a common theme of work and information overload problems associated with the job. They rarely have time to evaluate the evaluations, let alone read through the voluminous reports that come across their desks. This was at the root of the repeated call for executive summaries in the front matter of reports, which would allow them to judge the relevance of the contents and determine whether further reading for substance was necessary. Although 16 (61%) of the staffers complained of an information overload problem, 19 also indicated that they were often forced to generate their own data relevant to political and policy questions. As one staffer put it, "We have no overload of useful and understandable information."

The timing of study reports and their relevance to questions before the Congress were major barriers repeatedly mentioned by congressional staff. A senior policy analyst for the Assistant Secretary of Education compared the policy process to a moving train. She suggested that information providers have the obligation to know the policy cycle and meet it on its own terms. The credibility problem is also one that plagues social inquiry. The Deputy Director of the White House Domestic Policy staff said that all social science suffers from the perception that it is unreliable and not policy-relevant. His comments were reflected by several of the staffers interviewed; for example, "Research rarely provides definitive conclusions," or "For every finding, others negate it," or "Educational research can rarely be replicated and there are few standards that can be applied to assess the research products." One went so far as to call project evaluations lies, then reconsidered and called them embellishments.

It must be pointed out that the distinctions among different types of inquiry research, evaluation, data collection, and so on are rarely made by the recipients of knowledge and information. If project evaluations are viewed as fabrications, it reflects negatively on the entire educational inquiry community. Even when policy-relevant research is presented in time to meet the moving train, staffers complain of having too much information that cannot be easily assimilated, or that studies are poorly packaged, contain too much technical jargon, and are too

(Continued)

Exhibit 12-G
(Continued)

self-serving. Several said that researchers write for other researchers and rarely, except in congressionally mandated studies, tailor their language to the decision-making audiences in the legislative process.

SOURCE: Adapted from D. H. Florio, M. M. Behrmann, and D. L. Goltz, "What Do Policy Makers Think of Evaluational Research and Evaluation? Or Do They?" *Educational Evaluation and Policy Analysis*, 1979, 1(6):61-87. Copyright © 1979 by the American Educational Research Association, Washington, DC. Adapted by permission of the publisher.

Epilogue: The Future of Evaluation

There are many reasons to expect continued support of evaluation activities. First, decisionmakers, planners, project staffs, and target participants are increasingly skeptical of common sense and conventional wisdom as sufficient bases on which to design social programs that will achieve their intended goals. Decades of attempts to solve the problems represented by explosive population growth, the unequal distribution of resources within and between societies, popular discontent, crime, educational deficiencies among adults and children, drug and alcohol abuse, and weaknesses in traditional institutions such as the family have led to a realization that these are obstinate and difficult issues. This skepticism has, in turn, led policymakers and decisionmakers to seek ways to learn more quickly and efficiently from their mistakes and to capitalize more rapidly on measures that work.

A second major reason for the growth of evaluation research has been the development of knowledge and technical procedures in the social sciences. The refinement of sample survey procedures has provided an important information-gathering method. When coupled with more traditional experimental methods in the form of field experiments, these procedures become a powerful means of testing social programs. Advances in measurement, statistical theory, and substantive knowledge in the social sciences have added to the ability of social scientists to take on the special tasks of evaluation research.

Finally, there are the changes in the social and political climate of our times. As a society—indeed, as a world—we have come to insist that communal and personal problems are not fixed features of the human condition but can be ameliorated through the reconstruction of social institutions. We believe more than our ancestors did that societies can be improved and that the lot of all persons can be enhanced by the betterment of the disadvantaged and deprived. At the same time, we are confronted with severely limited resources for welfare, health, and other social programs. It is tempting simply to wish away unemployment, crime, homelessness—all the social ills we are too familiar with—and to believe that "moral reconstruction" will diminish the need for effective and efficient social programs. But it is catastrophically naive to think that doing so will solve our problems.

The prognosis is troublesome, in the short term at least, when we contemplate both the variety and number of concerns that require urgent action and the level of resources being committed to controlling and ameliorating them. It is clear that sensible, orderly procedures are required to choose which problems to confront first, and which programs to implement to deal with them. Our position is clear: Systematic evaluations are invaluable to current and future efforts to improve the lot of humankind.

Summary

■ Evaluation is purposeful, applied social research. In contrast to basic research, evaluation is undertaken to solve practical problems. Its practitioners must be conversant with methods from several disciplines and able to apply them to many types of problems. Furthermore, the criteria for judging the work include its utilization and hence its impact on programs and the human condition.

■ Because the value of their work depends on its utilization by others, evaluators must understand the social ecology of the arena in which they work.

■ Evaluation is directed to a range of stakeholders with varying and sometimes conflicting needs, interests, and perspectives. Evaluators must determine the perspective from which a given evaluation should be conducted, explicitly acknowledge the existence of other perspectives, be prepared for criticism even from the sponsors of the evaluation, and adjust their communication to the requirements of various stakeholders.

■ Evaluators must put a high priority on deliberately planning for the dissemination of the results of their work. In particular, they need to become "secondary disseminators" who package their findings in ways that are geared to the needs and competencies of a broad range of relevant stakeholders.

■ An evaluation is only one ingredient in a political process of balancing interests and coming to decisions. The evaluator's role is close to that of an expert witness, furnishing the best information possible under the circumstances; it is not the role of judge and jury.

■ Two significant strains that result from the political nature of evaluation are (1) the different requirements of political time and evaluation time and (2) the need for evaluations to have policy-making relevance and significance. With respect to both of these sets of issues, evaluators must look beyond considerations of technical excellence and pure science, mindful of the larger context in which they are working and the purposes being served by the evaluation.

■ Evaluators are perhaps better described as an aggregate than as a profession. The field is marked by an absence of strong communication among its practitioners and by diversity in disciplinary training, type of schooling, and perspectives on appropriate methods. Although the field's rich diversity is one of its attractions, it also leads to unevenness in competency, lack of consensus on appropriate approaches, and justifiable criticism of the methods used by some evaluators. Among the enduring controversies in the field has been the issue of qualitative and quantitative research. Stated in the abstract, the issue is a false one; the two approaches are suitable for different and complementary purposes.

■ Evaluators are also diverse in their activities and working arrangements. Although there has been considerable debate over whether evaluators should be independent of program staff, there is now little reason to prefer either inside or outside evaluation categorically. What is crucial is that evaluators have a clear understanding of their role in a given situation.

■ A small group of elite evaluation organizations and their staffs occupy a strategic position in the field and account for most large-scale evaluations. As their own methods and standards improve, these organizations are contributing to the movement toward professionalization of the field.

■ With the growing professionalization of the field of evaluation has come a demand for published standards and ethical guidelines. While efforts have been made along these lines, it will probably take some time to develop detailed standards and ethical rules. Meanwhile, evaluators must be guided by general principles and a recognition that their work inevitably involves ethical issues as well as judgments about the quality of their work.

■ Evaluative studies are worthwhile only if they are used. Three types of utilization are direct (instrumental), conceptual, and persuasive. Although in the past, considerable doubt has been shed on the direct utility of evaluations, there is reason to believe they do have an impact on program development and modification. At least as important, the conceptual utilization of evaluations appears to have a definite effect on policy and program development, as well as social priorities, albeit one that is not always easy to trace.

KEY CONCEPTS

Conceptual utilization

Long-term, indirect utilization of the ideas and findings of an evaluation.

Direct (instrumental) utilization

Explicit utilization of specific ideas and findings of an evaluation by decisionmakers and other stakeholders.

Policy significance

The significance of an evaluation's findings for policy and program development (as opposed to their statistical significance).

Policy space

The set of policy alternatives that are within the bounds of acceptability to policymakers at a given point in time.

Primary dissemination

Dissemination of the detailed findings of an evaluation to sponsors and technical audiences.

Secondary dissemination

Dissemination of summarized often simplified findings of evaluations to audiences composed of stakeholders.

Glossary

Accessibility

The extent to which the structural and organizational arrangements facilitate participation in the program.

Accountability

The responsibility of program staff to provide evidence to stakeholders and sponsors that a program is effective and in conformity with its coverage, service, legal, and fiscal requirements.

Accounting perspectives

Perspectives underlying decisions on which categories of goods and services to include as costs or benefits in an efficiency analysis.

Administrative standards

Stipulated achievement levels set by program administrators or other responsible parties, for example, intake for 90% of the referrals within one month. These levels may be set on the basis of past experience, the performance of comparable programs, or professional judgment.

Articulated program theory

An explicitly stated version of program theory that is spelled out in some detail as part of a program's documentation and identity or as a result of efforts by the evaluator and stakeholders to formulate the theory.

Assessment of program process

An evaluative study that answers questions about program operations, implementation, and service delivery. Also known as a process evaluation or an implementation assessment.

Assessment of program theory

An evaluative study that answers questions about the conceptualization and design of a program.

Attrition

The loss of outcome data measured on targets assigned to control or intervention groups, usually because targets cannot be located or refuse to contribute data.

Benefits

Positive program outcomes, usually translated into monetary terms in cost-benefit analysis or compared with costs in cost-effectiveness analysis. Benefits may include both direct and indirect outcomes.

Bias

As applied to program coverage, the extent to which subgroups of a target population are reached unequally by a program.

Black box evaluation

Evaluation of program outcomes without the benefit of an articulated program theory to provide insight into what is presumed to be causing those outcomes and why.

Catchment area

The geographic area served by a program.

Conceptual utilization

Long-term, indirect utilization of the ideas and findings of an evaluation.

Control group

A group of targets that do not receive the program intervention and that is compared on outcome measures with one or more groups that do receive the intervention. Compare *intervention group*.

Cost-benefit analysis

Analytical procedure for determining the economic efficiency of a program, expressed as the relationship between costs and outcomes, usually measured in monetary terms.

Cost-effectiveness analysis

Analytical procedure for determining the efficacy of a program in achieving given intervention outcomes in relation to the program costs.

Costs

Inputs, both direct and indirect, required to produce an intervention.

Coverage

The extent to which a program reaches its intended target population.

Direct (instrumental) utilization

Explicit utilization of specific ideas and findings of an evaluation by decisionmakers and other stakeholders.

Discounting

The treatment of time in valuing costs and benefits of a program in efficiency analyses, that is, the adjustment of costs and benefits to their present values, requiring a choice of discount rate and time frame.

Distributional effects

Effects of programs that result in a redistribution of resources in the general population.

Effect size statistic

A statistical formulation of an estimate of program effect that expresses its magnitude in a standardized form that is comparable across outcome measures using different units or scales. Two of the most commonly used effect size statistics are the *standardized mean difference* and the *odds ratio.*

Efficiency assessment

An evaluative study that answers questions about program costs in comparison to either the monetary value of its benefits or its effectiveness in terms of the changes brought about in the social conditions it addresses.

Empowerment evaluation

A participatory or collaborative evaluation in which the evaluator's role includes consultation and facilitation directed toward the development of the capabilities of the participating stakeholders to conduct evaluation on their own, to use it effectively for advocacy and change, and to have some influence on a program that affects their lives.

Evaluability assessment

Negotiation and investigation undertaken jointly by the evaluator, the evaluation sponsor, and possibly other stakeholders to determine whether a program meets the preconditions for evaluation and, if so, how the evaluation should be designed to ensure maximum utility.

Evaluation questions

A set of questions developed by the evaluator, evaluation sponsor, and other stakeholders; the questions define the issues the evaluation will investigate and are stated in terms such that they can be answered using methods available to the evaluator in a way useful to stakeholders.

Evaluation sponsor

The person, group, or organization that requests or requires the evaluation and provides the resources to conduct it.

Ex ante efficiency analysis

An efficiency (cost-benefit or cost-effectiveness) analysis undertaken prior to program implementation, usually as part of program planning, to estimate net outcomes in relation to costs.

Ex post efficiency analysis

An efficiency (cost-benefit or cost-effectiveness) analysis undertaken after a program's outcomes are known.

Focus group

A small panel of persons selected for their knowledge or perspective on a topic of interest that is convened to discuss the topic with the assistance of a facilitator. The discussion is used to identify important themes or to construct descriptive summaries of views and experiences on the focal topic.

Formative evaluation

Evaluative activities undertaken to furnish information that will guide program improvement.

Impact

See *program effect*.

Impact assessment

An evaluative study that answers questions about program outcomes and impact on the social conditions it is intended to ameliorate. Also known as an impact evaluation or an outcome evaluation.

Impact theory

A causal theory describing cause-and-effect sequences in which certain program activities are the instigating causes and certain social benefits are the effects they eventually produce.

Implementation failure

The program does not adequately perform the activities specified in the program design that are assumed to be necessary for bringing about the intended social improvements. It includes situations in which no service, not enough service, or the wrong service is delivered, or the service varies excessively across the target population.

Implicit program theory

Assumptions and expectations inherent in a program's services and practices that have not been fully articulated and recorded.

Incidence

The number of new cases of a particular problem or condition that arise in a specified area during a specified period of time. Compare *prevalence*.

Independent evaluation

An evaluation in which the evaluator has the primary responsibility for developing the evaluation plan, conducting the evaluation, and disseminating the results.

Internal rate of return

The calculated value for the discount rate necessary for total discounted program benefits to equal total discounted program costs.

Intervention group

A group of targets that receive an intervention and whose outcome measures are compared with those of one or more control groups. Compare *control group.*

Key informants

Persons whose personal or professional position gives them a knowledgeable perspective on the nature and scope of a social problem or a target population and whose views are obtained during a needs assessment.

Management information system (MIS)

A data system, usually computerized, that routinely collects and reports information about the delivery of services to clients and, often, billing, costs, diagnostic and demographic information, and outcome status.

Matching

Constructing a control group by selecting targets (individually or as aggregates) that are identical on specified characteristics to those in an intervention group except for receipt of the intervention.

Mediator variable

In an impact assessment, a proximal outcome that changes as a result of exposure to the program and then, in turn, influences a more distal outcome. The mediator is thus an intervening variable that provides a link in the causal sequence through which the program brings about change in the distal outcome.

Meta-analysis

An analysis of effect size statistics derived from the quantitative results of multiple studies of the same or similar interventions for the purpose of summarizing and comparing the findings of that set of studies.

Moderator variable

In an impact assessment, a variable, such as gender or age, that characterizes subgroups for which program effects may differ.

Needs assessment

An evaluative study that answers questions about the social conditions a program is intended to address and the need for the program.

Net benefits

The total discounted benefits minus the total discounted costs. Also called net rate of return.

Nonequivalent comparison design

A quasi-experimental design in which intervention and control groups are constructed through some means other than random assignment.

Odds ratio

An effect size statistic that expresses the odds of a successful outcome for the intervention group relative to that of the control group.

Opportunity costs

The value of opportunities forgone because of an intervention program.

Organizational plan

Assumptions and expectations about what the program must do to bring about the transactions between the target population and the program that will produce the intended changes in social conditions. The program's organizational plan is articulated from the perspective of program management and encompasses both the functions and activities the program is expected to perform and the human, financial, and physical resources required for that performance.

Outcome

The state of the target population or the social conditions that a program is expected to have changed.

Outcome change

The difference between outcome levels at different points in time. See also *outcome level*.

Outcome level

The status of an outcome at some point in time. See also *outcome*.

Outcome monitoring

The continual measurement and reporting of indicators of the status of the social conditions a program is accountable for improving.

Participatory or collaborative evaluation

An evaluation organized as a team project in which the evaluator and representatives of one or more stakeholder groups work collaboratively in developing the evaluation plan, conducting the evaluation, or disseminating and using the results.

Performance criterion

The standard against which a dimension of program performance is compared so that it can be evaluated.

Policy significance

The significance of an evaluation's findings for policy and program development (as opposed to their statistical significance).

Policy space

The set of policy alternatives that are within the bounds of acceptability to policymakers at a given point in time.

Population at risk

The individuals or units in a specified area with characteristics indicating that they have a significant probability of having or developing a particular condition.

Population in need

The individuals or units in a specified area that currently manifest a particular problematic condition.

Pre-post design

A reflexive control design in which only one measure is taken before and after the intervention.

Prevalence

The total number of existing cases with a particular condition in a specified area at a specified time. Compare *incidence*.

Primary dissemination

Dissemination of the detailed findings of an evaluation to sponsors and technical audiences.

Process evaluation

A form of program evaluation designed to determine whether the program is delivered as intended to the target recipients. Also known as implementation assessment.

Process theory

The combination of the program's organizational plan and its service utilization plan into an overall description of the assumptions and expectations about how the program is supposed to operate.

Program effect

That portion of an outcome change that can be attributed uniquely to a program, that is, with the influence of other sources controlled or removed; also termed the program's impact. See also *outcome change*.

Program evaluation

The use of social research methods to systematically investigate the effectiveness of social intervention programs in ways that are adapted to their political and organizational environments and are designed to inform social action in ways that improve social conditions.

Program goal

A statement, usually general and abstract, of a desired state toward which a program is directed. Compare with program objectives.

Program monitoring

The systematic documentation of aspects of program performance that are indicative of whether the program is functioning as intended or according to some appropriate standard. Monitoring generally involves program performance related to program process, program outcomes, or both.

Program objectives

Specific statements detailing the desired accomplishments of a program together with one or more measurable criteria of success.

Program process monitoring

Process evaluation that is done repeatedly over time.

Program theory

The set of assumptions about the manner in which a program relates to the social benefits it is expected to produce and the strategy and tactics the program has adopted to achieve its goals and objectives. Within program theory we can distinguish *impact theory,* relating to the nature of the change in social conditions brought about by program action, and *process theory,* which depicts the program's organizational plan and service utilization plan.

Quasi-experiment

An impact research design in which intervention and control groups are formed by a procedure other than random assignment.

Randomization

Assignment of potential targets to intervention and control groups on the basis of chance so that every unit in a target population has the same probability as any other to be selected for either group.

Randomized field experiment

A research design conducted in a program setting in which intervention and control groups are formed by random assignment and compared on outcome measures to determine the effects of the intervention. See also *control group; intervention group.*

Rate

The occurrence or existence of a particular condition expressed as a proportion of units in the relevant population (e.g., deaths per 1,000 adults).

Reflexive controls

Measures of an outcome variable taken on participating targets before intervention and used as control observations. See also *pre-post design; time-series design.*

Regression-discontinuity design

A quasi-experimental design in which selection into the intervention or control group is based on the observed value on an appropriate quantitative scale, with targets scoring above a designated cutting point on that scale assigned to one group and those scoring below assigned to the other. Also called a cutting-point design.

Reliability

The extent to which a measure produces the same results when used repeatedly to measure the same thing.

Sample survey

A survey administered to a sample of units in the population. The results are extrapolated to the entire population of interest by statistical projections.

Secondary dissemination

Dissemination of summarized often simplified findings of evaluations to audiences composed of stakeholders.

Secondary effects

Effects of a program that impose costs on persons or groups who are not targets.

Selection bias

Systematic under- or overestimation of program effects that results from uncontrolled differences between the intervention and control groups that would result in differences on the outcome if neither group received the intervention.

Selection modeling

Creation of a multivariate statistical model to "predict" the probability of selection into intervention or control groups in a nonequivalent comparison design. The results of this analysis are used to configure a control variable for selection bias to be incorporated into a second-stage statistical model that estimates the effect of intervention on an outcome.

Sensitivity

The extent to which the values on a measure change when there is a change or difference in the thing being measured.

Service utilization plan

Assumptions and expectations about how the target population will make initial contact with the program and be engaged with it through the completion of the intended services. In its simplest form, a service utilization plan describes the sequence of events through which the intended clients are expected to interact with the intended services.

Shadow prices

Imputed or estimated costs of goods and services not valued accurately in the marketplace. Shadow prices also are used when market prices are inappropriate due to regulation or externalities. Also known as accounting prices.

Snowball sampling

A nonprobability sampling method in which each person interviewed is asked to suggest additional knowledgeable people for interviewing. The process continues until no new names are suggested.

Social indicator

Periodic measurements designed to track the course of a social condition over time.

Social program; social intervention

An organized, planned, and usually ongoing effort designed to ameliorate a social problem or improve social conditions.

Social research methods

Procedures for studying social behavior devised by social scientists that are based on systematic observation and logical rules for drawing inferences from those observations.

Stakeholders

Individuals, groups, or organizations having a significant interest in how well a program functions, for instance, those with decision-making authority over the program, funders and sponsors, administrators and personnel, and clients or intended beneficiaries.

Standardized mean difference

An effect size statistic that expresses the mean outcome difference between an intervention and control group in standard deviation units.

Statistical controls

The use of statistical techniques to adjust estimates of program effects for bias resulting from differences between intervention and control groups that are related to the outcome. The differences to be controlled by these techniques must be represented in measured variables that can be included in the statistical analysis.

Statistical power

The probability that an observed program effect will be statistically significant when, in fact, it represents a real effect. If a real effect is not found to be statistically significant, a Type II error results. Thus, statistical power is one minus the probability of a Type II error. See also *Type II error*.

Summative evaluation

Evaluative activities undertaken to render a summary judgment on certain critical aspects of the program's performance, for instance, to determine if specific goals and objectives were met.

Target

The unit (individual, family, community, etc.) to which a program intervention is directed. All such units within the area served by a program comprise its target population.

Theory failure

The program is implemented as planned but its services do not produce the immediate effects on the participants that are expected or the ultimate social benefits that are intended, or both.

Time-series design

A reflexive control design that relies on a number of repeated measurements of the outcome variable taken before and after an intervention.

Type I error

A statistical conclusion error in which a program effect estimate is found to be statistically significant when, in fact, the program has no effect on the target population.

Type II error

A statistical conclusion error in which a program effect estimate is not found to be statistically significant when, in fact, the program does have an effect on the target population.

Units of analysis

The units on which outcome measures are taken in an impact assessment and, correspondingly, the units on which data are available for analysis. The units of analysis may be individual persons but can also be families, neighborhoods, communities, organizations, political jurisdictions, geographic areas, or any other such entities.

Utilization of evaluation

The use of the concepts and findings of an evaluation by decisionmakers and other stakeholders whether at the day-to-day management level or at broader funding or policy levels.

Validity

The extent to which a measure actually measures what it is intended to measure.

References

Advisory Committee on Head Start Research and Evaluation
1999   *Evaluating Head Start: A Recommended Framework for Studying the Impact of the Head Start Program.* Washington, DC. Department of Health and Human Services.

Affholter, D. P.
1994   "Outcome Monitoring." In J. S. Wholey, H. P. Hatry, and K. E. Newcomer (eds.), *Handbook of Practical Program Evaluation* (pp. 96-118). San Francisco: Jossey-Bass.

Aiken, L. S., S. G. West, D. E. Schwalm, J. L. Carroll, and S. Hsiung
1998   "Comparison of a Randomized and Two Quasi-Experimental Designs in a Single Outcome Evaluation." *Evaluation Review* 22(2):207-244.

American Evaluation Association, Task Force on Guiding Principles for Evaluators
1995   "Guiding Principles for Evaluators." *New Directions for Program Evaluation*, no. 66 (pp. 19-26). San Francisco: Jossey-Bass. Available from http://www.eval.org/Publications/ publications.html#Guiding%20Prin

Ards, S.
1989   "Estimating Local Child Abuse." *Evaluation Review* 13(5):484-515.

AuClaire, P., and I. M. Schwartz
1986   *An Evaluation of Intensive Home-Based Services as an Alternative to Placement for Adolescents and Their Families.* Minneapolis: Hubert Humphrey School of Public Affairs, University of Minnesota.

Averch, H. A.
1994   "The Systematic Use of Expert Judgment." In J. S. Wholey, H. P. Hatry, and K. E. Newcomer (eds.), *Handbook of Practical Program Evaluation* (pp. 293-309). San Francisco: Jossey-Bass.

Baron, R. M., and D. A. Kenny
1986   "The Moderator-Mediator Variable Distinction in Social Psychological Research: Conceptual, Strategic and Statistical Considerations." *Journal of Personality and Social Psychology* 51:1173-1182.

Berk, R. A., and D. Rauma
1983   "Capitalizing on Non-Random Assignment to Treatment: A Regression Continuity Analysis of a Crime Control Program." *Journal of the American Statistical Association* 78 (March): 21-28.

Berkowitz, S.
1996   "Using Qualitative and Mixed-Method Approaches." In R. Reviere, S. Berkowitz, C. C. Carter, and C. G. Ferguson (eds.), *Needs Assessment: A Creative and Practical Guide for Social Scientists* (pp. 121-146). Washington, DC: Taylor & Francis.

Bernstein, I. N., and H. E. Freeman
1975 *Academic and Entrepreneurial Research.* New York: Russell Sage Foundation.

Besharov, D. (ed.)
2003 *Child Well-Being After Welfare Reform.* New Brunswick, NJ: Transaction Books.

Besharov, D., P. Germanis, and P. H. Rossi
1998 *Evaluating Welfare Reform: A Guide for Scholars and Practitioners.* College Park: School of Public Affairs, University of Maryland.

Bickman, L. (ed.)
1987 "Using Program Theory in Evaluation." *New Directions for Program Evaluation,* no. 33. San Francisco: Jossey-Bass.
1990 "Advances in Program Theory." *New Directions for Program Evaluation,* no. 47. San Francisco: Jossey-Bass.

Biglan, A., D. Ary, H. Yudelson, T. E. Duncan, D. Hood, L. James, V. Koehn, Z. Wright, C. Black, D. Levings, S. Smith, and E. Gaiser
1996 "Experimental Evaluation of a Modular Approach to Mobilizing Antitobacco Influences of Peers and Parents," *American Journal of Community Psychology* 24(3): 311-339.

Boruch, R. F.
1997 *Randomized Experiments for Planning and Evaluation: A Practical Guide.* Thousand Oaks, CA: Sage.

Boruch, R. F., M. Dennis, and K. Carter-Greer
1988 "Lessons From the Rockefeller Foundation's Experiments on the Minority Female Single Parent Program." *Evaluation Review* 12(4):396-426.

Boruch, R. F., and W. Wothke
1985 "Seven Kinds of Randomization Plans for Designing Field Experiments." In R. F. Boruch and W. Wothke (eds.), *Randomization and Field Experimentation. New Directions for Program Evaluation,* no. 28. San Francisco: Jossey-Bass.

Braden, J. P., and T. J. Bryant
1990 "Regression Discontinuity Designs: Applications for School Psychologists." *School Psychology Review* 19(2):232-239.

Bremner, R.
1956 *From the Depths: The Discovery of Poverty in America.* New York: New York University Press.

Brindis, C., D. C. Hughes, N. Halfon, and P. W. Newacheck
1998 "The Use of Formative Evaluation to Assess Integrated Services for Children." *Evaluation & the Health Professions* 21(1):66-90.

Broder, I. E.
1988 "A Study of the Birth and Death of a Regulatory Agenda: The Case of the EPA Noise Program." *Evaluation Review* 12(3):291-309.

Bulmer, M.
1982   *The Uses of Social Research.* London: Allen & Unwin.

Burt, M., and B. Cohen
1988   *Feeding the Homeless: Does the Prepared Meals Provision Help?* Report to Congress on the Prepared Meal Provision, vols. 1 and 2. Washington, DC: Urban Institute.

Calsyn, R. J., G. A. Morse, W. D. Klinkenberg, and M. L. Trusty
1997   "Reliability and Validity of Self-Report Data of Homeless Mentally Ill Individuals." *Evaluation and Program Planning* 20(1):47-54.

Campbell, D. T.
1969   "Reforms as Experiments." *American Psychologist* 24 (April): 409-429.
1991   "Methods for the Experimenting Society," *Evaluation Practice* 12(3):223-260.
1996   "Regression Artifacts in Time-Series and Longitudinal Data." *Evaluation and Program Planning* 19(4):377-389.

Campbell, D. T., and R. F. Boruch
1975   "Making the Case for Randomized Assignment to Treatments by Considering the Alternatives: Six Ways in Which Quasi-Experimental Evaluations in Compensatory Education Tend to Underestimate Effects." In C. A. Bennett and A. A. Lumsdaine (eds.), *Evaluation and Experiment* (pp. 195-296). New York: Academic Press.

Campbell, D. T., and J. C. Stanley
1966   *Experimental and Quasi-Experimental Designs for Research.* Skokie, IL: Rand McNally.

Caplan, N., and S. D. Nelson
1973   "On Being Useful: The Nature and Consequences of Psychological Research on Social Problems." *American Psychologist* 28 (March): 199-211.

Card, J. J., C. Greeno, and J. L. Peterson
1992   "Planning an Evaluation and Estimating Its Cost." *Evaluation & the Health Professions* 15(4):75-89.

Chelimsky, E.
1987   "The Politics of Program Evaluation." *Society* 25(1):24-32.
1991   "On the Social Science Contribution to Governmental Decision-Making." *Science* 254 (October): 226-230.
1997   "The Coming Transformations in Evaluation." In E. Chelimsky and W. R. Shadish (eds.), *Evaluation for the 21st Century: A Handbook* (pp. 1-26). Thousand Oaks, CA: Sage.

Chelimsky, E., and W. R. Shadish (eds.)
1997   *Evaluation for the 21st Century: A Handbook.* Thousand Oaks, CA: Sage.

Chen, H.-T.
1990   *Theory-Driven Evaluations.* Newbury Park, CA: Sage.

Chen, H.-T., and P. H. Rossi
1980   "The Multi-Goal, Theory-Driven Approach to Evaluation: A Model Linking Basic and Applied Social Science." *Social Forces* 59 (September): 106-122.

Chen, H.-T., J. C. S. Wang, and L.-H. Lin
1997   "Evaluating the Process and Outcome of a Garbage Reduction Program in Taiwan." *Evaluation Review* 21(1):27-42.

Ciarlo, J. A., and D. L. Tweed, D. L. Shern, L. A. Kirkpatrick, and N. Sachs-Ericsson
1992   "Validation of Indirect Methods to Estimate Need for Mental Health Services: Concepts, Strategies, and General Conclusions." *Evaluation and Program Planning* 15(2):115-131.

Cicirelli, V. G., et al.
1969   *The Impact of Head Start.* Athens, OH: Westinghouse Learning Corporation and Ohio University.

Cohen, J.
1988   *Statistical Power Analysis for the Behavioral Sciences,* 2nd ed. Hillsdale, NJ: Lawrence Erlbaum.

Coleman, J. S., et al.
1966   *Equality of Educational Opportunity.* Washington, DC: Government Printing Office.

Cook, T. D., and D. T. Campbell
1979   *Quasi-Experimentation Design and Analysis Issues for Field Settings.* Skokie, IL: Rand McNally.

Cooper, H., and L. V. Hedges (eds.).
1994   *The Handbook of Research Synthesis.* New York: Russell Sage Foundation.

Cordray, D. S.
1993   "Prospective Evaluation Syntheses: A Multi-Method Approach to Assisting Policy-Makers." In M. Donker and J. Derks (eds.), *Rekenschap: Evaluatie-onderzoek in Nederland, de stand van zaken* (pp. 95-110). Utrecht, the Netherlands: Centrum Geestelijke Volksgezondheid.

Coyle, S. L., R. F. Boruch, and C. F. Turner (eds.)
1991   *Evaluating Aids Prevention Programs.* Washington, DC: National Academy Press.

Cronbach, L. J.
1982   *Designing Evaluations of Educational and Social Programs.* San Francisco: Jossey-Bass.

Cronbach, L. J., and Associates
1980   *Toward Reform of Program Evaluation.* San Francisco: Jossey-Bass.

Culhane, D. P., and R. Kuhn
1998   "Patterns and Determinants of Public Shelter Utilization Among Homeless Adults in New York City and Philadelphia." *Journal of Policy Analysis and Management,* 17(1):23-43.

Datta, L.
1977   "Does It Work When It Has Been Tried? And Half Full or Half Empty?" In M. Guttentag and S. Saar (eds.), *Evaluation Studies Review Annual,* vol. 2 (pp. 301-319). Beverly Hills, CA: Sage.
1980   "Interpreting Data: A Case Study From the Career Intern Program Evaluation." *Evaluation Review* 4 (August): 481-506.

Dean, D. L.
1994   "How to Use Focus Groups." In J. S. Wholey, H. P. Hatry, and K. E. Newcomer (eds.), *Handbook of Practical Program Evaluation* (pp. 338-349). San Francisco: Jossey-Bass.

Dennis, M. L.
1990   "Assessing the Validity of Randomized Field Experiments: An Example From Drug Abuse Research." *Evaluation Review* 14(4):347-373.

Dennis, M. L., and R. F. Boruch
1989   "Randomized Experiments for Planning and Testing Projects in Developing Countries: Threshold Conditions." *Evaluation Review* 13(3):292-309.

DeVellis, R. F.
2003   *Scale Development: Theory and Applications,* 2nd ed. Thousand Oaks, CA: Sage.

Devine, J. A., J. D. Wright, and C. J. Brody
1995   "An Evaluation of an Alcohol and Drug Treatment Program for Homeless Substance Abusers." *Evaluation Review* 19(6):620-645.

Dibella, A.
1990   "The Research Manager's Role in Encouraging Evaluation Use." *Evaluation Practice* 11(2):115-119.

Dishion, T. J., J. McCord, and F. Poulin
1999   When interventions harm: Peer groups and problem behavior. *American Psychologist* 54:755-764.

Duckart, J. P.
1998   "An Evaluation of the Baltimore Community Lead Education and Reduction Corps (CLEARCorps) Program." *Evaluation Review* 22(3):373-402.

Dunford, F. W.
1990   "Random Assignment: Practical Considerations From Field Experiments." *Evaluation and Program Planning* 13(2):125-132.

Eddy, D. M.
1992   "Cost-Effectiveness Analysis: Is It Up to the Task?" *Journal of the American Medical Association* 267:3342-3348.

Elmore, R. F.
1980   "Backward Mapping: Implementation Research and Policy Decisions." *Political Science Quarterly* 94(4):601-616.

Fetterman, D. M., S. J. Kaftarian, and A. Wandersman (eds.)
1996   *Empowerment Evaluation: Knowledge and Tools for Self-Assessment & Accountability*. Thousand Oaks, CA: Sage.

Figlio, D. N.
1995   "The Effect of Drinking Age Laws and Alcohol-Related Crashes: Time-Series Evidence From Wisconsin." *Journal of Policy Analysis and Management* 14(4):555-566.

Fink, A.
1995   *Evaluation for Education and Psychology*. Thousand Oaks, CA: Sage.

Florio, D. H., M. M. Behrmann, and D. L. Goltz
1979   "What Do Policy Makers Think of Evaluational Research and Evaluation? Or Do They?"
        Educational Evaluation and Policy Analysis 1 (January): 61-87.

Fournier, D. M.
1995   "Establishing Evaluative Conclusions: A Distinction Between General and
        Working Logic." *New Directions for Evaluation*, no. 68 (pp. 15-32). San Francisco: Jossey-
        Bass.

Fowler, F. L.
1993   *Survey Research Methods,* 2nd ed. Newbury Park, CA: Sage.

Fraker, T. F., A. P. Martini, and J. C. Ohls
1995   "The Effect of Food Stamp Cashout on Food Expenditures: An Assessment of the Find-
        ings From Four Demonstrations." *Journal of Human Resources* 30(4):633-649.

Fraker, T., and R. Maynard
1984   *The Use of Comparison Group Designs in Evaluations of Employment-Related Programs.*
        Princeton, NJ: Mathematica Policy Research.

Freeman, H. E.
1977   "The Present Status of Evaluation Research." In M. A. Guttentag and S. Saar (eds.), *Eval-
        uation Studies Review Annual,* vol. 2 (pp. 17-51). Beverly Hills, CA: Sage.

Freeman, H. E., K. J. Kiecolt, and H. M. Allen III
1982   "Community Health Centers: An Initiative of Enduring Utility." *Milbank Memorial Fund
        Quarterly/Health and Society* 60(2):245-267.

Freeman, H. E., and P. H. Rossi
1984   "Furthering the Applied Side of Sociology." *American Sociological Review* 49(4):
        571-580.

Freeman, H. E., P. H. Rossi, and S. R. Wright
1980   *Doing Evaluations.* Paris: Organization for Economic Cooperation and
        Development.

Freeman, H. E., and M. A. Solomon
1979   "The Next Decade in Evaluation Research." *Evaluation and Program Planning* 2 (March):
        255-262.

French, M. T., C. J. Bradley, B. Calingaert, M. L. Dennis, and G. T. Karuntzos
1994   "Cost Analysis of Training and Employment Services in Methadone Treatment." *Evalua-
        tion and Program Planning* 17(2):107-120.

Galster, G. C., T. F. Champney, and Y. Williams
1994   "Costs of Caring for Persons With Long-Term Mental Illness in Alternative Residential
        Settings." *Evaluation and Program Planning* 17(3):239-348.

Glasgow, R. E., H. Lando, J. Hollis, S. G. McRae, et al.
1993 "A Stop-Smoking Telephone Help Line That Nobody Called." *American Journal of Public Health* 83(2):252-253.

Glasser, W.
1975 *Reality Therapy.* New York: Harper and Row.

Gramblin, E. M.
1990 *A Guide to Benefit-Cost Analysis.* Englewood Cliffs, NJ: Prentice Hall.

Gramlich, E. M., and P. P. Koshel
1975 *Educational Performance Contracting: An Evaluation of an Experiment.* Washington, DC: Brookings Institution.

Gray, T., C. R. Larsen, P. Haynes, and K. W. Olson
1991 "Using Cost-Benefit Analysis to Evaluate Correctional Sentences." *Evaluation Review* 15(4):471-481.

Greenberg, D. H., and U. Appenzeller
1998 *Cost Analysis Step by Step: A How-to Guide for Planners and Providers of Welfare-to-Work and Other Employment and Training Programs.* New York: Manpower Demonstration Research Corporation.

Greene, J. C.
1988 "Stakeholder Participation and Utilization in Program Evaluation." *Evaluation Review* 12(2):91-116.

Greene, J. C., and V. J. Caracelli (eds.)
1997 "Advances in Mixed-Method Evaluation: The Challenges and Benefits of Integrating Diverse Paradigms." *New Directions for Evaluation*, no. 74. San Francisco: Jossey-Bass.

Greene, W. H.
1993 "Selection-Incidental Truncation." In W. H. Greene, *Econometric Analysis* (pp. 706-715). New York: Macmillan.

Guba, E. G., and Y. S. Lincoln
1987 "The Countenances of Fourth Generation Evaluation: Description, Judgment, and Negotiation." In D. Palumbo (ed.), *The Politics of Program Evaluation* (pp. 203-234). Beverly Hills, CA: Sage.
1989 *Fourth Generation Evaluation.* Newbury Park, CA: Sage.
1994 "Competing Paradigms in Qualitative Research." In N. K. Denzin and Y. S. Lincoln (eds.), *Handbook of Qualitative Research* (pp. 105-117). Thousand Oaks, CA: Sage.

Gueron, J. M., and E. Pauly
1991 *From Welfare to Work.* New York: Russell Sage Foundation.

Halvorson, H. W., D. K. Pike, F. M. Reed, M. W. McClatchey, and C. A. Gosselink
1993 "Using Qualitative Methods to Evaluate Health Service Delivery in Three Rural Colorado Communities." *Evaluation & the Health Professions* 16(4):434-447.

Hamilton, J.
1994   *Time Series Analysis.* Princeton, NJ: Princeton University Press.

Hamilton, Rabinowitz, and Alschuler, Inc.
1987   *The Changing Face of Misery: Los Angeles' Skid Row Area in Transition—Housing and Social Services Needs of Central City East.* Los Angeles: Community Redevelopment Agency.

Hatry, H. P.
1994   "Collecting Data From Agency Records." In J. S. Wholey, H. P. Hatry, and K. E. Newcomer (eds.), *Handbook of Practical Program Evaluation.* San Francisco: Jossey-Bass.
1999   *Performance Measurement: Getting Results.* Washington, DC: Urban Institute Press.

Haveman, R. H.
1987   "Policy Analysis and Evaluation Research After Twenty Years." *Policy Studies Journal* 16(2):191-218.

Hayes, S. P., Jr.
1959   *Evaluating Development Projects.* Paris: UNESCO.

Heckman, J. J., and V. J. Hotz
1989   "Choosing Among Alternative Nonexperimental Methods for Estimating the Impact of Social Programs: The Case of Manpower Training." *Journal of the American Statistical Association,* 84(408):862-880 (with discussion).

Heckman, J. J., and R. Robb
1985   "Alternative Methods for Evaluating the Impact of Interventions: An Overview." *Journal of Econometrics* 30:239-267.

Hedrick, T. E., L. Bickman, and D. Rog
1992   *Applied Research Design: A Practical Guide.* Thousand Oaks, CA: Sage.

Heinsman, D. T., and W. R. Shadish
1996   "Assignment Methods in Experimentation: When Do Nonrandomized Experiments Approximate the Answers From Randomized Experiments?" *Psychological Methods* 1:154-169.

Henry, G. T.
1990   *Practical Sampling.* Newbury Park, CA: Sage.

Herman, D. B., E. L. Struening, and S. M. Barrow
1994   "Self-Reported Needs for Help Among Homeless Men and Women." *Evaluation and Program Planning* 17(3):249-256.

Hoch, C.
1990   "The Rhetoric of Applied Sociology: Studying Homelessness in Chicago." *Journal of Applied Sociology* 7:11-24.

Hsu, L. M.
1995   "Regression Toward the Mean Associated With Measurement Error and the Identification of Improvement and Deterioration in Psychotherapy." *Journal of Consulting & Clinical Psychology* 63(1):141-144.

Humphreys, K., C. S. Phibbs, and R. H. Moos
1996   "Addressing Self-Selection Effects in Evaluations of Mutual Help Groups and Profes-sional Mental Health Services: An Introduction to Two-Stage Sample Selection Models." *Evaluation and Program Planning* 19(4):301-308.

Jerrell, J. M., and T.-W. Hu
1996   "Estimating the Cost Impact of Three Dual Diagnosis Treatment Programs." *Evaluation Review* 20(2):160-180.

Joint Committee on Standards for Educational Evaluation
1994   *The Program Evaluation Standards,* 2nd ed. Newbury Park, CA. Sage.

Jones-Lee, M. W.
1994   "Safety and the Saving of Life: The Economics of Safety and Physical Risk." In R. Layard and S. Glaister (eds.), *Cost-Benefit Analysis,* 2nd ed. (pp. 290-318). Cambridge, UK: Cam-bridge University Press.

Kanouse, D. E., S. H. Berry, E. M. Gorman, E. M. Yano, S. Carson, and A. Abrahamse
1991   *AIDS-Related Knowledge, Attitudes, Beliefs, and Behaviors in Los Angeles County*. Santa Monica, CA: RAND.

Kaye, E., and J. Bell
1993   *Final Report: Evaluability Assessment of Family Preservation Programs*. Arlington, VA: James Bell Associates.

Kazdin, A. E.
1982   *Single-Case Research Designs.* New York: Oxford University Press.

Keehley, P., S. Medlin, S. MacBride, and L. Longmire
1996   *Benchmarking for Best Practices in the Public Sector: Achieving Performance Break-throughs in Federal, State, and Local Agencies.* San Francisco: Jossey-Bass.

Kennedy, C. H., S. Shikla, and D. Fryxell
1997   "Comparing the Effects of Educational Placement on the Social Relationships of Inter-mediate School Students with Severe Disabilities." *Exceptional Children* 64(1):31-47.

Kershaw, D., and J. Fair
1976   *The New Jersey Income-Maintenance Experiment*, vol. 1. New York: Academic Press.

Kirschner Associates, Inc.
1975   *Programs for Older Americans: Setting and Monitoring. A Reference Manual.* Washington, DC: U.S. Department of Health, Education and Welfare, Office of Human Development.

Kraemer, H. C., and S. Thiemann
1987   *How Many Subjects? Statistical Power Analysis in Research*. Newbury Park, CA: Sage.

Krueger, R. A.
1988   *Focus Groups: A Practical Guide for Applied Research*. Newbury Park, CA: Sage.

LaLonde, R.
1986   "Evaluating the Econometric Evaluations of Training Programs." *American Economic Review* 76:604-620.

Landsberg, G.
1983   "Program Utilization and Service Utilization Studies: A Key Tool for Evaluation." *New Directions for Program Evaluation*, no. 20 (pp. 93-103). San Francisco: Jossey-Bass.

Levin, H. M., G. V. Glass, and G. R. Meister
1987   "Cost-Effectiveness of Computer-Assisted Instruction." *Evaluation Review* 11(1):50-72.

Levin, H. M., and P. J. McEwan
2001   *Cost-Effectiveness Analysis,* 2nd ed. Thousand Oaks, CA: Sage.

Levine, A., and M. Levine
1977   "The Social Context of Evaluation Research: A Case Study." *Evaluation Quarterly* 1(4):515-542.

Levine, R. A., M. A. Solomon, and G. M. Hellstern (eds.)
1981   *Evaluation Research and Practice: Comparative and International Perspectives.* Beverly Hills, CA: Sage.

Leviton, L. C., and R. F. Boruch
1983   "Contributions of Evaluations to Educational Programs." *Evaluation Review* 7(5):563-599.

Leviton, L. C., and E. F. X. Hughes
1981   "Research on the Utilization of Evaluations: A Review and Synthesis." *Evaluation Review* 5(4):525-548.

Lipsey, M. W.
1990   *Design Sensitivity: Statistical Power for Experimental Research.* Newbury Park, CA: Sage.
1993   "Theory as Method: Small Theories of Treatments." *New Directions for Program Evaluation*, no. 57 (pp. 5-38). San Francisco: Jossey-Bass.
1997   "What Can You Build With Thousands of Bricks? Musings on the Cumulation of Knowledge in Program Evaluation." *New Directions for Evaluation*, no. 76 (pp. 7-24). San Francisco: Jossey-Bass.
1998   "Design Sensitivity: Statistical Power for Applied Experimental Research." In L. Bickman and D. J. Rog (eds.), *Handbook of Applied Social Research Methods* (pp. 39-68). Thousand Oaks, CA: Sage.

Lipsey, M. W., and J. A. Pollard
1989   "Driving Toward Theory in Program Evaluation: More Models to Choose From." *Evaluation and Program Planning* 12:317-328.

Lipsey, M. W., and D. B. Wilson
1993   "The Efficacy of Psychological, Educational, and Behavioral Treatment: Confirmation From Meta-Analysis." *American Psychologist* 48(12):1181-1209.
2001   *Practical Meta-Analysis.* Thousand Oaks, CA: Sage.

Loehlin, J. C.
1992   *Latent Variable Models: An Introduction to Factor, Path, and Structural Analysis.* Hillsdale, NJ: Lawrence Erlbaum.

Luepker, R. V., C. L. Perry, S. M. McKinlay, P. R. Nader, G. S. Parcel, E. J. Stone, L. S. Webber, J. P. Elder, H. A. Feldman, C. C. Johnson, S. H. Kelder, and M. Wu
1996   "Outcomes of a Field Trial to Improve Children's Dietary Patterns and Physical Activity: The Child and Adolescent Trial for Cardiovascular Health (CATCH)." *Journal of the American Medical Association* 275 (March): 768-776.

Lynn, L. E., Jr.
1980   *Designing Public Policy.* Santa Monica, CA: Scott, Foresman.

MacKinnon, D. P., and J. H. Dwyer
1993   "Estimating Mediated Effects in Prevention Studies." *Evaluation Review* 17:144-158.

Madaus, G. F., and D. Stufflebeam (eds.)
1989   *Educational Evaluation: The Classic Works of Ralph W. Tyler.* Boston: Kluwer Academic Publishers.

Mark, M. M., and R. L. Shotland
1985   "Stakeholder-Based Evaluation and Value Judgments." *Evaluation Review* 9:605-626.

Martin, L. L., and P. M. Kettner
1996   *Measuring the Performance of Human Service Programs.* Thousand Oaks, CA: Sage.

Mathematica Policy Research
1983   *Final Report of the Seattle-Denver Income Maintenance Experiment*, vol. 2. Princeton, NJ: Author.

McCleary, R., and R. Hay, Jr.
1980   *Applied Time Series Analysis for the Social Sciences.* Beverly Hills, CA: Sage.

McFarlane, J.
1989   "Battering During Pregnancy: Tip of an Iceberg Revealed." *Women and Health* 15(3):69-84.

McKillip, J.
1987   *Need Analysis: Tools for the Human Services and Education.* Newbury Park, CA: Sage.
1998   "Need Analysis: Process and Techniques." In L. Bickman and D. J. Rog (eds.), *Handbook of Applied Social Research Methods* (pp. 261-284). Thousand Oaks, CA: Sage.

McLaughlin, M. W.
1975   *Evaluation and Reform: The Elementary and Secondary Education Act of 1965/Title I.* Cambridge, MA: Ballinger.

Mercier, C.
1997   "Participation in Stakeholder-Based Evaluation: A Case Study." *Evaluation and Program Planning* 20(4):467-475.

Meyers, M. K., B. Glaser, and K. MacDonald
1998   "On the Front Lines of Welfare Delivery: Are Workers Implementing Policy Reforms?" *Journal of Policy Analysis and Management* 17(1):1-22.

Mielke, K. W., and J. W. Swinehart
1976 *Evaluation of the "Feeling Good" Television Series*. New York: Children's Television Workshop.

Miller, C., V. Knox, P. Auspos, J. A. Hunter-Manns, and A. Prenstein
1997 *Making Welfare Work and Work Pay: Implementation and 18 Month Impacts of the Minnesota Family Investment Program*. New York: Manpower Demonstration Research Corporation.

Miller, G., and J. A. Holstein (eds.)
1993 *Constructivist Controversies: Issues in Social Problems Theory*. New York: Aldine de Gruyter.

Mishan, E. J.
1988 *Cost-Benefit Analysis,* 4th ed. London: Allen & Unwin.

Mitra, A.
1994 "Use of Focus Groups in the Design of Recreation Needs Assessment Questionnaires." *Evaluation and Program Planning* 17(2):133-140.

Mohr, L. B.
1995 *Impact Analysis for Program Evaluation*, 2nd ed. Thousand Oaks, CA: Sage.

Mosteller, F., and R. Boruch (eds.)
2002 *Evidence Matters: Randomized Trials in Education Research*. Washington, DC: Brookings Institution.

Moynihan, D. P.
1991 "Educational Goals and Political Plans." *The Public Interest* 102 (winter): 32-48.
1996 *Miles to Go: A Personal History of Social Policy*. Cambridge, MA: Harvard University Press.

Murray, D.
1998 *Design and Analysis of Group-Randomized Trials*. New York: Oxford University Press.

Murray, S.
1980 *The National Evaluation of the PUSH for Excellence Project*. Washington, DC: American Institutes for Research.

Nas, T. F.
1996 *Cost-Benefit Analysis: Theory and Application*. Thousand Oaks, CA: Sage.

Nelson, R. H.
1987 "The Economics Profession and the Making of Public Policy." *Journal of Economic Literature* 35(1):49-91.

Newman, D. L., and R. D. Brown
1996 *Applied Ethics for Program Evaluation*. Thousand Oaks, CA: Sage.

Nowacek, G. A., P. M. O'Malley, R. A. Anderson, and F. E. Richards
1990 "Testing a Model of Diabetes Self-Care Management: A Causal Model Analysis With LISREL." *Evaluation & the Health Professions* 13(3):298-314.

Nunnally, J. C., and I. H. Bernstein
1994   *Psychometric Theory,* 3rd ed. New York: McGraw-Hill.

Office of Income Security
1983   *Overview of the Seattle-Denver Income Maintenance Final Report.* Washington, DC: U.S. Department of Health and Human Services.

Oman, R. C., and S. R. Chitwood
1984   "Management Evaluation Studies: Factors Affecting the Acceptance of Recommendations." *Evaluation Review* 8(3):283-305.

Palumbo, D. J., and M. A. Hallett
1993   "Conflict Versus Consensus Models in Policy Evaluation and Implementation." *Evaluation and Program Planning* 16(1):11-23.

Pancer, S. M., and A. Westhues
1989   "A Developmental Stage Approach to Program Planning and Evaluation." *Evaluation Review* 13(1):56-77.

Parker, R. N., and L. Rebhun
1995   *Alcohol and Homicide: A Deadly Combination of Two American Traditions.* Albany: State University of New York Press.

Patton, M. Q.
1986   *Utilization-Focused Evaluation,* 2nd ed. Beverly Hills, CA: Sage.
1997   *Utilization-Focused Evaluation: The New Century Text,* 3rd ed. Thousand Oaks, CA: Sage.

Phillips, K. A., R. A. Lowe, J. G. Kahn, P. Lurie, A. L. Avins, and D. Ciccarone
1994   "The Cost Effectiveness of HIV Testing of Physicians and Dentists in the United States." *Journal of the American Medical Association* 271:851-858.

Quinn, D. C.
1996   *Formative Evaluation of Adapted Work Services for Alzheimer's Disease Victims: A Framework for Practical Evaluation in Health Care.* Doctoral dissertation, Vanderbilt University.

Raudenbush, S. W., and A. S. Bryk
2002   *Hierarchical Linear Models: Applications and Data Analysis Methods,* 2nd ed. Newbury Park, CA: Sage

Reichardt, C. S., and C. A. Bormann
1994   "Using Regression Models to Estimate Program Effects." In J. S. Wholey, H. P. Hatry, and K. E. Newcomer (eds.), *Handbook of Practical Program Evaluation* (pp. 417-455). San Francisco: Jossey-Bass.

Reichardt, C. S., and S. F. Rallis (eds.)
1994   "The Qualitative Quantitative Debate: New Perspectives." *New Directions for Program Evaluation,* no. 61. San Francisco: Jossey-Bass.

Reichardt, C. S., W. M. K. Trochim, and J. C. Cappelleri
1995   "Reports of the Death of Regression-Discontinuity Analysis Are Greatly Exaggerated." *Evaluation Review* 19(1):39-63.

Reineke, R. A.
1991   "Stakeholder Involvement in Evaluation: Suggestions for Practice." *Evaluation Practice* 12(1):39-44.

Reviere, R., S. Berkowitz, C. C. Carter, and C. G. Ferguson (eds.)
1996   *Needs Assessment: A Creative and Practical Guide for Social Scientists*. Washington, DC: Taylor & Francis.

Rich, R. F.
1977   "Uses of Social Science Information by Federal Bureaucrats." In C. H. Weiss (ed.), *Using Social Research for Public Policy Making* (pp. 199-211). Lexington, MA: D.C. Heath.

Riecken, H. W., and R. F. Boruch (eds.)
1974   *Social Experimentation: A Method for Planning and Evaluating Social Intervention*. New York: Academic Press.

Robertson, D. B.
1984   "Program Implementation versus Program Design." *Policies Study Review* 3:391-405.

Robins, P. K., et al. (eds.)
1980   *A Guaranteed Annual Income: Evidence From a Social Experiment*. New York: Academic Press.

Rog, D. J.
1994   "Constructing Natural 'Experiments.'" In J. S. Wholey, H. P. Hatry, and K. E. Newcomer (eds.), *Handbook of Practical Program Evaluation* (pp. 119-132). San Francisco: Jossey-Bass.

Rog, D. J., K. L. McCombs-Thornton, A. M. Gilert-Mongelli, M. C. Brito, et al.
1995   "Implementation of the Homeless Families Program: 2. Characteristics, Strengths, and Needs of Participant Families." *American Journal of Orthopsychiatry*, 65(4):514-528.

Rosenbaum, P. R., and D. B. Rubin
1983   "The Central Role of the Propensity Score in Observational Studies for Causal Effects." *Biometrika* 70(1):41-55.
1984   "Reducing Bias in Observational Studies using Subclassification on the Propensity Score." *Journal of the American Statistical Association* 79(387):516-524.

Ross, H. L., D. T. Campbell, and G. V. Glass
1970   "Determining the Social Effects of a Legal Reform: The British Breathalyzer Crackdown of 1967." *American Behavioral Scientist* 13 (March/April): 494-509.

Rossi, P. H.
1978   "Issues in the Evaluation of Human Services Delivery." *Evaluation Quarterly* 2(4):573-599.
1987   "No Good Applied Research Goes Unpunished!" *Social Science and Modern Society* 25(1):74-79.
1989   *Down and Out in America: The Origins of Homelessness*. Chicago: University of Chicago Press.

1997   "Program Outcomes: Conceptual and Measurement Issues." In E. J. Mullen and J. Magnabosco (eds.), *Outcome and Measurement in the Human Services: Cross-Cutting Issues and Methods.* Washington, DC: National Association of Social Workers.

2001   *Four Evaluations of Welfare Reform: What Will Be Learned?* The Welfare Reform Academy. College Park: University of Maryland, School of Public Affairs.

Rossi, P. H., R. A. Berk, and K. J. Lenihan
1980   *Money, Work and Crime: Some Experimental Evidence.* New York: Academic Press.

Rossi, P. H., G. A. Fisher, and G. Willis
1986   *The Condition of the Homeless of Chicago.* Chicago, IL, and Amherst, MA: Social and Demographic Research Institute and NORC: A Social Science Research Institute.

Rossi, P. H., and K. Lyall
1976   *Reforming Public Welfare.* New York: Russell Sage Foundation.

Rossi, P. H., and W. Williams
1972   *Evaluating Social Programs.* New York: Seminar Press.

Rutman, L.
1980   *Planning Useful Evaluations: Evaluability Assessment.* Beverly Hills, CA: Sage.

Savaya, R.
1998   "The Potential and Utilization of an Integrated Information System at a Family and Marriage Counselling Agency in Israel." *Evaluation and Program Planning* 21(1): 11-20.

Scheirer, M. A.
1994   "Designing and Using Process Evaluation." In J. S. Wholey, H. P. Hatry, and K. E. Newcomer (eds.), *Handbook of Practical Program Evaluation* (pp. 40-68). San Francisco: Jossey-Bass.

Schorr, L. B.
1997   *Common Purpose: Strengthening Families and Neighborhoods to Rebuild America.* New York: Doubleday Anchor Books.

Schweinhart, L. J., and F. P. Weikart
1998   "High/Scope Perry Preschool Effects at Age 27." In J. Crane (ed.), *Social Programs That Work* New York: Russell Sage Foundation.

Scriven, M.
1991   *Evaluation Thesaurus,* 4th ed. Newbury Park, CA: Sage.

Sechrest, L., and W. H. Yeaton
1982   "Magnitudes of Experimental Effects in Social Science Research." *Evaluation Review* 6(5):579-600.

Shadish, W. R., T. D. Cook, and D. T. Campbell
2002   *Experimental and Quasi-Experimental Designs for Generalized Causal Inference.* Boston: Houghton-Mifflin.

Shadish, W. R., T. D. Cook, and L. C. Leviton
1991   *Foundations of Program Evaluation: Theories of Practice.* Newbury Park, CA: Sage.

Shadish, W. R., D. L. Newman, M. A. Scheirer, and C. Wye (eds.)
1995   "Guiding Principles for Evaluators." *New Directions for Program Evaluation*, no. 66. San Francisco: Jossey-Bass.

Shadish, W. R., Jr., and C. S. Reichardt
1987   "The Intellectual Foundations of Social Program Evaluation: The Development of Evaluation Theory." In W. R. Shadish, Jr., and C. S. Reichardt (eds.), *Evaluation Studies Review Annual* (pp. 13-30). Newbury Park, CA: Sage.

Shlay, A. B., and C. S. Holupka
1991   *Steps toward Independence: The Early Effects of the Lafayette Courts Family Development Center.* Baltimore: Institute for Policy Studies, Johns Hopkins University.

Shortell, S. M., and W. C. Richardson
1978   *Health Program Evaluation.* St. Louis: C. V. Mosby.

Skogan, W. G., and A. J. Lurigio
1991   "Multisite Evaluations in Criminal Justice Settings: Structural Obstacles to Success." *New Directions for Program Evaluation*, no. 50 (pp. 83-96). San Francisco: Jossey-Bass.

Smith, M. F.
1989   *Evaluability Assessment: A Practical Approach.* Norwell, MA: Kluwer Academic Publishers.

Solomon, J.
1988   "Companies Try Measuring Cost Savings From New Types of Corporate Benefits." *Wall Street Journal*, December 29.

Solomon, M. A., and S. M. Shortell
1981   "Designing Health Policy Research for Utilization." *Health Policy Quarterly* 1 (May): 261-273.

Solomon, P., and J. Draine
1995   "One-Year Outcomes of a Randomized Trial of Consumer Case Management." *Evaluation and Program Planning* 18(2):117-127.

Soriano, F. I.
1995   *Conducting Needs Assessments: A Multidisciplinary Approach.* Thousand Oaks, CA: Sage.

Spector, M., and J. I. Kitsuse
1977   *Constructing Social Problems.* Reprinted 1987, Hawthorne, NY: Aldine de Gruyter.

SRI International
1983   *Final Report of the Seattle-Denver Income Maintenance Experiment*, vol. 1. Palo Alto, CA: Author.

Stolzenberg, R. M., and D. A. Relles
1997   "Tools for Intuition About Sample Selection Bias and Its Correction." *American Sociological Review* 62(3):494-507.

Stouffer, S. A., et al.
1949   *The American Soldier*, vol. 2: *Combat and Its Aftermath*. Princeton, NJ: Princeton University Press.

Suchman, E.
1967   *Evaluative Research.* New York: Russell Sage Foundation.

Sylvain, C., R. Ladouceur, and J. Boisvert
1997   "Cognitive and Behavioral Treatment of Pathological Gambling: A Controlled Study." *Journal of Consulting and Clinical Psychology* 65(5):727-732.

Terrie, E. W.
1996   "Assessing Child and Maternal Health: The First Step in the Design of Community-Based Interventions." In R. Reviere, S. Berkowitz, C. C. Carter, and C. G. Ferguson (eds.), *Needs Assessment: A Creative and Practical Guide for Social Scientists* (pp. 121-146). Washington, DC: Taylor & Francis.

Thompson, M.
1980   *Benefit-Cost Analysis for Program Evaluation.* Beverly Hills, CA: Sage.

Torres, R. T., H. S. Preskill, and M. E. Piontek
1996   *Evaluation Strategies for Communicating and Reporting: Enhancing Learning in Organizations.* Thousand Oaks, CA: Sage.

Trippe, C.
1995   "Rates Up: Trends in FSP Participation Rates: 1985-1992." In D. Hall and M. Stavrianos (eds.), *Nutrition and Food Security in the Food Stamp Program.* Alexandria, VA: U.S. Department of Agriculture. Food and Consumer Service.

Trochim, W. M. K.
1984   *Research Design for Program Evaluation: The Regression Discontinuity Approach.* Beverly Hills, CA: Sage.

Turpin, R. S., and J. M. Sinacore (eds.)
1991   "Multisite Evaluations." *New Directions for Program Evaluation*, no. 50. San Francisco: Jossey-Bass.

United Way of America Task Force on Impact
1996   *Measuring Program Outcomes: A Practical Approach.* Alexandria, VA: United Way of America.

U.S. Department of Justice, Office of Justice Programs, Bureau of Justice Statistics
2003, January   *Criminal Victimization in the United States, 2001 Statistical Tables.* Washington, DC: U.S. Department of Justice. Retrieved from www.ojp.doj.gov/bjs

U.S. General Accounting Office
1986   *Teen-Age Pregnancy: 500,000 Births a Year but Few Tested Programs.* GAO/PEMD-86-16BR. Washington, DC: Author.
1990   *Prospective Evaluation Methods: The Prospective Evaluation Synthesis.* GAO/PEMD Transfer Paper 10.1.10. Washington, DC: Author.
1995   *Mammography Services: Initial Impact of New Federal Law Has Been Positive.* GAO/HEHS-96-17. Washington, DC: Author.

van de Vall, M., and C. A. Bolas

1981   "External vs. Internal Social Policy Researchers." *Knowledge: Creation, Diffusion, Utilization* 2 (June): 461-481.

Vanecko, J. J., and B. Jacobs

1970   *Reports From the 100-City CAP Evaluation: The Impact of the Community Action Program on Institutional Change.* Chicago: National Opinion Research Center.

Viscusi, W. K.

1985   "Cotton Dust Regulation: An OSHA Success Story?" *Journal of Policy Analysis and Management* 4(3):325-343.

Weiss, C. H.

1972   *Evaluation Research: Methods of Assessing Program Effectiveness.* Englewood Cliffs, NJ: Prentice Hall.

1988   "Evaluation for Decisions: Is Anybody There? Does Anybody Care?" *Evaluation Practice* 9(1):5-19.

1993   "Where Politics and Evaluation Research Meet," *Evaluation Practice* 14(1):93-106.

1997   "How Can Theory-Based Evaluation Make Greater Headway?" *Evaluation Review* 21(4):501-524.

Weiss, C. H., and M. J. Bucuvalas

1980   "Truth Tests and Utility Tests: Decision-Makers' Frames of Reference for Social Science Research." *American Sociological Review* 45 (April): 302-313.

Wholey, J. S.

1979   *Evaluation: Promise and Performance.* Washington, DC: Urban Institute.

1981   "Using Evaluation to Improve Program Performance." In R. A. Levine, M. A. Solomon, and G. M. Hellstern (eds.), *Evaluation Research and Practice: Comparative and International Perspectives* (pp. 92-106). Beverly Hills, CA: Sage.

1987   "Evaluability Assessment: Developing Program Theory." *New Directions for Program Evaluation*, no. 33 (pp. 77-92). San Francisco: Jossey-Bass.

1994   "Assessing the Feasibility and Likely Usefulness of Evaluation." In J. S. Wholey, H. P. Hatry, and K. E. Newcomer (eds.), *Handbook of Practical Program Evaluation* (pp. 15-39). San Francisco: Jossey-Bass.

Wholey, J. S., and H. P. Hatry

1992   "The Case for Performance Monitoring." *Public Administration Review* 52(6):604-610.

Wilson, S. J., M. W. Lipsey, and J. H. Derzon

2003   "The Effects of School-Based Intervention Programs on Aggressive Behavior: A Meta-Analysis." *Journal of Consulting and Clinical Psychology* 71(1):136-149.

Winfree, L. T., F.-A. Esbensen, and D. W. Osgood

1996   "Evaluating a School-Based Gang-Prevention Program: A Theoretical Perspective." *Evaluation Review* 20(2):181-203.

Witkin, B. R., and J. W. Altschuld

1995   *Planning and Conducting Needs Assessments: A Practical Guide.* Thousand Oaks, CA: Sage.

Wu, P., and D. T. Campbell
1996   "Extending Latent Variable LISREL Analyses of the 1969 Westinghouse Head Start Evaluation to Blacks and Full Year Whites." *Evaluation and Program Planning* 19(3):183-191.

Yates, B. T.
1996   *Analyzing Costs, Procedures, Processes, and Outcomes in Human Services.* Thousand Oaks, CA: Sage.

Zerbe, R. O.
1998   "Is Cost-Benefit Analysis Legal? Three Rules." *Journal of Policy Analysis and Management* 17(3):419-456.

Author Index

Subject Index

About the Authors

Peter H. Rossi is Stuart A. Rice Professor Emeritus of Sociology and Director Emeritus of the Social and Demographic Research Institute at the University of Massachusetts at Amherst. He has been on the faculties of Harvard University, the University of Chicago, and Johns Hopkins University. He was Director, 1960 to 1967, of the National Opinion Research Center and has been a consultant on social research and evaluation to (among others) the National Science Foundation, the National Institute of Mental Health, the General Accounting Office, and the Rockefeller Foundation. His research centers on the application of social research methods to social issues and is currently focused on evaluating welfare reform. His recent books include *Feeding the Poor* (1998), *Thinking About Evaluation* (1999, 2nd ed., with Richard A. Berk), *Just Punishments* (1997, with Richard A. Berk), and *Of Human Bonding: Parent-Child Relations Throughout the Life Course* (1990, with Alice S. Rossi). He is past president of the American Sociological Association and the 1985 recipient of the Commonwealth Award. He has received awards from the Evaluation Research Society, the Eastern Evaluation Society, the American Sociological Association, and the Policy Studies Association. He has served as editor of the *American Journal of Sociology* and *Social Science Research*, and he is a Fellow of the American Academy of Arts and Science and of the American Association for the Advancement of Science.

Mark W. Lipsey is the Director of the Center for Evaluation Research and Methodology and a Senior Research Associate at the Vanderbilt Institute for Public Policy Studies at Vanderbilt University. He received a Ph.D. in psychology from Johns Hopkins University in 1972 following a B.S. in applied psychology from the Georgia Institute of Technology in 1968. His professional interests are in the areas of public policy, program evaluation research, social intervention, field research methodology, and research synthesis (meta-analysis). The topics of his recent research have been risk and intervention for juvenile delinquency and issues of methodological quality in program evaluation research. Professor Lipsey serves on the editorial boards of the *American Journal of Evaluation*, *Evaluation and Program Planning*, *Psychological Bulletin*, and the *American Journal of Community Psychology*, and boards or committees of, among others, the National Research Council, National Institutes of Health, Campbell Collaboration, and Blueprints for Violence Prevention. He is a recipient of the American Evaluation Association's Paul Lazarsfeld Award and a Fellow of the American Psychological Society.

Howard E. Freeman was Professor of Sociology, University of California, Los Angeles. He was Chair of his department from 1985 to 1989, and founding director of UCLA's Institute for Social Science Research, a position he held from 1974 until 1981. He also held appointments in UCLA's Department of Medicine and School of Education. He joined UCLA in 1974 after serving as the Ford Foundation's Social Science Advisor for Mexico, Central America, and the Caribbean. Prior appointments include Brandeis University, where he was Morse Professor of Urban Studies, Harvard University, and the Russell Sage Foundation. He published more that 150 articles and a number of monographs on the posthospital experience of psychiatric patients, on policy issues in the delivery of health services, and on research methods. He was coeditor of the *Handbook of Medical Sociology*, now in its fourth edition, and of *Evaluation Review*. He was the recipient of the Hofheimer Prize of the American Psychiatric Association and the Myrdal Award of the American Evaluation Association and was a member of the Institute of Medicine. He also was president of Litigation Measurements, Inc., a small consulting firm that undertakes social research for attorneys. He died in 1992.